COURTING DEATH

COURTING DEATH

The Supreme Court and Capital Punishment

Carol S. Steiker

and Jordan M. Steiker

THE BELKNAP PRESS OF HARVARD UNIVERSITY PRESS

Cambridge, Massachusetts
London, England
2016

First printing

Library of Congress Cataloging-in-Publication Data

Names: Steiker, Carol S. (Carol Susan), author. | Steiker, Jordan M., author.
Title: Courting death : the Supreme Court and capital punishment
/ Carol S. Steiker and Jordan M. Steiker.
Description: Cambridge, Massachusetts : The Belknap Press of Harvard University
Press, 2016. | Includes bibliographical references and index.
Identifiers: LCCN 2016015005 | ISBN 9780674737426 (hard cover : alk. paper)
Subjects: LCSH: Capital punishment—United States. | United States.
Supreme Court. | Judicial review—United States. | Discrimination in capital
punishment—United States. | Capital punishment—United States—History.
Classification: LCC KF9227.C2 S74 2016 | DDC 345.73/0773—dc23 LC record
available at https://lccn.loc.gov/2016015005

For our parents, our first teachers

Contents

COURTING DEATH

Introduction

Regulating the Death Penalty to Death

IN THE SUMMER OF 2014, Cormac J. Carney, a federal judge in California, struck down that state's system of capital punishment under the federal constitution. California houses the largest death row in the country, home to more than 700 inmates awaiting execution. The ruling was overturned on narrow procedural grounds the following year, but its announcement and reasoning cast a bright light on some critical dysfunctions of capital punishment in California and throughout the United States. Judge Carney explained that California's death penalty no longer serves any valid function of punishment because only a tiny fraction of those sentenced to death are executed—only thirteen of the 900 inmates sentenced to death since the state adopted its current system in 1978. The judge observed that the lengthy delays between sentence and execution have "quietly transformed" a sentence of death into a sentence that "no rational jury or legislature could ever impose: *life in prison, with the remote possibility of death.*"[1]

Executions are so rare that execution is not the leading cause of death on California's death row. Execution is not even the *second* leading cause of death there; it comes in third behind natural causes and suicide.[2] The dysfunction in California is extreme but not unique.

In Pennsylvania, where Governor Tom Wolf has declared a moratorium on executions, the chief justice of the Pennsylvania Supreme Court penned a 2013 paper on the state's broken capital justice system in which he quoted a colleague's comment that "in Pennsylvania, we do not have the death penalty, rather we have 'death by arteriolosclerosis.'"[3] A former prison superintendent in Oregon described a death row inmate who has been tried four times and is now sixty-two years old: "[He] may have 30 years of appeals ahead of him. This is the exact same outcome that would have been achieved by a sentence of life without parole, but with massive additional cost."[4] Nationwide, of the more than 8,000 inmates under a death sentence at some point between 1973 and 2013, only 16 percent have been executed. A much larger number, 42 percent, had their convictions or sentences overturned or commuted, and 6 percent died by other causes; the remaining 35 percent are on death row.[5]

What is wrong with such a system, aside from gross inefficiency? As Judge Carney explained, the "random few" who are executed "will have languished for so long on Death Row that their execution will serve no retributive or deterrent purpose and will be arbitrary."[6] The judge invoked arguably the most famous Supreme Court pronouncement on the death penalty: *Furman v. Georgia*. In this landmark 1972 decision, the Court in effect abolished the death penalty as it was then practiced across the country. Like the California ruling, *Furman* was short-lived: the Court backtracked just four years later in response to a wave of pro–death penalty backlash, and the death penalty was reinstated. But the rarity and randomness of the death penalty was a central concern animating the Court's temporary abolition. As Justice Potter Stewart memorably declared, the death penalty was "so wantonly and so freakishly imposed" that it was "cruel and unusual in the same way that being struck by lightning is cruel and unusual."[7] Ironically, the Court's decision to revive the American death penalty in 1976 ultimately recreated the lightning-like capital justice system that Justice Stewart had condemned. Today, executions are considerably *less* common than lightning strikes: in 2015, the twenty-eight executions conducted nationwide were far fewer than the yearly average number of deadly lightning strikes (forty-nine) in recent decades.[8]

The American death penalty has come full circle over the past fifty years. Capital punishment was the subject of a concerted constitutional litigation campaign in the 1960s that led to the Supreme Court's bold abolition in 1972, followed by its chastened reauthorization of the death penalty four years later. But the Court did more than press a reset button in 1976; it embarked on an extensive—and ultimately failed—effort to reform and rationalize the practice of capital punishment in the United States through top-down, constitutional regulation. The prevailing consensus is that what is most anomalous about the American death penalty is that the United States has retained it while all other Western democracies have abolished it. But what is truly unique about the American death penalty experience is that the United States has attempted to find a middle position between repealing and retaining capital punishment—by subjecting it to intensive judicial oversight under the federal constitution.

Justice Harry Blackmun called this project of constitutional regulation an "experiment."[9] Enough time has passed to analyze its results. In *Courting Death*, we begin by chronicling the life of the American death penalty before constitutional regulation. Next, we tell the story of the Court's momentous constitutional interventions into capital punishment in 1972 and 1976. We consider how the Court failed to address forthrightly the "original sin" of the death penalty—the stain of racial discrimination. The Court paid surprisingly scant attention in its constitutional rulings to the death penalty's long and ignoble history of race-based use, a history shaped by the practice of slavery and an intractable post–Civil War legacy of racial discrimination. At a moment when policing and mass incarceration are under scrutiny for gross racial disparities, attention to the death penalty helps illuminate the way that race has been woven into the history of American criminal justice and yet often ignored by the courts. Our attention then turns to the profound difficulty of regulating a controversial practice across the vast and diverse country in light of the independence that our federal system affords each state. The Court's constitutional rulings produced quite divergent effects when filtered through the various state and local institutions and actors of the capital justice system, reproducing regional divisions familiar from the Civil War period.

We give a critical accounting of the Court's constitutional regulation, evaluating both its intended and unanticipated effects. On its own terms, the Court's regulation has been a failure, unable to address the problems of arbitrariness and discrimination that animated its creation. At first, the Court's regulation inadvertently bolstered the revived death penalty by promoting unjustified faith among justice system participants and the general public in the reliability and fairness of the process. But over time, constitutional regulation, again unintentionally, contributed to the marked destabilization and diminution of the American death penalty, sowing the seeds for a likely categorical constitutional abolition: in essence, the Court has regulated the death penalty to death.

Just as constitutional regulation illuminates the challenges of the American death penalty, the Court's experience with the death penalty offers insight into the complexity of constitutional regulation. The death penalty story illustrates some recurring patterns that are observable in other widely diverse constitutional contexts, such as the regulation of abortion, police practices, voting rights, and same-sex marriage. Despite these important connections to other areas of constitutional law, the death penalty is unique in ways that compel attention. The regulation of capital punishment cropped up almost overnight. Most constitutional doctrines take decades to develop, but death penalty law proliferated at a furious pace, driven by condemned inmates' rights to legal review in state and federal courts. The evolution of an entire line of doctrine over a comparatively short period of time offers a case study of how legal change works—or doesn't. The Court's attempt to square the death penalty with constitutional guarantees demonstrates both the power and failings of the Constitution by showing how judges have struggled, often unsuccessfully, to give it meaning in the most macabre circumstances. Most striking is the number of justices of varying political commitments who have renounced wholesale their previous decisions upholding death sentences and embraced constitutional abolition of the death penalty. This extraordinary phenomenon suggests that the death penalty will not last much longer in the United States. We trace the likely future trajectory of the Court's death penalty rulings toward a categorical constitutional abolition. We conclude with a postmortem, reflecting on what a post–death penalty future will hold for American criminal justice.

We came to the topic of the death penalty from our shared experience as law clerks for Justice Thurgood Marshall in two separate terms (1987 and 1989). Marshall was the only justice on the Court who as a lawyer had represented defendants in death penalty cases. He retained a fierce interest in the topic as a justice, which we both inherited from our experiences in his chambers. Each week, large stacks of petitions seeking the Court's review would arrive in chambers, and Justice Marshall made it clear that the death penalty petitions submitted by indigent defendants were the highest priority. This was our education in death penalty law. When each of us joined the legal academy in the early 1990s, we began to teach courses on capital punishment. We have collaborated for more than twenty years (as siblings, not spouses) on scholarly, litigation, and law reform projects addressing the death penalty. We are not dispassionate observers, but our primary lens has been a scholarly one. It is our hope that this project marries the virtues while balancing the vices of the on-the-ground engagement of our activism and the broader perspective of our scholarly pursuits.

If extended study of the American experiment with capital punishment teaches anything, it is the difficulty of predicting the future. Again and again, the Supreme Court's constitutional interventions took unexpected turns and produced results that were not anticipated by the Court or by knowledgeable observers, ourselves included. We considered titling this book "Unpremeditated" to capture the extent to which the constitutional law of the death penalty lacked the very premeditation that many capital murder statutes require. Although we hazard some predictions about what the future holds for the American death penalty, if the past is any guide, things may well take unexpected turns yet again. Whatever the future may hold, the now almost fifty-year experiment with constitutional regulation of capital punishment offers insights into the meanings and functions of capital punishment in American society and into the promise and pitfalls of constitutional regulation of highly contested social issues.

CHAPTER ONE

Before Constitutional Regulation

M ARY DYER WAS HANGED for the crime of heresy in Boston on
June 1, 1660. Dyer, a Quaker, had repeatedly defied her ban-
ishment from Puritan Massachusetts Bay Colony, knowing that she
did so upon pain of death. A painting of Dyer being led to the gallows depicts a solemn woman in sober garb and a white bonnet with
her eyes raised to the heavens as drummers herald her impending
execution to an expectant crowd.[1] Today, we understand Dyer's fate
as a warning about the dangers of religious intolerance: a statue of
Dyer stands in front of the Massachusetts Statehouse in Boston with
the inscription "Witness for Religious Freedom."[2] However, in her
own time, Dyer's sentence was a warning of a different kind. Her execution dramatically conveyed the deepest commitments of the Puritans, who sought to make the Massachusetts Bay Colony a "City
upon a Hill" and who viewed Quakerism as a threat to their model
of Zion in America.[3]

Dyer's execution reflects a truth about capital punishment in
America from the earliest colonial days through the late twentieth
century. For most of American history, capital punishment was not
a subject of significant national regulation; rather, it was primarily a
tool of local criminal justice, invoked by local officials to address dis-

tinctively local concerns. Mary Dyer's execution was but one of four executions of "Quaker martyrs" in mid-seventeenth-century Boston, demonstrating the importance that Puritan authorities placed on excluding religious dissidents (or "heretics," as the Puritans saw it).[4] The relevance of theological concerns to capital punishment in the Massachusetts Bay Colony is clear from the colony's list of capital offenses, which reflected as much influence from the Bible as from English common law: one could be executed for idolatry, blasphemy, man-stealing, the cursing of a parent by a child over sixteen years of age, and the offense of being a rebellious son, among other more traditional capital offenses like murder.[5] These Biblical offenses were often treated more leniently than the letter of the law suggested,[6] but the threat of capital punishment was not an empty one. Mary Latham, wife of *Mayflower* passenger William Latham, was hanged for adultery in 1644.[7] In neighboring Plymouth Colony, also a Puritan community, Thomas Granger was hanged in 1642 for acts of bestiality with various livestock, which were themselves "executed" in accordance with Leviticus 20:15 of the King James Bible: "if a man lie with a beast, he shall surely be put to death: and ye shall slay the beast."[8]

The use of capital punishment in colonial Massachusetts to promote religious purity contrasted sharply with its use in Southern colonies (and later, Southern states) to protect the slave economy. Adultery, sodomy, and witchcraft featured prominently in the crimes resulting in execution in seventeenth-century New England, while property crimes and crimes by slaves received greater attention in Southern colonies.[9] Virginia expanded its capital code to include numerous offenses relating to the tobacco trade, and South Carolina made it a capital crime for slaves to maim or even "bruise" whites or to encourage other slaves to run away.[10] As slaves began to outnumber whites in parts of the South, white owners increasingly feared violence or insurrection by slaves. Slaves convicted of murdering their owners or of plotting revolt often were subject not merely to ordinary death by hanging, but to even more terrifying and gruesome forms of execution such as burning at the stake or breaking on the wheel.[11] The corpses of slaves executed for revolt might also be hung in chains or dismembered to intensify and extend the terrifying spectacle.[12]

Murder or revolt by a slave, along with murder of a husband by his wife, were considered forms of "petit treason" against slave owners and husbands who, as heads of household, literally embodied the state.[13] One infamous example of the special horrors reserved for rebellious slaves is the aftermath of the Stono slave revolt in South Carolina in 1739, when slave insurrectionists had their heads severed and mounted on mileposts.[14]

Today, of course, we do not punish adultery or slave insurrection at all, much less with death. However, two key features of the era of such outmoded practices have persisted until quite recently. First, the death penalty remained for centuries primarily a matter of state and local prerogative. Second, the officials who controlled the most important aspects of death penalty practices—legislatures, governors, attorneys general, and prosecutors—came from the political branches of government. Until the Supreme Court "constitutionalized" the practice of capital punishment, a process that began in earnest in the 1960s, the death penalty simply was not a subject of top-down, national regulation, and certainly not by federal courts. To be sure, the federal government has always controlled its own capital statutes and prosecutions, leading, for example, to the execution of the Rosenbergs for conspiracy to commit espionage in 1953. But prior to the Supreme Court's intervention, the federal government never claimed authority over state death penalty practices—how state legislatures defined capital crimes, how local prosecutors selected defendants for capital charges, how state courts conducted capital trials, or how local and state officials performed executions. And the states have always been where the main action is with regard to capital punishment. The federal government is a bit player in the national death penalty drama; it conducted only three of the more than 1,400 executions that have taken place nationwide since 1976.[15] By making federal constitutional law the most important source of guidance for death penalty practices across the country, the Supreme Court fundamentally altered who controlled the American death penalty. Power moved both from states and localities to the federal government, and from the political branches to the courts. Thus, the Supreme Court's constitutional intervention in the death penalty, which led the Court to take an ongoing regulatory role over state death penalty practices, represented a profound break with the long sweep of American history.

Waves of Death Penalty Reform

The absence of a framework for top-down, national regulation of the death penalty did not mean that death penalty practices remained static until the Supreme Court intervened. On the contrary, death penalty practices changed substantially over time and often in the same direction across multiple jurisdictions. From the founding era of the late eighteenth century to the constitutional era of the late twentieth century, the American death penalty experienced at least four fundamental transformations: (1) the range of crimes eligible for death narrowed substantially; (2) death sentences became discretionary rather than mandatory; (3) executions moved from public to private spaces and from local to centralized places; and (4) modes of execution shifted over time toward methods believed to be more humane. These waves of death penalty reform flowed from state-based legislative law reform movements in which the federal government played no significant role. The apparent coordination of these transformations across many states in relatively brief periods of time reflects similar conditions and interests in those states rather than any top-down coercion or inducement.

The first wave of American death penalty reform targeted the wide ambit of death penalty statutes. In the early days of the new republic, every state authorized the death penalty not only for murder, but for many other offenses as well. The long list of potentially capital crimes was part of the colonial inheritance from Mother England, which had a famously expansive capital code. From 1688 to 1820, English penal law expanded the scope of capital punishment from fifty to more than 200 offenses, including pickpocketing, shoplifting, and unlawfully cutting down trees in an orchard, earning its appellation as the "Bloody Code."[16] England would eventually pare down the scope of its capital sanction,[17] but reformers in the new American republic were leaders in narrowing the death penalty. The same

Enlightenment spirit of reason and republican ideology of equality that contributed to the American Revolution also generated criticism of the broad reach of the death penalty. As one historian of the era describes the prevailing *zeitgeist*, "In the Founding Fathers' time, talk of 'sanguinary' laws and practices—and the need to reform and replace them with more reasoned or Christian policies—was everywhere, especially on the tongues of American revolutionaries and other intellectuals."[18]

Many of the leaders of the American Revolution were profoundly influenced by the writing of Cesare Beccaria, an Italian Enlightenment thinker who penned the first sustained critique of capital punishment. Beccaria's *On Crimes and Punishments,* published in Italy in 1764, was quickly translated and widely read across Europe and in the American colonies.[19] George Washington and Thomas Jefferson both bought copies, and John Adams quoted Beccaria in his famous defense of the British soldiers charged in the Boston Massacre in 1770.[20] In the progressive ferment of the Revolutionary era, many key American political leaders worked to scale back the death penalty in their states. As governor of Massachusetts, John Hancock advocated the abolition of the death penalty for the crime of burglary. Similarly, Governors John Jay of New York and Patrick Henry of Virginia both sought to shorten the list of capital crimes.[21] In the 1770s, Thomas Jefferson drafted a bill for Virginia that would have limited the death penalty to only the crimes of murder and treason, and James Madison later led the (close but unsuccessful) effort in the Virginia legislature to pass Jefferson's bill—a failure Madison attributed to popular "rage against Horse stealers."[22]

The most radical successful legislative assault on the breadth of the death penalty in the Founding era was Pennsylvania's homicide reform statute of 1794. Promoted by Dr. Benjamin Rush, one of Beccaria's greatest American admirers who was sometimes called the "American Beccaria,"[23] the Pennsylvania statute limited the death penalty to the crime of murder and scaled back the use of the punishment even within the class of murderers. Under the now widely used Pennsylvania formula, only "first-degree" murders are eligible for the death penalty; all others must be punished with noncapital sanctions. The scope of first-degree murder to this day centers on the original Pennsylvania definition, which focused on "deliberate and premeditated" murder and murder committed in the course of other serious felonies.[24]

While only a handful of states followed Pennsylvania's lead before the turn of the nineteenth century, the trend toward major death penalty restrictions picked up steam from the 1820s to the 1850s.[25] During this period, the American innovation of the penitentiary reflected and reinforced a new belief in the social roots of crime and a new hope in the possibility of rehabilitation through social isolation, penitence, and labor.[26] Executions dwindled for lesser felonies like rape, robbery, burglary, and arson. This decline in usage was followed in many states by formal abolition of the death penalty for those offenses. As a consequence, historian Stuart Banner explained: "By 1860 no northern state punished with death any offense other than murder and treason."[27] A small number of Northern states went even further, as Beccaria and his many admirers urged. Michigan became the first English-speaking jurisdiction in the world to abolish the death penalty for murder (though retaining it for treason) in 1846, followed by the complete abolition of the death penalty in Rhode Island in 1852 and Wisconsin in 1853.[28] It is important to note that while Southern states, too, restricted the number of capital crimes, these restrictions applied only to crimes committed by whites.[29] Indeed, most death penalty reforms happened later, less completely, or not at all in the South.

The second significant reform of the death penalty, related to the first, was the decision of American jurisdictions to give juries discretion to withhold the death penalty, even for offenders convicted of first-degree murder. Prior to this innovation, the death penalty had been mandatory upon conviction of a capital crime. The only possible escape from execution was by clemency or pardon from state governors (or the president for federal crimes), who held the same discretionary powers as English monarchs. But such unpredictable mercy led jurors in the days of mandatory death sentences to spare the lives of sympathetic defendants by voting to acquit them of capital crimes even in the face of compelling evidence of guilt. Concerns about jury nullification motivated many death penalty enthusiasts to join death penalty skeptics in supporting jury discretion in capital cases, in addition to the elimination of capital punishment for less serious offenses.[30] The movement toward discretion proved to be a protracted process. It began in the 1840s and was substantially complete by the end of the nineteenth century, but mandatory capital sentencing was not abandoned by all capital jurisdictions for all crimes until the 1980s.[31]

The third major change in death penalty practices addressed the location of executions. In colonial times and the early decades of the new republic, executions took place in public in the locality where the crime occurred, like the hanging of Quaker Mary Dyer on Boston Common in colonial Massachusetts. This practice reflected the belief that executions served important spiritual and pedagogical functions for the condemned and for the attending public. In the nineteenth century, however, an emerging middle class that cultivated a sense of refinement began to regard public executions as the province of baser elements of society. Public executions were no longer viewed as religious, edifying rituals. Instead, they were perceived as raucous, coarsening spectacles—although it is not clear that actual practices had changed so significantly. This newly emerging sensibility led states to pass laws beginning in the 1830s that ordered the removal of executions from public view, usually to the walled yard of a jail or prison. Such statutes often required that private executions be witnessed only by a small number of "reputable" or "respectable citizens."[32] By the end of the nineteenth century, the vast majority of death penalty states had passed private execution statutes. The last public execution in America took place in Kentucky in 1936 and corroborated many of the concerns of the practice's critics. The spectacle was attended by a crowd of nearly 20,000, served by vendors selling hot dogs, popcorn, and drinks; *Time* magazine reported that "tipsy merrymakers rollicked all night."[33] Kentucky abolished public executions in 1938, and none has taken place since.

As with the move from mandatory to discretionary death sentences, the move from public to private executions drew support from both opponents and supporters of capital punishment. Abolitionists often supported privatizing executions by arguing that public executions failed to deter crime.[34] This argument had a self-fulfilling quality, because whatever deterrent value executions might have had was likely diminished by privatization. But many death penalty supporters also embraced privatization to avoid the unfavorable publicity surrounding particularly raucous or gruesomely botched executions, or to placate critics in the midst of credible abolitionist campaigns.[35] The breadth of support for privatizing executions reflected the changing role of capital punishment in the nineteenth century. As the political and religious roles of the death penalty diminished, and the death penalty became less a symbol of state or church authority than an ordinary exercise of modernizing criminal justice systems, the need for public execution ceremonies likewise diminished.[36]

Executions moved from public to private spaces and also from local to more centralized facilities. Until the Civil War, county sheriffs were in charge of executions. But with the growth of state penitentiaries and the centralization of penal authority in the post–Civil War period, executions increasingly came to be supervised by state prison wardens at a single state facility. This change reflected a more general transition from local, communal criminal justice practices to more bureaucratic, hierarchical institutions characteristic of modernizing societies. It also no doubt reflected the modernization of execution methods, as the gallows (which were relatively easily assembled in various localities) were replaced with other, more technically complex modes of execution. It was not feasible for local counties to own and operate their own electric chairs or gas chambers. The movement toward centralization began in 1864 with Vermont and Maine and continued over the next century. In the 1890s, 86 percent of executions were performed by local authorities, but by the 1920s, the balance had shifted, and almost 80 percent of executions were performed by centralized state officials.[37]

The replacement of the gallows with other, purportedly more humane execution methods was the fourth wave of death penalty reform, and it is still continuing today. The successive development of new modes of execution in the United States stands in sharp contrast to England, which maintained hanging as its execution method until it abolished the death penalty in 1969, and to France, which used the guillotine until abolition in 1981.[38] Starting in the late nineteenth century, American jurisdictions repeatedly experimented with new modes of execution to render the process less painful and less visibly destructive of the body. Because county sheriffs kept control of executions for most of the nineteenth century, the risk of inexpert hangings was substantial, leading to prolonged death, decapitation, or some other mishap. The torturous hanging of three men in Ozark, Missouri, in 1889 exemplified the horrors of inexpert hangings, as the three struggled and groaned for many minutes, with one of them carried back to the gallows spitting blood for a second drop to finish the job. A newspaper reported: "The execution today was a horrible piece of butchery owing to the blunders of the sheriff."[39] At the other extreme, the hanging of Eva Dugan, the first woman to be executed in Arizona, was not prolonged, but it decapitated her, catapulting her headless body to the floor.[40]

The invention of the electric chair in the late nineteenth century seemed to promise a more refined mode of execution through American technological innovation. Although the first electrocution was botched, improvements of the method led to greater enthusiasm for it, and many states moved from hanging to electrocution between 1890 and 1950. In the century after its first use in New York in 1890, more than 4,000 people were put to death in the electric chair in twenty-six states.[41] As the number of deaths by electrocution grew, however, malfunctioning electric chairs produced their own horrifically torturous executions. In 1928, it took six separate shocks and more than seventeen minutes to execute Philip Jackson, a black man convicted of raping a white woman in the District of Columbia.[42] More than a half century later, in 1990 and then again in 1997, Florida's electric chair, nicknamed "Old Sparky," caused flames to shoot from the heads of executed inmates during the electrocution process.[43] As an alternative to either hanging or electrocution, some state legislatures moved to lethal gas, developed as a result of experimentation with chemical agents for trench warfare during World War I. The gas chamber, inaugurated in 1924, seemed to offer even less pain and destruction of the body. Twelve states eventually adopted the gas chamber, and eleven of them carried out at least one execution by lethal gas for a total of 594 such executions by the time the last one took place in Arizona in 1999.[44] The gas chamber's promise of a "swift and painless" death proved elusive, however, with prolonged and convulsive executions reported on a number of occasions.[45] More recently, virtually all jurisdictions have moved to lethal injection—again motivated by a desire to inflict minimal pain and minimal visible injury. Whereas in the past, part of the punishment of death was the pain, degradation, and disfigurement of the execution itself, in the late nineteenth and twentieth centuries, the punishment of death gradually became the loss of life, not the manner of death.

In the past decade, however, lethal injection, too, has come under increasing attack for causing unnecessary and prolonged suffering. Until recently, when drug shortages have forced states to improvise with substitutions, the most common lethal injection protocol was a three-drug combination that included a barbiturate sedative, a paralytic agent, and a heart-stopping drug. The paralytic agent renders the inmate unable to show pain, even though the commonly used heart-stopping drug would cause excruciating pain in the absence of adequate sedation. There is clearly some risk that execution by lethal injection will cause pain that is masked by an inmate's paralysis: medical professionals often refuse to participate in executions, and it can be difficult for nonprofessionals to maintain adequate sedation through an intravenous line in inmates whose veins may be compromised by drug use, old age, or poor health. While the prevalence of masked pain is unknown precisely because it is masked, there have been numerous documented cases of botched lethal injections, in which the execution has been demonstrably prolonged and painful. Recent research suggests that executions by lethal injection are botched at a higher rate than any of the other methods used since the late nineteenth century.[46] The increasing refusal of pharmaceutical companies to supply states with drugs for the purposes of execution has led states to scramble to modify their lethal injection protocols, resulting in the use of less reliable or untested drugs, alone or in combination.[47] In 2014, four separate executions using new drug protocols were seriously botched in Ohio, Oklahoma, and Arizona, with inmates writhing, choking, and gasping. One cried out, "I feel my whole body burning," and another took almost two hours to die.[48] The Supreme Court has twice recently upheld lethal injection protocols against constitutional challenges, but litigation continues in state and lower federal courts regarding the provenance of lethal injection drugs and the risk of unnecessary severe pain in the execution process.[49] As a result of both drug shortages and the risk of botched lethal injections, some states are again seeking to develop new methods of execution—or to resurrect old ones. In 2015, lawmakers in Oklahoma approved an entirely new execution method—death by nitrogen asphyxiation—that is also being considered by other states.[50] In 2014, the Tennessee legislature brought back the electric chair in the event that lethal injection drugs cannot be obtained, and in 2015, Utah brought back the firing squad for the same purpose.[51] The long process of successive experimentation with modes of capital punishment is clearly not yet complete.

The continuing saga of evolving execution methods exemplifies the nature of the substantial changes that death penalty practices have undergone throughout American history. These changes have been the product of statewide rather than national regulation and have been driven by politicians rather than courts. Given the political origins of death penalty reform, successful state initiatives usually have had the backing of both opponents and supporters of capital punishment. Death penalty opponents often promoted reforms hoping to lay the groundwork for complete abolition or to make a repellent practice less inhumane. Death penalty supporters often promoted reforms to quell criticism in light of unfavorable media attention, as well as to stabilize and modernize the practice. State legislative initiatives to reform death penalty practices no doubt were influenced by forces beyond state borders—for example, by the work of national abolitionist organizations and by the experiences of other states. However, these external influences were lateral rather than top-down; the national government and the federal courts played no substantial role in any of the waves of changes in death penalty practices until the Supreme Court's constitutional intervention in the late twentieth century.

North and South

Although the waves of death penalty reform described above reached across the country, change often came more slowly, if at all, in the South. The history of the American death penalty has been one of broad-based change over time, yes—but it has also been a history of profound regional division that is still clearly visible in death penalty practices today. Scholars and activists often refer to the swath of currently active death penalty states in the American South as the "death belt," a play on the term "Bible Belt" that is used to describe essentially the same region. The distinctive Southern embrace of capital punishment is in large part a product of the South's historical practice of chattel slavery and of slavery's enduring racial legacy long after the end of the Civil War. One of the strongest predictors of a state's propensity to conduct executions today is its history of lynch mob activity more than a century ago.[52] Given this connection, it is no surprise that the current map of active death penalty states is predominantly a map of the former Confederacy; not a single state from that region is among the twenty-nine states that either have abolished capital punishment or have conducted no more than three executions since 1976.[53] The South's distinctive history with regard to the death penalty is central for our purposes because it played a significant role in eventually prompting the Supreme Court's constitutional scrutiny of capital punishment.

The South's disproportionate use of capital punishment began early in American history. The South conducted the most executions of any region during every historical period except for the 1600s, the first century of European settlement—when colonial populations were small, black inhabitants few, and executions of any kind rare. After the end of the seventeenth century, the South consistently outstripped every other region in total number of executions, the majority of which were of black people.[54] Although no less a figure than Virginia's Thomas Jefferson was an early questioner of the practice

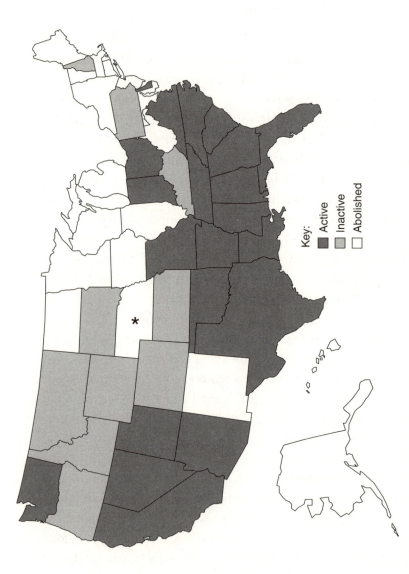

Status of the death penalty in the United States, 2016.

"Inactive" refers to states that currently retain the death penalty but have conducted no more than three executions since 1976. The asterisk (*) reflects that the Nebraska legislature's 2015 repeal of the death penalty has been suspended by a petition drive that will put the question up for a statewide referendum in November 2016 (Julie Bosman, "Nebraska to Vote on Abolishing Death Penalty After Petition Drive Succeeds," *New York Times*, October 16, 2015).

Key:

■ Active
▨ Inactive
☐ Abolished

of capital punishment, his position was exceedingly rare among Southern leaders. From the colonial era to the present day, Southern states have resisted both reform and abolition of the death penalty to a degree and with a consistency unique in the United States.

The South's intransigence on the issue speaks to the death penalty's practical uses and its symbolic significance. On the practical side, the large increase in executions, especially of blacks, in the South during the eighteenth century was the direct result of the large influx of African slaves to that region. As the South's slave labor economy grew, so did the demand by slave owners for state assistance in disciplining the growing enslaved population, to promote economic productivity and to protect the increasingly outnumbered white population from much-feared slave violence or revolt.[55] The extent to which capital punishment for slaves was perceived as a public good is demonstrated by the provision of state compensation to the owners of executed slaves, in the same way that property owners today are compensated when their land is taken by the state for a public use such as a highway.[56] For slaves, the threat of incarceration was not likely to serve as much of a deterrent. Hence, Southern states perceived a greater need than other states for maintaining corporal and capital punishment, often in extreme forms.[57] The use of torturous execution methods such as burning at the stake, as well as the public display of the corpses or body parts of those executed for slave revolt, were clearly meant as dire warnings to slaves about the harsh consequences of insurrection or violence against slave owners. After the Civil War and the abolition of slavery, Southern fears turned to potential violence from the newly freed and impoverished black population. Southern resistance to scaling back capital punishment thus continued in the aftermath of the Civil War, amid growing vigilante violence against freed blacks.

On the symbolic side, it is important to recognize that the use of capital punishment in the South served as a means of marking race and slave status. In eighteenth-century Europe and England and their colonies, different classes and races of people were punished in different ways. The choice of fine, whipping, hanging, or burning at the stake was imbued with meaning about the offender's place in society. As a result, in effect if not in explicit intent, "one of the functions of the death penalty . . . was *to create race:* to segregate the myriad social positions of the New World into hard and fast categories of white and black, free and enslaved."[58] After the Civil War and the end of slavery, the use of capital punishment in the South continued to have strong racial overtones—echoing and being echoed in return by the race-based mob violence of the practice of lynching. The racial resonances of the death penalty extended well beyond the era of Reconstruction. Franklin Zimring, who documented the connection between executions today and lynchings at the turn of the twentieth century, hypothesized that executions appeal to contemporary Southerners because of the South's long tradition of vigilante values, of which lynchings were the most dramatic manifestation.[59] Sociologist David Garland offered a broader, complementary account of the contemporary meanings of capital punishment in the South: "Support for the death penalty [in the South in the late twentieth century] became a marker of respect for states' rights and traditional authority; a respectable (that is to say, not openly racist) means of asserting that the civil rights movement had gone too far; and a vehicle for Southern resentment about interference by Northern liberals."[60]

The South's distinctive history of slavery, lynch mob violence, and racial division produced a distinctive Southern relationship to the waves of death penalty reform that moved across the country during the nineteenth century and after. The substantial narrowing of the ambit of the death penalty down to murder and treason, which was complete in the North by the time of the Civil War, never fully took hold in the South. While many Southern states did narrow their capital statutes in the antebellum period, they did not narrow them as radically as Northern states, and the narrowing that occurred applied only to whites. This differential treatment of whites and blacks reflected the widespread practice throughout the South prior to the Civil War of designating many offenses as capital on the basis of slave status and on the basis of race, regardless of slave status. In antebellum Virginia, death penalty scholar Sheri Lynn Johnson explains, "free African Americans (but not whites) could get the death penalty for rape, attempted rape, kidnapping a woman, and aggravated assault—all provided the victim was white; slaves in Virginia were eligible for death for commission of a mind-boggling sixty-six crimes."[61] At the same time, whites in Virginia could face the death penalty for just four crimes.[62] Although Southern states did not narrow their capital statutes, even for whites, as much as the North, actual executions of whites for crimes other than murder became increasingly rare in the South as the nineteenth century progressed. Historian Stuart Banner reported: "By the Civil War capital punishment for whites was, with a few exceptions, *in practice* reserved for murder throughout the South nearly as much as in the North."[63]

The elimination of capital punishment for whites other than for the crime of murder was achieved in the South less by the statutory narrowing adopted throughout the North than by discretion in the application of broad capital statutes. This discretion allowed Southern juries to mete out different punishments to black and white defendants in capital cases. The first states in the country to jettison mandatory capital statutes in favor of jury discretion were Tennessee and Alabama in 1841, followed by Louisiana in 1846—states that were slow to adopt any other restrictions on their death penalty practices. Scholars have speculated that Southern states were at the forefront of this—and only this—wave of death penalty reform because of the South's tolerance, indeed enthusiasm, for differential leniency for whites and blacks in capital cases.[64]

The narrowing of the ambit of the death penalty often led to legislative initiatives for wholesale abolition of capital punishment in the North, but never in the South. From the 1830s to the 1850s, lawmakers in New York, Massachusetts, Pennsylvania, Connecticut, Maine, New Hampshire, Vermont, New Jersey, Ohio, Illinois, and Indiana considered serious calls for abolition, though no wholesale abolition bills succeeded in these states. Michigan, Rhode Island, and Wisconsin became the first three American states to abolish the death penalty in the years between 1846 and 1853. Meanwhile, abolition of the death penalty was inconceivable in the antebellum South because of the widely held belief that capital punishment was needed to maintain the South's slave economy and society. The death penalty abolition movement's failure even to develop a toehold in the South also reflected the overlap in people and ideology between the death penalty abolition movement and the slavery abolition movement.[65] The two movements may have mutually reinforced each other in the North, but in the South, their linkage led them to fail together.

The split between the North and South means that the United States is in both the vanguard and the rearguard of worldwide death penalty abolition. The state of Michigan has the distinction of being the first government in the English-speaking world to abolish capital punishment for murder and lesser crimes.[66] Michigan has maintained its 1846 abolitionist stance to the present day; indeed, it amended its constitution in 1962 to prohibit the death penalty, thus precluding legislative reinstatement. At the same time, the United States is also the only Western democracy that still retains the death penalty; it is one of the top five executioners in the world today, along with China, Iran, Saudi Arabia, and Iraq.[67] This schizophrenic posture is a direct result of regional division on the issue of capital punishment within the United States, which was born of differing attitudes regarding the race-based practice of chattel slavery.

Even after the abolition of slavery, the death penalty abolition movement failed to gain any traction in the South. In the aftermath of the Civil War, capital punishment offered "an alternative form . . . of racial subjugation," explained Stuart Banner, a curb necessary in the eyes of some white Southerners "to restrain a primitive, animalistic black population."[68] White Southerners feared violent revenge and property crimes by the impoverished freed population, but above all, they seemed to fear sexual aggression by black men against white women. As historian William Carrigan observed, "Especially in the South, the late nineteenth century was beset with white paranoia on the topic [of the rape of white women by black men]."[69] These attitudes not only supported the use of capital punishment but also prompted rampant private violence against the newly freed black population, resulting in what Carrigan called a "reign of terror" and an "orgy of racial violence" in the postbellum South.[70] Between 1880 and 1930, more than 3,000 lynchings of blacks were recorded in Southern states, where the vast majority of such events took place.[71]

The practice of lynching constituted "a form of unofficial capital punishment" that in its heyday was even more common than the official kind.[72] The prevalence of lynching in the South at the turn of the century was illustrated by the ingenious argument of a defense lawyer to the jury in a case of alleged interracial attempted rape in Louisiana in 1907; his client *must* be innocent, he said, because otherwise he surely would already have been lynched![73]

But lynchings were not merely additional, informal executions. Rather, the practice of lynching helped to insulate the institution of capital punishment from lasting abolition. The Progressive Era saw one of the most active periods of death penalty repeal and reinstatement in America; ten states abolished capital punishment between 1897 and 1917, though eight of them reinstated the death penalty by the end of the 1930s, some within only a few years of abolition. During this period of flux, one of the primary considerations in favor of retention (and of reinstatement after abolition) of the death penalty was the need to maintain capital punishment to reduce the incidence of lynch mob violence. With the exception of Tennessee, all of the states that abolished the death penalty during this era were in the West or Midwest rather than the heartland of lynchings in the South. Nonetheless, a study of abolition during the Progressive Era concluded that lynchings were "*the* most important common triggering event in reinstatement of the death penalty" after abolition, occurring in each of the four states with the shortest periods of death penalty abolition.[74] The need to maintain the death penalty to deter lynching was a mainstay in debates about abolition and reinstatement during this period. As one Tennessee politician argued in opposition to abolition, "if this bill should become law it would be almost impossible to suppress mobs in their efforts to punish colored criminals."[75]

The most striking fact about Tennessee's abolition of capital punishment (aside from its brevity, as reinstatement occurred only four years later) is that, despite the common listing of Tennessee among the ten Progressive Era abolitionist states, Tennessee's bill did not actually abolish the death penalty. Rather, Tennessee's measure abolished the death penalty only for most forms of murder. The death penalty was retained for murder committed by a prisoner serving a life sentence (rare) and for the crime of rape (not so rare), which was in practice punished by death only when the perpetrator was black.[76] Tennessee's retention for rape was unique among the rest of the Progressive Era abolition bills. It reflected the widespread Southern belief that lynch mob violence simply could not be suppressed in cases of black men accused of the rape of white women, especially if the law refused to treat such outrages as capital crimes.

Concerns about lynch mob violence also played a role in delaying the move from public to private executions in the South. In part, Southern states were slower to abandon public executions because many of their citizens, white and black, wanted to attend such rituals.[77] While several Southern states had banned public executions by the end of the nineteenth century,[78] public opinion lagged behind official action. In the words of one Kentucky citizen in the late nineteenth century, viewing a public execution was "every tax-paying citizen's right."[79] The popularity of public executions in the South, according to law professor Franklin Zimring, reflected the South's greater embrace of "vigilante values" by which citizens "identify more closely with the punishment process [and] think of punishments as a community activity rather than the conduct of a governmental entity separate from community processes."[80] Although Southern blacks likely did not view executions as the authentic products of their own communities, black crowds nonetheless gathered at executions to hear religious leaders speak and to sing and pray with the condemned.[81] Southern sheriffs often accommodated local crowds by only partially enclosing the scaffold or by allowing hundreds into the putatively private jail yard.[82] These accommodations reflected not merely official indulgence of a popular pastime but also fear of the violent potential of a thwarted crowd.

Such fears were especially powerful and well-founded with regard to the execution of black men convicted of raping white women. Never was the (white) crowd's desire to see lethal justice done stronger than in cases involving black rapists. In two Southern states, "legislatures hastily revived public, local executions in response to white mobs threatening to lynch black rapists."[83] The day after the Arkansas legislature hurriedly brought back public executions for rapists in

1901, a crowd of thousands assembled to see a black man hanged. Two decades later, the Kentucky legislature also brought back public hanging for rape after a lynch mob sparked a riot in which five died and seventeen were wounded in the mob's unsuccessful attempt to snatch a black rapist from official custody.[84] Indeed, when Kentucky executed Rainey Bethea in 1936—the last public execution in the United States—Bethea was charged only with rape (despite having also committed murder) because public executions were authorized only for the crime of rape.[85] The threat of mob violence, targeted especially at black men accused or convicted of interracial rape, was so common in the South during the era of lynchings that it could seem foolhardy, sentimental, or simply counterproductive to restrict the more vulnerable, but morally and socially more benign, practice of public execution. In a world in which state-imposed death was *not* the worst or even the most likely fate that could befall a convicted black rapist, public executions were deployed by state officials to undermine the power of lynch mobs.

Finally, concerns about excessive pain or bodily mutilation, which played a prominent role in motivating the successive waves of experimentation with new, supposedly more humane execution methods, found more muted expression in the South than in other parts of the country. When Kentucky brought back public hangings for rape in 1920, it did so despite the fact that the state had substituted the electric chair for the gallows ten years previously. Humanitarian concerns took a back seat to the public's demand for public vengeance. Here, too, the South's distinctive history of lynchings plays an explanatory role. In the extrajudicial executions carried out by lynch mobs, it was common and intended for victims to suffer intense physical pain as well as fear. The lynching ritual (sometimes called "lynchcraft") often involved long abandoned punishments such as branding, eye gouging, and the cutting off of ears. Lynching victims also were frequently castrated, burned, or otherwise mutilated, and their clothing or even body parts claimed as souvenirs by spectators.[86] In short, the lynching victim's experience of extreme pain and bodily mutilation was considered a feature, not a bug, of the practice. It is unsurprising that concerns about the suffering of the condemned during legal executions generated less anxiety among Southerners than among those less accustomed to the graphic violence of lynchcraft.

The South's distinctive history—especially its history of race-based slavery and lynch mob violence—created a distinctively Southern relationship to the death penalty and to its possible abolition or reform. The South's more retrograde death penalty practices would eventually provide the impetus for the Supreme Court's first forays into constitutional regulation of capital punishment in the 1920s and 1930s and for the systematic attack on capital punishment as an issue of racial justice launched by civil rights litigators in the 1960s and 1970s. But for the dramatic regional divide on the death penalty, the Supreme Court might never have stepped in at all.

The Supreme Court Stays Out

Although the Supreme Court did not undertake its project of constitutional regulation of capital punishment in earnest until the 1960s, it was not for lack of invitations. Starting in the nineteenth century, capital litigants sought the Court's intervention in the conduct of capital trials and executions, primarily under constitutional provisions guaranteeing "due process of law" and forbidding the imposition of "cruel and unusual punishments." Despite these invitations, the Supreme Court largely stayed out of the business of regulating state death penalty practices, with only a few notable exceptions. The Court's *laissez faire* stance reflected both the state of constitutional law and the realities of federal power on the ground in the late nineteenth and early twentieth centuries—both of which would have to change in order to enable the Court's ultimate intervention.

The most common early constitutional challenges that specifically addressed capital punishment practices concerned methods of execution. The American colonies had inherited the gallows from England, and hanging remained the dominant execution method for the first hundred years of the new republic. However, the waves of experimentation with innovative execution methods that began in the late nineteenth century brought a number of constitutional challenges to the Supreme Court. The federal territory of Utah, first settled by Mormon pioneers, used the firing squad more than the gallows because Brigham Young, who led the Mormon church in the mid-1800s, argued that Mormon doctrine called for "blood atonement" for murder (a position rejected today by the Mormon Church), and hangings failed to produce the blood that shootings did.[87] The first constitutional challenge to a method of execution considered by the Supreme Court was brought in 1878 by Wallace Wilkerson, who was sentenced to death by firing squad for the murder of William Baxter in an altercation over a saloon card game in the Utah territory.

The supreme court of the territory upheld Wilkerson's sentence as within the trial judge's discretion to choose any authorized execution method (Utah law permitted shooting, hanging, and beheading). The U.S. Supreme Court granted review and held that criminal punishments imposed by territorial courts must comply with the federal Constitution, but that execution by firing squad did not constitute one of the "cruel and unusual punishments" forbidden by the Eighth Amendment. The Court reasoned that the firing squad had a long history of usage by military courts for crimes like mutiny and desertion, and that it did not constitute a punishment of "torture" or "unnecessary cruelty."[88] The Court was surely right that the firing squad, unlike the innovations that would follow it, was not a novel method of execution. However, the Court turned out to be wrong about the firing squad's lack of "cruelty" in Wilkerson's own case. Wilkerson declined to be blindfolded at his execution, and he flinched or braced himself at the sheriff's command to fire so that the shooters missed their mark, hitting Wilkerson's arm and torso but not his heart. It took more than twenty-seven minutes for Wilkerson to bleed to death "in front of astonished witnesses and a helpless doctor."[89]

On the heels of Wilkerson's case came a constitutional challenge to the first truly novel execution method—the electric chair. Thomas Edison, the father of modern electricity, veered quickly from supporting wholesale abolition of capital punishment in 1887 to promoting electrocution as a humane means of "instant" and "painless" death for the condemned in 1889.[90] Edison's advocacy regarding the electric chair was motivated by his bitter battle with industrial rival

George Westinghouse. Edison backed the marketing of direct current, while Westinghouse backed the use of alternating current. Edison shrewdly encouraged the use of Westinghouse's alternating current in the operation of the electric chair, hoping that it would support Edison's frequent claim that alternating current was more dangerous to human life than direct current; Edison even encouraged the press to use the term "westinghousing" for inducing death by electrocution.[91]

In 1889, when William Kemmler was sentenced to death in New York for the gruesome axe murder of his common-law wife, Mathilda "Tillie" Ziegler, he became the first person in the world to be sentenced to execution by electrocution. One of New York's most famous (and most expensive) lawyers, William Bourke Cockran, took on Kemmler's case and filed a constitutional challenge arguing that the electric chair constituted cruel and unusual punishment. It later became public that Cockran had been retained by the Westinghouse Electric Company, which hoped to get the electrocution law repealed so as to avoid a "gruesome display . . . of the dangers of a Westinghouse generator."[92] During the extensive hearings held in the case, the state introduced detailed testimony on how fast and painless death by electrocution would be, and how low the risk "that the criminal would be burnt."[93] Thomas Edison himself testified at the court hearings in favor of the effectiveness of the electric chair, and his testimony was widely credited as the decisive factor in the litigation. The New York courts upheld Kemmler's sentence, and the U.S. Supreme Court granted review to settle the question of whether electrocution was a "terrible torture," in the words of Kemmler's counsel, or a product of "the thoughts of eminent humanists," as New York's Attorney General contended.[94]

As with the firing squad, the Supreme Court held the electric chair constitutional. In the most quoted language of its *Kemmler* decision, the Court expounded on the meaning of the Eighth Amendment: "Punishments are cruel when they involve torture or a lingering death; but the punishment of death is not cruel within the meaning of that word as used in the Constitution. It implies there something inhuman and barbarous, something more than the mere extinguishment of life." What is often not understood about the decision in *Kemmler* is that the Court never directly resolved whether the electric chair was "cruel" under the Eighth Amendment. As the Court explained, the Eighth Amendment (along with the rest of the Bill of Rights) applied only to the federal government, not to the states. It was not until the 1960s that the Eighth Amendment, along with most of the rest of the Bill of Rights, was held to apply to the states as well as the federal government.[95] Thus, Kemmler's argument had to take a circuitous route: his lawyers argued that a cruel punishment imposed by a state would abridge "the privileges or immunities of citizens of the United States" or violate "due process of law" under the Fourteenth Amendment, which by its terms *did* apply to the states. To win under these legal rubrics, however, required something different from proof of "cruelty." The Court said that Kemmler had to offer proof of "an error *so gross* as to amount in law to a denial by the State of due process of law to one accused of crime, or of some right secured to him by the Constitution of the United States." The Court observed that New York had followed proper legislative procedure in adopting the electric chair, even appointing a commission to advise it on "the most humane and practical method known to modern science of carrying into effect the sentence of death in capital cases." Under these circumstances, the Court concluded, "We cannot perceive that the State has thereby abridged the privileges or immunities of the petitioner, or deprived him of due process of law."[96]

As with Wilkerson's torturous death by firing squad, Kemmler's execution turned out to be far more grisly than Edison's confident testimony predicted. After electrical current was run through Kemmler's body for seventeen seconds, the execution appeared to be complete. But it quickly became apparent that Kemmler was still alive, frothing at the mouth, heaving at the chest, and groaning through clenched lips. The current was turned on again for at least seventy more seconds, though some witnesses estimated that it was considerably longer. Smoke rose from Kemmler's head, and the smell of his burning flesh filled the room. The autopsy revealed that parts of his head and back, where the electrodes had been attached, had been scorched and blackened.[97] As the sensationalist *New York World* reported, "Part of his brain had been baked hard. Some of the blood in his head had been turned into charcoal."[98] The electric chair's highly publicized inaugural mishap called into question Edison's easy confidence in the new technology and the courts' reliance on Edison's expertise.

To be fair to the Supreme Court, it had no particular reason to predict that either Wilkerson's execution by firing squad or Kemmler's execution by electric chair would be botched. However, the challenge brought on behalf of Willie Francis, a black teenager convicted of murdering a popular white pharmacist in Louisiana, was a different matter. When Francis's case got to the Court, his execution *already* had been botched: when the state of Louisiana had tried to execute Francis in its electric chair in 1946, the chair had malfunctioned, running insufficient current through Francis's body to produce death. The constitutional question was whether Louisiana could put Francis in the electric chair a second time. Francis's counsel argued that it would be "cruel and unusual" to subject Francis to a second attempt at execution because of the physical pain of suffering further electrocution and the mental anguish of preparing for death a second time. The Court rejected these arguments, reiterating that the electric chair was not inherently cruel; rather, the Court explained, the chair's malfunction was "an unforeseeable accident" that could not be said to "add an element of cruelty to a subsequent execution."[99] The four dissenting justices were outraged, arguing that Francis's "death by installments" constituted a clearer constitutional violation "than would be presented by many lesser punishments prohibited by the Eighth Amendment or its state counterparts."[100]

Justice Felix Frankfurter wrote separately to explain why he cast the crucial fifth vote for allowing Louisiana a second chance to execute Willie Francis. Despite his acknowledged "personal feeling of revulsion against a State's insistence on its pound of flesh," Frankfurter noted, as the *Kemmler* Court had done, that the Eighth Amendment applied only to the federal government and not to the states. Thus, Frankfurter explained, the Court should not consider arguments based on "the historic meaning of 'cruel and unusual punishment.'" Rather, Francis's challenge should be considered under the more general and less demanding requirements of the due process clause, which allow the Court to strike down state policies only if they violate "immutable principles of justice, which inhere in the very idea of free government." Under this test, Frankfurter contended, "great tolerance toward a State's conduct is demanded of this Court."[101] Thus, as late as 1947, the year of its Willie Francis decision, the Supreme Court maintained its long-standing reluctance to interfere with state executions or to create any demanding constitutional standards to govern challenges to state execution methods.

In addition to seeking the Supreme Court's constitutional intervention on execution methods, litigants also repeatedly asked the Court to rule on the constitutionality of trial procedures in capital cases. These procedural challenges at first had no more success than the execution methods challenges. But in the 1920s and 1930s, the Court did reverse some capital convictions on grounds of unconstitutional trial procedures. In the process, it made its first forays into the constitutional regulation of capital punishment. The slowness of the Court to intervene in capital cases before the 1920s suggests what circumstances needed to change before the Court could undertake its more comprehensive constitutional regulatory project in the 1960s. And the Court's early interventions illustrate the kinds of concerns that would later impel the Court to intervene more extensively.

First, consider the procedural challenges that failed in the Supreme Court before the 1920s and the reasons for their failure. In 1884, the Supreme Court considered and rejected Joseph Hurtado's challenge to the capital charges brought against him for the murder of his wife's lover. Hurtado argued that he had a right to have his case presented to a grand jury for indictment—to have a group of his fellow citizens determine whether "probable cause" existed to bring formal charges against him. California law permitted all charges, even capital ones, to be brought by a prosecutor rather than a grand jury and to have probable cause determined by a magistrate at a subsequent preliminary hearing. If Hurtado had been prosecuted without an indictment in a federal court, his challenge would have succeeded without question, because the Fifth Amendment provides that "No person shall be held to answer for a capital, or otherwise infamous crime, unless on a presentment or indictment of a grand jury" except in wartime military cases. However, the *Hurtado* Court explained that the Fifth Amendment (like the Eighth Amendment) applied only to the federal government, not to the states. Thus, for Hurtado to prevail, he would have to demonstrate a violation of due process under the Fourteenth Amendment. The Court found no such violation, taking a narrow, historical view of due process and noting that prosecution without a grand jury's indictment had deep roots in the common law. Given this historical imprimatur, the Court concluded that a magistrate's probable cause determination after a preliminary hearing was adequate to safeguard a (state) defendant's rights at the charging stage. As for what kinds of state procedures might be held to violate due process, the Court invoked the same kind of general, abstract language that Frankfurter would later invoke in the Willie Francis case: due process requires adherence to those "general principles of public liberty and private right, which lie at the foundation of all free government."[102]

Despite this high-flown language, the Court remained slow to find violations of due process even in cases far more egregious than Hurtado's. In 1884, the year *Hurtado* was decided, Leo Frank was born to a New York Jewish family. When Frank was twenty-nine, he was charged on flimsy evidence with the capital murder of Mary Phagan, a thirteen-year-old girl who worked at the National Pencil Company in Atlanta, Georgia, where Frank was superintendent. Anger at the death of Mary Phagan and prejudice against Frank as a Yankee and a Jew led enraged crowds to gather outside the courthouse during Frank's trial, shouting threats through the open windows such as "Hang the Jew, or we'll hang you!"[103] The trial judge advised Frank's lawyers that both they and their client might be in danger should Frank be acquitted. To the cheers of the waiting crowd, Frank was convicted and sentenced to death. Frank challenged the outcome of his trial on the grounds that the mob's influence violated his rights to a fair trial and an impartial verdict—the very heart of "due process of law." The Supreme Court rejected his challenge, holding that the state had supplied Frank with adequate "corrective process" by allowing consideration of his motion for a new trial and his appeal to the Georgia Supreme Court. Because the Georgia courts rejected Frank's claims of unfairness "save in a few minor particulars not amounting to more than irregularities," the Supreme Court concluded that he had not been denied due process of law.[104]

Justice Oliver Wendell Holmes wrote a stinging dissent, declaring: "Mob law does not become due process of law by securing the assent of a terrorized jury." Holmes emphasized, "We are not speaking of mere disorder, or mere irregularities in procedure, but of a case where the processes of justice are actually subverted."[105] In some ways, Holmes's view of the case won the day. National outrage at the inadequacy of the legal proceedings in Frank's case led the governor of Georgia to commute Frank's death sentence to life imprisonment in 1915, and Frank later received a posthumous pardon from the Georgia Board of Pardons and Paroles in 1986. Moreover, as we shall see, Holmes's due process analysis would prevail in similar cases in the two decades following Frank's case. But in the way that mattered most, Leo Frank lost: after the governor's commutation, he was abducted from his prison cell and hanged by a lynch mob in front of a jubilant crowd of thousands.

Frank's fate suggests that even if the Supreme Court had found a violation of due process in his case, it would not have availed him, because a reversal by the Court would have enraged the lynch mob just as surely as the governor's commutation did. Indeed, the Court's own experience in another, similar case suggested as much. In 1906, Ed Johnson, a black man, was charged with the rape of a white woman in Chattanooga, Tennessee. Johnson was convicted and sentenced to death by an all-white jury on extremely flimsy evidence (the victim and sole witness to the crime testified, "I will not swear that he is the man") in a hasty proceeding suffused with the threat of mob violence, just as Leo Frank's trial was. The supreme court of Tennessee rejected Johnson's appeal, but Justice John Marshall Harlan, after consulting with his brethren, accepted review of the case on habeas corpus as the circuit justice hearing emergency appeals from the federal circuit that included Tennessee. The day following Justice Harlan's order, a mob removed Johnson from his cell with the tacit permission of jail officials and the county sheriff. The mob brought Johnson to the county bridge that spanned the Tennessee River, where he was hanged and also shot more than fifty times. One of those involved was a deputy sheriff who fired five shots at point-blank range and left a note pinned to Johnson's body, which spoke not to the public of Chattanooga, but rather to the Supreme Court in Washington. The note read, "To Justice Harlan. Come get your nigger now." After the first and only criminal trial ever held under the Supreme Court's original jurisdiction, the Court sentenced several of the Tennessee officials involved in Johnson's lynching to short prison terms for contempt of court. But there was nothing that the Court could do for Ed Johnson.[106]

The Johnson lynching was a dramatic demonstration of the fragility of legal order and federal power in the South around the turn of the twentieth century—especially in the context of alleged crimes by blacks against whites. During the heyday of lynchings in the South in the 1890s, extrajudicial executions by lynch mob outnumbered legal executions—something every court, including the Supreme Court, had to keep in mind. The possibility that intrusive federal judicial review of state court trials would lead to mob violence was very real, and it likely played a role in the Court's unwillingness to read the Fourteenth Amendment's promise of due process of law too expansively. During this period, interpreting the due process clause to require state courts to afford criminal defendants rights equivalent to those in the federal Bill of Rights might well have been unenforceable, at least in the South. Before the Supreme Court could attempt any comprehensive constitutional regulation of state death penalty practices, it needed to have confidence in the enforceability of its assertions of federal judicial power over state criminal processes, especially in the context of highly charged interracial capital crimes in the South. And the Court needed to develop a broader conception of due process of law, one that would encompass the right to be free from "cruel and unusual punishments."

The Supreme Court took some small, tentative steps in the direction of these changes in federal power and federal constitutional law in the 1920s and 1930s. Less than a decade after rejecting Leo Frank's challenge to his mob-dominated trial in Marietta, Georgia, the Court reversed the convictions of five black men sentenced to death in Phillips County, Arkansas, on grounds similar to those urged by Frank. The case arose from an incident in which a group of whites shot into a church during a meeting of black unionists and the blacks fired back, killing a white man. In the days that followed this incident, a race riot ensued in which dozens of blacks were hunted down and killed; a handful of white men were killed as well. Almost eighty blacks, but no whites, faced charges for their actions during the mayhem, twelve of whom received the death penalty after truncated trials before all-white juries in a courthouse surrounded by huge crowds of angry whites threatening a lynching.[107] Five of these capital convictions were reviewed by the Supreme Court in *Moore v. Dempsey.*

This time, less than a decade after his fiery *Frank* dissent, Justice Holmes wrote the majority opinion for the Court in *Moore.* Holmes described the facts as alleged by the petitioners: the lynch mob was held off only by the promise of officials that speedy convictions and executions would ensue; the defense counsel failed to consult with his clients or to make any legal challenges or to call any witnesses for the defense (even though witnesses were available); the trial at issue took only three-quarters of an hour followed by less than five minutes of jury deliberation; and "if any prisoner by any chance had been acquitted by a jury he could not have escaped the mob." Holmes claimed that he was applying rather than overruling the *Frank* decision, but he took a much less deferential posture toward state "corrective processes." He insisted that the federal courts on habeas corpus review must consider for themselves "whether the facts alleged are true." Holmes concluded, "if the case is that the whole proceeding is a mask—that counsel, jury and judge were swept to the fatal end by an irresistible tide of public passion, and that the State Courts failed to correct the wrong, [then nothing] can prevent this Court from securing to the petitioners their constitutional rights."[108]

The *Moore* Court's more expansive view of the role of the federal courts in ensuring due process in state criminal trials was a harbinger of further expansions in the 1930s. In *Brown v. Mississippi,* the Court reversed the convictions of three black men sentenced to death for the murder of a white man because their "confessions" had been extracted from them by prolonged torture. The Court could barely contain its disgust at the (uncontested) description of the treatment of the suspects by state officials which, the Court remarked, "reads more like pages torn from some medieval account, than a record made within the confines of a modern civilization which aspires to an enlightened constitutional government." The Court acknowledged that the Fifth Amendment right to be free from compelled self-incrimination applied only in federal and not in state courts—the same observation that generally preceded its rejection of challenges to capital convictions in earlier cases—but this time the Court went on to say that the right against physically coerced confessions was one "so rooted in the traditions and conscience of our people as to be ranked as fundamental." The Court pungently observed: "The rack and torture chamber may not be substituted for the witness stand."[109]

Although both *Moore* and *Brown* were capital cases, the Court's more expansive due process rulings in these cases did not formally turn on the fact that the death penalty was in play. The constitutional rejection of mob-dominated trials and confessions extracted by torture applied to capital and noncapital cases alike (though such extreme events were more likely to occur in capital cases). However, the Supreme Court took a further, novel step toward the constitutional regulation of capital punishment in the famous case of the "Scottsboro Boys." In Alabama in 1931, nine young black men and boys were accused, on extremely scanty evidence, of raping two white women who had been riding in the same rail freight car. They were all quickly charged and tried. Eight of them were sentenced to death, after having been afforded virtually no legal representation in the sketchiest of trials. The case was so flimsy that the state of Alabama eventually issued an official pardon (albeit in 2013).[110] In 1932, the Supreme Court reversed the Scottsboro convictions and for the first time created new constitutional law specific to capital cases. The Court held that defendants were entitled to representation by counsel in capital trials, a holding it would not extend to noncapital cases until the landmark case of *Gideon v. Wainright* more than thirty years later.[111]

The Court's willingness to expand due process and to make new constitutional law for capital cases was undoubtedly motivated by the Court's outrage at the "appalling injustices" produced by "farcical trials" in the South where blacks were accused, often falsely, of serious crimes against whites—a system that could fairly be described, according to legal historian Michael Klarman, as "legal lynching."[112] Although such cases occurred with frequency well before the 1920s and 1930s, the Court's first interventions came later, at a time when actual lynchings were far less common. The incidence of lynching had peaked around 1890, and by the 1920s and 1930s the practice had fallen off dramatically, to less than a tenth of what it had been at its height.[113] The Court could thus have greater confidence that its rulings sparing black defendants in the South would not be overruled by the lynch mob.

The Court's interventions, especially its novel ruling on the constitutional distinctiveness of capital punishment in the Scottsboro case, were forerunners of a revolution to come forty years later. In the 1960s, the conditions that produced the Court's initial interventions would reappear in heightened form. The constitutional law of due process would be revolutionized and grow to incorporate virtually all of the federal Bill of Rights. This expansion coincided with increasing national discomfort about the treatment of blacks in the South, not least in the criminal justice system. This discomfort helped to drive the expansion of constitutional rights; in turn, the new constitutional order offered new tools to address Southern injustices. Moreover, the Civil Rights Movement had demonstrated that the federal government was able, when it chose, to enforce unpopular judicial rulings in Southern states. The situation was ripe for the launching of a full-scale constitutional attack on capital punishment, motivated by its race-based applications in the South. Scottsboro turned out to be a shot across the bow of the American death penalty, though the warning went unheard and unheeded for nearly four decades.

CHAPTER TWO

The Supreme Court Steps In

THE 1960S WAS A TIME of great change in the United States. The decade saw a wholesale transformation of race relations, reflected in and reinforced by the Civil Rights Act of 1964 and the Voting Rights Act of 1965. It also saw the expansion of the welfare state with President Lyndon Johnson's War on Poverty, the growing cultural instability in part resulting from the deeply unpopular Vietnam War, and the beginning of the struggle for sex equality. These challenges to long-standing practices forged an environment conducive to a rethinking of the American death penalty.

Even with these dramatic upheavals, the speed and scale of change regarding the death penalty was startling. At the beginning of the 1960s, capital punishment in the United States seemed relatively stable despite some signs of decline. Executions and death sentences had fallen significantly from the highs they had reached during the Great Depression (per capita rates fell even further), and a few jurisdictions considered or achieved abolition in the 1950s and early 1960s. But there were no signs pointing toward nationwide reconsideration of the punishment. Like other criminal justice issues, the death penalty was generally considered a state and local issue, and the prospects for widespread political rejection of capital punishment were remote. Although waves of political reform (including abolition) of the death penalty punctuated our history, the most robust periods saw only a minority of states abolish, and no state in the Deep South had ever done so, a fact that remains true to this day. Moreover, the virtual absence of federal judicial regulation of capital punishment made it unlikely that the U.S. Supreme Court would enter the fray and declare the death penalty unconstitutional. In the decades preceding the 1960s, the Court's interventions were few and relatively modest, focusing on extreme malfunctions in the adversary process and not on the death penalty itself. Given this record, the influential legal scholar Alexander Bickel, writing in 1962, declared it "quite unthinkable" that the Court would soon declare capital punishment unconstitutional, given the Court's "willfully passed" opportunities to engage the issue. Bickel wrote that the "moment of judgment" for the American death penalty was likely "a generation or more away."[1]

Only a decade later, in 1972, the Supreme Court effectively struck down capital punishment as it was then practiced across the country in *Furman v. Georgia,* emptying the nation's death rows. The six-column banner headline that appeared in the *New York Times* the next day was "as large and as bold as when, equally improbably, men had landed on the moon in 1969."[2] At the time of the decision, many informed observers—including some of the justices on the Court—believed that the American death penalty had run its course. Had the Court's decision stuck, the United States would have been somewhat early but essentially on the same track as its Western democratic peers in abandoning capital punishment. But in relatively short order, politicians denounced the Court's intervention, states revised their death penalty statutes, and the Court gave its imprimatur to many of the new schemes in a set of landmark decisions in 1976. The death penalty was revived. By the 1980s, death sentences and executions had again become routine events. In roughly a two-decade span, the American death penalty had moved full circle. A familiar and stable fixture of state criminal justice systems in the early 1960s, capital punishment came perilously close to extinction in the early 1970s. Just as quickly, the death penalty was revived and emerged in a more robust and stable form, inaugurating a new era in which the

United States would become the leading executioner—and eventually lone—among Western democracies.

The "new" American death penalty differed in a fundamental respect from its previous incarnation; it would be subject to ongoing extensive regulation by the federal courts, particularly the Supreme Court. The United States thus charted a novel third course between the options of retention and abolition: it authorized the continued use of capital punishment, but sought to tame its arbitrary, discriminatory, and excessive applications through a growing set of constitutional doctrines. This choice of retention with regulation has had enormous consequences for the shape of the American death penalty as well as the prospects for its eventual abolition.

How did the American death penalty become so vulnerable so quickly? And how did the seeming demise of the death penalty so swiftly reverse course, with the United States emerging as the sole Western democracy engaging in an otherwise disappearing practice? These two stories are essential to understanding the current (and exceptional) American situation of retention and regulation.

The Road to (Near) Abolition

The triggering event for the near abolition of the American death penalty was a striking reprise of the Scottsboro case from the 1930s—a petition to the U.S. Supreme Court from Frank Lee Rudolph, a black man sentenced to death for raping a white woman in Alabama. Nothing in Rudolph's petition was particularly notable. The Court, which had been essentially absent in regulating the American death penalty, chose yet again not to intervene, declining review in 1963. But unlike past denials of review, in this case three justices called on the Court to get involved. Justice Arthur Goldberg, writing for himself and two other justices dissenting from denial of review, announced that he thought the Court should decide whether the Eighth and Fourteenth Amendments to the Constitution permitted the imposition of death for the crime of rape. The announcement was striking for several reasons. Justices rarely say anything when the Court declines to hear a case, reflecting the Court's general reluctance to tip its hand about constitutional issues not yet decided or to engage in interpretation outside a live case or controversy. Moreover, Justice Goldberg raised a constitutional question that was neither litigated in the courts below nor presented to the Court. The defendant's petition had sought relief on narrower grounds (he argued, among other things, that the presence of "vicious police dogs" during his interrogation rendered his confession involuntary).[3] Perhaps most importantly, the Court had never declared any significant feature of the American death penalty unconstitutional, so Justice Goldberg was suggesting an unprecedented limitation on state capital practices.

We know now that Justice Goldberg's dissent from denial was the product of his remarkable calculated effort to subject capital punishment to constitutional review (and perhaps abolition). Prior to the 1963 Supreme Court term, he had asked Alan Dershowitz, his law clerk (later a famous law professor and defense attorney), to produce a memorandum addressing the constitutionality of capital punishment. Rather than reaching his constitutional position in response to cases presented to the Court, he searched for cases that could serve as vehicles to vindicate his constitutional position. Indeed, Justice Goldberg's brief tenure on the Court was characterized by his "untamed exuberance for constitutional claims of both liberty and equality."[4] Ultimately, Justice Goldberg was unable to persuade enough of his colleagues to take up the issue in the 1963 term (he needed just one more vote to grant review). Perhaps Justice Goldberg did not even want the Court to intervene at that point but instead hoped to inspire legal challenges in future cases. If this was his purpose, he clearly succeeded. The abbreviated version of Dershowitz's memorandum became the dissent from denial of review that galvanized the concerted constitutional litigation campaign against the death penalty.

The dissent caught the attention of the NAACP Legal Defense Fund, the preeminent civil rights law firm in the country. The LDF's legal staff was very familiar with Supreme Court practice, having engaged in decades of litigation before the Court on numerous fronts, most famously its efforts to desegregate schools and other public facilities. The LDF understood the significance of three justices registering their doubts about the constitutionality of the death penalty for rape. But it was unclear whether and how the LDF should enter the fray. As an organization devoted to racial equality, the LDF believed that capital punishment generally and the death penalty for rape in particular were engines of racial injustice, so it seemed natural for the LDF to pursue the dissent's challenge. The LDF had involved itself in numerous capital cases over the preceding decades. It chose its cases carefully, focusing primarily on defendants it regarded as innocent and framing its claims relatively modestly (it never challenged the death penalty itself as an unacceptable form of punishment). But the LDF's work on capital cases was especially difficult as well as dangerous. At trial, sometimes the best the LDF could hope for was a guilty verdict with a non-death sentence. Thurgood Marshall, who led the LDF during that period, used to say that when a jury returned a life sentence in a highly aggravated case with a white victim and a black defendant, he knew the jury believed the defendant to be innocent.

Marshall put himself at great risk personally in the LDF's capital cases. Mark Tushnet's biography describes Marshall's near lynching following his representation of two black men in a capital case in Columbia, Tennessee.[5] Gilbert King's account of Marshall's subsequent involvement in an interracial rape case from Groveland, Florida, likewise documents the peril that accompanied efforts to vindicate the rights of blacks accused of violence toward whites. During the Groveland case, Harry Moore, the Florida Executive Director of the NAACP, and his wife were killed when their house was firebombed after Moore spoke out about the local sheriff's mistreatment of the suspects. In King's view, the Groveland case became the "impetus" for the LDF's decision to take up the anti–death penalty campaign in the 1960s.[6]

By the mid-1960s, the LDF arrived at a strategy to end the American death penalty. The centerpiece of the strategy was to bring executions in the United States to a halt. If the LDF could secure a moratorium on executions, there would be enormous pressure on courts, particularly the Supreme Court, not to let the practice resume. "The politics of abolition boiled down to this: for each year the United States went without executions, the more hollow would ring claims that the American people could not do without them," explained Michael Meltsner, an LDF lawyer, in his compelling first-hand account of the effort. "The longer death-row inmates waited, the greater their numbers, the more difficult it would be for the courts to permit the first execution."[7]

The mechanics of securing a moratorium were unusually complex. The LDF had only a handful of lawyers working on capital cases, and they were certainly not equipped to represent the hundreds of death-sentenced inmates nationwide. The LDF prepared "Last Aid Kits" for distribution to lawyers across the country who had clients facing execution. The kits contained a variety of stock legal claims aimed at securing stays of execution. Lawyers were encouraged to assert newly available procedural rights applicable to all criminal defendants, including the right to *Miranda* warnings during police interrogations and the exclusion of evidence seized in violation of the Fourth Amendment, which emerged as part of the Warren Court's revolution in constitutional criminal procedure. But the LDF's greatest contribution was its innovative set of new constitutional arguments directed specifically at the administration of the death penalty.

The biggest obstacle to a comprehensive challenge to the death penalty was the plain fact that a large majority of states had capital statutes on the books. The widespread legislative embrace of the death penalty undermined the claim that the death penalty was contrary to "evolving standards of decency"—the Court's touchstone for assessing whether punishments are "cruel and unusual" under the Eighth Amendment. Anthony ("Tony") Amsterdam, the architect of the LDF strategy, constructed a set of claims that targeted weaknesses in prevailing capital practices while cleverly laying the groundwork for a more encompassing challenge. One central claim focused on the absence of standards to guide the sentencing decision between life and death. By the 1960s, every capital jurisdiction afforded absolute discretion to jurors to impose or withhold the death penalty.[8] The American Law Institute (ALI), a highly influential, nonpartisan law reform organization, addressed the death penalty in the early 1960s and suggested refining capital statutes to guide the capital sentencing decision. The Model Penal Code—the ALI's influential blueprint for state criminal laws—promulgated aggravating and mitigating factors to make jurors' decisions more principled and consistent across cases. But capital jurisdictions essentially ignored the ALI's proposed reforms. By the late 1960s, the standardless discretion allowed by capital statutes seemed especially problematic in light of the rarity of capital verdicts. The breadth of states' death penalty schemes made a large number of offenders eligible for the death penalty—not just for murder, but also, in some jurisdictions, for rape, kidnapping, robbery, and burglary, among other offenses. Yet jurors (and prosecutors) exercised their absolute discretion to limit the actual use of the death penalty to a small number of cases. The absence of guidance or standards meant there was no guarantee that the few persons sentenced to death were truly more deserving of death than the vast majority of offenders who received lesser punishment.

The LDF separately emphasized three pervasive problems in the administration of capital punishment in addition to the problem of general arbitrariness. First, the distribution of death sentences was not merely random, but infected with racial bias. Allowing—but not requiring—the death penalty for rape meant that in practice the punishment was reserved for black defendants convicted of raping white women. Blacks constituted the overwhelming majority of those executed for rape in the twentieth century (of the 455 inmates executed for rape during the period 1930–1967, 405 were black[9]). Second, because of its rare, haphazard, and discriminatory use, the LDF argued that the death penalty for rape (as well as robbery and other nonhomicidal crimes) amounted to disproportionate punishment, following the lead of Justice Goldberg in his dissent from denial of review in *Rudolph*. Finally, the LDF highlighted the odd "unitary" structure of death penalty decision making—in which jurors decided the question of punishment at the same time (and based on the same limited evidence) that they adjudicated guilt or innocence, without a separate sentencing hearing. As a practical matter, that approach meant that jurors often had minimal information about a defendant as they decided the question of life or death, because defendants often declined to offer evidence at trial that explained why they should not be sentenced to death for fear that a jury might regard such evidence as an indirect admission of guilt.[10]

As the LDF litigated these discrete issues—discretion without standards, racial discrimination, lack of proportionality, and unitary proceedings—it also constructed a plausible basis for the broader claim that the death penalty violated contemporary standards, notwithstanding its legislative authorization and broad availability. Amsterdam contended that the death penalty remained on the books and was tolerated by the public only because of these distorting practices. On the one hand, these practices produced death verdicts that did not reliably express popular values. Unitary proceedings facilitated the imposition of death sentences that jurors otherwise would have rejected had they been afforded a meaningful opportunity to consider mitigating aspects of the offender and the offense. This risk was exacerbated by the practice of "death qualifying" capital juries, a process for excluding potential jurors based on their unwillingness to consider imposing the death penalty. On the other hand, the distorting practices challenged by the LDF prevented the community from having to live with large numbers of death sentences and executions. Unbridled discretion meant the death penalty could serve a symbolic rather than practical function. Legislators and the general public could take a tough stand on crime by espousing a general belief in the death penalty, knowing that its actual use could and would be avoided through routine grants of unregulated "mercy." That same discretion allowed the death penalty to operate at the margins of society, reserving the punishment for poor and minority defendants (and in cases involving valued victims) while exempting less despised offenders. In short, as the LDF told it, Americans tolerated the death penalty on the books only because they did not have to confront its regular, evenhanded enforcement.

The litigation of these issues in the Supreme Court was a rollercoaster ride during the latter half of the 1960s. In 1968, the Supreme Court delivered the first major victory for the abolitionist movement, rejecting Illinois's overbroad standard for death qualification. The Court held that states could not exclude potential jurors simply because they harbored some concerns ("conscientious scruples") about the death penalty. To strike such jurors for "cause," the state would have to demonstrate that they were so fixed in their anti–death penalty views that they would reject death in every case.[11] Given the rising number of Americans opposed to the death penalty and the historical practice of requiring unanimity in criminal cases, many observers believed that this limit on death qualification would radically reduce states' abilities to secure capital sentences.

The same year, the Court also agreed to hear two significant cases. In *Maxwell v. Bishop,* the Court granted review on the issues of discretion without standards and unitary proceedings, and in *Boykin v. Alabama,* the Court decided to address whether the death penalty amounted to excessive punishment for the crime of armed robbery.[12] These grants of review fit perfectly within the LDF approach. Both cases had potentially broad reach. Standardless discretion was the norm in capital jurisdictions, and many states employed the unitary procedure. Even though it was extremely rare to receive a death sentence for robbery, *Boykin* offered an unprecedented opportunity for the Court to find an application of the death penalty disproportionate—too harsh for the crime. Neither case challenged the death penalty categorically. The LDF first wanted a series of smaller victories before a comprehensive challenge reached the Court. The LDF had urged the Court *not* to decide whether death qualification of capital juries unfairly skewed the guilt-innocence determination (as opposed to the determination of sentence), fearing that the broader challenge to death qualification had reached the Court prematurely. The organization advised the Court to await further empirical studies of the prejudicial impact of prevailing death qualification practices.[13]

By the end of 1968, the moratorium strategy was in full gear. No one had been executed in the United States in over a year. The Court's inclusion of *Maxwell* and *Boykin* on the docket meant that executions were unlikely for the foreseeable future, as the Court's anticipated decisions in those cases could well affect the legality of the sentences of other death row inmates. Cautious optimism that *Maxwell* and *Boykin* would provide momentum toward a comprehensive challenge, however, quickly dissipated. The Court resolved *Maxwell* and *Boykin* on narrow grounds, granting relief to the individual defendants but declining to address the potentially broad capital issues implicated by the cases. The Court selected two other cases to serve as vehicles for the standardless discretion and unitary procedure issues, but the Court's resolution of those issues in 1971 seemed calamitous to the abolitionist cause. In *McGautha v. California,* a solid majority of the Court rejected the idea that due process requires states to develop standards to decide who should live and die. Justice John Marshall Harlan II, writing for the majority, expressed grave doubts that death penalty decision making could be improved by additional instructions. On the one hand, any list of relevant considerations would inevitably be incomplete, given the range of circumstances that might bear on the appropriateness of the death sentence. On the other hand, instructing the jury to consider all potentially relevant factors would amount to "meaningless 'boiler-plate' "—no more helpful than California's instruction that the choice between life and death "shall be fixed to the judgment, conscience, and absolute discretion of the jury." In the end, Justice Harlan appeared to view the argument against standardless discretion as naïve, suggesting, "Those who have come to grips with the hard task" of taming the death penalty decision with standards have learned the unhappy fact that it is impossible: "To identify before the fact those characteristics of criminal homicides and their perpetrators which call for the death penalty, and to express these characteristics in language which can be fairly understood and applied by the sentencing authority, appear to be tasks which are beyond present human ability."[14]

The loss in *McGautha,* with its rejection of the broadest and most promising challenge to prevailing capital procedures, caused the LDF to rethink whether the Supreme Court was the right arena in which to pursue abolition. The LDF began to shift its focus to the states, hoping to persuade executive officials to prevent executions and state legislatures to reconsider the punishment. Inside the Court, the prospects for judicial intervention seemed dim. William Brennan, the justice most troubled by the continued retention of the death penalty, was resigned to move on. The sole remaining broad challenge to the death penalty was rooted in the Eighth Amendment—the claim that the death penalty was "cruel and unusual" and no longer comported with evolving standards of decency. That claim seemed unlikely to find sufficient support from a Court that had just rejected a challenge to state death-sentencing procedures. The liberals on the Court were willing to deny review of the Eighth Amendment claim because it had little chance to prevail and would represent a jurisprudential obstacle to a similar sort of claim down the road. But Justice Black wanted to put an exclamation point on the Court's work and make clear that executions could resume.[15] So the Court granted review in several cases, including *Furman v. Georgia,* to decide whether the death penalty constituted cruel and unusual punishment under the Eighth Amendment.

The facts of *Furman* underscored the broad reach and arbitrary implementation of the American death penalty. William Henry Furman, an uneducated, mentally ill black man, had broken into the home of William and Lanell Micke in Savannah, Georgia. Hearing the intrusion, William Micke went to investigate, but Furman ran away, slamming the kitchen door behind him as he left. Furman stated at trial that he tripped over a cord on the porch while backing away and accidentally discharged his gun. In contrast, a detective testified that Furman had told him that, after slamming the door, he turned around and fired one shot before fleeing. Whether or not the gun went off accidentally, it was clear that William Micke was killed by a single bullet that passed through a closed wooden door. At trial, the jury was instructed that it could find Furman guilty of murder on a "felony murder" theory even if the shooting was accidental. The judge instructed the jury to choose between life in prison and death by electrocution as it saw fit, adding that the jury was not required to give "any reason for its action in fixing the punishment at life or death." After deliberating on the combined questions of guilt and punishment for about an hour and a half, following a trial that had lasted less than a single day, the jury convicted Furman of murder and sentenced him to death.[16] The imposition of the death penalty against a thwarted burglar who shot—quite possibly accidentally—

toward a closed door while fleeing illustrated how the death penalty was not confined to the "worst of the worst" offenders.

As the LDF prepared for argument in the newly granted cases, the prospects for success seemed increasingly remote. The lack of votes in *McGautha* was troubling enough, but the Court's composition was also changing in ways unlikely to aid the cause. President Nixon, who had already replaced Chief Justice Earl Warren and Justice Abe Fortas with Warren Burger and Harry Blackmun prior to *McGautha*, had two more appointments with the departures of Justices Hugo Black and John Marshall Harlan. Neither of the new justices— Lewis Powell and William Rehnquist—seemed like plausible votes against the death penalty.

When the LDF argued the cases in early 1972, it used many of the same facts underlying the standardless discretion argument but deployed them in a new way. Rather than arguing that states needed to add standards to ensure consistent application of the death penalty, the LDF claimed that standardless discretion allowed states to retain the death penalty without actually using it. Standardless discretion was not unconstitutional in its own right. It was the mechanism that propped up a form of punishment that lacked meaningful public support and that would not be tolerated if regularly implemented. The claim, in essence, was that the death penalty was no longer embraced by the American people and that the Court should reject it as cruel and unusual punishment.

Remarkably, given its recent decision in *McGautha*, the Court agreed that the prevailing administration of the death penalty violated the constitution. The five justices in the *Furman* majority issued a brief opinion indicating that the "imposition and carrying out of the death penalty" in the cases before it would amount to "cruel and unusual punishment." But the agreement ended there. Each of the five wrote a separate opinion reflecting his distinctive view about the constitutionality of the American death penalty. Worse still, in terms of communicating clearly the Court's constitutional position, none of the justices in the majority joined anyone else's opinion. The five concurring opinions spanned over 130 pages of the U.S. Reports. Two of the justices—Marshall and Brennan—embraced the LDF claim that the death penalty was no longer consistent with prevailing societal values. Justice Brennan emphasized the distinctiveness of the death penalty and argued that it is "uniquely degrading to human dignity." Justice Marshall insisted that the average citizen, if informed about the facts surrounding the death penalty, would "find it shocking to his conscience and sense of justice." But the other three justices focused on the prevailing administration rather than the overall constitutionality of the death penalty. Justice William O. Douglas worried that the discretion of judges and juries allowed for the discriminatory application of the death penalty against defendants who were poor, despised, or members of unpopular minority groups. Justices Potter Stewart and Byron White focused on the arbitrariness caused by the combination of infrequent death sentences and the absence of standards. Justice Stewart, for example, declared that "the petitioners are among a capriciously selected random handful upon whom the sentence of death has in fact been imposed." Given this capricious selection, he memorably insisted that the death sentences before the Court were cruel and unusual "in the same way that being struck by lightning is cruel and unusual." Justice White maintained that the infrequency of death sentences and executions undermined any claim that the death penalty meaningfully served important purposes of punishment, such as deterrence or retribution.[17] The concerns of Stewart and White were taken by most legal observers to be the crux of the decision. Their opinions provided the narrowest rationale supporting the result. More crucially, they alone among the justices in *McGautha* abandoned their position on the constitutionality of standardless discretion, making the *Furman* majority possible.

Only Justices Brennan and Marshall condemned the death penalty as a punishment (as opposed to its present administration), but many observers on and off the Court believed that *Furman* marked the end of the American death penalty. In his opinion, Justice Marshall announced that the United States had achieved "a major milestone in the long road up from barbarism" by joining "the approximately 70 other jurisdictions in the world which celebrate their regard for civilization and humanity by shunning capital punishment."[18] In private, Justice Stewart told his clerks that the death penalty in America was finished.[19] But the decision would face enormous backlash, and its effects would be short-lived. Before turning to the unraveling of *Furman*, we address the compelling question of how *Furman* happened. How was it possible that the relatively stable American death penalty of the 1950s and early 1960s—a penalty that had been subject to virtually no federal judicial oversight throughout American history—was deemed unconstitutional only a decade later?

Why *Furman*?

The sudden fragility of the American death penalty emerged from several developments. The weakening of the death penalty in other Western democracies strengthened Justice Goldberg's interest in having the Supreme Court consider whether capital punishment was still lawful under the constitution. The Court's unprecedented extension of constitutional criminal procedure rights to state criminal defendants—rights previously limited to the much smaller pool of defendants charged with federal crimes—also made constitutional regulation of the death penalty thinkable and feasible. The Court's decision to regulate state criminal procedures was traceable in large part to concerns about racial justice, which had also motivated the Court's earlier interventions in *Moore v. Dempsey, Brown v. Mississippi,* and the Scottsboro cases. Perhaps most fortuitously, the Legal Defense Fund heard Justice Goldberg's call for constitutional review and was very well suited to answer it. The LDF had the institutional knowledge and the inspired leadership necessary to carry out an abolitionist campaign within the courts. The LDF's moratorium strategy changed the nation's use of the death penalty, limiting executions and likely contributing to a decline in death sentencing as well. The courts, in turn, could point to the declining use of capital punishment as evidence in support of the constitutional claim. Perhaps most importantly, the legal campaign against the death penalty occurred at precisely the right moment in terms of public opinion. National support for the death penalty dropped to its all-time low in the mid-1960s, reflecting in part the enormous political and cultural change wrought by the social movements of that era as well as the relatively low levels of violent crime experienced in the 1950s and early 1960s. The combined effect of increased international and domestic misgivings about the death penalty on the one hand, and a new legal environment in which the Supreme Court sought to police many state criminal practices in order to curb racial discrimination on the other, provided the fuel for the Court's dramatic intervention.

The federal courts exerted little control or influence over state criminal processes for most of our country's history. This limited role resulted in part from the Court's view that the protections of the Bill of Rights constrained federal, not state, authorities. The Court narrowly interpreted the Fourteenth Amendment's due process clause—which does protect state criminal defendants—leaving most state prisoners to the mercy of the protections afforded within the state systems. As a result, many criminal defendants, especially in the Deep South, were subject to perfunctory trials with rudimentary protections. The 1960s, though, saw a dramatic reversal of this long-standing practice. Responding to manifestly unfair and discriminatory state criminal prosecutions and trials, the Warren Court extended many of the protections of the Bill of Rights to state prisoners through the due process clause. This shift on the Court was possible largely because of the changing racial attitudes in the country. The Civil Rights Movement had exposed the apartheid of the American South. The nonviolent protests—from the freedom rides to the marches in Selma and elsewhere—had conferred moral legitimacy on those challenging the status quo and underscored the urgency of the demands for racial justice. Without these developments, it is unlikely that the Court would have attempted to regulate state criminal justice systems, and criminal procedure (as well as the death penalty itself) would have remained topics for local resolution.

The extension of constitutional protections to state criminal defendants facilitated the Court's regulation of the death penalty in two ways. First, the expansion of the rights available to state prisoners (including, for example, the right to exclude illegally-seized evidence and the right to *Miranda* warnings before being interrogated in custody) made it possible for the moratorium strategy to succeed. Inmates facing execution had a broad set of new federal constitutional claims that they could assert to reverse their convictions or at least prolong the period between trial and execution. Second, the extension of the Bill of Rights to state prisoners made it more thinkable to directly challenge the death penalty. In 1962, just before Justice Goldberg's 1963 dissent, the Court recognized for the first time that the Eighth Amendment's prohibition of cruel and unusual punishment applied to state practices, when it invalidated criminal punishment for drug addiction.[20] State death row inmates now had a new vocabulary for arguing that the death penalty was unconstitutional: it had become "cruel and unusual."

Just before the Eighth Amendment was deemed to apply to state practices, it had acquired new force in the federal context. In the late 1950s, in *Trop v. Dulles,* the Court struck down the punishment of loss of citizenship imposed for desertion during World War II. Declaring that the "basic concept underlying the Eighth Amendment is nothing less than the dignity of man," a plurality of the Court (less than a majority, but the largest bloc of justices supporting the result in the case) insisted that the scope of the Eighth Amendment's protection is not "static" but instead "must draw its meaning from the evolving standards of decency that mark the progress of a maturing society." Interestingly, *Trop* addressed the death penalty in response to the claim that loss of citizenship was permissible because it was less cruel than the alternative of death. The plurality rejected the idea that the existence of the death penalty is "a license to the Government to devise any punishment short of death within the limit of its imagination." The plurality also suggested in a backhanded way that the death penalty itself was not vulnerable to Eighth Amendment attack, at least not *yet:* "Whatever the arguments may be against capital punishment, both on moral grounds and in terms of accomplishing the purposes of punishment—and they are forceful—the death penalty has been employed throughout our history, and, in a day when it is still widely accepted, it cannot be said to violate the constitutional concept of cruelty." *Trop* appeared to acknowledge that the constitutionality of the American death penalty was contingent on changing attitudes and was not conclusively and irrevocably established. As public support for the death penalty weakened over the next decade, the extension of the Eighth Amendment to state inmates was crucial to the possibility of striking down the death penalty.[21]

Justice Goldberg's opinion urging review of the constitutionality of the death penalty in the context of rape would have mattered little had the LDF not responded to his call. One possible reason that Justice Goldberg spoke for only a minority of the Court might have been the reluctance of his colleagues to challenge a practice on the basis of such a sparse factual and legal record. Prior to Justice Goldberg's dissent, opponents of the death penalty simply hadn't viewed the courts as a promising venue for abolition. The sorts of claims raised by inmates on death row tended to be specific to their cases and modest in scope, developed by local lawyers with little interest or investment in challenging the lawfulness of capital punishment. The petition in *Rudolph* reflected the extraordinarily low level of capital practice—the entire argument section was less than a page long. At the time, there was generally little coordination among lawyers who handled capital cases. Occasionally the LDF would assist in a troubling case, but there was no organized capital defense bar focused on limiting or defeating the practice. Even the ACLU, one of the most likely candidates to lead such an effort, did not consider capital punishment "a civil liberties issue" until two years after Goldberg's dissent.[22]

At the same time, the LDF, though it had only a handful of attorneys, had developed valuable experience in "cause" lawyering. In the fight against Jim Crow and state-sponsored segregation, the LDF had carefully selected cases to develop good factual records and identify the most vulnerable state practices. Early on, this meant challenging disparate pay for black and white schoolteachers and the practice of segregating interstate buses. In its most sustained litigation, the LDF focused first on segregation in higher education, particularly graduate programs (rather than secondary and elementary schools), because the contrasting opportunities for black and white students were most stark (many states did not offer graduate opportunities to black students) and popular opposition to segregation was less emotional and vociferous in the graduate school context. The desegregation litigation taught the LDF the importance of planning, strategy, and coordination. If the wrong case arrived too early in the Supreme Court, it could set back the overall effort. Even victories could be problematic if they moved the courts too far too fast and engendered political backlash.

The LDF's initial reaction to Goldberg's dissent was to provide an empirical foundation for what the Court undoubtedly already knew—that the death penalty for rape was administered in a racially discriminatory manner. The LDF enlisted the help of a prominent social scientist to study death and non-death outcomes in rape cases in the South. Ultimately this work did not prompt any state or federal court to grant relief, but it was precisely the sort of cause lawyering that paved the way for *Furman*. Documenting racial discrimination provided extremely valuable information and context that helped move the Court toward regulating the death penalty despite the Court's reluctance to grant relief on explicitly race-based terms. The LDF also adapted some of the tools of its desegregation litigation to the moratorium and abolition campaign. One of the consequences of the Court's refusal to give immediate relief to individual schoolchildren in *Brown v. Board of Education* was the emergence of innovative litigation geared to benefit an entire class of litigants. The LDF successfully (and surprisingly) was able to obtain class relief in Florida to prevent the execution of significant numbers of inmates while the broader constitutional issues they raised were heard in federal court. This use of civil rights litigation tactics appears to be the first time death row prisoners (or even state prisoners more generally) were able to avail themselves of class action procedures as they sought relief from their criminal sentences.[23]

Perhaps the most important fortuity related to the LDF effort was the participation of Tony Amsterdam. A law professor at the University of Pennsylvania, Amsterdam came to the LDF abolition campaign almost by accident, consulting on a capital rape case in the early days of the effort as a stand-in for another professor.[24] His brilliance and work ethic quickly catapulted him to the head of the campaign. Amsterdam engineered the moratorium strategy, which required extending the LDF's resources to both white and black death-sentenced inmates and working with lawyers all across the country. Amsterdam's insight was essential to crafting and selecting the types of arguments to advance in state and federal courts in anticipation of Supreme Court review. As cases piled up at the Court, the LDF devoted enormous energy to getting the right issues before the Court at the right time, in the right posture. Amsterdam wrote with an unusual combination of eloquence and indignation in the numerous briefs the LDF filed in the run-up to *Furman* and in the subsequent 1976 cases. He was a master at criticizing the unfairness or inadequacy of particular death penalty procedures while simultaneously insisting that the entire practice was irredeemable. In the critical 1976 cases, for example, he wrote:

> None of the justifications advanced to support the cruelty of killing a random smattering of prisoners annually survives examination in light of the realities of this insensate lottery; and none begins, of course, to justify the killing of any particular human being while his indistinguishable counterparts are spared in numbers that attest to our collective abhorrence of what we are doing to an outcast few.[25]

It is hard to imagine the Court would have addressed the broad constitutional challenges to the death penalty without the insistence of the LDF and Amsterdam. It is harder still to imagine the victory in *Furman*.

Justice Goldberg's memorandum to his colleagues in 1963 linked his plea to address the constitutionality of the death penalty to "the worldwide trend toward abolition."[26] International support for and use of the death penalty began to decline in the late eighteenth and early nineteenth centuries, inspired by Enlightenment critiques and the emergence of lengthy incarceration as an alternative punishment. The "long road up from barbarism" described by Justice Marshall in *Furman* was also a winding one, with gradual reforms ultimately culminating in significantly reduced use or abolition of the death penalty throughout most of the Western world. In Europe, abolition for peacetime offenses was achieved early in Portugal (1867), the Netherlands (1870), and Norway (1902), and the pace of abolition accelerated in the wake of World War II (with Austria, Finland, West Germany, and Italy all abolishing or severely limiting between 1945 and 1950). By the 1950s, use of the death penalty in Europe had become rare, though the penalty was formally retained by most European countries, at least for high crimes such as treason. In Central and South America, most countries formally abolished or informally abandoned the death penalty in the late nineteenth and early twentieth centuries (including, for example, Colombia, Costa Rica, Ecuador, Panama, Uruguay, and Venezuela). As in Europe, the path in Central and South America was tortuous, with military regimes sometimes reimplementing capital punishment in a region otherwise at the forefront of abolition due to Enlightenment, anticolonial, and Catholic influences.[27]

At the time of Justice Goldberg's dissent, the United States was not an outlier among Western democracies in its formal retention of the death penalty—as of 1965, only twenty-five countries worldwide had formally abolished the penalty. But in many other countries, there was a palpable sense of the possibility of abolition through the political process. In the United Kingdom, for example, the postwar Labor government undertook review of the death penalty with an eye toward repeal, eventually producing legislation that temporarily suspended the death penalty for murder in 1965 and made that suspension permanent in 1969.[28]

On the heels of post–World War II abolition (at least for ordinary offenses) in Italy, West Germany, and Austria, the fate of the death penalty in Western Europe seemed very precarious. In the United States, on the other hand, the prospect of full legislative abolition appeared (and continues to appear) remote. State-by-state repeal removed the death penalty from some dormant capital jurisdictions, but abolition in active capital jurisdictions, particularly in the Deep South, was simply off the table. Abolition at the national level through Congress was doubtful both politically and constitutionally. Justice Goldberg saw an opportunity for the Supreme Court to accomplish what the political branches could not. He (rightly) believed that the rest of the democratic world was moving inexorably in that direction.

Domestic public opinion in the mid-1960s moved in the same direction as international developments, making it an auspicious time for the Court to take up the issue of the death penalty. The 1966 Gallup Poll remains the only time in that poll's history in which more Americans opposed the death penalty (47 percent) than favored it (42 percent). The decline in support represented an enormous shift from just thirteen years before, when supporters enjoyed a whopping 43 percent edge over opponents (68 percent to 25 percent).[29] Numerous developments likely contributed to the advantage of the opposition. By the early 1960s, use of the death penalty had declined from its 1930s highs (averaging about 167 executions per year) to fewer than forty per year in the period 1960–65.[30] Some of the most visible uses of the death penalty had triggered substantial controversy. For example, the 1960 execution of Caryl Chessman for a series of nonhomicidal crimes after twelve years of litigation was widely criticized by prominent intellectuals and writers (Chessman had penned several best-selling books while on death row). Some critics opposed the use of the death penalty given that the crime for which Chessman had been convicted involved no loss of life, a critique that might well have influenced the manner in which Justice Goldberg framed his dissent three years later. Others pointed to the cruelty of executing Chessman so long after his conviction, with Alexander Bickel insisting that the Court should have forbidden Chessman's execution on the grounds that, coming twelve years after he was convicted, it amounted to a "punishment infinitely more ghastly than killing him in 1948 would have been"—a striking criticism given that the average time between sentence and execution today exceeds fifteen years.[31]

Elite and religious opinion in the United States was moving away from the death penalty by the early 1960s, mirroring the decline in international support for the practice. Within the criminal justice system, capital punishment seemed at odds with the rehabilitative ideal that had become dominant among those charged with administering punishment. The ALI considered recommending abolition of the death penalty when it devised the Model Penal Code (MPC) in the early 1960s, but chose not to do so in order to remain influential in the debate surrounding its administration and in fear of under-cutting the prospects for other parts of the code.[32]

Public support for the death penalty was also weakened by the emerging concern for marginalized groups—particularly blacks and the poor—reflected in the Civil Rights Movement and the War on Poverty. The late 1950s and early 1960s had shone a bright light on the discriminatory treatment of blacks in the South, and the passage of the Civil Rights Act of 1964 and the Voting Rights Act of 1965 illuminated the heightened prospects for social transformation. As the country seemed poised to discard its outdated past for a new future—which included national rights trumping state and local prerogatives—it is unsurprising that the public's support for the death penalty diminished.

Perhaps most importantly, the United States had experienced a steep drop in violent crime from the 1930s (with a murder rate of about ten per 100,000) to the 1950s and early 1960s, with the murder rate reaching its low around 1960 (of about five per 100,000). The drop was not uniform. Southern cities tended to have lower homicide rates in the early 1960s (compared to 1950), whereas Northern and Midwestern cities experienced higher rates. But the overall dynamic was evident—the United States seemed safer (and *was* safer) in the early 1960s than it ever had been in terms of murder. The year before Justice Goldberg's dissent, the United States had its modern-day low of 8,530 murders. The combination of declining executions and declining murders undercut the sense that the death penalty was essential as a deterrent. Moreover, the Cold War—together with declining domestic crime—undermined the perception that ordinary criminals constituted America's most pressing enemy.[33]

When the Court hinted in *Trop* that the death penalty might become cruel and unusual if no longer "widely accepted," it almost certainly did not anticipate that the decline in public support would appear within less than a decade. But the 1965 and 1966 Gallup Polls (where opposition to the death penalty ranged from 43 percent to 47 percent) painted a very different picture of American attitudes about capital punishment than any of the polls dating back to 1936, in which those opposed never exceeded 38 percent and amounted to as few as 25 percent in 1953. The apparent shift in public opinion undoubtedly led the Court to believe that elite and popular opinion were converging and moving steadily toward the abolitionist camp. In addition to the groundbreaking 1966 Gallup Poll, but even closer in time to the *Furman* decision, the media on both the left and the right, along with academic observers, were noting "mounting zeal for abolition" and predicting the likely eventual success of the abolition movement.[34] It was this seeming rise in public opposition to the death penalty that caused Justice Stewart to join Justice White to make up the bare *Furman* majority.[35]

Regulation, Not Abolition

The confluence of events that made *Furman* possible did not make it inevitable. From the beginning, the Court was reticent about reckoning with the death penalty and constitutionalizing what was widely understood to be a permissible political choice for state and local decision makers. The Court had either rejected or refused to address several of the LDF's most pressing claims prior to *Furman*. They included the challenge to racial discrimination in rape cases, the challenge to unitary proceedings, the challenge to applications of the death penalty for crimes other than murder, and the challenge to standardless discretion under the due process clause. When *Furman* did arrive, it did not present itself in the trappings usually associated with decisive landmark cases. The Court was divided five to four, and the discordant set of opinions by the five justices who joined the terse judgment generated no clear holding. Undoubtedly, some of the justices in the majority hoped and expected that the long, diverse, and intricate indictments of prevailing capital practices in *Furman* would have the effect of abolishing the death penalty because states might simply choose to avoid the difficulties of navigating the Court's concerns. But capital jurisdictions would not be nudged toward abolition. National and state leaders greeted *Furman* with vehement objection. President Nixon expressed his hope that the death penalty would survive the decision and announced plans to revive the federal death penalty for kidnapping and hijacking, among other offenses.[36] More colorfully, Lester Maddox, the lieutenant governor (and former governor) of Georgia, described *Furman* as a "license for anarchy, rape, [and] murder."[37] The denunciations were followed by swift legislative action across the country. In the four years following *Furman*, thirty-five states passed new capital statutes.

The distinctive feature of all of the new statutes was an effort to limit the discretion characteristic of death penalty schemes before *Furman*. Everyone understood that states could no longer ask jurors to choose between sentences of life in prison and death by execution without any discernible standards. But the amount of discretion permitted by *Furman* was unclear. Chief Justice Burger's dissent in *Furman* voiced concern that *Furman* might prompt states to adopt a mandatory death penalty, a development he regarded as more problematic than unrestrained discretion. It seemed odd that the constitution would require a return to the mandatory sentencing that states had universally rejected over the previous 150 years as unduly rigid and harsh. The other alternative was to adopt some form of "guided discretion" in which statutes would identify factors to guide prosecutors and sentencers (jurors or judges) in exercising their discretion. Such schemes would communicate the state's theory of offenses and offenders deserving (or undeserving) of death and would limit the reach of the death penalty compared to the breadth given by the pre-*Furman* statutes.

The capital punishment provisions of the MPC offered a blueprint for this sort of approach. The MPC allowed the death penalty only for the crime of murder, not for crimes such as kidnapping, treason, and rape (among others), as many state statutes had permitted. It required that the sentencer find at least one of eight enumerated "aggravating circumstances." These factors ranged from the relatively objective ("The murder was committed by a convict under sentence of imprisonment") to the more subjective and qualitative ("The murder was especially heinous, atrocious or cruel, manifesting exceptional depravity"). And it required the sort of bifurcated proceedings that the LDF had (unsuccessfully) urged the Court to mandate in *McGautha*, in which the sentencer would first decide guilt or innocence and, if guilt were established, decide whether to impose death in a separate sentencing proceeding in which all "relevant mitigating evidence" could be considered.[38]

A number of states responded to *Furman* with statutes eliminating discretion altogether and mandating the imposition of a death sentence for every offender convicted of any capital crime. This approach was attractive because of its seeming 180-degree turn away from the problem of excess discretion. If sentencers lacked the power to bestow mercy, the resulting death sentences would no longer be vulnerable to the charge of arbitrariness and discrimination. Mandatory statutes had two additional virtues. Justice White's opinion in *Furman* had highlighted the rarity of death sentences and executions, arguing that the sheer infrequency of death sentences undermined any claim that it served important goals of punishment, such as deterrence or retribution. The mandatory death penalty would presumably reverse the trend of limited death sentencing and make capital punishment a more regular part of state criminal justice systems. In this respect, the mandatory death penalty would not simply respond to the constitutional challenge of *Furman;* it would revitalize a practice that had been in decline for several decades. A related virtue was the message mandatory statutes would send to the Supreme Court. For those who doubted the states' commitment to the death penalty, the mandatory death penalty communicated an unqualified embrace of the punishment and made it more difficult to credit the LDF's claim that the American people had turned their backs on capital punishment.

Most states, however, chose the "guided-discretion" approach and adopted some variation of the MPC death penalty provision. Unlike the mandatory schemes, the guided-discretion statutes appeared to be moving forward rather than backward, with an innovative effort to tame the death penalty through the enumeration of aggravating and mitigating factors and the requirement of carefully structured, bifurcated proceedings. The guided schemes likewise had the comparative advantage of the imprimatur of the American Law Institute.

The states' rush to enact new statutes in the wake of *Furman* made it inevitable that the Court would revisit the Eighth Amendment question and decide whether the death penalty could be administered constitutionally. And if the statutes satisfied the concerns of *Furman* in terms of administering the death penalty in a nonarbitrary and nondiscriminatory manner, the Court might also have to decide the looming larger question left unanswered in *Furman*—whether the death penalty remained consistent with evolving standards of decency.

The LDF was faced with a difficult strategic question as it prepared to challenge the constitutionality of the new statutes. Its approach to the guided-discretion statutes was straightforward: the LDF could argue that the purported guidance of the new statutes was insufficient to assure evenhanded administration of the death penalty. Many of the new guided-discretion statutes had followed the MPC's lead in using amorphous aggravating factors (like the "especially heinous, atrocious or cruel" factor), so that the claim of meaningful guidance as to who should receive a death sentence was illusory. The guided-discretion statutes also still afforded prosecutors and sentencers an unaccountable veto of the death penalty. Despite the fact that the new statutes had a veneer of structure and guidance, they continued to permit decision makers to seek and impose the death penalty against virtually any offender while not requiring them to seek or impose it even in the most aggravated cases. The LDF could claim, as Justice Harlan had argued for the Court in *McGautha,* that the effort to tame the death penalty was doomed to failure. This position, of course, was in tension with the LDF claim in *McGautha* that due process mandated the articulation of standards. But now that *Furman* had condemned standardless discretion as a violation of the Eighth Amendment, it was strategically prudent to shift from the claim that capital sentencing standards are necessary to the position that capital sentencing standards are necessary but impossible to achieve.

The harder question concerned the mandatory statutes. The most obvious problem with such statutes was their failure to permit consideration of any aspects of the offender (for example, youth, intellectual disability, or mental illness short of insanity) or the circumstances of the offense (including minor participation, lack of intent to kill, influence of a codefendant) in the death penalty decision. Conviction of a capital crime required death in every case. The rejection of mandatory statutes prior to *Furman* reflected legislative and popular distaste for automatic death sentencing. Given this history, Chief Justice Burger was on strong ground in suggesting that the complete absence of discretion might be worse from a constitutional perspective than the excessive discretion *Furman* condemned.

But if the LDF attacked the mandatory statutes along these lines, it risked demanding the impossible: states had to avoid both too much and too little discretion. It would be awkward to argue to the Court that one set of statutes gave too much room for judgment while the other set gave too little. That sort of Catch-22 would suggest that the LDF was not really interested in finding the right procedures for capital sentencing, but instead was trying to compel the Court to invalidate the death penalty. If the LDF pursued the "too little discretion" line of argument against the mandatory statutes, it would increase the odds that the Court would sustain the guided-discretion schemes, as they seemed to occupy the middle ground between the pre-*Furman* world of unbridled discretion and the post-*Furman* mandatory approach. The LDF *was* trying to abolish the death penalty, and it was not going to pursue a constitutional line of attack—even a persuasive one—if it meant preserving capital punishment.

Instead, the LDF designed a unified attack against both post-*Furman* approaches: they both afforded too much discretion and risked arbitrary and discriminatory results. How could the LDF claim that the mandatory death penalty permitted too much discretion? In the LDF's view, the absence of discretion at sentencing would be replaced by the exercise of discretion elsewhere in the process. Prosecutors would decline to charge capital murder in cases where the elements were satisfied but death was not appropriate. Jurors, too, would refuse to convict on capital murder to avoid the imposition of a death sentence, and their nullification would be unreviewable. And executive officials would grant commutations to mitigate the harshness of mandatory sentencing. In short, discretion would still be routinely exercised, but in an ad hoc manner with no guidance from the legislature. The death penalty lottery would remain in place, but the tickets would be cashed at different moments in the process.

By the time the new statutes reached the Court in 1976, the dynamics of the constitutional battle had dramatically changed. In 1972, the Court could plausibly have believed that the death penalty was on a slow march toward extinction and that its intervention in *Furman* would be enough to complete the process. But the extraordinary legislative backlash to *Furman* suggested otherwise. Whether inspired by genuine commitment to the punishment or by the political advantages flowing from renouncing *Furman*, political leaders loudly and clearly communicated their desire to preserve the death penalty.

The 1976 cases reviewed five new capital schemes, all from the South. Two statutes, from North Carolina and Louisiana, made imposition of the death penalty mandatory. Two others, from Georgia and Florida, were "guided-discretion" schemes emulating the Model Penal Code. The fifth, from Texas, was a strange amalgam. A conviction for capital murder required the state to prove an aggravating factor during the guilt/innocence phase, and the punishment phase made the death penalty mandatory if the jury answered "yes" to three yes/no questions, the most important of which focused on the likely dangerousness of the defendant. The oral arguments in the cases were grueling, and the Court did not seem impressed with either of the LDF's two central positions—that none of the new statutes satisfied *Furman*'s implicit demand for standards and that the death penalty itself was contrary to evolving standards of decency. The justices appeared openly incredulous of the claim that the opportunity for any discretion within the system—whether by prosecutors, juries, or executive officials—rendered the death penalty unconstitutional, especially given that such discretion is a defining feature of the American criminal justice system. They also seemed troubled by Amsterdam's unwillingness during oral argument to concede that any procedural framework would satisfy the constitution. When Amsterdam was pressed to rank the new statutes in terms of their constitutional sustainability, he insisted that all of them were so far from the constitutional mark that he would not engage the question. On the broader issue, Amsterdam likewise ceded no ground regarding the significance of the massive legislative response to *Furman*. The willingness of states to put statutes on the books was not the appropriate gauge of meaningful popular support, he said, especially if discretionary outlets in practice facilitated freakish application of the penalty against an unlucky few.

A new wrinkle in the 1976 arguments was the appearance of the United States government as an *amicus* ("friend" of the Court) in vigorous support of the constitutionality of the death penalty. Robert Bork, the Solicitor General, filed an extensive brief disputing the petitioners' claims. Included among Bork's arguments was new empirical work claiming to show a deterrent effect from executions (work that would subsequently receive sharp criticism and even rebuke from the academic community). At oral argument, Bork challenged the LDF's positions on several grounds, emphasizing the death penalty's long-standing pedigree within the American criminal system and the Court's limited role in reviewing the constitutionality of punishments. Bork hammered home that the LDF was unwilling to endorse any of the new statutes and that its arguments about discretionary outlets applied as powerfully to the noncapital context. Bork went further than just insisting that the new statutes complied with *Furman*. He maintained that *Furman* had amounted to an overreach by the Court and should be directly overruled.

The Court upheld the guided-discretion statutes. The most important opinion was jointly authored by Justices Stewart, Powell, and newly appointed Justice John Paul Stevens. They began by addressing the fundamental question that Justice Goldberg and the LDF had hoped would lead to the end of the death penalty—whether the punishment remained consistent with evolving standards of decency. The plurality maintained that the developments in the four years since *Furman* "undercut substantially the assumptions on which [that] argument rested." Thirty-five state legislatures and the federal government had passed new statutes, California voters had passed a referendum to sustain the punishment, and juries had returned substantial numbers of death sentences. These events were sufficient for the plurality to conclude that the death penalty remained "acceptable" to contemporary society.[39]

But the plurality insisted that societal acceptance was not enough; the death penalty must also comport with human dignity so that its imposition "cannot be so totally without penological justification that it results in the gratuitous infliction of suffering." The plurality then identified two legitimate bases for states' retention of the death penalty: retribution and deterrence. Retribution had been in decline as a ground for punishment, a decline that would be reversed over the next few decades. Anticipating this nascent shift, the plurality recognized a place for society to express its "moral outrage at particularly offensive conduct." Somewhat surprisingly, given the nearly half century since the most active period of lynching, the plurality suggested that the retributive outlet of the death penalty might be necessary to prevent private violence: "When people begin to believe that organized society is unwilling or unable to impose upon criminal offenders the punishment they 'deserve,' then there are sown the seeds of anarchy—of self-help, vigilante justice, and lynch law." The plurality also embraced deterrence as a legitimate basis for states to retain the death penalty, even as it acknowledged the uncertain empirical record in terms of actually establishing a deterrent effect. Overall, the plurality was simply unwilling to strike down capital punishment without a much stronger showing that society had rejected it.[40]

The backlash against *Furman* had put the Court on the defensive. The plurality's deferential approach—asking only whether the Georgia legislature was "clearly wrong" in its judgment "that capital punishment may be necessary in some cases"—reflected the changed circumstances. It is interesting to note, though, that the backlash against *Furman*'s tentative opinion evoked only a tentative response from the Court. Nothing in the plurality's opinion was a strong endorsement of the death penalty. Nor did the plurality disclaim the possibility that the death penalty could be declared unconstitutional in the future. In the end, the plurality demanded "more convincing evidence" before deeming capital punishment "unconstitutionally severe." The plurality also noted that it did not have occasion to decide whether the death penalty was constitutional as applied against persons convicted of nonhomicidal crimes (such as rape, kidnapping, and armed robbery, which remained capital in the new Georgia scheme), because the cases it selected for review all involved offenders convicted of murder. The plurality's insistence that the death penalty was proportional as applied to murderers left open the door to challenges (like the one in *Rudolph*) that the death penalty is excessive in other contexts.[41]

On the specific issue regarding the structure of the new capital statutes, the plurality found that the guided-discretion schemes sufficiently addressed *Furman*'s concerns about arbitrariness and discrimination. The plurality held that guidance is necessary to tame the death penalty and that Georgia's use of aggravating factors seemed suited to that task. The plurality noted that the MPC had demonstrated the viability of structuring the death penalty decision by narrowing those eligible for the penalty through the use of aggravating factors. From the plurality's perspective, it was premature to reject the enterprise on the ground that some of Georgia's aggravating factors, particularly the "outrageously or wantonly vile" factor, appeared overly broad and potentially applicable to every murder. The plurality noted that the Georgia Supreme Court could interpret the language to constrain its reach. The plurality also highlighted the bifurcated structure of Georgia's capital system and its provision for automatic proportionality review in the Georgia Supreme Court. It rejected the LDF's position that absolute discretion not to impose the death penalty would lead to the sort of arbitrariness condemned by *Furman*. The plurality contrasted arbitrariness in choosing who should die—which it deemed impermissible and within the state's power to control—with arbitrariness in choosing who should be spared, which it regarded as an inevitable and unproblematic boon to particular offenders: "Nothing in any of our cases suggests that the decision to afford an individual defendant mercy violates the Constitution."[42]

While the plurality controlled the middle of the Court, two groups of justices gravitated toward the poles. Justice White, who had been part of the *Furman* majority, wrote for himself and two other justices

(Chief Justice Burger and Justice Rehnquist) to more emphatically reject the constitutional challenge to the new guided-discretion statutes. Justice White viewed as "considerably overstated" the claim that the guided-discretion approach would reproduce the arbitrary and discriminatory pre-*Furman* regime.[43] He rejected the assumption that prosecutors would use their discretion to discriminate or that discretion to withhold the death penalty is constitutionally problematic. He acknowledged: "Mistakes will be made and discriminations will occur which will be difficult to explain," but rejected the attack on the new statutes as reflecting a "lack of faith in the ability of the system of justice to operate in a fundamentally fair manner."[44] The tone of Justice White's opinion displayed frustration with the LDF's unwillingness to view the new statutes as a clear break from the standardless discretion of the past. In his view, the LDF's absolutist position rejecting any discretion as intolerable (even the discretion traditionally accorded prosecutors and jurors) amounted to a belief that government was "incompetent to administer" the death penalty—a position he was not willing to endorse in light of the states' new efforts to improve their capital systems. Justice Blackmun, who had dissented in *Furman,* continued to believe that the Court lacked the power and authority to invade this area of state prerogative, even though as a personal matter he viewed the death penalty as abhorrent and contrary to "childhood's training and life's experiences."[45]

At the opposite pole, Justices Brennan and Marshall maintained that the death penalty violated evolving standards of decency. Justice Brennan insisted that the death penalty denies the intrinsic worth of individuals and should be jettisoned like the punishments of the rack, the screw, and the wheel. Justice Marshall disputed that retribution is a permissible basis for retention and argued extensively about the inadequacy of studies purporting to show a deterrent effect for the death penalty. While he acknowledged that the raft of new statutes in response to *Furman* had "a significant bearing" on whether the death penalty was acceptable in American society, he reiterated his view that an informed citizenry would reject the punishment, citing a recent study supporting the "Marshall hypothesis" that individuals' opposition to the death penalty grew in relation to their information about it.[46] From *Gregg* on, Justices Brennan and Marshall never again voted to sustain a death sentence. Unlike the ALI, they made the decision to adhere to their views of the necessity of abolition, even as that position made it more difficult for them to contribute to the shape of constitutional regulation that the Court would impose.

Even though no advocate stood before the Court challenging the *absence* of discretion in the mandatory statutes, the same plurality that defended the guided-discretion statutes rejected North Carolina's mandatory scheme in *Woodson* on this ground. The plurality noted the long history in which states unanimously came to regard mandatory death sentencing as "unduly harsh and unworkably rigid." It also argued that mandatory statutes merely "papered over" the problem of unguided discretion because some jurors in mandatory schemes would refuse to convict in cases where they regarded the death penalty as excessive. The plurality regarded the use of discretion in this manner as potentially worse than the guided-discretion alternative because: "Instead of rationalizing the sentencing process, a mandatory scheme may well exacerbate the problem identified in *Furman* by resting the penalty determination on the particular jury's willingness to act lawlessly." Perhaps most importantly, the plurality insisted that "death is different" from all other punishments and therefore requires heightened safeguards for capital defendants. Although mandatory sentencing provisions are permissible in the noncapital context, when a defendant faces the death penalty, the plurality said that "fundamental respect for humanity . . . requires consideration of the character and record of the individual offender and the circumstances of the particular offense as a constitutionally indispensable part of the process of inflicting the penalty of death." In poetic language, the plurality explained that the mandatory imposition of capital punishment wrongly "treats all persons convicted of a designated offense not as uniquely individual human beings, but as members of a faceless, undifferentiated mass to be subjected to the blind infliction of the penalty of death." *Woodson* saw the Court embrace two new and potentially far-reaching constitutional doctrines respecting the death penalty: that capital sentencing must be individualized and permit consideration of unique aspects of the defendant calling for a lesser sentence; and, more generally, that the difference between death and all other punishments requires distinctive protections in capital cases.[47]

The 1976 decisions thus abandoned the path to abolition that *Furman* had seemed to initiate. The Court declined to find the death penalty inconsistent with evolving standards of decency, which was critical to the resurgence of the death penalty over the coming decades. But the Court also declined the invitation of Bork and others to overrule *Furman* and return the death penalty to the states. Instead, the Court embraced at least four principles that would guide its extensive constitutional doctrine going forward: (1) states must guide sentencing discretion and narrow the class of offenders subject to the punishment; (2) the death penalty must be proportionate to the offense triggering the punishment; (3) defendants must receive an individualized assessment of the appropriateness of the death penalty that includes consideration of their character, background, and the circumstances of the offense; and (4) the categorical difference between death and all other punishments ("death is different") requires that capital proceedings be especially fair and reliable.

American Exceptionalism and the Death Penalty

The near death of the American death penalty in 1972 and its emergence as a revived but regulated practice following the 1976 cases bear on a principal question surrounding capital punishment in America: why is the United States the sole Western democracy to retain and implement the death penalty? A rich scholarly literature has addressed this question, as well as the related phenomenon of the broader punitive turn in the United States over the past half century. The United States emerged as the lone executing state among its Western democratic peers at the same time as it veered toward its practice of mass incarceration (with imprisonment rates increasing fivefold between 1972 and 2007), and embraced other punitive criminal justice policies such as "zero tolerance" policing initiatives, "three strikes" statutes enhancing punishment for recidivists, the increased use of criminal sanctions for juvenile offenders, and the widespread authorization of sentences of life without possibility of parole.[48]

The most common explanations for American punitiveness focus on distinctive aspects of American culture, American politics, and their combustible interaction. In terms of culture, the United States is an outlier in several respects, including its high rate of violent crime, unusual embrace of individual gun ownership, and lack of social solidarity, reflected in high levels of income inequality and a relatively weak welfare state.[49] The cultural divide between the United States and Europe is even more evident in the American South, where fundamental Protestantism is quite strong and racial division is most pronounced. Frank Zimring has argued that the divergence between Europe and the United States with respect to the retention of capital punishment is traceable to the distinctive culture of vigilante justice that prevailed in some parts of the United States in the early twentieth century. Looking specifically at execution rates (rather than formal retention of the death penalty or even death sentencing rates), Zimring finds an illuminating connection between a history of lynching early in the twentieth century and the willingness to conduct executions in the 1980s and 1990s. This account focuses not on American culture as a whole, but on the distinctive experience with lynching—which had both regional and racial components.[50]

With regard to the structure of American politics, many scholars point to American federalism and localism as contributing strongly to American punitiveness in the modern era. Criminal justice in the United States is primarily a local function, and the politics surrounding criminal justice tend to be more populist than bureaucratic, with the central actors—state legislators, district attorneys, and even judges—subject to partisan elections and direct political control. David Garland offers a nuanced account of how the relative weakness of the American state has led to the devolution of authority over capital punishment to local political communities. Garland notes the relative weakness of mediating institutions like political parties and bureaucratic elites in the United States compared to their European counterparts. This weakness further contributes to the power of populist forces in policy making, resulting in what Garland terms a "hyperdemocracy." In his account, this vacuum of state power at the center helped to create and continues to reinforce a powerful localism and populism in the United States. These institutional and political features undergird and interact with other features of American society and culture that Garland argues are centrally implicated in America's death penalty story. The cultural features emphasized by Garland echo many of Zimring's themes: the lack of social solidarity and conflict among social groups, particularly along racial lines; high levels of interpersonal violence, especially in the South; and distinctively American "cultural commitments," including not only populism and localism but also antistatism, individualism, religiosity, and the conflicting pulls of "ruggedness and refinement."[51]

These illuminating cultural and political accounts partly explain why the United States did not abolish the death penalty in the same manner as European states—where centralized political elites imposed abolition despite popular support for the punishment.[52] They explain why the mechanism of national legislative abolition is unavailable in the United States, and why attachment to the death penalty by both politicians and the broader public might be more pronounced in the United States, given our inheritance of Puritan values, racial division, and high rates of violence. These accounts also offer insightful explanations as to the *form* of American retention, in which the United States is not so much a monolithic entity retaining the death penalty as it is a divided land in which some states retain and use the death penalty, others retain it in name only (with token death sentences, executions, or both), and others have abolished it.

But these various theories of American exceptionalism with respect to retention of capital punishment fail to capture three important dimensions of the American death penalty. First, for most of our history, our death penalty practices were on a similar trajectory to our Western European peers, with the same trends of restricting the crimes for which it could be imposed, moving executions behind prison walls, humanizing execution methods, and limiting its overall use. By basing their accounts on long-standing cultural and political differences between the U.S. and Europe, these theories minimize commonalities and fail to account for how recently (since 1970) a sharp divergence between American and European practices emerged. Second, the U.S. has embraced not simple retention, but retention plus constitutional regulation, and this aspect of retention is exceptional in its own right. Theories of American exceptionalism with regard to retention treat the current American death penalty as continuous with its unregulated past, failing to account for its remarkable new form. Third, the American death penalty came perilously close to extinction, to the point that it is contingent not only that the U.S. did not abolish, but that it did not abolish at a slightly earlier point than much of Europe. Claims of exceptionalism rooted in deep cultural or political differences suggest, wrongly, that American retention of the death penalty was somehow fated.

This latter point regarding contingency is especially important because the current shape of the American death penalty has been forged by an unusual sequence of events—temporary abolition, restoration, and regulation. None of the steps in this sequence was foreordained. Instead of temporary abolition and restoration, we might have had permanent abolition given the weakness of the death penalty in the 1960s and 1970s. Death sentences had declined, polls registered low support for capital punishment, a de facto moratorium on executions was initiated in 1967, and the Supreme Court declared prevailing statutes unconstitutional in *Furman*. What modestly different circumstances might have produced permanent rather than temporary abolition? One possibility would have been a slightly earlier decision by the Court. If the Court had taken up the constitutionality of capital punishment sometime between 1963 and 1968, when Earl Warren was still chief justice and before Nixon was elected president, the dynamics on the Court would have been very different than those that produced the tentative and fractured set of opinions in *Furman* in 1972. The chances of a definitive ruling against the death penalty would have been especially high after Justice Marshall replaced Justice Clark in 1967. Although Chief Justice Warren was not eager to engage the constitutional issue in 1963 (as demonstrated by his vote against review in *Rudolph*), he subsequently made his opposition to capital punishment clear, announcing upon his retire-ment that he found the death penalty "repulsive."[53] And Justice Fortas, who replaced Justice Goldberg in 1965, shared Justice Goldberg's abhorrence for the death penalty, penning a widely circulated argu-ment against the practice less than a decade after he, along with Chief Justice Warren, left the Court in 1969.[54] A majority composed of Chief Justice Warren and Justices Douglas, Brennan, Fortas, and Marshall might well have voted against the death penalty on broad and decisive grounds in the mid-1960s (deeming the punishment contrary to evolving standards of decency), and it is possible that Jus-tice Stewart or Justice White, both of whom voted with the *Furman* majority in 1972, would have joined such an opinion or at least con-curred on narrower grounds.

Had the Court issued such an opinion in the mid-1960s, it might have encountered a backlash, just as the Court's subsequent decision in *Furman* did. But that backlash would not have been as strong or as effective given the timing. Southern states protesting judicial abo-lition of the death penalty would have had less traction in the mid-to-late 1960s, coming on the heels of ugly and violent resistance to the Civil Rights Movement. By 1972, the controversy over busing and President Nixon's successful politicization of criminal justice issues intensified the backlash in ways that likely would have been avoided a half decade earlier. More importantly, a constitutional abolition that firmly rejected the death penalty as inconsistent with con-temporary values would have rendered later attempts to reinstate capital punishment extremely difficult to mount. The more ambig-uous *Furman* decision focusing on procedural and administrative defects contained an obvious invitation to future legislation and therefore litigation; a more decisive, categorical ruling would have contained no such invitation and likely would have stuck.

Alternatively, had Nixon not prevailed in the 1968 election, the Court that decided *Furman* would have included the five justices from the *Furman* majority (Douglas, White, Brennan, Marshall, and Stewart), plus four new justices appointed by a Democratic president. Such a Court would have been much more inclined to produce the sort of decisive, categorical ruling that would have both prevented and withstood potential backlash. If either the Warren Court or the "new" *Furman* Court had produced an enduring constitutional abolition of capital punishment, the United States would have been at the forefront of the wave of abolition that swept Europe in the 1970s through the 1990s and would have received (or at least assigned itself) credit for being a leader in this human rights revolution, a position that might have made backsliding more unattractive, just as it has been in Europe. An enduring constitutional abolition would have rendered moot any question of American exceptionalism with regard to the death penalty.

An equally plausible scenario is one in which *Furman* came out the other way, and we ended up with neither temporary abolition, permanent abolition, nor significant regulation. The Court offered a powerful rationale for such a result when it rejected a due process challenge to capital punishment in 1971 in *McGautha*, maintaining that the discretionary American death penalty could not be improved by quixotic attempts to rationalize it. Justices Stewart and White were both members of the *McGautha* majority, and if one or both of them had failed to be swayed by a similar attack on unguided discretion under the Eighth Amendment the following year, the *Furman* challenge would have been defeated. If so, the strong conviction of the Court's Nixon appointees that the question of capital punishment belonged to the states (and to Congress in the federal system) would have been resoundingly vindicated. Perhaps the Court might have gone on to police the borders of capital punishment, eventually rejecting it for crimes less than murder or offenders with reduced culpability, such as juveniles. But if the Court had rejected the challenge in *Furman*, states would not have recrafted their statutes dramatically and simultaneously, and the Court would have been much less inclined to construct a complex body of Eighth Amendment regulatory law. The consequences for the path of capital punishment in America would have been profound.

If the Supreme Court had not temporarily invalidated the death penalty, the backlash that *Furman* unleashed, strongest in the South, could have been avoided. It is possible that without that galvanizing momentum, the death penalty would have continued to wither, and that death sentences and executions would not have climbed at all, or at least not as rapidly as they did in the two decades following *Furman*. It is also possible that the death penalty would not have become as much of an issue of states' rights and the kind of masthead symbol for law-and-order politics or shibboleth in the culture wars that it became when it was so strongly linked with the liberal wing of the Supreme Court—the same Court that had imposed *Brown*, *Miranda*, and *Roe v. Wade*.

Overall, deterministic explanations for American retention of the death penalty miss how close the United States was to being at the vanguard of abolition. They also miss how distinctive its path of retention has been in light of the Court's resulting turn toward constitutional regulation. Contingency much more than determinism characterized the tumultuous foundational death penalty era of the 1960s and 1970s.

Just as the Court's decision to regulate the American death penalty (rather than to abolish or unconditionally endorse it) was neither determined nor foreordained, so too the shape and focus of the Court's regulation could have taken many different forms. One particularly pressing question was whether the Court's regulatory efforts would address the concerns about racial discrimination that haunted the American death penalty practically from its inception. These concerns provided the impetus for the LDF to mount its constitutional campaign against the death penalty, and the issue of race provided the framework for the LDF's arguments to the Court. But would the Court confront directly what was then and remains today an uncomfortable, divisive, even explosive issue? Would capital punishment become the new face of the Court's efforts to confront America's legacy of its other exceptionalism—the ongoing dilemma of discrimination against the descendants of American slaves?

CHAPTER THREE

The Invisibility of Race
in the Constitutional Revolution

SOMETIMES THE HISTORICAL CONTEXT in which important constitutional doctrines are born or elaborated may influence deciding judges in subtle, perhaps even unconscious, ways. Consider, for example, how the Cold War imperative for the recognition of civil rights for black Americans may have affected midcentury court rulings on racial equality,[1] or how the intrusive policing of gay men in public lavatories may have influenced consideration of the constitutionality of the bugging of phone booths and other forms of surveillance.[2] Arguments that these background conditions influenced constitutional law are necessarily speculative given that the salience of the background conditions may have lurked below the level of consciousness.

The racial context informing the foundational constitutional challenges to capital punishment is different. The justices who "constitutionalized" the death penalty in the 1960s and 1970s could not have avoided consciously reflecting on the racial history of capital punishment in America, given that the constitutional campaign against the death penalty was led by the nation's preeminent racial justice organization, the NAACP Legal Defense and Educational Fund (LDF). Moreover, the litigants and their *amici* (organizations submitting briefs as "friends of the court") consistently thrust the issue of race to the forefront in their legal arguments. Nobody with even a modicum of historical awareness could have missed the salience of race to the American practice of capital punishment.

Strangely, though, the birth of the Supreme Court's constitutional regulation of capital punishment was largely devoid of mention of the racially inflected history of the law and practice of the death penalty, despite how central the issue of race was to the litigation effort that forced the Court's hand. One can read the entire canon of the Court's pathbreaking cases on capital punishment during the 1960s and 1970s without getting the impression that the death penalty was an issue of major racial significance in American society.

The Court's silence regarding race is at once mysterious and understandable. There are a variety of plausible motivations, both personal and institutional, that help account for what otherwise might seem to be a strange and glaring lacuna in the hundreds of pages of ruminations that the justices offered in their inaugural constitutional opinions on capital punishment. We explore the fears and anxieties, as well as the hopes and incentives, that may have made the choice of avoidance attractive at the time. While the justices' evasion may be explicable, it is doubtful that they fully anticipated the costs of their silence or its potential long-term effects on the future of the death penalty. Only after the unfolding of several more decades of constitutional regulation of capital punishment can we see how the Court's early avoidance of the race issue had important and unanticipated consequences.

Hiding in Plain Sight

The tremendous influence of race on American capital punishment law and practice, especially in the South, was undoubtedly a powerful impetus both for the Supreme Court's early forays into constitutional regulation of capital trials in the 1920s and 1930s, and for the constitutional litigation campaign initiated by the LDF in the 1960s. The legal claims that LDF advanced in the Supreme Court, as well as the evidence offered in support of those claims, focused on the persistence of racial discrimination in the operation of the death penalty. This emphasis on discrimination was echoed and even amplified in the briefs filed by a variety of *amici* in the key foundational cases. And yet a cursory—indeed, even a careful—reading of the Court's opinions in the defining era (roughly from 1963 to the late 1970s) reveals little attention to racial discrimination. The result of this mismatch between litigation strategy and judicial rulings was an odd dialogue between death penalty litigants and the Court, with the litigants repeatedly urging the Court to limit or abolish the death penalty because of its racially discriminatory administration and the Court's consistent unwillingness to use race as the lens for understanding or regulating the American death penalty.

Before the 1960s, defense lawyers challenged various aspects of capital convictions but rarely challenged the constitutionality of the death penalty itself. For the most part, lawyers representing defendants in capital cases raised generic claims available to all criminal defendants, challenging discrimination in jury selection, coercive interrogation techniques, improper venue, and so forth. The constitutionality of capital punishment as a punishment went unquestioned in part because of its long-standing pedigree (a continuous practice in most states from the colonial and founding eras through the 1950s), and in part because of the textual acknowledgments of the practice in the Constitution itself.

But the same concerns about racial injustice that had produced *Brown v. Board of Education* and the Supreme Court's broader criminal procedure revolution led the Court to invite constitutional scrutiny of the death penalty.[3] "Invite" is the appropriate word, given Justice Goldberg's unusual decision in 1963 to raise the question—unprompted by the litigants—whether the death penalty for the crime of rape amounts to disproportionate punishment. Goldberg framed his dissent from denial of review of this question in light of Alan Dershowitz's extensive memorandum addressing potential constitutional challenges to capital punishment. Dershowitz was skeptical about the success of a full frontal assault on the death penalty in light of its long usage, so his memorandum focused instead on the problem of its racially discriminatory administration and its excessive harshness in cases other than murder. But at Chief Justice Warren's urging, as Goldberg went through the task of cataloguing the best arguments in the memorandum for his published dissent, he omitted any reference to race. Instead, Goldberg announced his view that several questions surrounding the use of the death penalty in rape cases were "relevant and worthy of argument and consideration," including whether imposing death for the crime of rape violates "evolving standards of decency," whether taking life to protect a value other than life constitutes excessive punishment, and whether the permissible aims of punishment can be achieved in such cases with punishments less than death.[4]

Despite the absence of any overt argument about race, Justice Goldberg's dissent in *Rudolph* immediately caught the attention of the LDF. In the preceding decades, the LDF had taken an interest in a limited number of capital cases, focusing primarily on cases involving black defendants who had a plausible claim of actual innocence, as well as some systemic issues like racial discrimination in grand jury selection.[5] Now, though, three members of the Court had revealed their discomfort with the one aspect of the American death penalty—its use in rape cases—that was undeniably linked to racial prejudice. The LDF's lawyers responded by pursuing an ambitious empirical study of rape cases in the South to document racial discrimination in the application of the death penalty. They engaged Marvin Wolfgang, a leading criminologist at the University of Pennsylvania, to design the study, and they sent a cohort of law students to courthouses throughout the Deep South during the summer of 1965 to gather raw data.[6] The nature of the project and the manner of its execution—young liberals traveling to the Deep South to uncover evidence of racial discrimination—made clear that the LDF's work on the death penalty was of a piece with its other civil rights work of the same era.[7]

The resulting litigation in *Maxwell v. Bishop* challenged discriminatory patterns in capital rape cases in Arkansas. Wolfgang had found that black-on-white rape cases in Arkansas were more likely to yield capital sentences than any other racial combination, controlling for twenty-two nonracial variables.[8] When the case reached federal court on habeas corpus review, the district court rejected the claim of racial discrimination by faulting Wolfgang's study on methodological grounds. The Court of Appeals for the Eighth Circuit (then-Judge Harry Blackmun writing for the panel) affirmed, holding that Maxwell had failed to establish discrimination in his individual case. Blackmun went even further, expressing skepticism that proof of statewide discrimination would ever suffice in an individual case: "We are not certain that, for Maxwell, statistics will ever be his redemption."[9]

By the time Maxwell lost in the Eighth Circuit, the LDF's approach to capital cases had expanded dramatically. Instead of focusing solely on black defendants, or primarily on issues of racial discrimination, the LDF embarked on a more encompassing effort to bring the American death penalty to a halt. The LDF's "moratorium" strategy was to prevent any executions, regardless of the inmate's race, by raising all available procedural claims.[10] Some of those claims were garden-variety challenges to illegal searches, questionable confessions, and the like, relying on the Warren Court's dramatic extension of criminal procedural protections to defendants in state courts. But many of the claims focused specifically on defects in capital litigation, including the ubiquitous practice of excluding potential jurors who had any qualms about the death penalty, the use of "unitary" trials in which defendants had no separate opportunity to seek mercy apart from the guilt-innocence trial, and the failure of state capital schemes to provide any guidance as to who should receive the ultimate punishment.

The decision to attack the death penalty itself involved complicated judgments both pragmatic and principled. The LDF's lawyers realized that the Court might not embrace its claims of racial discrimination and that the best hope for many death-sentenced black inmates might rest on broader reforms—or perhaps even abolition—of the capital system. In addition, LDF lawyers were themselves opposed to the death penalty apart from its racially discriminatory administration, and when they realized their strategies could benefit a broader swath of inmates, they felt obligated to expand their charge. Tony Amsterdam, the architect of the LDF effort, explained, "We could no more let men die that we had the power to save . . . than we could have passed by a dying accident victim sprawled bloody and writhing on the road without stopping to render such aid as we could."[11]

Not coincidentally, many of the LDF's newly formed stock of capital-specific claims drew upon and reinforced concerns about racial discrimination. The exclusion of jurors who expressed qualms about the death penalty (death qualification) was a common means of excluding minorities from capital juries. Standardless discretion in state capital statutes allowed prosecutors and juries to reach different results in similar cases and insulated racial disparities from judicial review.

When the LDF sought review of Maxwell's case in the Supreme Court, it focused primarily on the extensive evidence of racial discrimination in Arkansas rape cases and the ways in which standardless discretion facilitated that discrimination. The petition seeking review declared that the "detailed and exhaustive examination" of the Arkansas cases "graphically demonstrates the grim consequences of leaving unfettered and uninformed discretion to juries to choose between death and lesser penalties for rape in a state which has historically practiced racial discrimination." The petition evocatively compared the sort of discrimination evident in the Arkansas system to the practice of lynching in an earlier era: "Decisions of this Court have long recognized that violence may emanate from the state as well as from the mob, and that violence under color of law is as dangerous to the social fabric as that not cloaked with legitimate authority."[12]

Ultimately, the Court granted review on Maxwell's claims regarding standardless discretion and Arkansas's unitary trial structure, but declined to review the claim of racial discrimination. Notwithstanding the Court's limited grant, both Maxwell's lawyers and *amici* continued to press the issue of racial discrimination. An *amicus* brief on behalf of various Jewish organizations argued extensively that the death penalty for rape constituted a "badge of slavery," and offered an elaborate chart demonstrating the near perfect overlap between states that practiced racial segregation and those that authorized the death penalty for rape.[13] An *amicus* brief on behalf of a group of national civic leaders (including William Coleman, Burke Marshall, and Cyrus Vance) argued that the Arkansas procedure for selecting jurors, which tied eligibility to having paid a poll tax, likely contributed to the jurors' understanding of their charge "as authorizing them to take race into account in deciding [Maxwell's] fate."[14]

While *Maxwell* was pending, the Court ruled in *Witherspoon v. Illinois* that the state's approach to death qualification was unconstitutionally overbroad because it excluded jurors who should have been permitted to serve in capital cases despite having some conscientious scruples about the death penalty.[15] In light of this development, Maxwell's lawyers from LDF filed a supplemental pleading to the Court. The lawyers realized that Maxwell was entitled to relief under *Witherspoon* because his case, too, involved unconstitutional death qualification of the jury. Nonetheless, they urged the Court to address the issues on which review had been granted. In their view, if the Court were to grant Maxwell relief on narrow grounds and decline to address the broader questions of standardless discretion and unitary proceedings, those choices "could only be characterized as incredibly heedless of human life" given the large number of inmates potentially affected by the broader claims. Maxwell's lawyers used the opportunity presented by the supplemental brief to ask the Court to *broaden* the scope of its consideration and revisit its decision not to grant review on the underlying claim of racial discrimination.[16]

The Court declined the LDF's invitation to rule broadly and instead reversed Maxwell's sentence on *Witherspoon* grounds, doing so in a short opinion that made no mention of race. In describing the earlier proceedings in the case, the Court indicated that Maxwell had claimed "among other things" that the Constitution prohibited the standardless discretion and unitary trial procedure of the Arkansas capital scheme, conspicuously omitting the empirical challenge to Arkansas's use of the death penalty to punish almost exclusively interracial rapes involving black defendants and white victims. The Court then concluded that the wholesale exclusion of jurors with any conscientious reservations about the death penalty required reversal for Maxwell, as it had for Witherspoon. At the end of the opinion, the

Court noted that it had granted review in two other cases presenting the standardless discretion and unitary proceeding challenges.[17]

Both *Rudolph* and *Maxwell* were missed opportunities in the sense that the Court flagged troublesome capital cases involving black men sentenced to death for raping white victims in the Deep South and ultimately chose not to comment upon—much less address or remedy—the widely appreciated fact of racial discrimination in capital prosecutions for rape in that region. But the Court's silence about race extended to the other foundational cases before the Court in which litigants highlighted the ubiquitous risk of racial discrimination in capital trials more broadly. In *Witherspoon* itself, Witherspoon's lawyers argued that the exclusion of "scrupled" jurors—those who harbored doubts about the death penalty—undermined capital defendants' rights to have a fair cross section of the community decide their cases; the lawyers explicitly noted the disproportionate exclusion of blacks in the operation of Illinois's death qualification process.[18] Likewise, the LDF's *amicus* brief contended that the death qualification process in many states allowed prosecutors to do indirectly what they could not do directly—to prevent blacks from sitting on capital juries. Even though Witherspoon had been convicted of murder rather than rape, the LDF highlighted in its statement of interest its particular concern about racial discrimination in the operation of capital punishment; the statement observed that Wolfgang's recent empirical work confirmed "that the death penalty is administered in the United States in a fashion that makes racial minorities, the deprived and downtrodden, the peculiar objects of capital charges, capital convictions, and sentences of death." The LDF also noted in the body of its brief that the risk of disproportionately excluding blacks was particularly high "when persons opposed only to the death penalty for rape are excluded as scrupled."[19] The ACLU's *amicus* brief argued that the discriminatory application of the death penalty itself might cause blacks to harbor greater doubts about the punishment than other groups (citing evidence that 78 percent of blacks opposed the death penalty).[20] The various briefs together suggested the possibility of a troubling dynamic in which blacks experienced the death

penalty as racially discriminatory, thereby enabling their disproportionate exclusion from capital juries based on their "scruples," which
in turn would contribute to discriminatory results.

Despite the numerous references to race in the pleadings, the Court's
resulting opinions in *Witherspoon* made no mention of race. Justice Stewart's opinion for the majority emphasized that the issue before the Court was a "narrow one," declining to address whether
death qualification undermined a defendant's right to a fair trial at
the guilt stage and affirming that states retained the power to exclude
prospective jurors who clearly indicated their refusal to vote for death.
Though the Court cited a recent Gallup Poll indicating relatively
low support for the death penalty nationwide, it failed to report the
much larger number of blacks who opposed the death penalty and
the corresponding disproportionate exclusion of black jurors under
Illinois's death qualification practices; it likewise failed to confront
the continuing disproportionate exclusion of blacks that would result from permissible death qualification measures untouched by the
decision.[21]

The standardless discretion question avoided in *Maxwell* resur-
faced first in *McGautha v. California* in 1971 as a "due process" claim
and then in *Furman v. Georgia* in 1972 as a claim of "cruel and unusual punishment" under the Eighth Amendment.[22] The *McGautha*
briefing made less of race than the similar briefing in *Maxwell,* perhaps in part because the litigation strategy in *Maxwell* emphasized
the connection between standardless discretion and the discriminatory results contained in the Wolfgang study. By the time of *McG-
autha,* the stock language framing the standardless discretion claim
denounced the "arbitrariness," "discrimination," and "irrationality"
wrought by the absence of standards, and virtually all of the briefs
used these terms frequently and interchangeably.[23] Both the brief for
McGautha and some of the *amicus* briefs made explicit the claim that
standardless discretion produced racially discriminatory outcomes,
though the briefs as a whole did not make this the primary point.[24]
In response, California offered empirical data purporting to support
its claim that "a defendant's race plays no part" in capital jury decisions in California, with the raw data showing that black offenders

constituted a smaller percentage of death-sentenced inmates than of non-death-sentenced inmates convicted of first-degree murder.[25]

When the Court rejected the standardless discretion claim in *McGautha* (as well as the companion claim regarding unitary trials), many observers thought that global challenges to capital punishment were essentially exhausted.[26] But the Court immediately granted review in four new cases—collected in *Furman*—that asked whether the death penalty could be imposed consistent with the Eighth Amendment's prohibition of cruel and unusual punishments. Like McGautha, the defendants in all four cases were black. But the *Furman* briefing emphasized to a greater extent the ways in which racial discrimination permeated state capital systems. The inventive LDF strategy did not directly encourage the Court to invalidate the death penalty because of racial discrimination. Rather, the litigants argued that the fact of racial discrimination accounted for capital statutes staying on the books despite dwindling popular support. The standardless discretion in state schemes permitted the application of capital punishment solely against marginalized groups, particularly blacks, and the broader public's concerns about the death penalty were likely muted by the knowledge of its limited reach. In the California case, *Aikens v. California,* which was rendered moot by the invalidation of the California statute under state law, the petitioner's brief captured this argument poignantly: "A legislator may not scruple to put a law on the books (still less, to maintain an old law on the books) whose general, even-handed, non-arbitrary application the public would abhor—precisely because both he and the public know that it will not be enforced generally, even-handedly, non-arbitrarily." More directly, Aikens's brief stated: "Those who are selected to die are the poor and powerless, personally ugly and socially unacceptable. In disproportionate percentages, they are also black."[27]

Furman's own brief also suggested that the absence of standards could produce discriminatory outcomes. Furman argued that the jury that sentenced him to die (for a homicide that might well have been accidental but was bumped up to capital murder because it occurred during a burglary) knew very little about him or his circumstances apart from the facts of his crime, his age, and his race.[28]

Georgia responded that it could "hardly be presumed that the juries in this country have conspired to sentence only certain classes of persons within our society, or that the juries responsible for the death penalties now outstanding were infected with an impermissible discrimination." Georgia, like California in *McGautha,* maintained that the evidence did not support an inference of "rampant" discrimination, and that the high concentration of blacks on death row in Georgia was likely attributable to the high offending rates of blacks.[29]

The *amicus* briefs in *Furman* extensively documented the role of race in American capital punishment. A coalition of Jewish organizations again drew the Court's attention to the connection between segregation and retention of the death penalty.[30] A brief on behalf of several civil rights organizations (including the NAACP and the Southern Christian Leadership Conference) provided a broad overview of race's shadow over the American death penalty. The brief proclaimed, "The total history of the administration of capital punishment in America, both through formal authority, and informally, is persuasive evidence that racial discrimination was, and still is, an impermissible factor in the disproportionate imposition of the death penalty upon non-white American citizens." The brief recounted racial discrimination in the administration of the death penalty during slavery, the experience of lynching and vigilantism stretching from the post-Reconstruction era through the mid-1930s, and explicitly argued: "The disproportionate numbers of non-white persons executed by formal capital punishment" violated the Eighth Amendment.[31] Another *amicus* brief, filed on behalf of various churches, argued that the death penalty denied condemned persons their religious freedom by depriving them of the opportunity to seek salvation. It further argued that the application of the death penalty disproportionately to men who are from "less-favored ethnic and socio-economic groups" compounds the violation by adding to the mental suffering of such offenders who are aware of the invidious discrimination directed at their groups.[32]

Five justices in *Furman* agreed that the prevailing administration of the death penalty violated the Eighth Amendment. Notwithstanding the briefs' sustained, evocative references to the role of racial discrimination in the American death penalty, the five individual opinions supporting the judgment are relatively sparse in their references to the problem of race, especially in light of their extraordinary collective length (about 135 pages in the U.S. Reports). Justices Brennan and White made no arguments about racial discrimination at all. Justice Douglas alone offered a sustained critique of the discriminatory administration of the death penalty, quoting a presidential study that had observed: "The death sentence is disproportionately imposed and carried out on the poor, the Negro, and the members of unpopular groups." Douglas discussed the race and crimes of the offenders before the Court, two black men convicted of raping white women and one black man convicted of murder in the course of a burglary. He then added that he could not conclude, based on the records before the Court, "that these defendants were sentenced to death because they were black." Instead, he criticized the unbridled discretion afforded sentencers in capital cases, concluding that the "discretionary statutes are unconstitutional in their operation" because they are "pregnant with discrimination."[33] Justice Stewart likewise indicated that "racial discrimination ha[d] not been proved," and found the administration of the death penalty unconstitutional because it had been "wantonly and freakishly imposed."[34]

Justice Marshall—the only black justice on the Court and a former LDF attorney—offered an extensive history of capital punishment in the United States, moving from the colonial period to the founding era and then through the nineteenth and twentieth centuries. None of this history made any reference to race or racial discrimination. Marshall then focused on whether capital punishment was necessary to achieve permissible goals of punishment, which he identified as retribution, deterrence, incapacitation, encouragement of pleas, eugenics, and efficiency. Finally, Marshall asked whether the death penalty remained consistent with prevailing morality, focusing not on polling data (which he argued was of limited value) but instead on whether American citizens would support the death penalty if aware "of all information presently available." The facts developed by Marshall included the absence of any proven deterrent effect beyond life imprisonment, the rarity of death sentences in relation to convictions for murder, the low recidivism rate for convicted murderers released from prison, and the generally good behavior of such convicts while incarcerated. In Marshall's view, these facts alone would be sufficient to persuade "the great mass of citizens . . . that the death penalty is immoral and therefore unconstitutional." He then added three supplemental facts that would likely "convince even the most hesitant of citizens to condemn death as a sanction"— its discriminatory administration, its application against innocent persons, and its adverse effects on the rest of the criminal justice system. On the discrimination point, Marshall cited studies providing evidence of racial discrimination, as well as evidence of discrimination on the basis of sex, class, intelligence, and privilege. His entire treatment of discrimination occupied three paragraphs in his sixty-page concurrence, and only one of those paragraphs focused on race. Notably absent in his lengthy history of the American death penalty, or in his discussion of the purposes of capital punishment, is any indication that the death penalty was used to subordinate minorities. Like Douglas, Marshall appeared equally troubled by the apparent under-enforcement of the death penalty against the privileged as he was by the application of capital punishment against minorities and the poor.[35]

As a whole, the five concurrences convey the impression that the majority justices were extremely reluctant to assert that the defendants before them (even the two defendants condemned for rape) might have been victims of racial discrimination. Despite ample ammunition in the *amicus* briefs, none of the justices seemed willing to offer a detailed history of the role of race in shaping capital statutes and practices for over 200 years; Justices Douglas and Marshall, the only two justices who addressed race at all, both stopped short of placing the practice in its historical, slavery-rooted context. Instead, each seemed content to focus on relatively recent, twentieth-century patterns that showed discrimination along both racial and nonracial lines. Perhaps most tellingly, none of the justices seemed willing to describe, much less embrace, the thrust of the LDF's argument—that the death penalty remained on the books in large part *because of* its racially discriminatory administration. Indeed, Marshall's hypothesis that most American citizens would reject the death penalty if only they knew about its discriminatory administration was in considerable tension with the LDF claim that most Americans (and legislatures) tolerated the retention of the death penalty precisely because they were aware of its exclusive application against the outcasts of society, including racial minorities.

When *Furman* invalidated prevailing capital statutes, many participants and observers believed they had witnessed the end of the American death penalty. Had *Furman* "stuck"—with states choosing to forego redrafting their statutes or the Court invalidating any such efforts—claims regarding the American death penalty's racially discriminatory administration would have been buried alongside the death penalty itself. The LDF would have known that concerns about racial justice at some level informed the Court's decisions, but the record of opinions would have reflected a sort of euphemistic code, with repeated condemnation of "arbitrariness," "wantonness," and "freakishness," rather than more forthright condemnations of racial prejudice.[36]

But just as Chief Justice Warren had underestimated the backlash that would follow the Court's "non-accusatory" opinion in *Brown*, which had whitewashed the long-standing connections between chattel slavery, white supremacist ideology, and state segregation of schools, the *Furman* Court misread public attitudes toward capital punishment and over-estimated the willingness of states to acquiesce in judicial abolition, even if framed in a similarly non-accusatory manner.[37] In the four years following *Furman*, thirty-five states re-enacted capital statutes, and the Court agreed to address whether death sentences obtained under five of the new capital schemes could be imposed consistently with the Eighth Amendment.

In many ways, the 1976 litigation before the Court was a reprise of *Furman*. The LDF controlled the litigation (although its lawyers were not named as lead counsel on the petitioners' briefs). The LDF strategy was to continue to emphasize the unreviewable discretion to impose or withhold the death penalty, despite the promulgation of "aggravating" factors to guide sentencer discretion in many of the new statutes, and the mandatory requirement of death upon conviction of first-degree murder in others. Whereas the *Furman* briefs emphasized the absence of standards within the capital statutes themselves, the 1976 briefs pointed to the numerous opportunities for unconstrained police, prosecutorial, and juror discretion to withhold the death penalty prior to sentencing, even under the purportedly mandatory statutes of Louisiana and North Carolina.[38]

As in *Furman,* the petitioners' briefs sought to document the role of racial discrimination in capital litigation. Though none of the five cases involved a capital conviction for rape, each petitioner's brief indicated that racial discrimination in capital rape cases was "sufficiently blatant to allow of overwhelming statistical proof."[39] Having worked so extensively with Wolfgang to produce the rape study, the LDF was aware of the empirical challenges in producing a comparable study for murder, especially given the rarity of death sentences as well as the costs of designing and implementing an empirically sound study.[40] That recognition prompted the petitioners' acknowledgment that a "similarly overwhelming comprehensive demonstration of racial discrimination has concededly not yet been made in connection with the death penalty for murder." But the petitioners nonetheless insisted that "very strong evidence" of such continuing discrimination in murder cases could be inferred from a variety of empirical studies, informed observation of state capital systems, and "the intuitive implausibility of the hypothesis that the same people, operating through the same procedures in rape and murder cases, have practiced racial discrimination in the rape cases but risen scrupulously above its influence when the charge is murder." The petitioners also noted the "sobering" fact that the percentage of nonwhites in the death row population post-*Furman* was not significantly different from the percentage in the pre-*Furman* death row population.[41] Despite the fact that the death-sentenced inmates in three of the five cases were white—Troy Gregg (Georgia), Charles William Proffitt (Florida), and Jerry Lane Jurek (Texas)—several of the briefs in those cases included appendices listing the race of death-sentenced defendants in all post-*Furman* cases in the state.[42] In addition, the petitioners alluded to recent findings that blacks faced harsher punishment in cases involving white victims, representing a shift from the focus on race-of-the-defendant discrimination in earlier cases.[43] The overall message of the petitioners' briefs regarding racial discrimination was clear. The briefs in both *Gregg* and *Jurek* concluded their passages regarding racial discrimination with the following evocative plea: "The time is too late now to rectify the errors of the past; such, of course, is the nature of capital punishment. It is not too late—nor is it too early—to prevent the repetition of those errors in the future."[44]

The issue of race was particularly salient in the *amicus* briefs. The LDF filed a brief in *Gregg* on its own behalf, indicating in its statement of interest that its experience "in handling capital cases over a period of many years convinced us that the death penalty is customarily applied in a discriminatory manner against racial minorities and the economically underprivileged." The LDF went further, arguing that "the evil of discrimination was not merely adventitious, but was rooted in the very nature of capital punishment."[45] Amnesty International filed an *amicus* brief in the five cases making a similar point, explaining that it "is the worldwide experience of Amnesty International that the death penalty is applied in a highly discriminatory fashion against ethnic and religious minorities, against political prisoners, against the disadvantaged."[46] On the other side, in its extensive *amicus* brief rejecting the proposition that the death penalty is unconstitutional per se, the United States devoted an entire section to the proposition that "Capital Punishment Is Not Imposed On The Basis of Race."[47] The brief, filed by Solicitor General Bork, is best known for its claim of empirical support for the death penalty's deterrent effect, an argument that appeared central to the Court's ultimate embrace of the death penalty as a permissible punishment in three of the cases. But the brief also engaged the empirical studies the petitioners cited to support claims of racial bias. According to the United States, those studies did not support a claim of continuing racial discrimination in murder cases, as they focused primarily on discrimination in cases litigated at a time when blacks were excluded from jury service. Similarly, the United States "[did] not question" the conclusion of Wolfgang's study of racial discrimination in rape cases in the South during the period 1945–1965, but argued that the study neither proved continuing discrimination in such cases, nor discrimination in murder cases. The brief also foreshadowed some vulnerabilities of framing the constitutional claim against the death penalty on racial grounds, arguing that none of the defendants offered evidence of racial discrimination in their individual cases, and "the possibility that racial discrimination exists upon occasion in the criminal justice system is not an argument against the penalty imposed upon petitioners."[48]

The Court subsequently upheld the "guided discretion" statutes and invalidated the "mandatory" ones.[49] Given the widespread reauthorization of the death penalty in many states, the Court could not credit the view that the death penalty was inconsistent with prevailing standards of decency. The Court refused to conclude that the newly designed means of guiding sentencer discretion were incapable of ameliorating the "arbitrariness" and "caprice" of the old standardless discretion schemes. More broadly, the Court maintained that states could validly invoke deterrence and retribution as grounds for retaining the death penalty.[50] Strikingly absent from the decisions is any mention of the problem of racial discrimination. Justice Douglas was no longer on the Court, and Justice Marshall's dissent focused on the weakness of the deterrence claim and the inadequacy of retribution to justify capital punishment. Justice Brennan, the sole other dissenter, wrote in abstract terms how the death penalty denies human dignity. Though the 1976 opinions collectively occupy slightly fewer pages than those in *Furman* and its companion cases, it is nonetheless remarkable that the issue of racial discrimination was never mentioned in the 210 or so pages of analysis by justices on both sides of the issue in the landmark decision that made the affirmative case for the first (and to date, only) time that the American death penalty is a constitutional form of punishment. The absence of race is especially notable given that the Court chose to review statutes from five states in the Deep South (Georgia, Louisiana, North Carolina, Florida, and Texas).

The Court's decisions endorsing three of the new capital schemes were issued in July 1976, at the end of the 1975 term. When the Court returned to begin the 1976 term, it immediately agreed to address the question that Justice Goldberg had broached more than a decade earlier—whether the death penalty was permissible for the crime of rape. The grant was encouraging to the LDF; with the Court's invalidation of the mandatory schemes, Georgia alone authorized capital punishment for the rape of an adult woman, and it seemed unlikely that the Court would engage the issue if it were inclined to uphold the practice. Interestingly, the Court selected the case of a white inmate as the vehicle to address the claim. Throughout the 1960s and 1970s, the justices paid close attention to the varying facts and procedural postures of the underlying cases as they decided which inmates raising common claims would be the face of the claims as opposed to those whose cases would simply be held pending resolution of the issue. Chief Justice Burger, for example, unsuccessfully sought to include an extremely aggravated Georgia case in the 1976 litigation because he thought the high level of aggravation would convince the Court to resurrect capital punishment.[51] Justice Powell, on the other hand, wanted to exclude Woodson from the 1976 cases because Woodson was black and his victim was white.[52]

That the Court chose Coker, a white rapist, as the face of the claim suggested strongly that the Court wanted to avoid racial bias as the primary—or even a significant—ground for the decision. If the Court had believed the underlying practice to be racially discriminatory and had wanted to invoke that fact as a basis for relief, the presence of a white defendant would complicate the decision, requiring the Court to explain why discrimination in *other* cases justified overturning Coker's death sentence (exactly the sort of problem Solicitor General Bork highlighted in his *amicus* brief in *Gregg*). Moreover, as legal scholar and litigator Sheri Lynn Johnson describes in her account of the *Coker* litigation, at the time Coker sought review, the Court had petitions for review pending in two other Georgia rape cases with black defendants raising the same claim; her examination of the records in those cases led her to conclude that the race of the defendant was the only significant ground of distinction.[53]

Despite the signal reflected in the Court's choice of Coker, the LDF emphasized racial discrimination in its brief. The LDF documented in a chart the declining use of the death penalty to punish rape, identifying the number of executions for rape per year since 1946 and separating white and black offenders. The LDF discussed historical evidence supporting the claim that, "in Georgia, the death penalty for rape was specifically devised as a punishment for the rape of white women by black men." Citing the Wolfgang study, the LDF argued: "Recent statistical studies have proved the fact of discrimination conclusively." Ultimately, the LDF maintained that acceptance of the death penalty for rape rested on "racial, not penal, considerations" and that "where race does not enter the picture, its acceptance is positively aberrational." Hence, just as in *Furman*, the LDF insisted in *Coker* that racial prejudice and discriminatory enforcement permitted the continued retention of a practice that society otherwise would already have rejected.[54]

An *amicus* brief on behalf of the leading advocacy groups for women's equality, including the National Organization for Women Legal Defense and Education Fund and the Women's Law Project, reinforced the claim of racial bias, asserting that the practice of punishing rape with death was tied to Southern traditions "which valued white women according to their purity and chastity and assigned them exclusively to white men." The brief, authored by future Supreme Court justice Ruth Bader Ginsburg, powerfully exposed the ways in which the death penalty for rape fundamentally rested on both sexist and racist beliefs. The brief detailed the ways in which the crime of rape was long regarded as a crime against the property of a woman's husband or father. It described efforts by women in the 1930s to bring an end to lynching by mobs who "commit acts of violence and lawlessness in the name of women." It also recalled the racially discriminatory laws that treated black-on-white rapes differently from other racial combinations in antebellum Georgia. It concluded that "the death penalty for rape is an outgrowth of both male patriarchal views of women no longer seriously maintained by society and gross racial injustice created in part out of that patriarchal foundation."[55] On the state's side, the respondent's brief omitted any reference to race in its lukewarm defense of its capital rape verdicts, conceding that "Georgia, of course, has no interest in executing all rapists" (exactly the point made by the LDF), and suggesting that "at some future date" the practice might be deemed excessive. The state's nonresponsiveness to claims of racial discrimination was exacerbated by its unelaborated declaration at the end of the brief: "Tradition and history support the retention of the death penalty for rape."[56] Indeed.

The Court in *Coker* declared the death penalty a "grossly disproportionate and excessive punishment for the crime of rape" and "therefore forbidden by the Eighth Amendment." The plurality opinion devised a new methodology for gauging excessiveness, looking first at the current judgment reflected in state statutes and jury decision making. The plurality observed that the decline in state capital rape statutes (which Georgia attributed to the Court's intervention in *Furman*) signaled declining societal support for the punishment, as did the relatively few capital verdicts for rape obtained in Georgia post-*Furman*. The plurality then brought its own judgment "to bear on the question of the acceptability of the death penalty under the Eighth Amendment." Borrowing from a theme in Ginsburg's *amicus* brief, the plurality concluded that the crime of rape "does not compare with murder" in terms of "moral depravity and of the injury to the person and to the public."[57] Justices Brennan and Marshall concurred in the result, but did so based on their categorical rejection of the death penalty as a permissible punishment.

Neither the plurality opinion nor the dissenting opinions made any reference to race. Given the long-standing historical connection between race and capital punishment for rape, the role of the LDF in developing empirical evidence of racial discrimination in the Wolfgang study of rape cases, the acknowledgment of the persuasiveness of that study in Solicitor General Bork's brief in the 1976 cases, and the continued emphasis on racial bias by the litigants in *Coker*, it is astonishing that concerns about race did not merit even a mention in the ultimate *Coker* opinions. *Coker* represents the height of the Court's avoidance of race, because Georgia's continued authorization of death for rape was simply impossible to explain or understand without examining the racial history surrounding that practice.

Coker is in many respects the appropriate bookend to *Rudolph*, Justice Goldberg's dissent from denial of review fourteen years earlier.

In the years spanning those two decisions, the Court embarked on a remarkable project to assess the constitutionality of the American death penalty. The Court initiated the conversation and ultimately produced the first moratorium on executions in the United States followed by the first—and only—brief period of judicial abolition. Even as it initiated the conversation, the Court took great pains to separate the questions of race and capital punishment. Justice Goldberg and his colleagues declined to mention race in their initial inquiry into the appropriateness of death for rape. The Court refused to grant certiorari in *Maxwell* on the issue of racial discrimination in rape cases in the South and declined to respond to claims of racial discrimination in several of its foundational cases, including *Witherspoon.* And when the Court finally invalidated prevailing statutes in *Furman,* the justices supporting that result were reluctant to suggest that the black petitioners (two of whom had been sentenced to death for raping white women) might have been victims of racial discrimination, and instead highlighted the generally "wanton" and "freakish" nature of American death verdicts.[58] When the death penalty was resurrected in 1976, the Court selected three white inmates as the face of the constitutional challenges to the Georgia, Florida, and Texas schemes and ultimately upheld the new schemes without engaging the lingering question of racial discrimination. *Coker* followed quickly on the heels of the 1976 cases, as the Court sought to excise the most obviously objectionable part of what was now going to be an ongoing practice. But in shoring up the death penalty against continuing fears of racial discrimination, the Court managed to say nothing about the racial discrimination that its members—and everybody else—knew it was addressing.

Explaining the Gap

The Court's deafening silence on the subject of race in its foundational capital punishment cases is striking but, on reflection, perhaps not altogether surprising. Ample reasons of various kinds—strategic, institutional, ideological, and psychological—help explain what otherwise might appear to be a baffling obtuseness. Not every consideration

applies to every justice in every case, though more than one explanation might be at work at any given time even with regard to the work
of individual justices. Moreover, not every consideration necessarily
operated at a conscious level. Rather, what follows is an attempt to
consider why a "race neutral" constitutional approach to the issue of
capital punishment may have been appealing to the Supreme Court
even—perhaps especially—in the racially charged era of the 1960s
and 1970s.

As a strategic matter, the Court had already committed itself to a
challenging racial justice agenda with regard to school desegregation
in *Brown* in 1954. Though the Court bought time with its 1955 decision in a second case in the *Brown* litigation ("*Brown II*"), which
promoted a gradualist "all deliberate speed" approach to the enforcement of its desegregation mandate, the Court returned to
school desegregation in the late 1960s and early 1970s at exactly the
same time that it took on capital punishment.[59] In 1968, the same
year as the Court's death penalty decision in *Witherspoon,* the Court
decided *Green v. County School Board,* holding that a Virginia school
board's "freedom of choice" plan was not adequate to promote compliance with *Brown*'s desegregation mandate.[60] And in 1971, just one year
prior to *Furman,* the Court decided *Swann v. Charlotte-Mecklenburg
Board of Education,* upholding court-ordered busing as an equitable
remedy to achieve integration in a large public school system in North
Carolina.[61] These controversial rulings, though more publicly palatable
than they would have been in the 1950s, embroiled the Court, the
public, and the LDF (which litigated both cases) in controversy in the
South and beyond.[62]

In light of the Court's ongoing role in the school desegregation
battle, it is no wonder that Chief Justice Warren, the architect of
the Court's unanimous opinion in *Brown,* hesitated to add capital
punishment to the simmering pot of racial issues. Black murderers
and especially rapists presented a much less sympathetic face for civil
rights enforcement than did schoolchildren. Not only did Warren decline to make a fourth vote for certiorari in *Rudolph,* he also asked
that Goldberg cut the race argument out of his dissent from denial
of review, despite the prominence of that argument in the memo that

Goldberg had circulated to the Court. Warren explained to Goldberg that the public would not accept any softening of the punishment for rape given widespread white fears of sexual violence by blacks. The same concern for public sensibilities led Warren to delay confronting the constitutionality of laws prohibiting interracial marriage, which were not invalidated by the Court until 1967.[63]

In addition to protecting its ongoing project of school desegregation from controversial entanglements, the Court doubtless sought (unsuccessfully, as it turned out) to move on the issue of capital punishment in a way that would avoid generating a new version of the backlash that had greeted its handiwork in the school desegregation context. There were good reasons for the Court to worry that constitutional limitation or abolition of capital punishment for explicitly race-based reasons would inspire more spirited public resistance than apparently race-neutral interventions. If the Court chose the racial route, it would be accusing hundreds to thousands of jurors of at least implicit racism, most of them from the South. The death penalty was (and always had been) more popular, widely authorized, and vigorously employed in the South than in any other region of the country. The Warren Court's desegregation rulings and its criminal procedure revolution already seemed to target Southern institutions, and these decisions engendered substantial backlash in that region.[64] The Court might well have feared that a ruling against capital punishment that focused on its racial aspects would further stoke fires that were already burning, especially given that the only non-Southern state in the *Furman* litigation (California) dropped out before the Court's decision when its case was rendered moot by a state constitutional ruling on the death penalty.[65]

Moreover, throughout the 1960s and 1970s, crime rates were rising across the country, especially crime in inner-city minority communities. The race riots of the late 1960s and the increasingly militant stance of black radicals fed into growing fears of black violence.[66] Indeed, the Republican Party sought to capitalize on these fears by using crime as a racially coded wedge issue to appeal to Southern white Democrats as part of its "Southern strategy" to convince "Dixiecrats" to switch party affiliation.[67] Rising crime rates and fear of black crime not only increased the likelihood of political backlash to a race-based judicial curtailment of capital punishment, they also may have engendered ambivalence among some of the justices about the underlying racial discrimination claim. While the LDF had very strong evidence, based both on raw numbers and on Wolfgang's statistical analysis, of racial discrimination in the use of the death penalty for rape, the same was not true for the crime of murder, which comprised the majority of capital prosecutions. The raw numbers on the race of capital murder defendants did not present the same striking prima facie case for an inference of discrimination as the rape numbers did—a point that California made in its brief in the *McGautha* litigation and that Solicitor General Bork noted in the brief for the United States in *Gregg*.[68] Nor did the LDF have the resources to undertake the expansive—and expensive—statistical analysis of capital murder necessary to prove its discrimination case, as it acknowledged in its brief.[69] Consequently, the Court may have entertained the alternative inference explicitly urged by Georgia in *Furman*—that the overrepresentation of blacks on death row was attributable to their overrepresentation among murderers.[70]

Given the difference in the strength of the discrimination inference with regard to capital prosecutions for rape on the one hand and murder on the other, the Court may well have preferred to deal with the issue by eliminating the most obviously problematic cases on some other ground, thus avoiding the need to dig deep into the statistical morass. This explanation fits perfectly with what the Court in fact did: only a year after *Gregg*, the Court constitutionally invalidated the death penalty for rape on proportionality grounds in *Coker*—a case with a white defendant and a decision devoid of any discussion of race. A Court sympathetic to the racial discrimination claim in capital rape cases but skeptical of it in its broader form could thus do away with the most obviously troubling racial aspects of capital punishment without committing itself on the larger, technically fraught issue of what constituted adequate proof of racial discrimination in sentencing outcomes.

The technical expertise needed to evaluate claims of racial discrimination also may have made avoidance of the issue attractive to the Court. As the more sophisticated litigants recognized, raw numerical disparities (of the kind referenced by Justice Douglas in his solo concurrence in *Furman*) are insufficient to prove discrimination. Further analysis is necessary to demonstrate that the disparities are caused by racial discrimination as opposed to other, nonracial factors, such as differences in crime rates, differences in the severity of the crimes committed, or differences in the records or other characteristics of the offenders. The best tool to sort through these possibilities—multiple-regression analysis—is difficult for nonstatisticians to use or understand, and the justices may have appropriately doubted their capacity to evaluate the reliability of evidence of this type.

Justice Powell was the author of the majority opinion in *McCleskey v. Kemp*, which finally directly addressed in 1987 the race issue that the Court had avoided in its foundational death penalty cases in the 1970s. Powell wrote the five-to-four decision upholding a death sentence imposed on a black defendant convicted of killing a white police officer, rejecting the defendant's claim of racial discrimination premised on a statistical study that used multiple-regression analysis.[71] While working on the case, Powell acknowledged in a memo to his law clerk that his "understanding of statistical analysis— particularly what is called 'regression analysis' range[d] from limited to zero."[72] The move that Powell ultimately made in *McCleskey*—raising questions about the methodological soundness of the statistical study, but ultimately deciding the case on legal grounds while assuming without deciding the validity of the study—is a move that recurs in the Court's constitutional decision making.[73] Powell, who joined the Court just in time for the *Furman* litigation, was certainly not alone among the justices in his uneasiness with statistical proof. As a result, many of the justices may have felt that their personal legitimacy as jurists was threatened in cases involving statistical proof and thus may have preferred to render decisions on purely legal rather than statistical grounds.[74] This same sense of an appropriate judicial role may have informed the Court's ultimate conclusion in *McCleskey* that judging in general—and with regard to claims of racial discrimination in particular—requires evaluating proof in individual cases rather than examining broader statistical evidence.[75]

In addition to concerns about the legitimacy of their judicial role, the justices may have avoided the racial aspects of the capital punishment litigation in part because of concerns about the legitimacy of the Court as an institution. Addressing a controversial topic like capital punishment through the lens of procedural justice, as illustrated most clearly by the decisions of swing Justices Stewart and White in *Furman,* may have seemed less socially divisive than applying the lens of racial justice. Moreover, the procedural justice focus may have seemed more distinctively judicial and less potentially legislative than a focus on racial equality. The workings (and failings) of the judicial process are well within the special expertise of courts, in contrast to the evaluation of expert, technical proof of racial discrimination in outcomes, which may seem more suited to the legislative venue. The Court's timing of its entrance into the capital punishment fray was important with respect to this consideration. The Warren Court had faced frequent and vociferous criticism for stepping beyond the appropriate boundaries of what was supposed to be the "least dangerous branch" of government, given that the judiciary controls neither army nor purse.[76] The Court's foundational capital punishment cases came on the heels of this criticism, in the waning days of the Warren Court and the early days of the Burger Court. Thus, the swing justices may have sought to dispose of the death penalty issue in the way least likely to feed into this critique—once again unsuccessfully, given that the dissenting justices repeatedly sounded the theme that the Court was inappropriately intruding in the legislative sphere.[77]

Interestingly, the South African Constitutional Court's decision invalidating capital punishment under the post-apartheid constitution in 1995 in the very first case presented to it for review also largely eschewed race-based argumentation—a silence perhaps even more surprising than that of the U.S. Supreme Court, given the overt and extreme racism of the apartheid regime.[78] In an exploration of the reasons for the South African court's apparent avoidance of race in its ruling on capital punishment, one commentator suggests a similar motivation to that posited above—that is, to establish the court as the appropriate adjudicator of the issue in contrast to the legislative branch, a motivation especially strong in the context of establishing an inaugural constitutional court with the power of judicial review. "In this setting, the Justices may have sought to elevate purely legal decision making over considerations that require the pragmatic, fact-based wisdom of legislators." Under this view, the South African court sought "a lens that privileged the expertise and position of the judiciary" so as to "legitimize that body's elevation over its parliamentary rival."[79]

On a broader ideological level, the U.S. Supreme Court's relative silence on the issue of race in capital punishment was of a piece with its approaches in the two most closely related constitutional areas: the regulation of criminal justice and the promotion of racial equality. In the broader criminal justice area, the Court presaged its approach to capital punishment by largely avoiding explicit discussion of race, even in cases in which the racial context was undeniably significant.[80] More generally, instead of focusing on *outcomes* in the criminal justice context—the kinds of punishments imposed, the length of criminal sentences, or the distribution of criminal penalties—the Court focused on the *procedures* by which punishment was imposed.[81] The Warren Court viewed the most significant constitutional problems with the American criminal justice system as procedural ones and hoped to ameliorate them by extending the rights to counsel and trial by jury and by regulating police interrogations and lineups. Consequently, it seemed natural, or at least plausible, to focus on procedural deficiencies in the capital punishment system, even under the more outcome-oriented Eighth Amendment, which forbids cruel and unusual punishments rather than mandating any special procedural protections.

In the context of constitutional litigation regarding racial equality, the Court obviously did not eschew discussions of race, but it did consistently express the hope that race-based remedies were merely temporary stopgap measures necessary to achieve a race-blind future. For example, in the school busing context, the Court referred to the court-ordered busing plan that it approved in 1971 as an "interim corrective measure" that would not necessarily require yearly court monitoring or updating once desegregation was achieved.[82] Similarly, in the affirmative action context, the Court in 1978 struck down the use of racial quotas in university admissions but upheld the voluntary use of race for the promotion of diversity, a remedial measure that Justice Sandra Day O'Connor later explicitly maintained should be "limited in time"—specifically, to 25 years—before evolving into constitutionally favored race-neutral policies.[83] This aspiration toward a race-blind future, present even in the era in which the Court most endorsed race-conscious remedial measures to give effect to the constitutional guarantee of equality, made a race-neutral approach to the constitutionality of capital punishment that much more appealing.

Both the Court's commitment to procedural justice and its aspiration toward a color-blind ideal reflect a larger and deeper commitment, one more rooted in the 1960s and 1970s than in the present: the Court's deeply optimistic faith in the constitutional perfectibility of social and legal institutions. To have invalidated the death penalty on the ground of racial disparities in its administration would have betrayed this faith by giving up hope that such disparities could be remedied by the right procedural interventions or "interim corrective measures." A race-based abolition would have amounted to an acknowledgment that the effects of institutionalized racism could not be erased by constitutional intervention—the very last message that the Supreme Court wanted to send in the era of constitutionally mandated school desegregation and criminal procedure reform. The LDF's opponents cleverly and powerfully appealed to this reluctance by arguing that evidence of past disparities should be discounted in light of the Court's own constitutional interventions. For example, Georgia argued that inferences of current racial discrimination from past disparities were not justified because "safeguards against arbitrariness or other lack of due process for disadvantaged persons have increased substantially in the last several decades . . . [including] the right to effective assistance of counsel for the indigent."[84] And Solicitor General Bork argued: "The only studies that even inferentially suggest a possibility of racial discrimination were conducted in the

South during a time when blacks were often excluded from grand and petit juries. They do not demonstrate that discrimination persists now that blacks sit in judgment on other blacks."[85] Once again, the South African context offers a similar dynamic—the new justices acted with the hope that conditions would improve with the official end of apartheid and the belief that "inequality . . . may be curable in the long run" through legal intervention.[86]

The Court's belief that procedural innovations might provide a cure for discrimination took center stage when the Court squarely addressed the issue of racial disparities in capital sentencing in *McCleskey* in 1987. In rejecting McCleskey's claim, the Court relied in part on other "safeguards designed to minimize racial bias in the process."[87] Primary among these safeguards was the Court's *Batson* doctrine. In *Batson v. Kentucky*, decided just one year prior to *McCleskey*, the Court made it easier to challenge the discriminatory exercise of peremptory strikes.[88] Prosecutors are permitted to use such strikes to dismiss prospective jurors for any reason or no reason, but not on the basis of race. The *Batson* Court shifted the burden to the prosecution to provide race neutral explanations for strikes when the nature or pattern of strikes in an individual case gave rise to a prima facie inference of discriminatory intent. The *Batson* decision did in fact permit the litigation of many more claims of discrimination in the use of peremptory strikes than previous law had done, and the Court has granted relief on *Batson* grounds in a few recent capital cases involving clear and unquestionable racial bias in jury selection.[89]

But the Court's reliance on *Batson* as a means of preventing racial discrimination in capital sentencing was profoundly misplaced. *Batson* did not purport to address disparities in capital charging decisions by prosecutors, which themselves contribute substantially to disparities in sentencing outcomes. Even in terms of preventing discrimination in jury selection, studies of the effectiveness of *Batson* in reducing the race-based use of peremptory strikes have demonstrated only an extremely modest effect.[90] This is not surprising in light of the incentives that exist to base peremptory strikes at least in part upon the race of prospective jurors and the ease with which "race neutral" explanations for strikes can be offered. With regard to incentives, if the race-based use of peremptory strikes depended on racial hatred or the belief in the inferiority of minority jurors, then there would undoubtedly be much less race-based use of peremptories than is evident today. However, there is clearly a great deal of what economists call "rational discrimination" in jury selection. Counsel on both sides make decisions about the desirability of jurors from particular demographic groups based on generalizations about attitudes that the group as a whole tends to hold. There is good reason, based on polling data, to believe that blacks as a group are more sympathetic to criminal defendants and less trusting of law enforcement than whites, and that blacks as a group are less supportive of capital punishment than whites. Under such circumstances, capital prosecutors who harbor no personal racial animosity may well see strong reasons to use race as a proxy for viewpoint in using peremptory challenges in capital cases. With regard to the easy availability of "race neutral" explanations, prosecutors can always offer explanations for striking prospective jurors based on their demeanor (the juror appeared hostile, nervous, bored, made poor eye contact, made too much eye contact, smiled or laughed inappropriately, frowned). Because no judge can simultaneously monitor the demeanor of all prospective jurors throughout the entire jury selection process, there is no way to disprove a prosecutor's claim that a particular juror appeared more "hostile" to him than the others. To reject such an explanation, a trial judge would have to make a credibility determination against a prosecutor—something judges are not prone to do lightly and in the absence of hard evidence. Although the Court's faith in *Batson* turned out to be ill-founded, it fit well with the Court's preference for procedural justice remedies in response to claims of substantively unjust outcomes.

Even as the *McCleskey* Court embraced the possibility of achieving substantive equality through procedural means, surely the justices entertained doubts about the speed and completeness of change over time, especially given the baseline of long-standing racial inequality that the Court was starting from in the 1960s and 1970s. In light of these plausible doubts, the justices may have hesitated to treat racial disparities as a ground for invalidating capital punishment because of the likelihood that similar disparities existed and would continue to exist in the imposition of noncapital punishments, which—unlike the penalty of death—could not be simply excised from the legal system. This concern about the potential scope of a substantive remedy was also paramount in the *McCleskey* opinion. As Justice Powell explained, "McCleskey's claim, taken to its logical conclusion, throws into serious question the principles that underlie our entire criminal justice system."[91] This concern was heightened by the Court's decision a decade earlier to invalidate the use of capital punishment for the crime of rape. The Court had seen the statistics on the race-based prosecutions for rape in the South, and it could not have believed that disparate charging and sentencing in rape cases would disappear simply because the death penalty was off the table. It was unthinkable to invalidate the entire criminal justice system if its workings could be shown—as they plausibly could—to be affected by racial prejudice. But if the Court relied on statistical racial disparities to invalidate capital punishment, it would be forced to explain why similar disparities must be accepted in the imposition of ordinary criminal punishment. The Court no doubt sought to avoid a public announcement that racism is unavoidable and therefore must be tolerated—both for the country's sake and for the justices' own psychological comfort.

The Court knew exactly what such a disheartening announcement would sound like, as Justice Antonin Scalia circulated a memo to his fellow justices in *McCleskey* suggesting that he might write a concurrence along precisely these lines. Scalia explained, "Since it is my view that the unconscious operation of irrational sympathies and antipathies, including racial, upon jury decisions and (hence) prosecutorial decisions is real, acknowledged in the decisions of this court, and ineradicable, I cannot honestly say that all I need is more proof."[92] Although Scalia never wrote this concurrence, his characteristic bluntness revealed the Court's dilemma with regard to evidence of racial disparities in capital sentencing. If the Court directly addressed the issue and declared the statistical proof of racial discrimination inadequate, then it would simply invite further litigation as armies of social scientists would seek to provide the missing proof. If the

Court declared the statistical proof adequate and granted relief, then it would have to face the inevitable challenge to the entire criminal justice system, without the possibility of granting similar relief. The *McCleskey* Court neatly skirted both unattractive options. It assumed without deciding the soundness of the statistical study, but it required individual rather than statistical proof for a successful discrimination case—proof that is essentially impossible to produce without a smoking-gun statement of purposeful racial discrimination by a prosecutor or jury. Thus, the Court avoided the enormity of the remedy sought for systemic discrimination while still maintaining, albeit disingenuously, that the Constitution prohibited racial discrimination in individual cases. The remedial difficulties that the Court ultimately confronted in *McCleskey* must have been apparent in the litigation regarding racial disparities in the Court's foundational cases, offering yet another powerful motivation to steer the discussions and ground the decisions in race-neutral terms.

The Court's focus on issues such as death qualification in *Witherspoon*, arbitrariness in the swing *Furman* concurrences, and proportionality in *Coker*—without any sustained discussion of the racial significance of these particular legal issues or of the broader racial context—turns out to be less mysterious than it appears at first blush. As the litigants pounded on the racial issues in the Court's foundational capital punishment cases, the justices had ample opportunity to consider the costs along many dimensions of opening up a public discussion about the evidence and constitutional significance of racial disparities in the administration of the death penalty. The Court's failure to engage robustly in this discussion could not have been inadvertent, and its silence reflected the power of the various anxieties that we have attempted to unearth and flesh out.

The Consequences of Avoidance

As in the school desegregation context in *Brown*, the Court's various death penalty opinions from *Rudolph* to *Coker* offered a woefully incomplete picture of the underlying practice. The price of omitting a discussion of race was to create the false impression that the greatest failings of the American death penalty system could be found in discrete, isolated problems such as the death qualification of jurors, unitary trials, and the absence of standards in state capital statutes. Of course, the Court might have had good reasons for resisting the most encompassing and speculative of the LDF's claims—that the death penalty remained on the books in large part because only blacks and other marginalized groups were caught in the execution net. But even if the Court was not persuaded by that assertion, it could have said much more about how race historically and at that time informed decisions at every level, including legislative selection of crimes punishable by death, prosecutorial decisions to charge capitally in individual cases, judge and jury verdicts, and appellate and executive discretionary outlets from the ultimate imposition of the punishment.

The most profound consequence of the Court's failure to address the issue of race in its capital jurisprudence is that the unjust influence of race in the capital punishment process continues unchecked. A recent study of the death penalty in the state of Louisiana since 1976 reveals racial disparities even more striking than the Georgia disparities the Court tolerated in its *McCleskey* decision nearly thirty years previously. In modern-era Louisiana, killers of whites are six times more likely to get a death sentence than killers of blacks, and fourteen times more likely to be executed; black men who kill white women are thirty times more likely to get a death sentence than black men who kill other black men. No white person has been executed in Louisiana for a crime against a black victim since 1752.[93] Quite apart from outcomes, evidence abounds of discriminatory attitudes and practices in capital cases in many jurisdictions. In Texas, a psychologist repeatedly offered "expert" testimony that blacks (and Hispanics) are more likely to pose a continuing threat to society—a required finding before a death sentence can be imposed under that state's statute.[94] A prosecutor convinced an all-white South Carolina jury to sentence a black defendant to death by referring to him as a "monster," a "caveman," and a "beast of burden" and likening him to "King Kong."[95] Although a federal judge recently threw out the death sentence in that case, a Georgia man was denied relief and executed despite the admission under oath by one of the jurors in the case that he had voted for the death penalty because "that's what that nigger deserved."[96] By failing to look at the death penalty through the lens of race, the Court has limited the capacity of death penalty law to see and respond to racial injustice.

More broadly, the Court's failure to address forthrightly the death penalty's racialized history and current practice has disserved the Court in its role as chronicler of history and social and political practices. Had the Court framed its constitutional regulation of capital punishment against the backdrop of antebellum codes, lynchings, mob-dominated trials, and disparate enforcement patterns, the Court would have done a much better job of explaining *why* the American death penalty deserved the sustained attention of the American judiciary. This would have been true even if the Court ultimately had framed its doctrines in nonracial terms. Moreover, to the extent that the Court's silence about race was calculated (as in *Brown*) to preserve the Court's capital and prevent popular backlash or resistance, it was spectacularly unsuccessful. Anyone who followed the LDF's capital punishment campaign understood that by intervening in the death penalty, the Court was taking sides in a culture war regarding racial status even as the Court omitted the history of deliberate discrimination that offered the greatest justification for its interventions.

The Court's silence also had consequences for the development of its death penalty jurisprudence. In the short term, the Court's failure to acknowledge racial discrimination in cases like *Rudolph* and *Coker* undermined the strength of that claim when *McCleskey* arrived at the Court in the late 1980s. As Sheri Lynn Johnson persuasively argues, *Coker* managed to erase the most racially discriminatory aspect of the death penalty (its use in rape cases) without giving the racial context surrounding that decision; thus, when the Court finally engaged a statistical study of racial discrimination in *McCleskey*, it was presented with a much less racially skewed death penalty and no "official" judicial record that race had ever played a substantial role in recent capital sentencing.[97] As a result, the Court was better able to give Georgia prosecutors and judges the benefit of the doubt and to "decline to assume that what is unexplained is invidious."[98] Johnson argues that a stronger opinion in *Coker* documenting the race-of-the-victim effects in rape cases would have made it more difficult to dismiss strong race-of-the-victim effects in the homicide study presented in *McCleskey,* and such a dynamic might have led to a different outcome in that case, given the Court's five-to-four division.[99] Perhaps so. But Justice Powell, the only available vote in *McCleskey* on the majority side, was undoubtedly aware of Wolfgang's rape studies even though they did not make their way into the *Coker* decision. His reluctance to side with the dissenters seems just as plausibly attributable to the problems of remedy and fears of spillover to the noncapital side, as to his need, in Justice Scalia's words, for "more proof."

The most far-reaching consequences of the Court's silence about race for the Court's broader death penalty jurisprudence were neither contemplated nor foreseeable. Three powerful strands of contemporary capital jurisprudence are traceable to the Court's framing of its decisions in its early cases, and thus in some way traceable to the Court's decisions to forego explicitly racial grounds of decision. The first two strands are the robust requirement of individualized sentencing and the accompanying heightened representational demands in capital trials. The Court's decision in *Maxwell* and later in *Furman* to focus on the problem of standardless discretion (rather than, say, racially discriminatory outcomes) has radically transformed capital practice, but in ways that were themselves contingent, complex, and unanticipated. The Court's regulatory intervention in *Furman* required states to constrain capital sentencing discretion if they sought to retain the death penalty. Numerous jurisdictions, including North Carolina and Louisiana, pursued what they saw as the clearest and most definitive path in this regard—the decision to make capital punishment mandatory for certain crimes. When the Court rejected the mandatory statutes, it formally recognized the significance of a defendant's character and background as well as the circumstances of the offense to the death penalty decision. That recognition required states to provide a statutory vehicle for the consideration of mitigating evidence, broadly defined. It also profoundly altered the responsibilities of defense counsel in investigating and presenting the case for life in capital trials.

The irony, of course, is that the Court's initial concern about the absence of guidelines for sentencers in capital cases ultimately produced a much more substantial commitment to open-ended individualized sentencing. That commitment has improved death penalty representation, but it has also proven extraordinarily costly. Contemporary capital trials are far more expensive than their counterparts in the 1960s and 1970s, and those costs have increasingly destabilized the practice. Capital prosecutions have declined dramatically over the past fifteen years, and the costs associated with capital trials—commonly borne by local rather than state governments—have contributed significantly to the decline.[100]

Would a race-conscious or race-focused capital jurisprudence have avoided these developments? If the Court had addressed the racially discriminatory application of capital rape statutes in *Rudolph* or *Maxwell*, it might have alleviated some of the pressure to address the "arbitrary" and "freakish" aspects of the American death penalty a few years later. It is difficult to assess, counterfactually, whether an early "win" on race grounds would have contributed momentum to the sort of temporary abolition achieved in *Furman* (with the unexpected consequences described above) or, on the other hand, would have defused a continuing commitment by the LDF to attack, or the Court to regulate, capital punishment.

The race avoidance in *Coker* produced a third powerful strand of contemporary death penalty law—the Court's proportionality doctrine. Prior to *Coker*, the Court had virtually no experience gauging whether particular punishments, though permissible generally, were excessive as applied to particular offenses or offenders. And *Coker* could have avoided this difficult enterprise by choosing a black defendant/white victim case and ruling that the long-standing (and continuing) racial discrimination in capital rape prosecutions required prohibiting the practice. Instead, the *Coker* Court sought to assess proportionality by looking at "objective" indicia of prevailing values (state statutes and jury decision making), and consulting its own judgment regarding the challenged practice and the purposes of punishment.[101] That proportionality approach yielded modest results in the first two decades after *Coker,* with the Court upholding the death penalty as applied to juveniles and offenders with intellectual disabilities, and carving a small layer of protection for some defendants convicted of murder as accomplices who did not themselves kill.[102] But the past fifteen years have seen a dramatic expansion of the doctrine. The Court reversed the earlier denials of protection for juveniles and offenders with intellectual disabilities and, in the context of a defendant sentenced to death for child rape, rejected the application of capital punishment to ordinary crimes other than murder.[103] In doing so, the Court substantially broadened the criteria for assessing prevailing standards of decency in a way that opens a potential doctrinal route to wholesale constitutional abolition of the death penalty.

In light of the unexpected growth of the individualization requirement (and the accompanying extraordinary costs of capital representation), as well as the contemporary expansion of the proportionality doctrine, the race avoidance of *Rudolph, Maxwell, Furman, Gregg,* and *Coker* might have yielded more substantial and intrusive regulation of state capital practices than more focused, race-based approaches. This dynamic is not unfamiliar. In the wake of the Civil War, advocates for racial justice sought explicit, simple declarations of racial equality in the Civil Rights Act of 1866 and the Fourteenth Amendment. For example, Congressman Thaddeus Stevens, leader of the Radical Republicans in the House of Representatives, proposed the following amendment: "All national and State laws shall be equally applicable to every citizen, and no discrimination shall be made on account of race and color."[104] And an original proposal for the Civil Rights Act would have condemned any racial discrimination with respect to "civil rights or immunities."[105] However, concerns about the potentially broad implications of general guarantees of racial equality (including their consequences for antimiscegenation laws, segregation, and voting restrictions) caused the Reconstruction Congress to embrace a narrower, targeted Civil Rights Act safeguarding specific rights of economic personhood.[106] Those same concerns likely informed the choice to forego Stevens's straightforward protection against racial discrimination in favor of the vague language of the Fourteenth Amendment, which does not mention race at all. Instead, the amendment protects "privileges and immunities" from abridgment, assures "due process of law" prior to deprivations of life, liberty, or property, and prohibits denial of "equal protection of the laws"—language that has been used to protect the rights of women, ethnic minorities, and gays and lesbians, as well as the rights to use contraceptives, terminate a pregnancy, and homeschool one's children, among other things.

The desire not to intrude too much on racial prerogatives ultimately paved the way for a dramatic expansion of the scope of equality and liberty protected by the Fourteenth Amendment apart from race, though it came at the price of helping to delay for at least three quarters of a century the dismantling of Jim Crow.[107] So, too, might race avoidance in the capital context produce more enduring and intrusive regulation of capital punishment—perhaps even laying the groundwork for eventual constitutional abolition—than the more limited, though more threatening, race-based intervention that the Court abjured.

CHAPTER FOUR

Between the Supreme Court
and the States

IN HIS HISTORY of capital punishment in America, Stuart Banner describes a little-remembered feature of colonial justice. The death penalty, of course, was a ubiquitous practice. Execution was, as Banner observes, the base point of punishment, as virtually all serious crimes were punishable—and in many cases punished—by death. Yet, in some cases throughout the seventeenth and eighteenth centuries, offenders were sentenced not to actual death but to the ceremony of execution. Banner describes a woman who had killed her child in 1677 and who was subsequently sentenced to a simulated hanging—to "stand a full ½ houre on the gallowes with a halter about her neck." Other offenders, Banner reports, were not informed that they would be spared death until the last moment, giving the simulation greater drama and terror.[1]

Banner speculates that simulated executions and last-minute reprieves permitted officials to "reap much of the benefit of the death penalty without actually having to kill." Perhaps by rehearsing the steps of a real execution and simultaneously demonstrating the state's power and restraint, officials could deter crime and yet ameliorate the harsh effects of a criminal justice system that did not yet have incarceration as a realistic alternative to death. As Banner notes, pardons also played a significant role in the United States prior to the modern (post-1972) era in reducing the deadly toll of capital verdicts.[2] In England, too, the vast reach of the death penalty in the eighteenth century (applicable to over 200 offenses) was cabined by discretionary grants of mercy at all stages of the process. Douglas Hay, observing the gap between those eligible for the death penalty and those spared, argued that England's frequent exercises of mercy helped promote an "ideology of justice" that reduced class tensions and tended to stabilize the social order overall.[3]

Today in the United States, we no longer have simulated executions, and we rarely have pardons or commutations. But a vast percentage of those sentenced to death have not been executed and appear to face no realistic risk of execution in the near future. Pronouncements of death sentences far exceed actual executions. This is a new phenomenon. In the past, death sentences by and large resulted in executions within a relatively short period of time, typically measured in months rather than years. Unlike the case of the woman sentenced to a simulated hanging, though, the death penalty today operates as a symbol in many states not as a result of deliberate, transparent decisions, but by a confluence of complicated, poorly understood forces traceable in large part to the Supreme Court's efforts to regulate the death penalty.

One of the central motivations for regulation is the desire to achieve uniformity—to make practices more "regular." This motivation was central to the Court's decision to enter the capital punishment fray, as members of the Court no doubt believed that federalizing capital punishment law would bring some consistency and stability to American death penalty practices. What the Court and observers likely underestimated, though, was the extent to which regulation of complex social phenomena creates extraordinary opportunities for divergence—the possibility that the regulation will mean quite different things in different places. Regulation is filtered through numerous actors—legislatures, multiple courts, executive officials—and affords numerous opportunities for both avoidance of the regulatory norms and their conscientious internalization. In the modern era, we have witnessed both extremes, with some jurisdictions resisting federal intervention and others using the fact of regulation to weaken the underlying practice of capital punishment. As a result, the shape of contemporary death penalty practice is in many respects less regular than what it replaced. The divergence, though, is less evident in the distribution of capital sentences than in the willingness and capacity of states to translate capital sentences into executions. Executions require a very high level of coordination and cooperation among governmental actors, and such coordination is evident in only a small number of jurisdictions. Accordingly, only a few death penalty jurisdictions execute a substantial percentage of those sentenced to death, whereas the rest have limited or no executions. We have replaced (or supplemented) a lottery for death sentences with a lottery for executions, and the engine behind that change is regulation.

The United States now houses four sorts of jurisdictions: states without the death penalty by law ("abolitionist states," such as Michigan and Vermont); states with the death penalty on the books but trivial numbers of death sentences and executions ("de facto or virtually abolitionist states," such as Colorado and Wyoming); states with significant numbers of death sentences but few executions ("symbolic states," such as California and Pennsylvania); and states with both the death penalty in law and in practice—states actively carrying out significant numbers of executions ("executing states," such as Texas and Oklahoma). These jurisdictions roughly correspond to geographic regions, with the abolitionist states distributed primarily in the Northeast and Midwest; the de facto abolitionist and symbolic states distributed more broadly, including in the heartland, the mid-Atlantic region, and the West; and the executing states confined almost exclusively to the South and its borders.

In the modern death penalty era (from the resumption of executions in 1977 to December 31, 2015), states carried out 1,422 executions. Of these executions, the vast majority—about 85 percent (1,209)—were conducted in ten southern states and two states bordering the South: Texas (531), Oklahoma (112), Virginia (111), Florida (91), Missouri (86), Georgia (60), Alabama (56), North Carolina (43), South Carolina (43), Louisiana (28), Arkansas (27), and Mississippi

(21). Indeed, the five top states in terms of executions account for almost two-thirds (931) of the executions nationwide. Only two other states carried out at least 25 executions (Ohio [53] and Arizona [37]), and over a quarter of executions conducted outside of the South and its borders (55 out of 201) involved "volunteers"—defendants who had given up their appeals. In contrast, only about 7 percent (83) of the 1,209 executions conducted in the twelve leading Southern and border executing states involved volunteers.[4]

The enormous disparity in executions between symbolic and executing states is not traceable to significant differences in death-*sentencing* rates. Indeed, the death-sentencing rates of some of the symbolic states are relatively high, with Pennsylvania, for example, producing more death verdicts per homicide in the first two decades post-*Furman* than the two states leading in sheer numbers of executions during that period (Texas and Virginia); similarly, California has a higher per capita death-sentencing rate than either Georgia or Virginia, two of the currently leading states in executions (and executions per death sentence). Even Harris County, Texas, the county with the most executed defendants, trails Philadelphia County, Pennsylvania, in its death-sentencing rate, though Pennsylvania is a symbolic state with just three executions in the past forty years (all involving defendants who gave up their appeals). As a result, the death row populations in symbolic states are considerably larger than those of executing states, with California, Pennsylvania, and Tennessee currently housing more than three times as many death row inmates (1,003) as the three states leading in executions in the modern era (Texas, Oklahoma, and Virginia [327]).[5]

The key issue, then, is translating death sentences into executions. At the top end, Virginia and Texas have managed to convert at least 50 percent of their death sentences into executions, with Virginia far and away ahead of all other states, having executed over 70 percent of those sentenced to death. Together, Virginia and Texas have carried out 642 executions in the modern era (about 45 percent of the executions carried out nationwide) despite the fact that the two states account for only about one-seventh of the death sentences obtained during this period (just over 1,100 out of the nation's 8,000 or so death sentences). At the other end of the spectrum, California and Pennsylvania, with more death sentences than Virginia and Texas (over 1,300), have executed only sixteen offenders, or just over 1 percent of those sentenced to death within their jurisdictions. Between these extremes, two other states with at least sixty death sentences—Missouri and Oklahoma—have execution rates above 35 percent (producing more than one execution for each three death sentences), five others have execution rates around 20 percent (Arkansas, South Carolina, Indiana, Georgia, and Louisiana), while the majority of such death penalty states have execution rates below 10 percent, including Florida, with an execution rate of about 9 percent (91 executions with about 950 death sentences). Many of the states that now have significant numbers of death sentences but trivial numbers of executions routinely executed offenders prior to the Court's regulation. California executed 501 inmates in its state penitentiary (1893–1967), Pennsylvania executed 350 inmates (1915–1962), and Tennessee executed 134 inmates (1909–1960). Today, these jurisdictions have large death rows but offenders face no prospect of execution in the short term. Execution is only the third leading cause of death for a death-sentenced inmate in California (behind natural causes and suicide).[6]

Most of the scholarly and popular attention to the death penalty chasm between the South and the rest of the country tends to focus on the question of Southern exceptionalism: What aspects of Southern politics and culture account for the region's continued, robust use of the death penalty? Many explanations have been offered, including those that emphasize the connection between the death penalty and racial fear and oppression, those that point to higher levels of violence generally in the South (including homicide rates), those that highlight the prevalence of fundamentalist religious beliefs (the near-perfect overlap of the "Bible Belt" and the "Death Belt"), and those that focus on the long-standing inadequacies of criminal defense representation in Southern jurisdictions. These explanations are pertinent to the questions of retention of the death penalty and death-sentencing rates, but they do not begin to explain the execution gap described above.

The phenomenon in need of explanation is not the continued willingness of Southern jurisdictions to execute death-sentenced offenders but the new normal of death sentences without executions outside of the South and its borders. The death penalty exists as law but not as practice in virtually all of these capital jurisdictions. As a result, their death rows have become the simulated gallows of the twenty-first century. The decoupling of death sentences and executions coincided with the Court's constitutional regulation of the death penalty, but the relationship is not coincidental. Regulation, which the Court embraced to make the administration of the death penalty more consistent and uniform, has produced state capital systems that are worlds apart.

Prior to the Court's intervention in *Furman* and subsequent decisions, capital cases were treated like other serious felony cases and received comparable resources and attention both at trial and in subsequent review. With the advent of constitutional regulation, capital practices have changed enormously as a new reservoir of death-specific constitutional claims is available in every capital case. Defendants can file pretrial motions challenging innumerable aspects of the new capital scheme adopted within their jurisdiction. Such challenges can focus on the breadth of aggravating factors, the absence of an adequate statutory vehicle to consider mitigating factors, and the manner in which the ultimate question of life versus death is framed for the jury. At trial, defendants can challenge the exclusion of jurors who harbor doubts about the death penalty, as well as the failure to exclude jurors intractably committed to capital punishment. Bifurcated trials entail numerous federal constitutional questions. What sort of evidence may be introduced at the punishment phase to support a death sentence? May the state introduce evidence relating to victims' personal qualities and the consequences of the crime for their family and loved ones? Are defendants permitted to introduce evidence unrelated to the offense concerning their own trauma and victimization? Are the parties permitted to present evidence relating to the real meaning of a life sentence (namely, whether and when the defendant might be eligible for parole)? After trial, death-sentenced inmates have substantial reason to challenge all of the decisions that culminated in a death sentence, because the police, prosecutor, defense attorneys, and trial judge all make important decisions bearing on the fairness, accuracy, and constitutionality of that sentence.[7]

The new body of federal constitutional law concerning the death penalty required new institutional structures to process the increased litigation. Outside of the courts, capital defense (and prosecution) became a legal specialty, and states and counties had to develop new ways to train and select lawyers capable of navigating the emerging complex doctrines. Inside the courts, the explosion of federal constitutional issues in capital cases meant that the ordinary processes for reviewing capital convictions were inadequate. Many states included provisions for mandatory state supreme court review of capital sentences in their new statutes, replacing the discretionary ad hoc attention to capital sentences under the prior regime.[8] In addition, states revamped their postconviction proceedings, which are designed to facilitate review of those constitutional claims that require developing new facts, such as the adequacy of trial counsel and whether the prosecution complied with its constitutional duty to disclose exculpatory evidence to the defense (evidence undercutting the state's case).

The emergence of new constitutional doctrines governing capital cases and the creation of new institutional structures for processing such claims have contributed to the extraordinary divergence in state execution rates. This divergence occurs because the new constitutional norms are enforced differently across jurisdictions. Although the U.S. Supreme Court ostensibly has the final word on the content of federal constitutional regulation, the sheer volume of cases makes it impossible for the Court to harmonize state and lower federal court rulings applying Court decisions. Some state and lower federal courts tend to construe those decisions narrowly, rarely finding constitutional error; others have enforced the Court's limits robustly, frequently sending cases back for new trials. More significantly, states have embraced different institutional mechanisms and different levels of legal process in response to the heightened constitutional requirements for the death penalty. These differences—ranging from the appointment of counsel, the movement of cases on direct appeal and in postconviction review, and the setting of execution dates—bear considerably on the speed from sentence to execution. The breadth and complexity of background constitutional norms also create moments of responsibility for numerous actors within the capital system, including local prosecutors, statewide prosecutors, prison officials, judges, and governors. Executions require all of these actors to cooperate in moving capital cases along. Circumspection or resistance at any point can prevent death sentences from becoming executions, and states vary greatly along these lines.

Reversal rates in capital cases vary significantly across jurisdictions. Capital litigation involves three tiers of review: the first two tiers, direct review and postconviction review, occur within the state system; after state death-sentenced inmates have exhausted their review in the state courts, they can seek review of their conviction and sentence in the federal courts, through federal habeas review. Although states differ greatly in the *speed* with which cases move within their tiers of review, and this processing speed in state courts accounts for a great deal of the difference in execution rates, a separate variable is *how* (not when) the state court rules. Unsurprisingly, states with very high execution rates tend to be states with relatively low reversal rates in state court. For example, Virginia—the most efficient state in converting death sentences into executions—had by far the lowest reversal rate among state courts in the first three decades post-*Furman*. Two other high-executing states, Missouri and Texas, likewise have had extremely low reversal rates in capital cases reviewed in state court.[9]

State court reversal rates do not, however, tell the whole story. Tennessee and California have also experienced relatively low reversal rates in state court, though they have carried out few executions. This is because the death sentences that survive state court review in Tennessee and California face a much higher risk of reversal in subsequent *federal* court review. Indeed, the federal court reversal rates for death sentences obtained in Tennessee and California have been among the highest in the nation. Ultimately, executions are much more likely where the cumulative (state plus federal court) reversal rate is very low, and the three leading states along this dimension—Virginia, Texas, and Missouri—have been three of the most prolific executing states in the country. Virginia's extreme outlier status in its execution rate (having executed over 70 percent of those sentenced to death, with no state even remotely close) is matched by its extreme outlier status in its low cumulative reversal rate (its cumulative reversal rate of 18 percent is far below the national average, with only one other state below 50 percent in the first two decades post-*Furman*).[10]

The raw numbers of reversal rates do not provide a full picture of the divergence in constitutional norm enforcement. The opinions of state and federal courts reveal varying receptivity to similar federal constitutional claims. For example, one of the key questions after the death penalty was upheld in *Gregg* was whether the various state schemes provided adequate vehicles for the consideration of mitigating evidence—a new requirement recognized by the Court in the 1976 cases. Two states—Texas and Oregon—had enacted the same unusual statute, which did not directly invite jurors to consider mitigating evidence or ask them whether the defendant deserved to die. Instead, the statute focused exclusively on whether the defendant committed the crime deliberately and whether the defendant would be dangerous in the future. Despite the difficulties with this approach, the Texas courts and the Court of Appeals for the Fifth Circuit (the federal court responsible for reviewing challenges in Texas cases) consistently rejected the claim that jurors were unable to give effect to mitigating evidence such as deprived circumstances, intellectual disability, difficult background, and mental illness. According to those courts, if jurors credited such evidence, they could give effect to it by concluding that the defendant would be less dangerous in the future. The obvious problem with this conclusion was that jurors could logically believe *both* that the defendant should be spared because of difficult circumstances *and* that the defendant would remain dangerous. Indeed, having a traumatic background, cognitive impairments, or mental illness can dangerously reduce one's ability to control one's behavior while at the same time diminishing the culpability for one's crime.[11]

For thirty years, the Texas and federal courts adhered to this flawed approach notwithstanding an intervening 1989 Supreme Court decision that found the statute inadequate in the case of a defendant with intellectual disabilities who had been severely abused as a child (the decision caused the Texas legislature to revise its statute, but the courts still needed to address the many sentences obtained under the former statute). As a result, hundreds of Texas inmates were executed even though the Texas statute had not permitted their juries to decide whether they deserved to die. In contrast, the Oregon courts, faced with the same statute and the same problem, responded to the intervening decision by vacating the death sentences of all twenty-three offenders sentenced under the problematic scheme; this choice contributed to Oregon's low execution rate (Oregon has executed only two offenders in the modern era). Had the state or federal courts reviewing Texas cases taken the same approach as the Oregon courts, Texas would have executed only a handful of offenders in the first three decades following *Gregg* rather than leading the country with over 300 executions, a majority of which involved sentences secured via the unconstitutional statute. Ultimately, though belatedly, the Supreme Court again intervened, declaring in 2007 that the Texas and lower federal courts had been wrong all along in viewing the statute as generally adequate for the consideration of mitigating evidence. In fact, the Court declared that the Texas courts' treatment of these claims was not simply wrong, but unreasonably so. By then, however, most of the Texas defendants sentenced under the unconstitutional scheme had been executed.[12]

Another area revealing discordant applications of Court doctrine concerns the constitutional requirements for attorney performance in capital cases. In the 1980s, the Court announced a general standard for evaluating whether a capital defendant had received constitutionally adequate representation. In order to receive a new trial, an inmate must establish that counsel's performance was deficient in light of prevailing practices and that counsel's errors were reasonably likely to have affected the case's outcome.[13] The breadth and open-endedness of this standard has yielded dramatically different results in different jurisdictions. In some state courts—such as Texas and Virginia—relief based on ineffective assistance of counsel is exceedingly rare. The highest criminal court in Texas, the Texas Court of Criminal Appeals (CCA), infamously denied relief even in cases where trial counsel slept during significant portions of a capital trial. The CCA also denied relief in cases where defense lawyers conducted no pretrial investigation, put on no evidence whatsoever during the sentencing phase, used derogatory ethnic terms in referring to their own clients, and offered no argument on behalf of their clients' lives. In contrast, other state and federal courts have more closely reviewed attorney performance in capital cases, reversing death sentences where trial counsel had failed to develop and present an appropriate case for sparing the defendant's life.[14]

The divergence among state and lower federal courts in their treatment of ineffective assistance of counsel claims has created an odd dynamic in which the Court seems to be unusually attentive to correcting outlying decisions. One faction on the Court appears to be interested in policing denials of relief in cases decided by courts that have rarely found constitutional deficiency. In 2000 and 2003, in two high-profile capital cases, the Court reversed denials of relief by the Court of Appeals for the Fourth Circuit where trial counsel had failed to discover and present powerful mitigating evidence, including evidence of cognitive impairment and horrific abuse.[15] The Court of Appeals for the Fourth Circuit, whose responsibility extends to Virginia cases, rarely had found constitutional error in state capital cases coming to its court in the decades following *Furman*. A different faction on the Court appears to be interested in reining in courts that have frequently granted relief based on ineffective representation. Over the past ten years, the Court has repeatedly reversed—sometimes in summary fashion without the benefit of briefing or argument—such decisions from two federal appeals courts (the Court of Appeals for the Sixth Circuit and the Court of Appeals for the Ninth Circuit).[16] The unusual, frequent interventions by the Court in this area reveal a struggle in which the Court itself appears to recognize and lament the inconsistent applications of its Sixth Amendment doctrine. Moreover, this dynamic has extended to other capital doctrines, with the Court seeming to police particular courts based on their perceived excessive solicitude or excessive hostility toward capital claims. The Kansas Supreme Court, for example, has had an astonishingly high reversal rate in its direct appeal review of capital convictions (nearly 100 percent). The U.S. Supreme Court, in turn, has heard a disproportionate number of Kansas capital cases, frequently reversing the Kansas Supreme Court's grants of relief (often in cases implicating no broad or interesting capital issue). In the 2015 Supreme Court term, the Court heard three Kansas cases, which represents one third of the inmates on Kansas's death row—this while Kansas has not carried out an execution in over a half century.[17] The Supreme Court's micromanaging of Kansas cases—far out of proportion to the significance of those cases (or of the death penalty as a practice in Kansas)—reflects the determination of one faction on the Court to prevent overenforcement of federal constitutional norms.

In some extreme cases, state courts not only have underenforced Supreme Court doctrines, they have expressed open skepticism about the wisdom of the Court's regulation. A little over a decade after *Gregg*, the Court addressed in a Texas case whether the Eighth Amendment forbids the execution of persons with intellectual disability (formerly "mental retardation"). Given the paucity of states prohibiting the practice, the Court sided with Texas and established no categorical bar. Thirteen years later, the Court, responding to a flood of new states condemning the practice, ruled that the execution of persons with intellectual disability violates prevailing standards of decency. Despite straightforward language in the decision affirming that "death is not a suitable punishment for a mentally retarded criminal," the Texas Court of Criminal Appeals, as it purported to implement the Court's decision, doubted whether *all* persons with intellectual disability should be exempt from execution. Instead, the CCA suggested that it should "define that level and degree of mental retardation at which a consensus of Texas citizens would agree that a person should be exempted from the death penalty."[18]

The CCA rejected the idea that all persons recognized as having intellectual disability under prevailing clinical norms should be spared, arguing instead that the exemption was more appropriate for persons like the fictional character Lennie in John Steinbeck's novel *Of Mice and Men*.[19] Accordingly, the CCA created its own, nonclinical approach to assessing intellectual disability with the avowed goal of weeding out offenders with mild intellectual disability whom Texans might regard as sufficiently culpable for execution. The nonclinical approach builds on and reinforces outdated stereotypes about intellectual disability, focusing, for example, on whether the offender can respond "rationally" to questions, lie in his own interest, and engage in planning. The approach explicitly invites the decision maker to consider facts of the capital offense, ostensibly to gauge whether the offense was "impulsive" or involved "forethought." But critics of the Texas approach argue that the effort to focus on the details of the offense is inconsistent with clinical practice (where the determination of intellectual disability is rooted in assessments of deficits in particular areas of adaptive behavior), and inappropriately encourages decision makers (jurors and judges) to reject the exemption where the circumstances of the crime are highly aggravated and disturbing.[20]

As a result of Texas's court-created ad hoc approach to intellectual disability, numerous Texas defendants who satisfy traditional clinical criteria for the diagnosis have nonetheless been sentenced to death and executed. Many of these inmates undoubtedly would be deemed exempt from the death penalty in other jurisdictions, and Texas offenders seeking relief based on intellectual disability have had a far lower rate of success than offenders outside the state.[21] The Supreme Court recently moved to rectify a related problem in Florida, where the Florida courts had imposed a strict IQ cutoff for the exemption in conflict with professional clinical norms (which include a "standard error of measurement"). The Texas courts, though, continue to adhere to their nonclinical approach, and the Court of Appeals for the Fifth Circuit has declined to intervene. In fact, the Court of Appeals recently explained that the Supreme Court decision in the Florida case did not call into question the Texas nonclinical approach because "the word 'Texas' nowhere appears in the [Supreme Court] opinion." The underenforcement in Texas of the Court's prohibition against executing persons with intellectual disabilities demonstrates how constitutional regulation can produce very different outcomes depending on a jurisdiction's willingness to embrace the principles animating the Court's intervention.[22]

The most significant variable affecting execution rates is the speed at which cases move through state and federal systems of review. Constitutional regulation of the death penalty profoundly altered state and federal review of capital sentences. Prior to the Court's constitutional engagement, cases moved relatively quickly through post-trial review; it was rare for a case to spend several years before heading to federal court or from federal court to execution. In the wake of *Furman* and *Gregg*, though, with numerous federal constitutional questions now surrounding every capital prosecution, states have had to provide additional resources and mechanisms to facilitate consideration of those claims. States have varied widely in their responses along numerous dimensions, including the selection and compensation of attorneys, the expectations regarding briefing and oral advocacy, the use of evidentiary hearings to resolve disputed facts, and a host of other mundane but important choices. Federal courts have also differed in their processing of claims by state death row inmates, and at the end of the process, states have embraced different mechanisms for setting execution dates. Taken together, these differences—in state court, federal court, and state executive procedures—have strongly influenced the speed to execution, because the modern era has witnessed quite divergent levels of legal process within capital jurisdictions.

The divergence in process is not random; outside of the South, states tend to move slowly and deliberately in their treatment of capital cases, which accounts for the relative rarity of executions in those jurisdictions. In contrast, the leading executing states, all located either in or bordering the South, have embraced procedures and practices which tend to clear the path to execution and move cases expeditiously.

Each state has its own complicated, idiosyncratic set of practices bearing on its execution rate. The stories of California and Texas, two outliers in the modern era at opposite extremes, can serve to illustrate how procedures facilitate or forestall executions. The culmination of a death verdict in an execution requires roughly four significant events: the resolution of issues on direct appeal in state court, the resolution of legal challenges in state postconviction review (addressing claims based on new facts), the resolution of challenges in federal court via federal habeas corpus review, and the setting of execution dates. Ultimately, executions require tremendous coordination, because obstacles at any stage can prevent the consummation of death sentences. Such coordination is confined to a small handful of capital jurisdictions, with Texas leading the way.

Capital cases in Texas proceed through direct appeal much more quickly than in California and most other states. Several factors contribute to the quick processing. For many years in Texas, it was common for trial counsel to serve as counsel on direct appeal (although this practice has declined in recent years). This continuity of representation accelerated direct appeals by removing a potentially time-consuming and cumbersome process of identifying and appointing appropriate appellate counsel. Perhaps more importantly, the culture surrounding the entire direct appeal is affected by the introduction of separate counsel at that stage. In California, where separate appellate counsel is appointed, appellate counsel is more likely to identify and pursue systemic challenges to the state death scheme as well as particularized claims relating to the specifics of the defendant's trial. Trial lawyers, on the other hand, are more likely to focus on discrete, nonrecurring (often evidentiary) issues. This focus results not merely from professional habit and lack of more general appellate expertise, but also from the very real demands trial practice places on lawyers occupied by such work.[23]

The difference in the expectations of appellate counsel in states that allow "continuous representation," like Texas did, and states that require new counsel (or even have special offices for capital appellate representation), like California, is reflected in the briefing and oral advocacy on direct appeal. Perhaps the most striking difference is the willingness in Texas for counsel to waive oral argument on direct appeal. Even today, lawyers representing death-sentenced inmates often decline to travel to Austin to present oral argument at the CCA in their sole opportunity to assert many claims without procedural barriers. Lawyers on the civil side in Texas and elsewhere would be loath to forego such an important opportunity, and the willingness of Texas defense lawyers to waive oral argument in a capital case (as well as the willingness of the CCA to tolerate such waivers) suggests a low standard of practice. Briefs filed in Texas direct appeals are considerably shorter than those submitted in other death penalty states, likewise reflecting the relatively low expectations and investment of counsel; California's page limit for such briefs, on the other hand, is more than twice the limit in Texas, and direct appeal briefs filed in California tend to be longer, more sophisticated, and more comprehensive. In addition, oral arguments in California are scheduled only after a tentative opinion is drafted by the California Supreme Court, and capital appellate attorneys would never consider waiving their oral arguments in such circumstances (and the California Supreme Court would likely not permit them to do so).[24]

In California, one somewhat significant but also perplexing contributor to delays on direct appeal is the process of perfecting the record for appeal. Although California has a nominal time limit for this process, extensions are granted in many cases to correct the record, augment the record with omitted materials, and resolve disputes about unreported oral proceedings. In Texas, on the other hand, the expectations and procedural requirements in this regard are quite minimal. In fact, in the first two decades post-*Furman,* delays in producing the trial record in Texas were more likely to be attributable to court reporters than to legal challenges, and the CCA, when it noticed a lag in this regard in the early 1990s, adopted a policy limiting extensions sought by court reporters.[25]

But an even greater source of delay in the movement of California death cases is the time spent identifying and appointing qualified counsel to handle capital appeals. The difficulty in securing appellate counsel stems from the fact that California's qualification requirements are quite demanding, and very few lawyers qualified for such appointments are interested in undertaking them. California compensates appellate attorneys lavishly in comparison to Texas, but the level of remuneration is not attractive in light of the very demanding expectations. California's institutional defenders available for appointment in capital direct appeals—the State Public Defender and the California Appellate Project—receive significant funds and are well-regarded organizations. These entities, however, are simply not equipped to handle the volume of capital appeals in the California system, especially in light of their own commitment to high-level advocacy (and the caseload limitations dictated by such a commitment).[26]

As a result of California's demand for qualified counsel and the absence of a corresponding supply, direct appeals languish for years in the state system. By 2004, estimates suggested a four-to-five-year delay in the appointment of appellate counsel in California capital cases, a period of total loss in terms of resolving challenges to the lawfulness of the underlying conviction and sentence. As of that time, more than one hundred death-sentenced inmates were without counsel for their direct appeal (a number greater than the current death row population of all but eight death penalty states). Even today, over fifty California inmates are without direct appeal counsel, in contrast to zero such inmates in Texas, where direct appeal counsel are appointed expeditiously after the imposition of a death sentence.[27]

The legal culture surrounding appeals is affected by the nature and structure of the highest criminal court in Texas. Texas is virtually alone in establishing a separate criminal court with the last say on criminal matters. In theory, such a design might yield benefits in terms of expertise. In practice, though, the isolation of a high criminal court from civil matters contributes to the lower standard of practice. The absence of a civil docket means that the CCA does not encounter the high-level private litigation practices seen on the civil side. Although civil appellate practice, even before the highest state courts, is not uniformly exemplary, the habits and practices of the most prominent civil appellate attorneys vastly surpass those on the criminal side. This is especially true in Texas for some of the reasons stated above: many death penalty appeals in Texas have been handled by trial lawyers without significant appellate expertise, financial resources, or time. Because it is not exposed to high-powered appellate practice (unlike its state supreme court counterparts in other jurisdictions), the CCA has less reason to question the standard of practice in its court. It is hard to imagine, for example, an experienced civil appellate attorney foregoing an opportunity to present oral argument to a state supreme court in any high-stakes litigation; it is likewise hard to imagine a court with civil and criminal jurisdiction permitting counsel to waive argument in capital cases if waivers were rarely if ever sought on the civil side.

The division of civil and criminal matters at the highest level tends to lessen the prestige of the CCA, which in turn might affect the level of practice within the court. In the vast majority of states, the highest court is denominated the "supreme" court, and its members are envisioned as embodying the profession's highest training, experience, and prestige. State supreme court justices in most jurisdictions (including California) are the central gatekeepers for the profession, charged with the twin responsibilities of supervising the admission of lawyers to the bar and disciplining attorneys for professional misconduct. By separating the civil and criminal side, Texas has produced a high criminal court without the substantial supervisory role exercised in other jurisdictions. Its values and norms are drawn not from general expectations or ideals about what duties lawyers ordinarily owe their clients, but from very particular expectations based on the prevailing practices within the criminal system.

One advertised benefit of the civil-criminal division contributes to the speed of direct appeals. Death cases do not compete with civil matters for the court's attention and resources. In Texas, death cases do not even necessarily compete with noncapital criminal cases, because the CCA's noncapital jurisdiction, unlike its capital jurisdiction, is entirely discretionary. Accordingly, Texas simply does not experience the backlog of capital cases awaiting decision on direct appeal common to other jurisdictions; the CCA ordinarily resolves such cases expeditiously. In California, on the other hand, given the high court's extraordinary capital and noncapital caseload (as well as the intricacy of the briefing), the process of drafting an opinion on direct appeal routinely takes many years—in some cases close to a decade. Thus, while the appointment of counsel, direct appeal briefing, and judicial resolution generally occur within a few years of a death sentence in Texas, those events routinely require well over a decade in California, and the CCA's unusually confined docket contributes significantly to that result. It is no coincidence that Oklahoma—the only other state with a similar civil-criminal court divide—has the highest execution rate per capita in the nation, with Texas second.[28]

The story on state habeas is similar to the story on direct appeal. The Texas system of postconviction review has facilitated the relatively speedy movement of cases from state to federal court, although the mechanisms responsible have shifted over the past three decades. During the 1980s and early 1990s, Texas did not have a comprehensive system for appointing or compensating postconviction counsel for indigent death-sentenced inmates, and state law did not mandate such appointments even in capital cases.[29] As a result, many death-sentenced inmates did not have counsel, and representation was provided in an ad hoc manner. In California, and in most other jurisdictions, the absence of state postconviction counsel puts cases in limbo in state court, but in Texas some trial courts pushed cases through the system by setting execution dates notwithstanding the absence of counsel. Unlike in many other jurisdictions, execution dates in Texas were at this time entirely a matter of trial court discretion, and no centralized decision maker (such as the governor, attorney general, or high state court) prompted or ratified execution date decisions. In most cases, the setting of an execution date generated a flurry of activity that resulted in the appearance (often pro bono) of postconviction counsel and a stay of execution. In some cases, however, the execution date prompted postconviction counsel to file a cursory habeas petition, which the trial court and the CCA promptly denied on the merits, pushing those cases into federal court. A few of those cases actually led to swift executions when the inmate subsequently lost on the merits in federal court. Indeed, in the early 1990s, some Texas cases moved through state and federal habeas to execution in mere months after counsel was obtained, a time frame otherwise unheard of in the modern era.[30] Even in the cases in which stays were obtained (either in state or federal court), the setting of execution dates kept the cases moving through the system. Thus, Texas was able to carry out executions at a time when most other jurisdictions were largely inactive because of its willingness to move ahead in cases involving unrepresented inmates. In fact, Texas carried out over 25 percent of the executions nationwide during the period 1987–1992.[31]

Despite its comparative success in achieving executions in the 1980s and early 1990s, Texas restructured its postconviction system in the mid-1990s to increase the speed from sentence to execution. The new legislation provided for the appointment of counsel to indigent death-sentenced inmates, assuring that cases would not languish because an inmate was unrepresented. The law also erected new procedural obstacles to relief, including restrictions on successive petitions and a new statute of limitations. In a concession to stabilizing the process, the law removed the ability of trial courts to set execution dates in advance of state and federal habeas review so that execution dates would no longer drive litigation.

The changes to state habeas practice were spectacularly successful. The combination of a right to counsel, a statute of limitations, filing deadlines, and procedural limits on successive petitions enabled Texas to move cases quickly through state postconviction review. The defense bar had hoped that the creation of a right to counsel in state postconviction proceedings would raise the prevailing level of practice in state habeas, which requires extensive factual investigation of the defendant, his crime, and his trial. Performed well, these tasks are in many ways more demanding than representing a defendant at trial, because state postconviction counsel must undertake sufficient investigation to evaluate whether trial counsel provided adequate representation and whether any other actors—the police, prosecutors, jurors—committed undetected errors or misconduct. But even after the Texas reforms, the level of representation in state postconviction proceedings remained distressingly poor. The CCA imposed presumptive limits on compensation (around $8,000), and lawyers appointed in these cases routinely failed to undertake any investigation—the heart of postconviction representation. In addition, many lawyers missed filing deadlines, resulting in the forfeiture of any further state and federal review. In the cases in which post-conviction lawyers actually performed well—by filing a petition in a timely manner and uncovering significant facts bearing on the constitutionality of the sentence—Texas trial courts almost uniformly declined to hold evidentiary hearings to evaluate the contested new evidence. Instead, trial courts engaged in euphemistically termed "paper hearings" in which the defense and prosecution would submit conflicting affidavits and the court simply endorsed the prosecution's account of the facts without hearing any of the witnesses uncovered by the defense. Indeed, it was and remains a common practice for Texas trial courts to issue their findings of fact by simply signing the "proposed findings" prepared by the state without so much as changing a comma in a pleading that often runs over one hundred pages.[32]

The failure of many state habeas lawyers in Texas to conduct meaningful investigation, coupled with the cursory consideration of facts in those cases where they were developed, facilitated the speedy movement of state habeas claims into federal court. The legislative reform of state habeas contributed to the radical acceleration of the pace of executions in Texas, from an average of eight per year in the decade before the reforms to an average of twenty-five per year in the decade after.[33] The speed of postconviction review in Texas was bolstered by the absence of any significant state-enforced mechanism for discovery in the postconviction process (the vehicle for obtaining information in the possession of state authorities). In some states, such as Florida and North Carolina, robust statutory or constitutional entitlements to discovery considerably extend post-conviction proceedings.[34] The absence of such discovery in Texas reinforces the perception of state habeas process as neither inviting nor requiring a thorough examination of the manner in which the underlying conviction was secured. By providing a forum for litigating claims based on new facts, albeit a relatively toothless and perfunctory one, Texas reaps the benefits of federal habeas law, which accords a presumption of correctness to any "determination of a factual issue made by a State court."[35] Although federal habeas attorneys have long argued that cursory fact-findings made without the benefit of live testimony and other procedural safeguards should not be deemed adequate determinations, such findings have routinely been accorded a presumption of correctness in federal litigation.[36]

In 2010, after a series of newspaper exposés of the malfunctioning of the state postconviction system (and the shockingly low level of attorney representation in that forum), Texas established a statewide office for postconviction representation. The level of practice in that office is vastly superior to the representation it replaced, and it appears Texas trial courts are now more willing to hold evidentiary hearings in cases of contested facts. But the vast majority of inmates currently on Texas's death row went through state postconviction review under the old regime, and they will likely move expeditiously toward execution in the same fashion as their predecessors.[37]

California's postconviction system departs from the Texas system in many of the same ways that the two systems diverge on direct appeal. California has comparatively demanding requirements for appointment of postconviction counsel, including practice and training requirements and demonstrated research and writing skills. California also has far greater expectations about the nature and extent of postconviction proceedings. California allocates $50,000 for postconviction investigation alone, a figure that would have covered all of the defense expenses, including attorney fees, in many of the Texas cases litigated between 1990 and 2010. As a matter of practice, postconviction lawyers in California spend vastly more on postconviction litigation, particularly in cases handled by the state-funded defender organizations, the Habeas Corpus Resource Center and the State Public Defender Office.[38]

Here again, as on direct appeal, the most significant source of delay is the insufficient supply of lawyers able and willing to accept appointments. As a result, approximately 300 California inmates currently lack postconviction counsel. This astonishing figure means that the number of unrepresented inmates in California exceeds the number of *total* inmates on any state death row other than Florida. In contrast, no one in Texas is currently without postconviction counsel, and many of California's 300 unrepresented inmates will wait longer to receive counsel than it will take for a Texas death-sentenced inmate to go through all levels of review and execution.

Even when California's death-sentenced inmates receive postconviction counsel, their cases often move at a glacial pace, in part because of crowded dockets. One California inmate, for example, recently received oral argument on his postconviction petition more than fourteen years after filing his brief in the California Supreme Court. Thus, even apart from differences in affirmance/reversal rates, California and Texas differ remarkably in the manner and speed of addressing challenges to capital convictions and sentences.[39]

Delays within the state systems have a much greater effect on ultimate execution rates than do subsequent delays in federal court review. But in this forum as well, cases move more quickly in the federal courts reviewing Texas cases than in those reviewing California cases, despite the fact that the federal courts in both jurisdictions have the same basic structure and are subject to the same operating rules (federal law). Texas cases are reviewed by the federal courts within the Fifth Circuit, and those courts have contributed significantly to the high execution rate in Texas. As Texas resumed executions in the 1980s, both federal district courts within the circuit and the court of appeals itself were more willing than other federal courts to deny stays of execution in capital cases, even in cases in which the ordinary processes (full adversarial proceedings in state and federal court) had not run their course. In this respect, the courts within the Fifth Circuit assisted in the policy of some Texas trial courts to move cases along by setting execution dates. Relatedly, the courts within the Fifth Circuit are less likely than courts in most other circuits to authorize full appeals of capital claims denied in federal district court (unlike in civil appeals, criminal appellants are not entitled to a full appeal as a matter of course). District courts within the Fifth Circuit have also been less inclined to hold evidentiary hearings than courts in other circuits, particularly those within the Ninth Circuit; between 1992 and 2003, district courts within the Ninth Circuit held such hearings about 50 percent more frequently than those within the Fifth.[40]

In 1996, Congress passed legislation to lessen the time between death sentences and execution by restricting the federal habeas forum. The Anti-Terrorism and Effective Death Penalty Act (AEDPA), like the postconviction reform in Texas, created new deadlines for filing petitions and established new barriers to multiple filings. Unlike the Texas reform, AEDPA also established a new, unprecedented, deferential standard of review, such that federal courts cannot ordinarily reverse state court decisions unless they are not simply wrong, but "unreasonably" wrong. AEDPA has significantly reduced the percentage of cases in which federal courts reverse state court judgments, and executions nationwide increased in the decade following its adoption before falling again to comparable pre-AEDPA totals. It is difficult to account precisely for the influence of AEDPA in speeding the path to executions, but two facts have limited its success in producing an "effective" death penalty. First, the lion's share of delays in capital cases occur in state court, and adjusting the procedures in federal court does not address those delays. Second, even though AEDPA makes ultimate success unlikely, federal courts must still sort through AEDPA's tremendously complicated procedural doctrines before denying relief.[41]

Accordingly, notwithstanding AEDPA, cases within the Ninth Circuit tend to move slowly, especially in the Eastern District of California, where the courts are burdened with one of the largest dockets among federal courts in the country. Although the federal district courts in Texas are likewise among the most burdened in terms of their overall docket, they still manage to process capital cases relatively quickly. One federal district judge in Texas is notorious for requiring lawyers appointed in his court to accept less time than contemplated by AEDPA to prepare and file a petition; if a prospective lawyer declines to agree to the accelerated schedule, he or she is denied the appointment. The federal courts within the Fifth Circuit are also more tolerant of less than zealous advocacy by appointed counsel. In a recent case, Texas lawyers informed their client that they would not pursue clemency despite their obligation to do so under the federal statute authorizing their appointment. The attorneys claimed that such efforts would be pointless because of the rarity of clemency grants in Texas. When other lawyers sought to intervene on the inmate's behalf (pro bono), the lawyers representing the inmate refused to step aside, the courts within the Fifth Circuit denied the substitution, and the inmate was executed. Justice Sonia Sotomayor, expressing concerns about the denial of review by the U.S. Supreme Court, argued that the refusal to substitute counsel was "an abuse of discretion" and that the Fifth Circuit was mistaken in "rejecting a substitution motion solely because it agrees with the appointed attorneys' premonitions about clemency."[42]

The most dramatic divide between the courts in the Fifth and Ninth Circuit is reflected in their respective roles in end-stage litigation, when inmates have exhausted their appeals. The Court of Appeals for the Ninth Circuit historically has been more reluctant than other federal appeals courts to move cases quickly to execution in such circumstances. The court's reputation as anti-execution was cemented in its highly visible efforts to block California's first execution in the modern era, when it repeatedly imposed stays to halt death row inmate Robert Alton Harris's execution. The complicated last-minute proceedings in the litigation ended with a highly irregular and controversial order by the U.S. Supreme Court barring any future stays of execution in Harris's case. In contrast, the courts in the Fifth Circuit have rarely granted stays despite their uncommon exposure to cases involving troublesome circumstances warranting intervention.[43]

The differences between Texas and California in their handling of capital litigation are mirrored in other jurisdictions, where officials face moments of discretion that can facilitate or forestall executions. In several states, for example, executive officials have imposed moratoria against executions. In Pennsylvania, Governor Tom Wolf recently declared he would not let executions proceed because of concerns about arbitrary and discriminatory capital sentencing. In Washington State, Governor Jay Inslee imposed a moratorium on executions based on geographical disparities and concerns about the utility of the death penalty in light of the availability of life without possibility of parole. Governors have taken similar actions in Colorado and Oregon. These sorts of interventions build on the norms of constitutional regulation and represent a striking departure from executive actions in the pre-*Furman* era. For most of our history, executive officials exercised their discretion in response to *individual* claims of excessive punishment, and commutations were a routine feature of the capital system. Indeed, in Texas, approximately 20 percent of those sentenced to death between 1920 and 1970 received such relief. Today, individual commutations have virtually disappeared (for example, much less than 1 percent in Texas), because executive officials tend to regard extended judicial review of individual sentences as supplanting the necessity of executive oversight. But executive officials now seem more concerned with addressing the *systemic* issues implicated by constitutional regulation, and the variation in such responses across jurisdictions can have strong effects on execution rates. Perhaps most dramatically, Governor George Ryan's concern about deficiencies in the Illinois capital system, brought to light after the exoneration of thirteen death-sentenced inmates, led him to impose a moratorium on executions in 2000. That moratorium was followed by his grant of mass commutations (clearing the state's death row) as the extent of the dysfunction in Illinois became apparent. Illinois subsequently abolished the death penalty.[44]

Even short of moratoria, executive officials are often confronted with choices that bear on the feasibility of executions. The recent and ongoing experience with lethal injection litigation illustrates the enormous differences in states' capacity and willingness to execute—and the possibilities for divergence opened by the fact of regulation. Beginning in the early 2000s, inmates began challenging the common lethal injection protocol used in virtually every death penalty jurisdiction. Opponents of the protocol argued that the common three-drug cocktail created an unnecessary and substantial risk of undetected suffering on the part of the condemned. The U.S. Supreme Court chose to address the issue after only a few years of its percolation in the state and lower federal courts, and the timing of the Court's intervention led many observers to suspect that the Court wanted to nip the challenge early and clear the way for executions to proceed. The Court's resulting opinion upheld the use of the protocol in Kentucky and established a high bar for future challenges to execution methods and protocols.[45]

Nonetheless, concerns surrounding lethal injection protocols slowed executions substantially in some jurisdictions, while other jurisdictions continued to execute without significant interruption. Texas and Virginia carried out executions within weeks of the Court's decision, while many other states became mired—and are still mired—in lethal injection litigation.[46] Again, the difference in reactions had less to do with the content of federal regulation (which is minimal) than with the legal and cultural norms within the different jurisdictions as well as the surrounding politics. In some states, restrictive administrative procedure laws made it cumbersome to alter execution protocols, whereas in other states, prison officials had broad discretion to adapt to concerns about particular drugs by changing protocols on the fly.[47]

By 2010, problems with lethal injection became more pronounced as both domestic and foreign suppliers of drugs used in lethal injections began to withdraw such drugs from the market. Some of those companies declared publicly that they did not want to see any of their products used in executions, and, for drugs that remained on the market, they asked purchasers to sign end-user agreements to steer their drugs away from execution chambers.[48] The crisis in the availability of drugs led to different state strategies. Some jurisdictions, like Oklahoma and Arizona, proceeded with executions using experimental protocols, and each experienced botched executions. In the Oklahoma case, the inmate, Clayton Lockett, was not sufficiently anesthetized, and prison officials stopped the execution fifteen minutes after the lethal drugs had been administered because Lockett was writhing on the gurney and not yet dead. After the execution was halted, Lockett died of a heart attack while still in the execution chamber. Prior to Lockett's execution, the Oklahoma Supreme Court had issued a stay to determine if the change in protocol complied with state procedures. Oklahoma Governor Mary Fallin decried the court's intervention and said the execution could proceed notwithstanding the state supreme court's ruling; in addition, her allies in the legislature threatened to pursue impeachment against the five justices who had supported the stay. In the face of this pressure, the Oklahoma Supreme Court reversed itself, clearing the path for the execution.[49]

In addition to using experimental protocols, some states committed to carrying out executions notwithstanding the drug shortage have sought to obtain execution drugs from shady overseas suppliers, in apparent violation of federal law. Others, like Texas and Georgia, have turned to compounding pharmacies, relatively unregulated suppliers of drugs that are able to manufacture pentobarbital, one of the execution drugs withdrawn from the market. States have also sought to carry out executions by obtaining drugs from other high executing states; Virginia recently performed an execution with pentobarbital supplied by Texas. Texas, in turn, had previously sought help in obtaining drugs from Oklahoma, and an e-mail exchange between Oklahoma officials reflected a flippant plan to provide such drugs in return for tickets to the annual Oklahoma-Texas football game.[50]

The experience with lethal injection litigation and subsequent state maneuvering provides a window into the ways regulation is filtered through layers of culture, law, and politics. States determined to execute—and that are oriented toward that goal at all levels, including their governors, state judges, and prison officials—have managed to continue to execute in the face of significant obstacles. In other states, these obstacles are difficult to surmount, and the absence of a zealous commitment to executions results in lengthy delays.

The numerous and varied particular institutional factors that drive the enormous difference in execution rates might suggest that such differences are best understood at a micro level. To a limited extent, this is true. Each death penalty state has its own peculiar mix of institutional arrangements that produce executions to varying degrees. No two states are identical, and even states that produce executions to similar degrees can vary quite significantly in the particulars of their institutional arrangements. But the distribution of executions across the United States is so regionally determined that some larger determinants are at work in generating the institutional arrangements and discretionary choices within those arrangements that ultimately produce or avoid executions.

What most needs explanation is not the high execution rate of some states like Texas, but rather the negligible execution rate of many other states, including California. It is not intuitively surprising that states sentencing large numbers of people to death end up executing large numbers of people. What is more surprising is that states sentencing large numbers of people to death manage to avoid executing almost anybody. The interesting phenomenon is not Texan exceptionalism or, more broadly, Southern exceptionalism in generating executions, but rather the combination of forces producing a significant swath of states with large death rows and negligible executions. Why do such states invest the enormous resources necessary to generate death sentences and yet fail to follow through with executions?

One answer, perhaps not surprisingly, is a political one. There are striking political differences between "symbolic" states, considered as a group, and "executing" states, and these political differences are the primary driving force behind the execution gap that exists between such states. However, the umbrella concept of "political differences" encompasses a number of more finely grained distinctions. The most significant of these distinctions are captured under the separate, though related, rubrics of political culture, political economy, and legal culture.

As to political culture, a cursory look at a map of the United States with capital sentencing rates and execution rates entered by state invites a political explanation for the divide between symbolic and executing states. The symbolic states are almost all Democratic "blue" states, and the executing states are almost all Republican "red" states—so much so that the electoral maps of recent presidential elections offer a fairly accurate model of the execution gap in this modern, post-*Furman* era. While there is clearly a substantial correlation between the Democratic and Republican divide in national electoral politics and the execution gap, there is a causal link as well. Most obviously, support for capital punishment is more widespread among Republicans than among Democrats, and there is reason to suspect that such support is more intense as well. This support itself is correlated with and may be caused or bolstered by a number of other aspects of the political culture of red states, such as populism, religious fundamentalism, and punitive, "tough-on-crime" responses to criminal acts generally.

One might fairly ask why this difference in overall support for capital punishment, whatever its source, might generate death sentences in both red and blue states, but executions only in red ones. The answer lies in the potentially higher costs and predictably lower benefits of proceeding with executions in blue states. In blue states, one is likely to find more and larger pockets of strong death penalty opposition (for example, in liberal San Francisco and parts of Los Angeles in California, or in relatively liberal Philadelphia and Pittsburgh in Pennsylvania). These pockets of opposition are not large or powerful enough to defeat capital punishment in state legislatures or to prevent capital charges or convictions wholesale. But such pockets can generate powerful, politically unwelcome criticism in particular cases, and this criticism tends to peak in the media around the executions themselves. Thus, executions in blue states can generate higher political costs than lower-visibility death sentences. The media circus and sharp criticism surrounding California's execution of Crips gang cofounder Stanley "Tookie" Williams at the end of 2005 is a case in point, in which an outpouring of opposition to the execution in the state emphasized Williams's good works in prison as an advocate against gang violence.[51] So sharp was the escalation of the movement to free Mumia Abu-Jamal from Pennsylvania's death row after then-Governor Tom Ridge signed his death warrant in 1995— more than a decade after Abu-Jamal's capital conviction for the murder of a Philadelphia police officer—that Abu-Jamal was ultimately resentenced to life in prison.[52] It is hard to imagine the same degree of protest and criticism regarding either of these execution dates, or other similar cases, in a red stronghold like Texas.

Moreover, the political benefits of proceeding with executions in blue states are lower than they are in red states, because high governmental officials in blue states—governors, state attorneys general, and state and federal appellate judges—are less likely to reap political rewards from promoting executions or from staking their political fortunes on close identification with capital punishment. They are also more likely to share the dominant liberal and cosmopolitan political values of their states and thus either oppose capital punishment or, at the least, have greater anxiety about its application in particular cases than do high governmental officials in red states. Capital sentences cannot become executions without commitment from the highest echelon of the legal and political elite, but the political benefits of capital punishment are weakest in this stratosphere, especially in blue states.

The diminishing returns of capital punishment at the highest governmental levels in blue states have an important corollary related to political economy: to a great degree, the political benefits of capital punishment are concentrated at the local level. Especially heinous murders tend to generate intense local outrage, and this outrage, in turn, puts pressure on local law enforcement actors to make arrests and to bring capital charges. The bringing of a capital charge and the return of a capital conviction and sentence can happen fairly quickly in the time frame of a capital case (this was especially true in the 1980s and 1990s), and these events go a long way toward addressing the immediate, local reaction to a particular crime. The charge, subsequent conviction, and sentence generate most of the expressive value of capital punishment, and thus most of the political points that the police and prosecutors possibly can score. The execution, if it happens at all, will necessarily happen years later, even in relatively expeditious jurisdictions. And if the execution never happens—because the conviction or sentence is set aside in the lengthy post-trial review process—the police and the prosecutors can and often do assume the mantle of outrage and pay little in the way of political costs (though the financial costs of retrial can be high). Although state prosecutors in the United States are almost universally local elected officials—and are thus easily disciplined by the political process—they have little political incentive (and not much power) to influence the degree to which death sentences are actually carried out. Thus, the political actors who are considered most responsible for capital punishment policy and who have the greatest political incentives to promote it satisfy their political interests almost entirely through death sentences rather than executions.[53]

In contrast, officials holding statewide offices, along with state and federal appellate judges, are more removed, both geographically and temporally, from the immediate local pressures to pursue capital charges arising out of specific murder cases. These more removed institutional actors remain more impervious to the politics of the death penalty in the absence of political institutions connecting them to issues of local law enforcement. It is notable that in Texas, the District and County Attorney's Association, in coordination with the state attorney general's office, is a powerful statewide lobbying force in the legislature on death penalty issues. Moreover, the death penalty is a very large and central part of the portfolio of the attorney general's office in Texas in contrast to California and many other states. This sort of statewide mobilization and coordination is necessary to prevent the primarily local impetus for executions from dissipating as the responsibility for administering the death penalty reaches more removed institutional actors.

In the absence of mobilization and coordination that will hold the feet of these more removed actors to the political fire, the final judicial and executive decisions that allow executions may not occur. Decisions that result in the delay or even the defeat of executions are often less visible, more technical, and more bureaucratic (in the sense of being the product of more than one person's sole discretionary authority) than the initial capital charging and trial. If the more removed institutional actors are more opposed to or ambivalent about the use of capital punishment than are local communities or local law enforcement officials—as they tend to be in blue states more than red states—they can greatly limit the ambit of the death penalty without very much direct confrontation. Such a strategy permits states to preserve both the expressive value of capital sentences to local communities and their political value to local law enforcement agents without actually resorting to many executions. As Professor Frank Zimring has noted, "the same endless processes of review detested by many in the system [of capital punishment] may also serve the interests of governments in moderating rates of execution without being visibly lenient."[54]

It is important to recognize, however, that it is not always antipathy or even ambivalence toward the death penalty that delays or prevents executions in symbolic states. Rather, the differences in political culture between symbolic and executing states are linked to important differences in legal culture as well. As illustrated in the comparison of Texas and California, in symbolic states, capital defense services are more likely to be organized and well-funded, state appellate and postconviction review of capital convictions is more likely to be intensive and demanding, federal habeas review of capital convictions is more likely to be intensive and demanding, and the appellate and postconviction process is more likely to be drawn out. In contrast, in executing states, the legal process that follows the return of a death sentence is far more likely to be nasty, brutish, and short: counsel are less likely to file substantial briefs; reviewing courts are less likely to hold hearings; oral arguments are viewed as less critical; the credentials and performance of attorneys are subject to less scrutiny; and the entire process moves much more quickly.

The precise differences in the legal processes available to capital defendants in symbolic states and executing states vary state by state, but a fairly consistent big picture emerges: symbolic states are far more likely to have what could be termed "due process" legal cultures. These cultures promote true adversary presentations by advocates and thus produce more searching review by courts of the myriad legal, especially constitutional, claims generated by capital litigation. This process necessarily delays, and in many cases ultimately defeats, the carrying out of capital sentences. Indeed, it is nearly impossible for any state to provide sufficient resources to allow its capital processes to maintain a high rate of death sentencing and a high rate of execution while simultaneously satisfying the demands of due process. As Frank Zimring observed, "A nation can have full and fair criminal procedures, or it can have a regularly functioning process of executing prisoners; but the evidence suggests it cannot have both."[55]

The difference in legal culture so evident between California and Texas is the legacy of a much older and broader phenomenon. It is no accident that so many of the executing states are concentrated in the South, as that region has a history of incomplete conversion to a due process culture of criminal adjudication. It is notable that the Supreme Court began its foray into the constitutionalization of criminal procedure in the capital trial of the Scottsboro Boys, which was emblematic of the "legal lynchings" that often passed for Southern justice, particularly in cases of alleged black-on-white violence. The wholesale criminal procedure revolution wrought by the Warren Court in the 1960s was in large part an attempt to bring outliers—again mostly Southern states—up to a national standard of due process in criminal cases.[56] The ability to expedite executions in many states is at least partly due to the incomplete success of the Warren Court's project—the result of Southern resistance to norms dictated by the same Court that sought to impose national values of racial justice. Or, from the perspective of the symbolic states, the *in*ability to expedite executions is attributable not merely to less deeply held political commitment at all levels to the policy of capital punishment but also to entrenched expectations about what the judicial process ought to look like in capital cases. For example, it would simply be unthinkable—far outside the norms of the reigning legal culture—for lawyers in California to fall asleep during capital trials, for trial judges to ignore such behavior, or for appellate courts to excuse it, as has happened in Texas more than once.[57]

The differing institutional arrangements, political dynamics, and legal cultures that have contributed to the execution gap between Texas and California (and, by extension, between executing and symbolic states more generally) may seem commonsensical, even obvious.[58] Yet, when these explanations are considered collectively and in detail, a surprising conclusion emerges: in the United States today, executions are *not* the natural and inevitable by-product of capital sentences. Rather, the flow of executions, even in states that routinely produce a significant number of capital sentences, can be disrupted, reduced, and even halted entirely by unrelated institutional actors operating independently from each other. It is only when these unrelated institutional actors achieve some degree of integration or political cohesion that one finds a steady stream of executions. It takes near-perfect institutional facilitation generated by strong political will to keep the pipeline clear from the courtroom to the death chamber.

Just as most explanations for the execution gap tend to focus on the exceptionalism of executing states, most criticisms of capital punishment policy tend to focus on those states as well. Texas has been lambasted for deficiencies in its capital system, including its quality of representation, racial bias, junk forensic evidence, wrongful convictions, and so on. These criticisms, whether of Texas or other states, are often well deserved. However, symbolic states—states that return large numbers of death sentences without producing many executions—are often given too much of a pass on the special problems raised by their own distinctive, though less visible, use of capital punishment.

Perhaps the most obvious problem is the enormous and senseless material cost of producing capital sentences without executions. It is hard to imagine that any legislature would publicly validate the decision to spend millions of dollars and to allocate scarce judicial resources for the mere issuance of death sentences, without any realistic likelihood of generating a substantial number of executions. Neither supporters nor opponents of capital punishment would find anything attractive about such an arrangement were they to recognize its de facto existence. David McCord captures this absurdity with grim humor by imagining the death penalty as a product subject to consumer protection laws—surely, the product would be recognized as a "lemon" in light of the fact that, among other deficiencies, so few of those sentenced to death actually end up being executed.[59]

Another obvious and much noted problem that attends the de facto conversion of death sentences into sentences of life without parole is the issue of "death row syndrome"—the psychological effect on capital defendants serving extraordinarily lengthy stays on death row under a putative sentence of death, whether or not execution ever occurs.[60] Capital defendants in such circumstances not only suffer from the fear and uncertainty generated by the sentence itself, they also are detained in restrictive and debilitating conditions, most frequently in solitary confinement. Both the European Court of Human Rights and England's Privy Council (in its role of overseeing capital punishment in several former British colonies) have concluded that lengthy confinement under sentence of death is an inhuman punishment that violates basic guarantees of fundamental rights.[61] Federal District Court Judge Cormac Carney recently reached a similar conclusion, holding that California's inability to carry out executions had rendered the state's death penalty unconstitutional.[62] According to the judge, "the dysfunctional administration of California's death penalty system has resulted, and will continue to result, in an inordinate and unpredictable period of delay," and such "delay has made execution so unlikely that the death sentence carefully and deliberately imposed by the jury has been quietly transformed into one no rational jury or legislature could ever impose: life in prison, with the remote possibility of death."[63] Although that decision was reversed on appeal, the appellate court notably reversed on a procedural point and did not disavow the thrust of the district court's reasoning.[64] A similar concern has frequently been advanced by Justice Stephen Breyer, and his recent conversion to the view that the death penalty is unconstitutional, voiced in a dissent in a lethal injection case, rests significantly on the cruelty of long-term death row confinement.[65] Interestingly, Justice Anthony Kennedy, the swing justice on the current Court, also recently lamented the cruelty of long-term solitary confinement, but he did so in a manner that explicitly did not call into question the continued permissibility of the death penalty. Justice Kennedy's unusual opinion—triggered by a passing reference at oral argument to the circumstances of confinement for a death-sentenced inmate—focused instead on prevailing confinement practices, which he seems to regard as intolerable.[66]

In addition to these obvious problems raised by the symbolic use of capital punishment in states like California, there is a less noted but no less important issue. Ironically, symbolic states, even more than executing states, reproduce the very constitutional problems that led to the initial (though temporary) constitutional invalidation of capital punishment in *Furman*. As several of the justices emphasized, the rarity of the death penalty's imposition relative to its breadth of potential applicability produced a degree of arbitrariness and inefficacy that was constitutionally intolerable. Recall Justice Stewart's insistence in *Furman* that the death sentences before the Court were cruel and unusual in the same way "that being struck by lightning is cruel and unusual."

These same concerns about the administration of the pre-*Furman* capital sentencing schemes are strikingly relevant to the administration of capital punishment in symbolic states today. The only difference is that in the pre-*Furman* era it was death sentences that were rarely imposed among those eligible, while in symbolic states it is executions that are rarely carried out among those sentenced to death. In both situations, however, the concerns about arbitrary administration have equal bite. As in the pre-*Furman* death penalty schemes, those who are actually executed in symbolic states today are not distinguishable from the much larger mass of those who are not executed by any relevant factors, such as their personal blameworthiness, their dangerousness, or their irredeemability. Rather, the few executions that have occurred in California and other symbolic jurisdictions over the last two decades are as apparently arbitrary—or wanton and freakish, in the words of Justice Stewart—as the few executions that occurred in the years leading up to *Furman*.

The only thing that could be said in favor of current symbolic states over pre-*Furman* states is that the current states get whatever symbolic or expressive value inheres in pronouncing sentences of death. While such pronouncements no doubt have some immediate expressive value and some obvious political benefit for the local political actors immediately responsible for producing them, that expressive value is inevitably undercut by the delay and attrition that make execution such an unlikely prospect. Indeed, the expressive value of death sentences in symbolic states depends on the general public being unaware or positively misinformed about the realistic likelihood of the defendant actually being executed, a state of affairs that is increasingly unlikely in the most prominent symbolic jurisdictions. This limited expressive value, premised on a lack of transparency that is both troubling and probably ephemeral, is hardly the kind of plausible criminal justice purpose that the Court has repeatedly suggested is necessary to justify the use of capital punishment under the Eighth Amendment. Such a purpose seems analogous to the expressive value that pre-*Furman* states could have claimed in maintaining capital punishment as a possible though almost never used sanction—a value that none of the justices in the *Furman* majority thought even worthy of comment.

In allowing executions to decline into near desuetude, symbolic states evince exactly the failure of political will that doomed the constitutionality of the pre-*Furman* capital sentencing regimes. It is commonplace for critics of contemporary capital punishment, ourselves among them, to note that executing states have failed to respond adequately to the concerns of *Furman*. What is far less noticed is that symbolic states eerily reproduce *exactly* some of the most disturbing aspects of the pre-*Furman* distribution of executions. While this form of rare and random distribution clearly makes no fiscal sense and may well pose a special kind of cruelty to those in lengthy isolation under uncertain sentence of death, these problems have not received much traction as constitutional problems outside of dissenting opinions. But the inevitable arbitrariness and inefficacy of such distributions have long been recognized as distinctive constitutional infirmities—ones that symbolic states should now confront as their own.

Is the divide between executing and symbolic states stable? The current regime in symbolic states of sentences without executions might simply be a bizarre product of constitutional regulation (and its accompanying fragmentation of responsibility for capital punishment) that satisfies no one, and we might therefore expect that such regimes will eventually be abandoned for one of the two poles of abolition or frequent executions. Alternatively, such regimes might reflect a unique compromise that serves an ongoing, if unrecognized, social purpose of mediating the demands for harsh punishment and the realities of modern legal processes and sensibilities. This function, more than any putative purpose of capital punishment, may explain the surprising persistence of the modern form of symbolic execution. Like our colonial forebears, who deliberately sentenced offenders to stand on the gallows without being executed, many jurisdictions today continue to "reap much of the benefit of the death penalty without actually having to kill."[67]

CHAPTER FIVE

The Failures of Regulation

A S DEATH PENALTY SUPPORTERS and opponents battled in the courts during the 1960s and early 1970s, increased regulation of the death penalty was no one's goal. Justice Goldberg's 1963 call to action sprang from his belief that the death penalty ought to be abolished. The litigators at the LDF likewise hoped that small victories in the U.S. Supreme Court would soon be followed by outright judicial abolition. Supporters of the death penalty regarded its administration as an issue for the states. They were skeptical that the Court had much to teach the states about improving capital practices. Thus, when the Court rejected abolition in its 1976 decisions while elaborating a set of Eighth Amendment constraints, it embarked on a course that seemed to please no one: retention of the death penalty with top-down regulation of capital practices by the American judiciary.

Now, forty years later, supporters and opponents of the death penalty remain united in their dislike of the status quo of retention and regulation. Supporters of the death penalty believe that the Court's efforts have burdened the administration of capital punishment with an overly complex, absurdly arcane, and minutely detailed body of constitutional law that, to borrow the words of the great American jurist Learned Hand from a slightly different context, "obstructs, delays, and defeats" the administration of capital punishment. Pro-death penalty critics highlight the sheer volume of death penalty litigation, the labyrinthine nature of the doctrines that litigation has spawned, and the lengthy delays that occur between the imposition of death sentences and their execution. Opponents of the death penalty believe that the Court's interventions have been insufficient to redress the arbitrary and discriminatory imposition of death that prompted the Court to intervene in the first place. These critics note that the American death penalty continues to strike like lightning, giving no confidence that the few offenders sentenced to death and executed are genuinely more deserving than the many more who are spared. Worse still, the arbitrariness is compounded by the continuing influence of race and poor representation on the distribution of capital sentences.[1]

Both sets of criticisms of the Court's work are substantially correct: the death penalty is, perversely, both over- and underregulated. The body of doctrine produced by the Court is enormously complex and its applicability to specific cases is difficult to discern. Yet, it remains unresponsive to the central concerns that inspired the Court to embark on its regulatory regime.

How did the Court manage to create a body of law at once so messy and so meaningless? The development of the Court's capital doctrines reveals that the complexity and high visibility of the Court's regulatory project masks its minimalism. States are not required to depart significantly from their pre-*Furman* regimes. The disruptive impact of the Court's regulation, particularly in the immediate aftermath of the Court's reinstatement of the death penalty, was attributable less to significant regulatory demands than to miscommunication between the Court and state actors regarding the Court's minimal requirements. In the end, regulation has not solved or significantly ameliorated the problems it was designed to address. Part of the failure is the result of the Court's choices, but part is rooted in inherent aspects of the enterprise. Even well-targeted judicial regulation has its limits.

The failure of regulation to solve the problems the Court identified, regrettable in itself, is made worse by a hidden cost of the Court's chosen path: regulation, by virtue of its visibility and complexity, managed to help legitimate and entrench the American death penalty in the first few decades following the 1976 decisions. Although perhaps unintended by any member of the Court or any advocate before it, the Court's interventions strengthened the status of the death penalty as a form of punishment in the eyes of actors within the capital system and of the public at large. The Court's many decisions and rules created the appearance of intensive regulation. That appearance provided unjustified comfort to actors within the system—prosecutors, jurors, executive officials—whose discretionary choices were made against the background of the Court's highly visible role. The public at large likewise drew reassurance from the fact that the administration of the death penalty was now unmistakably in the hands of the courts. By the late 1980s, the palpable national mood was one of frustration with the Court's extensive regulation, which many believed not only insured but *over*-insured against arbitrary or unjust executions. The comfort was short-lived, as the country's exposure to wrongful convictions ultimately undercut faith in the reliability of American capital punishment. But, for two decades, regulation managed to stabilize capital punishment despite its relatively modest contribution to the fairness and reliability of the American death penalty.

The Content of Constitutional Regulation

The failure of the Court's regulation on its own terms is illustrated by recalling the central problems identified in the Court's foundational decisions. In the pre-*Furman* world, state statutes cast an exceptionally broad net—permitting the death penalty to be imposed against a large number of offenders, including those convicted of nonhomicidal offenses such as rape, armed robbery, and kidnapping. But the number of those actually sentenced to death was quite small—a tiny fraction of those eligible for capital punishment. The rarity of the death penalty was in part the result of the absolute discretion provided in state schemes; in the Georgia statute reviewed in *Furman*, for example, jurors had the choice of imposing death, life imprisonment, or imprisonment from one to twenty years for the offense of forcible rape. The statute gave no criteria for choosing among those quite divergent options. As a pre-*Furman* court in Florida characteristically explained, the decision to impose death or a lesser punishment for murder was to be "determined purely by the dictates of the consciences of the individual jurors."[2]

This juxtaposition of broad death eligibility, rare death sentences, and no statutory guidance created several related problems. These features suggested that some offenders would be excessively punished. Prosecutors might seek, and juries might return, capital verdicts in run-of-the-mill cases that the larger community did not regard as warranting death. This fear was clearly a subtext in *Furman* itself; of the three petitioners, two had been sentenced to death for rape, which raised the possibility that the penalty was being applied when a community consensus was lacking. The features also suggested that the death penalty was being administered unfairly. Even if every defendant sentenced to death under a capital sentencing scheme "deserves" to die according to the larger community's considered judgment, the scheme could still be problematic if many other offenders, just as "deserving" as those condemned, are spared for arbitrary reasons. The extreme rarity of the death penalty—even in highly aggravated cases—contributed to Justice Stewart's perception that the death penalty struck like lightning. Most troubling was the perception that the distribution of the death penalty was not merely arbitrary but discriminatory. If the rare imposition of the death penalty is predictably limited to poor or minority defendants while other offenders (or those with minority victims) are routinely spared, the death penalty is fairly viewed as an engine of discrimination. This concern was most prominent in Justice Douglas's concurring opinion in *Furman,* where he highlighted the "equal protection" theme "implicit" in the Eighth Amendment. Douglas used anecdotal and statistical evidence to demonstrate that the death penalty in the United States was visited disproportionately upon the "poor, young, and ignorant," and upon "the Negro, and the members of unpopular groups." He noted explicitly that in each of the three cases before the Court in *Furman* the defendant was black, and in the two rape cases the victims were white. Douglas decried what he evocatively termed the "caste aspect" of the imposition of the death penalty and argued that the discretionary capital sentencing schemes at issue were "pregnant with discrimination."[3]

Another troublesome aspect of the pre-*Furman* era was the relative casualness of the entire capital process. The unitary proceedings in many states suggested that there was nothing special about the potential penalty, reflecting low expectations about the breadth and quality of evidence relevant to the capital sentencing decision. Lawyers representing capital defendants and death-sentenced inmates were taken from the same pool of lawyers operating in the noncapital sphere, with no special training or commitment. Jury selection was rudimentary and primarily aimed at preventing death penalty opponents from serving on capital cases. In short, death was emphatically "not different," and capital proceedings reflected that fact.

In response to such problems, the Court developed four major doctrines constraining state practices. These doctrines continue to provide the basic framework for the Court's regulatory efforts. The first, "narrowing," requires states to limit the types of murders punishable by death through the enumeration of aggravating factors. The second, "proportionality," places constitutional limits on offenses and offenders subject to the death penalty. The third, "individualized sentencing," insists that state statutes permit jurors to reject the death penalty based on mitigating aspects of the offense and the offender. The fourth, "heightened reliability," demands that capital proceedings provide additional safeguards given the categorical difference between death and all other punishments. At first blush, these doctrines might appear to be a reasonable response to the defects of the pre-*Furman* era. On close examination, though, these doctrines have neither improved capital practices nor solved the problems of arbitrariness, discrimination, and error.

The guided discretion statutes upheld in the 1976 cases responded to the *Furman* challenge by requiring more than a murder conviction to permit the imposition of the death penalty. Borrowing from the Model Penal Code (MPC), these statutes essentially created a new offense of "capital murder," insisting that jurors find the presence of at least one "aggravating factor" (or its functional equivalent) as a prerequisite to a death sentence. The hope was that the promulgation of such factors would ensure that offenders receiving death sentences would be among the "worst of the worst" offenders according to community standards. No longer would prosecutors and jurors be left to their own devices in deciding whether the offense and offender before them were truly deserving of the ultimate punishment. Moreover, given the observed rarity of death sentences in relation to the breadth of pre-*Furman* statutes, aggravating factors would presumably shrink the pool of death-eligible defendants and produce a more meaningful correspondence between the class of death-eligible defendants and those actually sentenced to death.

The problems with states' efforts in this regard surfaced immediately. The new Georgia statute reviewed in *Gregg*, for example, included as an aggravating circumstance that the offense "was outrageously or wantonly vile, horrible or inhuman in that it involved torture, depravity of mind, or an aggravated battery to the victim." The key terms of this factor are vague and undefined. Most murders can be characterized as "vile, horrible or inhuman," and the added modifiers, especially "depravity of mind," seem to invite subjective, idiosyncratic judgments. Georgia was hardly alone in using vague, open-ended terms in its list of aggravating factors. Most states, following the MPC's lead (a key MPC factor was whether "the murder was especially heinous, atrocious or cruel, manifesting exceptional depravity"), included at least one factor that seemed to function as a catchall—an aggravator that could be deployed in any case in which the jury seemed inclined to impose death. Overly broad and subjective aggravating factors defeat both of the ostensible purposes of statutory narrowing: they fail to limit the application of the death penalty in absolute terms to a narrow class of offenders, and they fail to afford advance notice of the community's views regarding the offenses deserving of death. Instead, such factors put prosecutors and jurors in essentially the same position as their pre-*Furman* counterparts, asking them to consult their own conscience and judgment—rather than clear legislative criteria—as they decide between life and death.[4]

Four years after *Gregg*, the Court reversed a capital sentence resting solely on the "outrageously or wantonly vile" circumstance, recognizing that the factor failed "to provide a meaningful basis for distinguishing the few cases in which [the penalty] is imposed from the many cases in which it is not." But the Court's resolve on this score waned over the ensuing years. In a series of cases, the Court upheld capital verdicts resting on similarly vague aggravators, including Arizona's factor borrowed from the MPC, which asks whether the defendant committed the offense in an "especially heinous, cruel or depraved manner." In these cases, the Court acknowledged that the bare language of the factor was impermissibly vague, but sustained the capital verdicts based on purported "limiting constructions" applied by state judges. In a similar vein, the Court sustained a capital verdict obtained via Idaho's absurdly indeterminate factor, whether: "By the murder, or circumstances surrounding its commission, the defendant exhibited utter disregard for human life." The notion that the death penalty should be applied or withheld based on whether a defendant exhibits "utter" versus (presumably) "ordinary" disregard for human life reveals the emptiness of the enterprise. With these more recent decisions, the Court seems to have retreated from the requirement that aggravating factors have some objective core content.[5]

Some aggravating factors, even when they are clear, often do little work to cabin the death penalty. One ubiquitous aggravator (again borrowed from the MPC) is whether a murder is accompanied by a separate dangerous felony, such as robbery, arson, burglary, kidnapping, or rape. Many murders fall into this category, transforming every killing during a convenience store or liquor store robbery into a "worst of the worst" offense. The "additional felony" aggravator means that taking some property from the dead victim (robbery) or temporarily restraining the victim before the killing (kidnapping) will convert an otherwise ordinary murder into a death-eligible offense.[6]

The problem is not merely that vague aggravating factors often replicate the unbridled discretion of the pre-*Furman* regime or that some objective factors cover too much ground. Though the Court goes through the motions of assessing whether *individual* aggravators narrow the class of death-eligible offenders, the Court has never inquired whether aggravating factors *taken collectively* accomplish anything along these lines. Many states started with long lists of aggravating circumstances in their initial statutes. But even those jurisdictions that started with just a handful are unlikely to have so few today, because the pressure to expand the ambit of the death penalty over time has proven politically irresistible. This dynamic is so common that experts have given it a label—"aggravator creep" (a play on the concept of "mission creep" referenced in military contexts)—in which a "statute is passed with a list of aggravating factors, and then structural impulses often push that list to become longer and longer as new aggravators are added." Scott Turow, a lawyer and writer who supported the death penalty for most of his legal career before changing his views while serving on the Illinois commission that recommended that the state abolish capital punishment, describes the emotions and politics behind this process: "The furious heat of grief and rage the worst cases inspire will inevitably short-circuit our judgment. . . . And the fundamental equality of each survivor's loss, and the manner in which the wayward imaginations of criminals continue to surprise us, will inevitably cause the categories for death eligibility to expand, a slippery slope of what-about-hims."[7]

Even if individual aggravating factors within state schemes achieve significant narrowing on their own, there remains a substantial risk that the factors collectively create an enormously broad death penalty net. Empirical evidence suggests that this is not a speculative possibility. The most detailed study of death eligibility within a state—conducted by the well-known Baldus research group—found that approximately 86 percent of all persons convicted of murder in Georgia over a five-year period after the adoption of Georgia's new statute were death-eligible under that scheme. Perhaps more revealing is the Baldus study's conclusion that over 90 percent of persons sentenced to death before *Furman* would also have been deemed death-eligible under the post-*Furman* statute. The Baldus group's work strongly suggests that Georgia has not articulated a circumscribed theory of what the state might regard as the worst murders. Instead, Georgia has simply described the various factors that collectively account for the circumstances surrounding *most* murders. Far from achieving the narrowing function suggested in *Furman* and *Gregg*, these aggravating factors merely create the illusion that the offense at issue truly falls within the select set of crimes that justifies imposition of the death penalty. The study suggests that higher death-sentencing rates after *Furman* might be the result of this dynamic, with jurors giving special weight in sentencing decisions to Georgia's adoption and endorsement of statutory aggravating circumstances.[8]

Despite the Court's minimal policing of the narrowing requirement, its work in this area generated extensive, disruptive litigation. Some of the litigation resulted from the unwillingness of states to withdraw their most obviously problematic aggravators, such as Georgia's "outrageously or wantonly vile" factor. But a large swath of litigation concerned the status of capital verdicts resting on both permissible (objective) and impermissible (overly vague) factors. As the Court applied its narrowing doctrine, all parties agreed that a death verdict must be reversed if the sole aggravating factor in the case was later deemed insufficient. But it remained unclear what should happen where a jury relied on both a valid factor and an invalid one. The Court created a complicated, convoluted doctrine, allowing some such verdicts to stand and others to fall depending on how the state scheme framed the ultimate sentencing decision for the jury. The Court's doctrine was intricate and nonsensical and, in 2006, the Court jettisoned it. For more than two decades, though, the state and federal courts wrestled with legions of cases involving this problem, causing many death sentences to be reversed and expending enormous judicial resources. The U.S. Supreme Court alone heard at least half a dozen cases focusing on this esoteric issue, giving the appearance of intensive judicial scrutiny even though it accomplished little in terms of improving the underlying practice.[9]

Ultimately, the effort to achieve meaningful narrowing through aggravating factors has failed. Before *Furman*, jurors could impose the death penalty against essentially any offender who committed murder. After *Furman*, the states' enumeration of numerous and broad aggravating factors, combined with the Court's minimalist policing, leaves jurors in virtually the same place—except now they are more likely to *believe* that the offense before them is especially deserving of death.

Narrowing can also be achieved by excluding certain offenders and offenses from the death penalty's reach. At the time of Justice Goldberg's dissent from denial of review in 1963, the Court had never found an otherwise permissible punishment unconstitutional because it had been imposed for an insufficiently grave offense. After the 1976 cases upheld many of the new capital statutes, the Court immediately returned to the problem of capital punishment for rape. It granted review in *Coker v. Georgia,* and in 1977 ruled that the death penalty could not be imposed for the crime of raping an adult woman. The Court emphasized that Georgia was alone among American jurisdictions in continuing to authorize death for rape and noted the relative rarity of capital verdicts for that crime in post-*Furman* Georgia.[10]

Coker seemed promising for the future of constitutional regulation. Court-imposed proportionality limits could help promote the narrowing of the death penalty that is so difficult to achieve through aggravating factors. But in the two decades following *Coker,* the Court resisted proportionality limits. After briefly holding that the death penalty could not be imposed on a defendant convicted of felony murder who neither killed, attempted to kill, nor intended to kill, the Court reversed itself, paving the way for offenders to receive the death penalty for the handiwork of others. Under the Court's approach, if two offenders rob a bank and one of them decides to shoot a teller, both can be sentenced to death, even if the nonshooter did not want the killing to occur, as long as his participation in the bank robbery was sufficiently substantial and he was reckless with regard to the possibility that a killing might occur. In 1989, the Court refused to exempt juveniles from the death penalty, upholding death sentences imposed against offenders aged sixteen and seventeen at the time of their crimes. On the same day, the Court declined to exempt persons with intellectual disability from execution. In both cases, the Court found no "national consensus" forbidding the execution of such offenders, relying primarily on the rarity of state legislative prohibitions against those practices.[11]

More recently, the Court has embraced several proportionality limits. In the early 2000s, the Court revisited the claims of juveniles and persons with intellectual disability and declared the exclusion of both types of offenders to be unconstitutionally severe. The Court also extended *Coker* by disallowing executions for rape even in cases involving minor victims (several states made child rape a capital offense beginning in the 1990s). This latter decision stated that the death penalty cannot be imposed for any nonhomicidal offense against persons (leaving open the possibility of the death penalty for nonhomicidal crimes against the state, such as treason or terrorism).[12]

The Court's recent proportionality decisions represent important regulatory constraints. Their contribution to the rationalization of the American death penalty, however, remains minimal. Almost by definition, proportionality limits apply only to the most marginal capital practices. At the time of the Court's decision exempting juveniles in 2005, for example, the United States was the last jurisdiction in the world to officially authorize the execution of juvenile offenders.[13] Likewise, the use of the death penalty for rape was already widely understood to be a remnant of Jim Crow justice when *Coker* was decided in 1977, even though the Court did not frame its decision in those terms. For proportionality limits to have a profound impact, they would have to limit the death penalty to the most highly aggravated cases (such as mass murder) rather than simply prohibiting its imposition in the most mitigated or inappropriate ones. But just as it is difficult for states to articulate a theory of the "worst of the worst" offenses, so too is the Court constrained in its ability to define that class. Moreover, even in policing the outer edges of the American death penalty, the Court has not acted robustly. Felony murderers who do not themselves kill remain death-eligible, and offenders with intellectual disability are routinely denied protection because of states' hostility to that exemption. In some states, such as Texas, the protection against executing offenders with intellectual disability is more fairly described as a protection against executing offenders with obvious or severe intellectual disability. Many offenders who meet the traditional clinical criteria for intellectual disability remain subject to the penalty, and the Court has declined to intervene despite abundant opportunities.[14] State and federal courts have been unwilling to extend proportionality protection to offenders with severe mental illness—yet another class of offenders with significantly reduced moral culpability who not infrequently get caught in the death penalty net.[15]

Unlike the Court's other regulatory doctrines, the guarantee of individualized sentencing—the right of a defendant to present and have considered mitigating evidence—was not a direct response to some defects in the pre-*Furman* regime. Instead, it was a response to problems generated by *Furman* itself. Some states believed that the best (or perhaps only) way to satisfy *Furman's* concerns about arbitrariness and discrimination was to make death a mandatory punishment. On this line of thought, eradicating discretion would allow state schemes to avoid random or unequal treatment of offenders. When the mandatory statutes reached the Court in 1976, the Court concluded that mandatory sentencing creates a false consistency. Executing all persons convicted of the same offense fails to account for meaningful differences in culpability. The Court held that jurors must be able to withhold the death penalty based on mitigating aspects of the offense and offender. The irony, of course, was that the Court seemed to be protecting as a matter of constitutional law the very discretion *Furman* had identified as constitutionally problematic. But according to the Court, the discretion to *withhold* the death penalty based on mitigating factors is categorically different from the discretion to *impose* the death penalty based on amorphous perceptions of the aggravating aspects of the offense. So was born the central tension in American death penalty law: its simultaneous command that states cabin discretion of who shall die while facilitating discretion of who shall live.[16]

Somewhat surprisingly, the constitutional requirement of individualized sentencing produced significant disruption in the several decades following the 1976 decisions. The Court was clear that mandatory statutes were unconstitutional. But lurking beneath that clarity were two unanswered questions: could states confine consideration of mitigation to certain state-endorsed factors, and could states adopt procedures constraining how juries give effect to mitigating evidence? The Court was soon confronted with state schemes or practices that limited the types of mitigation juries could consider. In 1980, for example, the Court held that Ohio's exclusive list of mitigating factors violated the Constitution by precluding the jury from considering mitigating evidence regarding the defendant's lack of specific intent to cause death, minimal participation in the crime, and age at the time of the offense. The death-sentenced inmate in that case, Sandra Lockett, had been the getaway driver when her accomplices killed a pawnshop owner while robbing the store. In subsequent cases, the Court invalidated sentences when a state judge refused to assign any mitigating weight to the defendant's turbulent family history and emotional disturbance and when state case law precluded consideration of a defendant's good behavior while awaiting trial.[17]

As the Court decided these cases, it never precisely identified the types of evidence that judges and juries *must* be allowed to consider. Eventually, almost three decades after invalidating the mandatory death penalty, the Court explicitly embraced the broadest possible conception of mitigation, insisting that judges and juries must be able to consider any evidence that could reasonably support a sentence less than death. The breadth of this test encompasses evidence of a defendant's background, intellectual or psychiatric impairments, circumstances of the offense, post-crime rehabilitation, and essentially anything else that sentencers might believe justifies rejecting the death penalty. During that three-decade period, many courts intuited the direction of the Supreme Court's approach, reversing dozens of capital sentences in jurisdictions with statutes that provided a limited list of mitigating factors.[18]

Apart from restricting what counts as mitigating evidence, some state statutes undermined the right to individualized sentencing by limiting the ways in which such evidence could be considered. In a series of cases, the Court struck down "unanimity" rules, which precluded jurors from considering particular mitigating factors unless all jurors agreed they were present; such rules created the bizarre possibility of requiring a death sentence when the jury was united in its belief that death should not be imposed but divided as to which mitigating factors justified leniency. The biggest problem occurred in Texas. The Texas statute did not enumerate mitigating factors. Instead, the Texas scheme asked the jury to answer specific questions about the deliberateness of the crime and dangerousness of the defendant. According to the Texas and lower federal courts, these questions allowed adequate consideration of mitigating evidence though they "structured" its consideration. However, defendants insisted that the Texas statute failed to afford "full" consideration of mitigating factors and was thus unconstitutional in many cases: evidence of a difficult background or mental impairment, for example, might call for a life sentence even if such evidence did not disprove deliberateness or dangerousness. For more than twenty-five years, cases bounced between these courts and the U.S. Supreme Court as they struggled to apply the individualization requirement to the unusual Texas scheme. Ultimately, the Court rejected the idea that states can "structure" consideration of mitigating evidence. As in its other decisions elaborating the individualization requirement, the Court adopted a maximalist approach: state capital schemes must allow unconstrained consideration of any factors that might call for a sentence less than death.[19]

The individualization requirement represents a broad death penalty principle and amounts to a significant constraint on state capital schemes. But the constraint seems particularly unsuited to solving the problems identified in *Furman*. The pre-*Furman* villain was unbridled discretion, and the individualization requirement demands *even more* discretion, at least on the mitigating side. Jurors in the pre-*Furman* world were told they could exercise mercy essentially for any reason, but states still put significant limits on the types of evidence that jurors could consider; in many states, the only mitigating evidence defendants could offer had to bear on their guilt or innocence for the underlying offense. The pre-*Furman* limitations on the presentation of mitigating evidence were thus paradoxically more restrictive than the Court's current expansive approach. The individualization requirement is simultaneously the most robustly enforced constitutional principle and the most threatening to the *Furman* project of ensuring consistency across cases. The Court was right to reject mandatory sentencing, and it is defensible (if not compelling) to maximize the opportunities for defendants to persuade jurors to spare their lives. But enshrining absolute, unaccountable discretion to withhold death based on any and all mitigating factors is difficult to reconcile with the *Furman* commitment to redressing the evils of "standardless discretion."[20]

The individualization requirement need not have created so many difficulties. States were slow to respond to the Court's decisions and needlessly imposed obstacles to the consideration of mitigating evidence. The Court, too, shares some blame in failing to communicate the breadth of the doctrine from the outset. Ultimately, and ironically, four decades of elaboration of the individualization requirement has functionally returned us to the pre-*Furman* world in which jurors must use their own judgment or conscience—rather than state-imposed guidelines—to decide whether a particular constellation of facts calls for a sentence less than death.

The Court's most amorphous doctrine to emerge in the 1976 decisions concerns the need for special procedural safeguards or "heightened reliability" in capital litigation. This doctrine requires states to treat capital cases with special care in order to prevent erroneous convictions and unreliable sentences. This "death-is-different" principle was pivotal to the recognition of the right to individualized sentencing (and the rejection of mandatory statutes) described above, as states are free to impose mandatory sentences for noncapital crimes (and often do). Over the next several decades, the Court echoed its death-is-different commitment in a number of subsequent cases, but close examination of the Court's decisions reveals that the constitutionally required procedural safeguards in death cases are minimal. Although the Court has carved out a series of protections solely applicable to capital trials, it has done so in an entirely ad hoc fashion and left untouched a substantial body of doctrine that relegates capital defendants to the same level of protection as noncapital defendants.

Most of the handful of decisions invoking heightened reliability to carve special protections in capital cases were issued in the first two decades following the reinstatement of the death penalty. The Court relied on the principle to invalidate a death sentence based in part on information about the defendant that was given to the sentencing judge and not revealed to defense counsel. The Court also insisted that heightened reliability entails a right of defense counsel to ask prospective jurors about potential racial prejudice in cases involving interracial murders, and to prevent prosecutors from deliberately misleading jurors about the consequences of their capital sentencing decision by misstating the scope of appellate review. In a series of decisions, the Court invoked heightened reliability to permit defendants to inform jurors of the real consequences of a life sentence when "life" means life without the possibility of parole as a matter of state law. Finally, the Court required states to provide a lesser-included offense instruction in cases in which the evidence would support a guilty verdict for a noncapital offense (such as noncapital murder or manslaughter), so that jurors do not choose death simply because they otherwise would have to allow a noncapital crime to go unpunished.[21]

These decisions, taken together with the cases elaborating the requirement of individualized sentencing, represent the sum total of the Court's applications of its death-is-different doctrine. It should be apparent from the brief summary of these decisions that the doctrine does not reflect a systematic effort to regulate the death penalty process so much as a series of responses to particular circumstances in which the Court deemed a state rule or practice manifestly unfair. Although certain themes unite some of the decisions, such as "truth in sentencing," the Court has not explained precisely how death is different from all other punishments other than to reassert that death is final and severe. As a result, the Court appears to invoke the death-is-different principle on a case-by-case basis without a more general theory of the fundamental prerequisites to a fair and principled death penalty scheme.

That these decisions essentially exhaust the death-is-different doctrine reveals the extent to which the death penalty is not different after all. Despite Justice Antonin Scalia's insistence that applications of the death-is-different doctrine reflect the success of a "guerrilla war" waged by "heavily outnumbered opponents of capital punishment," it is worth noting that there are numerous contexts in which capital defendants receive no special safeguards.[22]

When the Court first articulated the right of criminal defendants to receive effective assistance of counsel, it went out of its way to insist that the standard should not differ because a defendant faced the death penalty: "For purposes of describing counsel's duties . . . [a] capital sentencing proceeding need not be distinguished from an ordinary trial." The Court crafted a highly deferential approach in assessing whether a capital trial lawyer performed acceptably, cautioning that the purpose of reviewing claims for ineffective assistance "is not to improve the quality of legal representation" but to provide relief where the adversarial system totally broke down. To succeed, a defendant must show both that counsel's performance was "outside the wide range of professionally competent assistance" and that counsel's errors "actually had an adverse effect on the defense."[23] As a result of this lax approach, state and lower courts routinely denied relief in cases involving manifestly poor representation in capital cases. Especially during the first two decades post-*Furman,* capital defendants were often represented by court-appointed lawyers lacking the experience, resources, or commitment to mount an appropriate defense. In a number of states, attorney fees were capped at absurdly low amounts, effectively guaranteeing that defense lawyers would conduct minimal investigation, employ no experts, and confine their efforts to off-the-cuff cross-examination of state witnesses.[24]

One obvious consequence of the Court's undemanding standard for trial representation in capital cases was the perpetuation of the "caste" system Justice Douglas decried in *Furman.* When courts tolerate such an extraordinarily "wide range" of representation in capital cases, resulting sentencing decisions are more likely to reflect a divergence in representation than a divergence in the circumstances of the offense and offender. The Court's decision not to impose special representational requirements in the capital context undermines considerably the aspiration of "heightened reliability" espoused elsewhere in the Court's capital jurisprudence.

The Court's minimal policing of capital representation is reflected in the fact that its first reversal of a capital sentence based on poor lawyering did not occur until more than a quarter century after *Furman.* Beginning in 2000, the Court issued a trio of decisions reversing capital convictions based on inadequate development and presentation of mitigating evidence that might have made a difference at sentencing.[25] These decisions are important, but they illustrate the

Court following rather than leading the transition to acceptable capital lawyering. In finding deficient performance in those cases, the Court pointed not to its own specific requirements for death penalty representation, which it had declined to articulate, but to the American Bar Association's 1989 Guidelines for the Appointment and Performance of Counsel in Death Penalty Cases, which were revised in 2003.[26] In the twenty-five years leading up to the Court's first grants of relief, capital practices were changing on the ground. During the 1980s and 1990s, horror stories of poor lawyering—including drunk, sleeping, and inept lawyers—were commonplace in the press, and those concerns prompted some efforts by the bar and state legislatures to raise the level of attorney performance. The Court's regulation of the death penalty created new institutional actors, most importantly a new professionalized capital defense bar (including state-funded capital trial offices, federally funded capital habeas offices, and several nonprofits focused on capital representation) committed to higher standards and the training of appointed lawyers. Even though the Court continues to adhere to its highly deferential standard, that standard now requires relief in some cases because the "wide range" of acceptable representation has narrowed with the rise of capital defense offices, clear bar expectations, and increased resources.

Another area where death is emphatically not different is in the availability of postconviction review. Under the Court's current doctrine, states need not provide any postconviction proceedings in criminal cases, including capital ones. States could decide to end their review of criminal convictions with a single direct appeal, and provide no additional mechanism for gauging the fairness of a defendant's trial. The Court has recognized that this "greater" power to deny any mechanism for postconviction relief allows a state to exercise the "lesser" power of denying counsel to indigent inmates should the state choose to establish collateral proceedings. As a result, death-sentenced inmates—even when afforded counsel—cannot seek relief based on counsel's ineffectiveness in postconviction review. As a matter of practice, states have moved toward providing counsel in such proceedings because it gives state courts the power to shape the record for eventual federal review (and to receive deference from federal courts in their resolution of federal constitutional claims).[27]

Perhaps more importantly, over the past thirty years, the Court and Congress have imposed substantial new barriers to all federal habeas petitioners, making it extremely difficult for state prisoners to vindicate their federal constitutional rights in federal court. Federal habeas is the primary means for state inmates to have the opportunity for review of their convictions and sentences in federal court—whose judges, unlike those of most state courts, do not have to stand for election. The new restrictions on federal habeas review, including strict enforcement of state procedural rules, limits on successive petitions, and a new statute of limitations, apply both to capital and noncapital prisoners.[28] The most important restriction is Congress's new, highly permissive standard under which state court resolutions of federal law cannot be reversed merely for being wrong; to receive relief, state prisoners must ordinarily show that the state court resolution was *unreasonably* wrong. All of the Court's protections for capital inmates are thereby weakened when a state death-sentenced inmate litigates in federal court. The question for the federal court is not whether the right to effective representation was denied, or whether the state's aggravating factors were impermissibly vague, or whether a defendant's mitigating evidence was improperly constrained; the question instead is whether the state court was clearly wrong in concluding otherwise. As a result, the percentage of death-sentenced inmates prevailing on federal constitutional claims in federal court has diminished dramatically.[29] Capital litigation remains protracted and expensive, but much of the wrangling in federal court focuses on the many new procedural barriers the Court and Congress have erected. State prisoners have occasionally argued that the new procedural limits are unconstitutional, or that the stakes in capital cases are too high to allow procedural obstacles (such as filing deadlines) to crowd out substantive review of the "real" issues—whether an underlying conviction and sentence were obtained in compliance with the federal law. But the Court has shown no signs of protecting the scope of the federal habeas forum by ensuring review of the merits of state prisoners' claims. Given that constitutional rights are no more effective than the means of their enforcement, the "equal" treatment of capital and noncapital defendants in postconviction proceedings has the effect of diluting whatever heightened reliability is sought by other death penalty doctrines.

The most dramatic illustration of the limited opportunities for postconviction review is found in the Court's approach to claims of actual innocence. On the surface, the issue seems fairly simple. If a death-sentenced inmate discovers compelling—even airtight—evidence of his actual innocence, does the Constitution require courts to spare him from execution? Shockingly, the answer appears to be "no." Historically, states have put absolute limits on inmates seeking to raise claims of innocence based on newly discovered evidence. They typically require such evidence to be presented within a relatively short time of conviction, and if evidence is presented outside of that timeframe, the courts close their doors and require the inmate to seek executive clemency. In the early 1990s, a Texas inmate presented new evidence of his actual innocence to the Texas courts, and they refused to consider his claim because of the Texas rule requiring such evidence to be presented within thirty days of conviction. When the inmate went to federal court, he argued that the Constitution disallows the execution of an innocent man and that the Texas rule must give way in capital cases because of the difference of death. The U.S. Supreme Court expressed skepticism about the constitutional necessity of postconviction review of claims of "bare innocence"—claims unconnected to a separate constitutional violation, such as prosecutorial misconduct. The Court highlighted the importance of finality in criminal adjudication and the traditional role of clemency to address claims of gross injustice. The Court ultimately denied relief, finding the petitioner's (admittedly weak) evidence of innocence insufficient. In addition, the Court declined to squarely embrace the proposition that the Constitution requires judicial relief for a death-sentenced inmate who can prove his innocence.[30] Now, almost twenty-five years later, the Court has yet to insist on such heightened reliability in capital cases. In the wake of numerous exonerations of death-sentenced inmates in Illinois, several members of the Court lamented the inadequate protections against wrongful convictions. Justice David Souter, writing for four dissenting justices, insisted: "We are . . . [in a] new empirical argument about how 'death is different,'" and concluded that the "repeated exonerations" in the modern era require the Court to do more to prevent error in capital cases.[31]

The most significant missed opportunity for heightened reliability occurred in the *McCleskey* litigation, in which death-sentenced inmates in Georgia sought relief based on a comprehensive empirical study documenting the substantial role of race in post-*Furman* capital sentencing.[32] The Baldus study employed sophisticated multivariate regression analysis to isolate the impact of race. The study found that the race of the victim powerfully influenced the imposition of the death penalty in post-*Furman* Georgia and that cases with black defendants and white victims were much more likely to generate death sentences than any other racial pairing after controlling for nonracial variables. In many respects, the Baldus study findings were a more powerful indictment of the American death penalty than the facts before the Court in *Furman*. In 1972, the Court worried that arbitrary and discriminatory considerations influenced the distribution of the death penalty, but it lacked clear data to establish this point; as Justice Stewart stated in his *Furman* concurrence, "racial discrimination has not been proved."[33] But the fear of arbitrariness and discrimination, coupled with the absence of state standards to guide sentencer discretion, was sufficient in 1972 to clear the nation's death row and invalidate prevailing statutes.

Fifteen years later, the Court was confronted with evidence that the Georgia capital system—even with its post-*Furman* safeguards—was plagued by the influence of race. In rejecting the Eighth Amendment challenge, the Court seemed to disavow any authority to recognize one rule in the death penalty context and another for all other punishments. According to the Court, taking McCleskey's claim "to its logical conclusion" would throw "into serious question the principles that underlie our entire criminal justice system." Given that the "Eighth Amendment is not limited in application to capital punishment, but applies to all penalties," the Court worried that "if [it] accepted McCleskey's claim that racial bias has impermissibly tainted the capital sentencing decision, [it] could soon be faced with similar claims as to other types of penalty."[34]

The Court's answer to McCleskey's challenge, in perhaps the most provocative test of the reach of its death-is-different principle, was to deny that the Eighth Amendment permits a distinctive set of rules in the capital context. *McCleskey* confirms that the Court's death-is-different doctrine does not authorize any far-reaching challenges to the states' ability to administer the death penalty. In evaluating potential attacks on the death penalty, the Court simply will not construe the Constitution to place "totally unrealistic conditions on its use," notwithstanding the Court's expressed commitment to heightened reliability in capital proceedings.[35]

In sum, despite the appearance of an elaborate scheme of death penalty regulation, the Court's death-is-different doctrine is nothing more than a modest, ad hoc series of limitations on particular state practices. As with the Court's other death penalty doctrines, the seemingly intricate and demanding constraints appear quite marginal upon closer inspection.

It is understandable that advocates of capital punishment, as well as institutional actors charged with implementing state capital schemes, would look at the post-*Furman* era of federal constitutional regulation and see an obstructionist Court imposing a confusing morass of hyper-technical rules. Judged by the volume of cases the Court has heard, the intricacy of the Court's resulting opinions, and the malleability of the emerging doctrines, the Court has assumed a prominent and seemingly powerful role in regulating the death penalty.

Despite this perception, contemporary death penalty law is remarkably undemanding. The narrowing, proportionality, and individualization requirements can be simultaneously and completely satisfied by a hypothetical statute that defines capital murder as any murder accompanied by some additional, objective factor or factors and that provides for a sentencing proceeding in which the sentencer is asked simply whether the defendant should live or die. No longer can death be imposed for the crime of rape, or against juveniles or persons with intellectual disability, but beyond that, the state can seek the death penalty against virtually any murderer. As for the requirement of heightened reliability, it surfaces unpredictably at the margins of state capital schemes. In the post-*Furman* regime, the doctrine of heightened reliability, like the death penalty itself, seems to strike like lightning, randomly and with no broad effect.

The resemblance of this hypothetical scheme to the pre-*Furman* regime is striking in itself, but all the more striking because of the widespread perception that death penalty law is extremely demanding. Virtually all of the complexity of death penalty law since 1972 stems from a failure in translation rather than an insistence on fulfilling the ambitious goals of *Furman* and the 1976 decisions. This communication gap, in which the Court rarely identified in clear and unanimous terms the minimal obligations of states in the post-*Furman* era, and in which states failed to respond quickly (or in some cases at all) to obvious, correctable defects in their statutes in light of those minimal obligations, has left us with the worst of all possible regulatory worlds. The resulting complexity conveys the impression that the current system errs, if it all, on the side of heightened reliability and fairness. And the fact of minimal regulation, which invites if not guarantees the same kinds of inequality as the pre-*Furman* regime, is filtered through time-consuming, expensive proceedings that ultimately do little to satisfy the concerns that led the Court to regulate this country's death penalty practices in the first place. In short, the last four decades have produced a complicated regulatory apparatus that achieves extremely modest goals while maximizing political and legal discomfort.

Fated Failure?

The failure of the Court's regulation to succeed on its own terms raises a question: was the project destined to fail? Can judicial regulation rationalize or at least significantly improve the American death penalty? Many of the Court's regulatory choices were misguided, and judicial regulation, properly framed, can achieve greater fairness and reliability than that afforded by the present regime. However, legal regulation is unlikely to solve the numerous problems of the status quo, including arbitrariness, discrimination, inefficacy, and error. These problems are difficult to overcome given the seemingly stable parameters of the current regime: that the death penalty will be imposed rarely and through the unaccountable discretion of prosecutors and jurors. The inevitability of discretion means that the capital decision cannot be tamed through legal language. In addition, many of the current pathologies in American capital practices, even if they can be ameliorated, are not amenable to judicial reform alone. They require cooperation and leadership from the political branches, but those qualities are often absent because of the intense politicization of criminal justice in general and the death penalty in particular.

The Court's regulation of the death penalty could be improved in several ways, however. In assessing whether state schemes guide capital decision making, the Court could look more closely at whether state aggravating factors collectively accomplish much in terms of limiting the class of death-eligible offenders. The Court could require states to use aggravating factors that are subject to precise measurement (in terms of how frequently they are present in murder cases), such as killings involving more than one victim, killings of police officers, and killings while in prison. The Court would then be in a position to assess whether the breadth of death eligibility in a state scheme corresponds meaningfully to the number of offenders sentenced to death. If statutory aggravators in a given jurisdiction collectively apply to no more than 10 or 15 percent of murders, it is much more tolerable to have death sentences in only 1 percent or so of murders overall. This approach would require states to jettison subjective factors such as the "especially heinous, atrocious, and cruel" aggravator. Even if these factors capture something important along retributive lines, they present the greatest risk of arbitrary and inconsistent application. Nor would states be able to retain the possibility of the death penalty for every homicide that occurs in the course of a serious felony, because that aggravator, either alone or in combination with other factors, casts too wide a net given the rarity of capital sentences.

The Court could also strengthen its proportionality doctrine by expanding its application to other less culpable offenders, such as persons with severe mental illness, and more vigorously enforcing its current ban on the execution of persons with intellectual disability. It could also require states to engage in their own proportionality review of individual sentences, a choice the Court eschewed in 1984.[36] Many states, including Georgia, provide for appellate proportionality review, under which state supreme courts are charged with comparing the facts of a defendant's case with similar cases within the jurisdiction to ensure comparable treatment. Despite *Gregg*'s endorsement of comparative proportionality review as a potentially valuable safeguard in 1976, many states do not require such review and many others perform it in a highly perfunctory manner. Ideally, state supreme courts would compare a defendant's case with comparable cases, including cases culminating in life sentences, to determine whether application of the death penalty would be excessive or unfair. Of course, comparative proportionality review implicates some of the same difficulties involved in structuring the original sentencing decision: how can we tell that a particular constellation of facts makes a case similar enough to warrant similar treatment? Notwithstanding this difficulty, a robust practice of comparative proportionality review might discourage prosecutors from seeking death in marginal cases and would involve the state courts in an ongoing process to gauge the reliability and fairness of the state capital system as a whole, rather than focusing on error in discrete cases.

The Court could also modify its lenient review of attorney performance in capital cases. In 2001, Justice Ruth Bader Ginsburg declared in a public speech that she had yet to encounter a death-sentenced inmate who was well-represented at trial.[37] Although the level of practice nationwide has improved, poor representation continues to plague capital cases at every level—trials, appeals, and postconviction proceedings. As use of the death penalty has declined and prosecutors have become increasingly willing to settle capital charges with a life verdict, the risk that poor lawyering rather than the facts of the case will cause a particular case to yield a death verdict has increased dramatically. Talented and committed capital trial lawyers will do everything in their power to avoid trial, with its risk of a death sentence. Competent capital trial lawyers engage in exhaustive investigation, use of experts, and extensive client contact at an early stage. As in most litigation contexts, capital cases are won or lost by pre-trial zealousness; without aggressive efforts to document the costs of trial, cases may stumble toward trial even though effective lawyering could secure a plea. Judicial review of the effectiveness of trial counsel in death cases, however, does not account for this new reality in which pretrial efforts are the whole ballgame. Constitutional doctrine generally limits review of capital trial lawyers' performance to whether they mounted something resembling a defense, by cross-examining witnesses, presenting mitigating evidence, and making appropriate objections. This sort of bird's-eye view of trial may catch the sleeping and inept lawyers, but it will leave untouched many cases in which lawyers simply did too little too late to make a difference for their clients.

Finally, the Court could embrace Justice Souter's suggestion to recalibrate capital doctrines in light of the disturbing evidence of wrongful convictions. The low-hanging fruit in this regard is simply to insist upon a judicial forum for death-sentenced inmates with compelling new evidence of actual innocence, a modest requirement that the Court remarkably has yet to embrace. But the opportunity to litigate innocence claims in postconviction proceedings is plainly not enough. The Court should do more to address the primary causes of wrongful convictions at the trial stage, including reliance on bad forensic science evidence, testimony secured from codefendants and jailhouse informants (often with undisclosed incentives), flawed eyewitness testimony, and untrustworthy confessions. Problems with these sorts of evidence are endemic in the criminal justice system. The Court's minimal policing of the prosecutorial use of such evidence facilitates conviction of the innocent. There are reasons to believe that the problems associated with the use of such evidence are even greater in capital cases, because of the strong pressures to quickly identify perpetrators in the most highly aggravated offenses. A true death-is-different approach would impose heightened safeguards in each of these areas, insisting that evidence leading to capital convictions is not merely relevant to the question of guilt or innocence but highly accurate as well. Unfortunately, the Court's prevailing doctrine points in the other direction. In the sentencing context, for example, the Court has rejected constitutional challenges to highly questionable "expert" testimony regarding the likely dangerousness of capital defendants, notwithstanding the position of the American Psychiatric Association that the unreliability of such testimony is "an established fact within the profession."[38] As a result, scores of inmates have been sentenced to death based on what amounts to little more than guesswork. Notably, in defending the use of dangerousness experts, the Court simply pointed to noncapital contexts in which such evidence might be relevant and admissible. The Court placed no weight on the distinctiveness of the death penalty and instead allowed continued use of dangerous experts because defendants had not established "that such testimony is almost entirely unreliable."[39]

This sketch of potential improvements to the Court's regulatory approach should not be read as confidence that judicial regulation can cure the ills of the American death penalty. The bulk of the Court's regulation has sought to frame the capital punishment decision in a way that will both provide meaningful standards and permit jurors to respond to powerful mitigating grounds for withholding the death penalty. But the prospects for simultaneously achieving both goals remain dim. From the start, the tension between the demands of consistency and individualization was apparent. As early as a year prior to *Furman,* lawyers at the LDF argued that unregulated mercy was essentially equivalent to unregulated selection: "'Kill him if you want' and 'Kill him, but you may spare him if you want' mean the same thing in any man's language."[40] After more than a decade of attempting to administer both requirements, several members of the Court with widely divergent perspectives came to see the incoherence of the foundations of the Court's doctrine. In 1990, Justice Scalia argued that the second doctrine—or "counterdoctrine"—of individualized sentencing "exploded whatever coherence the notion of 'guided discretion' once had." Scalia rejected the view that the two doctrines are merely in tension rather than flatly contradictory: "To acknowledge that 'there perhaps is an inherent tension' [between the two doctrines] . . . is rather like saying that there was perhaps an inherent tension between the Allies and the Axis Powers in World War II." As a result, Scalia (later joined by Justice Clarence Thomas) chose between the two commands and rejected the requirement of individualized sentencing as without constitutional pedigree: "Accordingly, I will not, in this case or in the future, vote to uphold an Eighth Amendment claim that the sentencer's discretion has been unlawfully restricted."[41]

Four years later, Justice Blackmun came to the same recognition of the essential conflict between the doctrines, but reached a different conclusion. Blackmun found himself at a loss to imagine any sort of reform that could mediate between the two conflicting commands. Unlike Scalia and Thomas, however, Blackmun did not resolve to jettison either constitutional command—not merely because of the demands of adhering to precedent, but "because there is a heightened need for both in the administration of death." Consequently, Blackmun concluded that the "death penalty cannot be administered in accord with our Constitution."[42]

One justice's response to the conflict between the need for guidance and the need for individualization was to call for limiting eligibility for capital punishment to a very small group of the worst of the worst—"the tip of the pyramid" of all murderers, in the words of Justice Stevens. If unguided mercy reprieves some from this group, there will still be arbitrariness in choosing among the death eligible, but it will operate on a much smaller scale and with greater assurance that those who make it to the "tip" belong in the group of the death eligible.[43]

Whatever its merits in theory, Stevens's suggested path of sharply narrowing the scope of capital punishment seems to have failed in practice. The whole project of narrowing has vindicated Justice John Marshall Harlan's position in 1971, offered to support the Court's rejection of challenges to standardless capital sentencing under the Due Process Clause: "To identify before the fact those characteristics of criminal homicides and their perpetrators which call for the death penalty, and to express these characteristics in language which can be fairly understood and applied by the sentencing authority, appear to be tasks which are beyond present human ability."[44] The Court could require states to achieve more narrowing than is found under existing statutes, as suggested above, but the sort of super-narrowing contemplated by Stevens seems unachievable given the long-standing failure of states to achieve even modest narrowing. As for Scalia's suggestion of abandoning the individualization requirement as a constitutional essential, the Court's defense of that requirement in the 1976 cases remains compelling: "A process that accords no significance to relevant facets of the character and record of the individual offender ... [impermissibly] treats all persons convicted of a designated offense not as uniquely individual human beings, but as members of a faceless, undifferentiated mass."[45]

Accordingly, the American death penalty must live, if it continues to live at all, with a significant measure of unaccountable discretion and the accompanying arbitrariness such discretion entails. As Scalia conceded in his private memo to his colleagues in *McCleskey,* unaccountable discretion entails not merely arbitrariness but invidious discrimination as well.[46] The individualization requirement guarantees that prosecutors and jurors with a mind to discriminate will inevitably have an opportunity to discriminate. The widespread influence of race on capital sentencing is not amenable to constitutional regulation short of abolition, and the decision to retain the death penalty must accept what *Furman* and the 1976 cases seemed to regard as intolerable: a continuing caste system in the administration of the death penalty.

Apart from these inherent limits on rationalizing death penalty decisions, there remain important structural obstacles to meaningful reform. Many of the most promising interventions to improve the American death penalty require legislative action, executive action, or both. Enhancing death penalty representation, for example, is difficult to accomplish through post-trial review of attorney performance. States must create and fund institutional structures to support capital representation, and state decision makers must ensure that adequate resources are available on a case-by-case basis. Unfortunately, despite the very large costs that are currently incurred in the administration of capital punishment, there is also good reason to believe that the capital process remains substantially underfunded, especially in the area of defense counsel services.

The best reference point for what constitutes minimally adequate capital defense services has been provided by the American Bar Association (ABA). The ABA's *Guidelines for the Appointment and Performance of Defense Counsel in Death Penalty Cases,* originally adopted in 1989 and revised in 2003, offers specific guidance on such matters as the number and qualifications of counsel necessary in capital cases, caseload limits, the nature of investigative and mitigation services necessary to the defense team, and the performance standards to which defense teams should be held. The *Guidelines* also describe the need for a "responsible agency" (such as a public defender organization) to recruit, certify, train, and monitor capital defense counsel. To date, the vast majority of states do not comply with the *Guidelines,* and many do not even come close. In 2001, the ABA created the Death Penalty Moratorium Implementation Project (now the Death Penalty Due Process Review Project) to monitor states' efforts to improve their death penalty systems. Beginning in 2003, the Project specifically investigated the extent to which states were in compliance with the *Guidelines* and by 2015 had published twelve state assessments. The record of compliance is dishearteningly low, with not a single state among the twelve reviewed found to be fully in compliance with any aspect of the *Guidelines* studied. For example, the assessment described Alabama's indigent defense system as "failing" due to the lack of a statewide indigent defense commission, inadequate minimal qualifications and training of capital defense counsel, failure to ensure adequate staffing, failure to provide death-sentenced inmates with appointed counsel in state postconviction proceedings, and very low caps on compensation for defense services.[47]

The current version of the *Guidelines* insists that its requirements are not "aspirational" but rather the minimum necessary conditions for the operation of a fair and accurate capital system. The record of state compliance with the *Guidelines* suggests that the states agree that they are not aspirational—not because the states believe that the *Guidelines* are required, but rather because they simply do not aspire to meet them.

Failure to meet the *Guidelines* should not necessarily be written off as simple intransigence. The costs involved in providing the resources necessary for minimally fair capital justice process can be staggering. Instructive in this regard is the Brian Nichols prosecution in Atlanta. Nichols was charged in a fifty-four-count indictment for an infamous courthouse shooting and escape that killed a judge, a court reporter, a sheriff's deputy, and a federal agent in 2005. In the investigative stage of the case, Nichols's appointed counsel quickly generated costs totaling $1.2 million, wiping out Georgia's available indigent defense funds and requiring postponement of the trial.[48] This price tag covered only the early investigative costs and did not include the costs of Nichols's trial or the years of appellate and postconviction costs that would have followed had the jury returned a death verdict (Nichols was sentenced to life imprisonment). The provision of the resources necessary for fair capital trials and appeals might simply not be possible, or at least not possible without substantial diversion of public funds from other sources—something state legislatures have repeatedly shown themselves unwilling to do in the context of providing indigent defense services.

Another potential meaningful reform of the American capital system would be to insulate actors involved in the decision-making process from outside pressures and influence. For example, instead of leaving unilateral authority to seek death in the hands of local district attorneys, states could structure the charging decision at a state-wide level, utilizing a commission (or collection of state prosecutors) to decide whether death should be sought. Such a process might prevent enormous divergences in capital charging decisions state-wide and ensure that case characteristics—rather than geography—dictate capital outcomes. Or perhaps judges presiding over capital cases (or appeals) could be insulated from popular elections, so that their important decisions in appointing lawyers, approving fees, presiding over trial, and ruling on challenges would not be made in the shadow of electoral considerations.

These sorts of needed reforms are nonstarters in the American system because of the intense politicization of the death penalty. Capital punishment, like the rest of criminal justice in the United States, is politicized *institutionally,* in that some or all of the most important actors in the administration of capital punishment are elected (with the exception of lay jurors). At the same time, capital punishment is politicized *symbolically,* in that it looms much larger than it plausibly should in public discourse because it is a focal point for fears of violent crime and powerful political shorthand for law-and-order policies generally. These two aspects of politicization ensure that the institutional actors responsible for the administration of the capital justice process are routinely subject to intense pressures, which in turn contribute to its arbitrary, discriminatory, and inaccurate administration. There is little hope of successfully addressing these problems in the absence of profound change on the politicization front.

The vast majority of death penalty jurisdictions within the United States have elected rather than appointed prosecutors, and these prosecutors are usually autonomous decision makers in their own small locales (counties). Rarely is there any state or regional review of local decision making or coordination of capital prosecutions. These simple facts of institutional organization generate enormous geographic disparities within most death penalty jurisdictions; ten counties in the United States account for almost 30 percent of all death-sentenced inmates.[49]

In addition, the symbolic politics of capital punishment are very much in play in the election of local prosecutors. Candidates for local district attorney and state attorney general in a wide variety of jurisdictions have run campaigns touting their capital conviction records, even going so far as listing individual defendants sentenced to death. As a practical matter, an elected prosecutor's capital conviction record should be a relatively small part of any prosecutor's portfolio, given the limited number of capital cases that any prosecutorial office will handle—a small fraction of homicide cases, and an even smaller fraction of all serious crimes. But many prosecutorial candidates perceive that the voting public has a special interest in capital cases, both because of the fear generated by the underlying crimes that give rise to capital prosecution and because a prosecutor's support of capital punishment represents in powerful shorthand a prosecutor's "toughness" on crime. These general incentives are troubling in themselves, because they suggest that political incentives might exist to bring capital charges and to win death verdicts quite apart from the underlying merits of cases. Even more troubling is the incentive that might exist to favor those in a position to provide campaign contributions or votes. The racial disparities in capital charging decisions favoring cases with white victims mirror the disparities in political influence in the vast majority of communities.

Judges must also face the intense politicization that surrounds the administration of capital punishment. Almost 90 percent of state judges face some kind of popular election. Politicization of capital punishment in judicial elections famously ousted Chief Justice Rose Bird and colleagues Cruz Reynoso and Joseph Grodin from the California Supreme Court in 1986, as well as Justice Penny White from the Tennessee Supreme Court a decade later. More recently, the judges on the Oklahoma Supreme Court were threatened with impeachment after that court stayed executions pending a determination of whether changes to the state's lethal injection protocol complied with state law. These high-profile examples are only the tip of the iceberg of political pressure. No judge facing election could be unaware of the high salience of capital punishment in the minds of voters, especially with regard to high-profile murders. After an official visit to the United States, the U.N. Special Rapporteur on extrajudicial, summary, or arbitrary executions reported that many of those with whom he spoke in Alabama and Texas (which both have partisan judicial elections) suggested that "judges in both states consider themselves to be under popular pressure to impose and uphold death sentences whenever possible and that decisions to the contrary would lead to electoral defeat."[50]

Governors, too, are influenced by the intense politicization of capital punishment. Like prosecutors and judges, governors have often campaigned on their support for the death penalty, emphasizing their willingness to sign death warrants. While governors are less implicated in the day-to-day workings of the capital justice process than prosecutors and judges, they play a crucial role in the exercise of clemency powers, which the Supreme Court has recognized as an important safeguard against the conviction and execution of the innocent. Some governors, like George Ryan of Illinois, have not been afraid to use their clemency power to respond to concerns about wrongful conviction. However, the trend in the use of the clemency power in capital cases turned sharply downward in the decades since the reinstatement of capital punishment in 1976, at the same time that the trend in death sentencing and executions turned sharply upward. The persistent political salience of capital punishment, as reflected by its prominence at all levels of political discourse, has no doubt affected the willingness of governors to set aside death sentences.

The politicization of the death penalty is a problem in itself and an obstacle to its cure. Capital decisions are made by actors who have strong incentives to push forward in capital cases and support capital verdicts irrespective of the merits, and those actors have little reason to limit their own discretion or attempt to insulate the death penalty from untoward influences. The Supreme Court has little power to address such politicization, and the Court's efforts to ameliorate arbitrariness, discrimination, and error are undermined by its looming presence in the capital sphere.

Hidden Cost of Regulation

On its own terms, constitutional regulation of the death penalty has been unsuccessful—an enormous regulatory effort with little rationalizing effect. But its cost does not end there. At the time the Court intervened, many if not most observers of the American death penalty appreciated the manifold weaknesses of the prevailing regime. Capital trials were rudimentary, capital sentencing provisions were wholly discretionary, the application of the death penalty in Southern rape cases strongly indicated pervasive racial discrimination, and the extremely rare application of the death penalty overall undermined any claim that the death penalty secured significant social benefits.

But the dramatic introduction of judicial oversight seemed to revitalize the practice in the decades following *Furman*, in no small part because of the Court's ownership of the issue. The quarter century of regulation post-*Furman* can fairly be understood as a period in which judicial regulation appeared to legitimate the American death penalty by making participants in the criminal justice system and the public at large more comfortable with the death penalty than they otherwise would or should have been. By "legitimate," we do not mean a process in which the Court *actually* justified faith in the capital system, but rather one in which the Court induced a *false or exaggerated* belief in the normative justifiability of the workings of the American death penalty.

The legitimating effect of the Court's intervention worked on several levels. The Court's focus on controlling the discretion of capital sentencers created a false aura of rationality, even science, around the necessarily moral task of deciding life or death. Robert Weisberg, a Stanford law professor, has argued convincingly that the Court's attempt to tame the "existential moment" of decision in the capital sentencing process had the effect of reducing the anxiety that judges and juries feel about exercising their sentencing power. The Court's capital punishment law has permitted institutional actors "to reassure themselves that the sanctions they inflict flow inevitably from demands of neutral, disinterested legal principles, rather than from their own choice and power." Weisberg powerfully, if anecdotally, illustrated this point by comparing jury instructions and closing arguments in capital hearings before and after the innovations of *Furman* and *Gregg*. Whereas pre-*Furman* jury instructions "aggressively reinforced the notion that the jury could not look to the law for any relief from the moral question of the death sentence," post-*Furman* instructions and prosecutorial arguments urged capital jurors to "realize that their apparently painful choice is no choice at all—that the law is making it for them" through a form of "penal arithmetic" that tallies aggravating and mitigating circumstances. Weisberg's impressionistic account is bolstered by the empirical work of the Baldus group, whose study of sentencing patterns in Georgia revealed a higher per capita sentencing rate after the Court's "reform" of capital sentencing schemes.[51]

The extensive review process required by the Court's constitutionalization of capital punishment also diluted sentencers' sense of responsibility for imposing the death penalty. The Court's Eighth Amendment jurisprudence itself has recognized the ways in which knowledge of a lack of final responsibility for imposing the death sentence can impermissibly bias a sentencing jury's decision. In the mid-1980s, the Court reversed a death sentence imposed after a Mississippi prosecutor was permitted to argue to the sentencing jury that its decision to impose the death sentence would be reviewed by the state supreme court. Such an argument, opined the Court, impermissibly denigrated the jury's sense of "awesome responsibility" for imposing the death penalty, especially because it was simply not true that appellate courts redo the moral calculus assigned to the sentencing jury.[52] Yet, what the Court's Eighth Amendment law forbids the prosecutor or judge to tell a seated sentencing jury is exactly what the post-*Furman* law "tells" every potential juror. The Court's constitutionalization of capital punishment has necessarily entailed systematic federal review of all capital cases and has prompted much greater state appellate review as well. Given the wide coverage of such review in the popular press, as well as the high visibility of reversals of death sentences, capital sentencing juries (not to mention judges!) must know that their imposition of a death sentence is not the end of the matter, but rather the beginning of a lengthy chain of review. Yet this "fact," of which we presume a large number of jurors are aware, is no more "true" than is the Mississippi prosecutor's argument: appellate courts do not generally review the moral appropriateness of the imposition of the death penalty. Rather, as we have demonstrated, the vast majority of the decisions regulating state death penalty practices touch peripheral rather than core issues. The Court's death penalty law thus leaves sentencing juries with a false sense that their power is safely circumscribed.

Each of these arguments about capital sentencers can fairly be extended to other actors within the capital system. Just as sentencers may be comforted by the apparent mathematical precision of modern capital sentencing regimes, prosecutors may feel emboldened in seeking the imposition of the death penalty. And just as sentencers may be reassured by the existence of layers of review between their sentence and the moment of execution (if it ever comes), state appellate courts may be reassured by the existence of federal habeas review, and governors may feel that any sentence that survives both state and federal review is not an appropriate vehicle for exercising the power of clemency. Two death penalty scholars have made this type of argument in attempting to account for the drastic post-*Furman* decline in the use of the clemency power. Hugo Bedau has argued that the decline in clemency resulted from "the perception . . . that death sentences are now meted out by trial courts with all the fairness that is humanly possible, even if in the dark pre-*Furman* past they were not." Franklin Zimring has made a similar argument, observing that in the post-*Furman* world of capital punishment, executions are regarded as the "moral responsibility of Supreme Court justices" rather than of state governors. The diffusion of moral responsibility that occurs when a decision is perceived (correctly or not) to be divided among a number of participants—the aptly described "problem of many hands"—affects all participants in the decision-making process, which in the capital context may include everyone from law enforcement agents to the actual executioner.[53]

Some of the arguments concerning legitimation for participants in the capital process (what might be called "internal" legitimation) may carry over to society at large. Weisberg, one of the strongest proponents of the internal legitimation argument, doubts this broader legitimating effect on these grounds: "Most Americans are probably only barely aware how capital punishment operates or fails to operate, much less how the law of capital punishment has developed."[54] Alan Hyde has generalized this objection to apply to "external" legitimation arguments of all sorts: "If legal decisions and rules are largely unknown to the population [and] not well-regarded when known, how could they . . . legitimate an order?"[55] Although Weisberg and Hyde are probably correct that members of the general public do not know much about the intricacies of the Court's death penalty doctrine, our guess is that they *think* they know a great deal. They know about the extensive review of capital sentences, and their ignorance about the precise nature of such review actually enhances the legitimating effect of such "knowledge." Similarly, the delays that occur between death sentence and execution are matters of common popular knowledge; by the late 1980s, the pressure on state and federal lawmakers to address exactly those delays had become increasingly intense. Public perceptions about the nature of death penalty regulation legitimated the practice *not* because such regulation is "well-regarded" (in Hyde's parlance), but rather because the elaborateness of the Court's death penalty jurisprudence fueled the public's impression in the decades immediately following *Gregg* that any death sentences that were imposed and finally upheld were the product of a rigorous—indeed, *too* rigorous—system of constraints.

The first decades of judicial regulation of the death penalty in the wake of *Furman* illustrate how institutions can take on lives of their own and find a place for themselves different from the one envisioned by their creators. The death penalty abolitionists who self-consciously litigated *Furman* and *Gregg*, hoping that their arguments would lead to the end of capital punishment in America, and the coalition of centrist justices who took on a more limited reformist mission, would no doubt be surprised to observe the extent to which the creation of constitutional death penalty law legitimated capital punishment. This body of law did so by denying contradictions between individualized consideration and fairness over a range of cases, by masking the moral choice and wide discretion of capital sentencers, and by promoting the appearance of intensive regulation despite its virtual absence. It is deeply ironic that the impulse to abolish and reform the death penalty produced a body of law that substantially stabilized and perpetuated American capital punishment as a social practice, at least in the short term. By the mid-1990s, death sentences and executions had climbed dramatically, legislative energies were directed toward curtailing review of capital convictions, some states (such as New York) sought reinstatement of the death penalty, and polls revealed growing public support for the punishment. At that time, it seemed as though constitutional regulation had produced the worst of all possible worlds: the Court's detailed attention to the death penalty had generated negligible improvements over the pre-*Furman* era, yet that attention had helped people to accept to a much greater degree our failed system of capital punishment.[56]

The legitimating effects of the death penalty, while powerful, eventually were undermined by a confluence of factors, not least of which was the discovery of numerous wrongly convicted inmates on American death rows. Moreover, by the turn of the millennium, constitutional regulation showed another face. In addition to its legitimating power, constitutional regulation began to reveal some of its destabilizing potential—that is, the ways in which judicial regulation of the death penalty has sown the seeds for a period of surprising new fragility for capital punishment. This destabilizing dynamic is yet another unintended and underappreciated aspect of the modern American death penalty.

CHAPTER SIX

An Unsustainable System?

B Y THE MID-1990S, the death penalty appeared to be an entrenched American institution. Thirty-eight states embraced the penalty, and death sentences and executions reached their modern-era highs. Capital jurisdictions were searching for ways to expand rather than limit the death penalty's reach, and few public officials questioned the propriety of its escalating use. But the next two decades saw a stunning reversal of fortune. Executions nationwide began their decline in 2000, falling from their 1999 high of 98 to an average of fewer than 40 per year 15 years later. Death sentencing dropped even more dramatically, from a high of 315 per year nationwide in 1996 to a low of 49 in 2015—an 84 percent decline. Seven jurisdictions jettisoned capital punishment, reducing the number of states with the death penalty on the books to 31. Polling data also reflected declining public support for the death penalty, with opposition to the death penalty registering its highest levels since the pre-*Furman* era.[1]

These indicia, impressive as they are, fail to capture the magnitude of the shift in mood regarding American capital punishment. Whereas executions in the 1980s were often greeted by enthusiastic death penalty supporters outside the prison walls, such celebrations essentially disappeared by 2010. Political campaigns, which previously elicited nothing short of ardent support for the death penalty, now include candidates—even at the national level—whose support ranges from tentative to nonexistent. The media's coverage of the death penalty includes a constant stream of pronouncements heralding the end of days for American capital punishment. Despite the frequency of such declarations, it is difficult to find politicians, advocacy organizations, or ordinary citizens lamenting the death penalty's predicted demise.

The story of the death penalty's seemingly sudden fall, coming so quickly on the heels of its sudden rise, involves numerous plots and subplots. Among them, no doubt, are the dramatic drop in violent crime rates, the erosion of criminal justice policy as a wedge issue in American politics, and the increased isolation of the United States at the international level as a jurisdiction retaining the death penalty.

But a surprisingly significant contributor to the new fragility of the American death penalty is the same development that facilitated its rise: the continuing course of constitutional regulation by the federal courts. Just as judicial oversight legitimated the American death penalty in the short term, easing its growth by ameliorating concerns about its administration, so too has regulation undermined the prospects of the American death penalty for the long term, in ways that seem obvious in retrospect but that have rarely been acknowledged or explored.

The destabilizing power of constitutional regulation is reflected in numerous developments. Regulation has led to the creation of permanent institutional structures, including capital defender organizations, intricate and lengthy capital trials, and multiple tiers of judicial review, all of which exert enormous pressures on the capital system. Some of the pressures are fiscal: the skyrocketing costs associated with the death penalty have become perhaps the central threat to its continued viability. Apart from costs, though, regulation has turned the extended delays that were part of the moratorium strategy in the 1960s into a permanent and irreversible feature of the capital justice system. Executions are no longer the ordinary or even expected result of death sentences in many jurisdictions, and despite being relatively undemanding, constitutional regulation has contributed mightily to that result. The failure of states to consummate death sentences with executions is an existential threat to retention.

Two of the other primary causes of the present fragility— widespread concern about wrongful convictions and the introduction of life without parole as the default alternative punishment to death—are by-products of the newly regulated environment. Regulation has also established a new baseline of expectations for the rationality of the American capital system, and the failure of the system to meet those expectations has provided several important actors— including Supreme Court justices—a vantage point from which to challenge its continued administration. In short, regulation has contributed to the transformation of the death penalty into its current bloated, inefficient form, which hardly anyone endorses. At the same time, having made the choice to regulate based on genuine concerns of fairness and reliability, the Court cannot un-ring the bell and forego regulation altogether, much less tear down the edifice of institutional arrangements that has grown in response to its intervention. Judicial regulation, once embraced as the alternative to judicial abolition, may yet be the death penalty's greatest threat.

The Burdens of Regulation

The Court's actual demands on the capital system are quite minimal. But the content of the Court's regulation has mattered much less to capital practices on the ground than the simple fact of regulation itself. When the Court embarked on the regulatory enterprise, it triggered major shifts in the nature of capital representation, capital trials, and capital appeals. Those shifts, in turn, have dramatically raised the costs of capital punishment across many dimensions, undermining its sustainability going forward.

Before the modern era, capital cases were handled by appointed lawyers who generally had no specialized knowledge or training related to the death penalty. The standard of trial practice was quite poor, as these lawyers approached their cases with the same strategies operative in other serious felony cases, primarily aiming for an acquittal or conviction on a lesser included offense. The prevailing statutory schemes in the 1960s had discouraged the development and presentation of mitigating evidence, with many states forbidding the introduction of such evidence except to the extent that it bore on the underlying question of guilt or innocence.[2] The Court's rejection of mandatory schemes, though, generated a new interest in mitigation. Both trial lawyers and postconviction lawyers began to focus on more extensive investigation and development of mitigating evidence. By the late 1980s to early 1990s, a new professional role emerged for "mitigation specialists," who would coordinate the development of wide-ranging evidence, including a defendant's medical history, educational history, family and social history, and religious and cultural influences. By 2000, the gold standard for capital trial practice (though not the reality in all or even most cases) became the utilization of a capital defense "team" with much greater role differentiation between lawyers, investigators, and mitigation specialists. The Court had not directly required such intensive trial-phase efforts; indeed, the Court did not identify a case of ineffective capital trial representation until more than 25 years post-*Furman*. But the new state statutory schemes triggered by *Furman* highlighted the importance of mitigation, and the growing cadre of death penalty lawyers and related specialists began to focus on the newly established "punishment phase" in bifurcated trials.[3]

The range of organizations supporting capital trial efforts exploded in the decades following the 1976 cases. In the 1980s, federally funded resource centers opened both to provide direct representation and to train lawyers engaged in such representation. Although many of the resource centers focused on postconviction litigation, they also brought energy and expertise to trial-level capital defense efforts. The federal government subsequently withdrew support from the resource centers, but alternative funding saw many of these entities reemerge as nonprofits with an identical mission. In Texas, for example, after the Texas Resource Center was defunded and closed its doors in the mid-1990s, its lawyers immediately founded the Texas Defender Service, a nonprofit that continues to provide sample motions, support, and training to Texas capital trial lawyers through its "trial project." Some states have created public defender offices specializing in capital defense, ensuring that capital defendants will have attorneys both committed to and trained in best practices. Many law schools have created "capital punishment clinics" to train their students in capital advocacy and to provide assistance to lawyers engaged in such representation.

At the national level, a variety of high-powered nonprofits have emerged to raise the level of capital representation and to advocate for the restriction and abolition of the death penalty. The Equal Justice Initiative (EJI), for example, headed by Bryan Stevenson, has worked tirelessly to improve the level of representation in Alabama, a state that has lagged far behind other jurisdictions in supporting capital representation services. Prior to his work at EJI, Stevenson was trained as a staff attorney at the Southern Center for Human Rights (SCHR), which was established in 1976 in response to the reinstatement of the death penalty and concerns about deplorable conditions in Southern prisons. By the 1980s, Stephen Bright, the longtime director of SCHR, emerged as the successor to Anthony Amsterdam as the most visible and eloquent critic of and litigator against American capital practices. For example, in the Court's 2015–2016 term, almost four decades post-*Gregg*, Bright argued a case challenging a prosecutor's use of peremptory challenges to exclude black jurors from a capital jury sitting in judgment of a black man charged with the murder of a white woman in Georgia.[4]

Organizations such as EJI and SCHR attract dozens of young law students and young lawyers to the growing network of indigent capital defense attorneys. Stevenson and Bright have had ongoing relationships with Harvard, Yale, and NYU law schools where they teach classes on capital punishment. Through their capital work in the South and teaching in the North, Bright and Stevenson have created a pipeline of elite lawyers flowing to areas of critical need, in many ways mirroring the flood of civil rights activists from the Northeast to the South during the upheaval of the 1960s. The primary difference, though, is that this new pipeline seems permanent and institutionalized, with the assistance of private nonprofit funding and the support of elite law schools.

The breadth of institutional and organizational support for capital defense efforts is reflected in the extraordinary training opportunities available to lawyers working in the capital defense field. Law schools at several universities, including Santa Clara, Iowa, Michigan, and DePaul, host (or have hosted) "death penalty colleges" to provide intensive training in various aspects of capital defense. Capital lawyers routinely flock to Colorado for specialized training in capital jury selection, and the distinctive "Colorado Method" has emerged as the state-of-the-art approach for defense lawyers. The method involves identifying and empowering jurors disposed toward life, and encouraging pro-death jurors to respect the views of life-oriented jurors during the deliberation process.

None of these forms of training or support existed prior to *Furman*. States did not have capital defender offices or capital resource centers, law schools did not house capital punishment clinics, and there were no nonprofit organizations devoted primarily to improving capital lawyering or providing direct representation in capital cases. Today's specialized capital defense practitioners, which include probably hundreds of lawyers and many more professionals like mitigation specialists and investigators, stand in stark contrast to the small handful of lawyers working on capital cases at the LDF and a few other organizations in the pre-*Furman* world. Even though the quality of capital representation did not change overnight (and in some jurisdictions has not changed enough), constitutional regulation effectively created the profession of capital defense work, and that transformation ensured that capital litigation would never be the same.

The emergence of institutional structures supporting the defense mission in capital trials is directly responsible for numerous changes to capital trial practice. Capital trial lawyers are advised to seek extensive resources, including funding for investigators and a wide range of experts, such as forensic experts for guilt-innocence phase issues like ballistics or DNA evaluation, psychiatric experts for mental health and competency issues, and psychological experts for intellectual disability evaluation. Trial lawyers are encouraged to seek adequate time for investigation and preparation of their cases, which may require numerous postponements of trial dates that are often set without regard to the new tasks associated with capital defense. Most fundamentally, capital trial lawyers, working with their teams, must engage in comprehensive mitigation investigation uncovering all aspects of the defendant's personal and family history, documenting psychiatric and intellectual impairments, and identifying relevant aspects of the alleged offense. Capital trial lawyers are offered training in the presentation and negotiation of plea offers, which require not only extensive pretrial investigation but ongoing, meaningful client contact as well. Such efforts, performed professionally, can credibly document both the extensiveness of the mitigation case that could be presented at trial and the likely costs that would be incurred if the case continued to that phase. All of these defense efforts require a substantial commitment of resources prior to trial, and they ensure that capital trials, when they do occur, will be more contested and protracted than either the capital trials of the pre-*Furman* era or their noncapital counterparts in the present regime. As a consequence, the total cost of capital prosecutions far exceeds the costs associated with noncapital trials.

If settlement talks fail, defense lawyers often seek extensive, individual voir dire, in an effort to remove "automatic death" jurors from the pool and to identify strong and open-minded jurors who might vote for life and resist pressures to go along with the crowd. Whereas jury selection in noncapital cases rarely occupies more than a day or two of court and attorney time, capital jury selection can take weeks or even months. Again, the cost and length of such efforts is not commensurate with the level of protections the Court actually affords capital defendants in the process. The Court has not protected capital defendants against the wholesale exclusion of jurors skeptical of capital punishment despite its landmark decision prohibiting that practice. And the Court rarely finds error when state courts refuse to exclude jurors at the other extreme who are strongly skeptical of mitigation.[5] But the mere fact that jury selection in capital cases is subject to constitutional regulation makes capital voir dire extremely expensive and time-consuming in many cases.

When the capital trial starts, the professionals sitting next to the defendant frequently reflect the new norms of practice. The team will likely include two capital attorneys, and might include a lawyer charged with the responsibility of identifying and preserving potential points of error that could be asserted on appeal. The content of the defense at the guilt-innocence phase will often look much different from its pre-*Furman* counterpart. Instead of focusing primarily on securing an acquittal or a conviction on a lesser charge, the defense team will try to "build a bridge" to the punishment phase by developing a theme during the guilt-innocence portion that will improve the prospects for a life sentence at the punishment phase. Experience with bifurcated schemes has taught capital defense attorneys that jurors are largely unreceptive to the more traditional tactic of denying guilt and then seeking mercy ("I didn't do it, but if I did, I was provoked and mentally unstable"). To be successful, capital defense lawyers must plant the seeds of the mitigation case during the guilt-innocence phase and create a continuity of argument and evidence so that jurors who found the defendant guilty might find an easier—and less dissonant—path to a life sentence.

The transformation of capital trial practice is not uniform and the newly emerged standards are as frequently violated as they are observed. But the cost of these new professional norms are felt in virtually every capital prosecution, because the prosecution's choice to seek death and go to trial opens the door to enormous expenditures of both time and money. The prosecution must account for the possibility of resources flowing into the defense case and prepare accordingly. A capital trial can consume hundreds, even thousands, of hours of prosecutorial time. The threat of prolonged, expensive litigation both at trial and in subsequent appeals provides the single most important incentive to take the death penalty off the table.

The Court's constitutional intervention also triggered a transformation of capital appeals. Capital cases were generally accorded no special treatment in the pre-*Furman* era, and state supreme courts largely had discretion over whether to entertain challenges to particular capital verdicts. The claims raised by death-sentenced inmates in the pre-*Furman* regime were little different from the claims asserted by their noncapital counterparts, focusing on ordinary police or prosecutorial misconduct, including allegations of illegally seized evidence and coerced confessions. But beginning in the 1970s, states almost uniformly moved to mandatory appellate review in state supreme courts, partly to comply with *Furman's* perceived mandate of enhanced reliability in capital proceedings and partly to facilitate review of the many distinctive constitutional claims now implicated in every capital case. As a result, capital appeals in many jurisdictions have become expensive, time-consuming affairs, often stretching over several years or, in rare cases, close to a decade. In some jurisdictions, states have created special defender offices to represent death-sentenced offenders on direct appeal, and in those jurisdictions in particular, the briefing and argument can be extensive and intricate, with briefs running into the hundreds of pages. Again, nothing in the Court's jurisprudence *mandates* special treatment for capital cases on direct appeal, but the move to constitutional regulation predictably expanded the significance and scale of direct appeals in capital cases.

A similar story can be told about state postconviction and federal habeas proceedings. Prior to the 1960s and 1970s, states had complicated and inefficient systems for reviewing claims in postconviction proceedings (sometimes referred to as "state habeas"), which primarily focus on claims alleging "new facts" outside of the trial record, such as ineffective assistance of counsel or prosecutorial misconduct. After *Furman* and the 1976 cases, states recognized that it was to their advantage to modernize their systems to facilitate postconviction review of capital convictions and sentences. For the first time, many states authorized the appointment of counsel for indigent death-sentenced inmates to help them navigate state postconviction proceedings, even though states rarely if ever provide counsel to noncapital inmates for postconviction review. Congress likewise established an unprecedented right for indigent death-sentenced inmates to receive counsel in federal habeas proceedings. Such proceedings provide an opportunity to assert federal claims relating to the constitutionality of a state inmate's conviction and sentence in a federal court after the conclusion of state court review.[6]

These developments ensure that virtually every capital inmate will have access to counsel in state and federal habeas review. As a result, the level and intricacy of habeas practice have changed dramatically.

For most of the twentieth century, state and federal habeas claims were advanced by inmates themselves, with handwritten pleadings arriving at the courthouse in large numbers to be reviewed by skeptical judges (or judicial assistants). Such review was not thought to be part of the ordinary path of criminal adjudication, and that path was deemed essentially completed with the denial of an inmate's direct appeal. With the advent of constitutional regulation, and the Court's constant engagement with states' new capital schemes, the stakes involved in habeas litigation grew tremendously. The Court's yearly pronouncements often called into question the legitimacy of capital verdicts obtained years before, and inmates who had lost on direct appeal would seek the benefit of the Court's changing (and confusing) doctrines.

In the first two decades post-*Furman,* state habeas proceedings were often chaotic because the rules governing such proceedings were unclear and often improvised. Many states had not yet created a mechanism for appointing habeas counsel, and there were no real experts in conducting state postconviction litigation. Defense lawyers in noncapital cases would occasionally represent paying clients in such proceedings, but the vast majority of cases involved inmates representing themselves followed by predictably cursory reviews of their claims. The level of practice was slightly higher in federal court, but the same dynamic was present: few criminal defense attorneys representing state inmates regularly litigated in federal court, and claims by state prisoners (which included not only challenges to criminal convictions but claims relating to conditions of confinement) tended to receive less scrutiny than other matters on the federal court docket.

By conferring a right to paid counsel for death-sentenced inmates, state and federal habeas proceedings ultimately became a central part of the capital appeals process. For the first time in American history, a new group of lawyers emerged with expertise in litigating in the habeas context. On the state habeas side, lawyers began to understand their role as requiring intensive investigation of the circumstances culminating in their clients' convictions, particularly the level of representation provided at trial. Prior to the professionalization of the state habeas role, lawyers in state habeas proceedings tended to do minimal investigation and often simply resubmitted claims that had already lost on direct appeal.[7] In addition, many states now have created capital state postconviction offices, ensuring that death-sentenced inmates have access to lawyers with specialized knowledge about the functions of the state habeas forum and the corresponding obligations of state habeas counsel. On the federal habeas side, some capital jurisdictions have specially created federal offices providing representation to death-sentenced inmates in federal court ("Capital Habeas Units" or "CHUs"). Like their counterparts in state habeas offices, these lawyers have expertise relating to the increasingly complex procedural doctrines governing the habeas forum. In other jurisdictions, federally appointed lawyers representing death-sentenced inmates are guided by consulting attorneys funded by the Administrative Office of the U.S. Courts.

The story of the gradual professionalization of state and federal habeas representation should not obscure certain facts. Notwithstanding the general trend toward higher representational standards, many death-sentenced inmates receive poor representation in one or both of these forums. Even well-represented inmates face enormous obstacles to obtaining relief. State courts remain wary of "retrying" cases in state habeas and often are unwilling to credit new facts asserted by defense-side state habeas counsel, no matter how compelling. The scope of the federal habeas forum has been drastically reduced by Congress in direct response to the perceived threat of federal habeas review to the efficient operation of state capital systems.[8] In both state and federal habeas, death-sentenced inmates encounter increasingly strict procedural rules, which often prevent those courts from addressing the merits of the inmates' claims.

But in terms of their effect on the status of the death penalty, the ability of death-sentenced inmates to ultimately prevail in state and federal habeas matters less than their increased access to those forums. Congress and the states have made it much more difficult, expensive, and time-consuming to translate death sentences into executions by affording state death-sentenced prisoners a right to litigate in state and federal habeas and by providing increasingly professionalized lawyers to undertake that representation. Constitutional regulation transformed what were once peripheral mechanisms of review into part of the protracted main event. In jurisdictions with strongly embedded due process values, these proceedings now occupy decades of time and substantial resources. Even in jurisdictions with less commitment to providing adequate resources, counsel, and review, these proceedings significantly extend the time between conviction and sentence. Like many of the other transformations in capital representation, the increased importance of state and federal habeas review was inspired but not required by the Court's death penalty jurisprudence. The Court has never constitutionally mandated state postconviction review, even in capital cases, nor has it insisted that states afford death-sentenced inmates counsel in either state or federal habeas proceedings. The Court has also deferred to Congress in shaping the scope of the federal habeas forum.[9] But the Court's choice to subject capital cases to an ever-burgeoning set of constitutional rules caused institutional actors—legislators, judges, advocacy organizations—to insist upon new institutional arrangements to facilitate the processing of constitutional claims. And those institutional arrangements, more than the content of the Court's death penalty jurisprudence, has substantially eroded the power of states to conduct executions.

The two primary destabilizing consequences of the Court's constitutional regulation are increased cost and delay. Prior to the modern era, the issue of cost was almost exclusively a pro–death penalty argument. Defenders of the practice highlighted the expenses associated with the long-term incarceration of non-death-sentenced offenders. Today, the new institutional arrangements and practices flowing from constitutional regulation have transformed the issue of cost into the most pressing consideration on the anti–death penalty side. Capital prosecutions are now vastly more expensive than their noncapital counterparts, and numerous studies confirm this new reality. A recent study commissioned by the Nevada legislature revealed that prosecutions in which the death penalty is sought cost about $500,000 more than comparable cases in which death is not sought, almost doubling the state's expense. Similar studies in Indiana and North Carolina likewise have documented the significantly increased costs associated with capital prosecutions in those jurisdictions. In California, capital punishment costs are astonishingly higher, with a comprehensive study finding that the death penalty cost the state an additional $4 billion in the post-1976 era. The increased costs of capital trials (and subsequent appeals) are not offset by incarceration costs, in part because death row incarceration (often solitary confinement) tends to be vastly more expensive than confinement in the general prison population, and in part because of the increasingly extended time of death row incarceration. In states like California, death penalty expenses include both the extravagant costs of capital trials and appeals *and* the costs associated with life imprisonment, given that so few inmates reach the death chamber.[10]

The growing appreciation of the increased cost of the death penalty, both in absolute terms and in comparison to life imprisonment, has contributed to the striking decline in capital sentences. Media accounts of the financial consequences of capital trials for local communities began appearing with regularity about a decade ago. In Texas, the 2009 prosecution of Levi King received considerable attention because King was already under a life sentence in Missouri when a Texas prosecutor decided to seek death for killings King committed in Texas. The rural county spent almost 10 percent of its budget ($750,000) for the initial expenses in King's defense, and the prosecution resulted in a life sentence. News reports indicated that the costs associated with the decision to pursue the death penalty against King contributed to the decision of county commissioners to withhold employee raises and increase local tax rates. As the King episode suggests, prosecutors increasingly must defend their decisions to seek death in light of the large financial obligations that choice entails, whereas prosecutors in the very recent past were more likely to have to answer for their decisions to take death off the table.[11]

Apart from contributing to the radical decline in capital prosecutions, the issue of cost has been prominent in state decisions to repeal capital statutes in the modern era, especially in the jurisdictions that abolished the death penalty after the economic downturn of 2008 (New Mexico, Illinois, Connecticut, Maryland, and Nebraska).

The recent repeal in Nebraska, the only "red" state to abolish during this period, was successful in part because of the ability of conservative death penalty opponents to cast the capital system as "another big government program."[12] The issue of cost is especially compelling in states with few executions, as opponents can draw attention to the absurdity of the status quo with a new metric: cost per execution. In California, for example, dividing the additional costs California has spent on capital punishment since 1976 by the small number of executions consummated during that period (13) yields a cost per execution approaching $250 million, a truly mind-boggling figure.[13] In several of the other states that recently abolished the death penalty, the metric likewise reveals the fiscal folly of the modern death penalty enterprise (Nebraska, Connecticut, and New Mexico all have had three or fewer executions since 1976, despite spending tens of millions of dollars in capital-related costs).

Constitutional regulation has also produced enormous delays between sentences and executions. In the mid-1980s, the average time between death sentences and executions nationwide was about six years; by 2012, that time had grown to over fifteen years.[14] But that shift—reflecting the extended time on death row of inmates actually executed—does not capture the fact that executions are simply not occurring in a large number of jurisdictions. In 2015, only six out of thirty-one death penalty states conducted any executions at all, the fewest since 1988. If, for example, California and Pennsylvania were to resume executions and executed inmates in order of their arrival on death row, the average time prior to execution would skyrocket. Across the country, death row inmates are growing older, and many will likely die outside of the execution chamber. In California, inmates face the prospect of spending as many as four or five decades awaiting execution (or natural death).

These delays—which show no signs of abating and are likely to increase rather than decrease in the coming years—present numerous, interconnected problems. At the most basic level, delays raise costs because extended death row incarceration has become a huge expense for state capital systems. Delays also undermine three of the primary goals supporting retention: deterrence, retribution, and incapacitation. Deterrence is attenuated when it is widely understood that an execution will occur, if at all, only after many years or (more likely) decades of incarceration. Moreover, the retributive value of executions is diminished when the person executed has lived a "second lifetime" on death row, implicating deep psychological questions about whether a person executed twenty years after the offense is the "same" person who had been condemned two decades earlier.[15] The reliance on the death penalty to incapacitate dangerous offenders is also undermined when incarceration, rather than execution, prevents violent behavior as the inmate ages. Delays thus pose a special problem for jurisdictions like Texas, which require a finding of future dangerousness as a prerequisite to a death sentence. The prospect of executing elderly, infirm (and presumably nondangerous) inmates creates other problems as well. In Nevada, the legislature recently approved construction of a new death chamber at a cost of almost $1 million in part because the existing chamber was not compliant with the Americans with Disabilities Act (ADA). Among other things, legislators feared that the inability of disabled witnesses, prison personnel, and inmates facing execution to access the chamber would lead to disruptive litigation preventing executions.[16] It is hard to imagine a more fitting image of America's odd—and exceptional—commitment to both new-world regulatory values and old-world punishment.

Most significantly for the offender, extended death row incarceration presents special problems of cruelty, especially given the prevailing harsh conditions of death row confinement. Condemned inmates now face multiple punishments: lengthy incarceration in solitary-style conditions; the anguish of perpetually living under a sentence of death; and actual execution. Delays in achieving executions are thus an existential threat to the death penalty, because they deepen three of the central anxieties surrounding its use—its excessive cost, its overall effectiveness in achieving social goals, and its cruelty.

The destabilizing effects of the new costs and delays associated with capital punishment are aggravated by perhaps the most widely appreciated problem for the American death penalty: the issue of wrongful convictions. Prior to the late 1990s, the American public seemed relatively untroubled by the possibility of innocents getting caught in the death penalty net, in part because of the Court's new and highly visible role in supervising capital practices. The extent of the public's confidence in the death penalty system was reflected in the muted, almost nonexistent response to the Court's unwillingness in 1993 to answer "yes" to the provocatively framed question it declined to answer in *Herrera v. Collins:* "Do the Eighth and Fourteenth Amendments permit a state to execute an individual who is innocent of the crime for which he or she was convicted and sentenced to death?"[17] But that confidence was shaken by the alarming discovery of numerous innocents erroneously sentenced to death, particularly in Illinois. The *Chicago Tribune* detailed systemic problems in the Illinois criminal justice system traceable in part to prosecutorial misconduct.[18] Northwestern University subsequently hosted a landmark conference in 1998 on wrongful convictions and the death penalty attended by more than 1,000 lawyers, students, and death penalty opponents; the advertisement for the conference declared that 74 people had been wrongfully sentenced to death and invited attendees to "come meet them."[19] The discovery of innocents on Illinois's death row, combined with journalistic accounts of rampant prosecutorial misconduct and the advocacy of Northwestern University's newly created Center on Wrongful Convictions, contributed to the decision of Republican Governor George Ryan to declare a moratorium on executions that was ultimately followed by Illinois's decision to repeal its capital statute.[20]

At the same time, new developments in DNA technology during the 1990s made it possible to reevaluate evidence in dormant cases— particularly sex offenses—leading to the exoneration of both capital and noncapital prisoners. The 2000 publication of *Actual Innocence,* which recounted the efforts of Barry Scheck and Peter Neufeld— pioneers in the postconviction use of DNA to uncover erroneous convictions, contributed to the mounting perception that our criminal justice system is fallible even in, and perhaps *especially* in, capital cases. Concerns about innocence and the possibility of wrongful convictions triggered a wave of new circumspection about the wisdom of capital punishment. Those concerns no doubt have contributed to many of the key developments—declining death sentences, declining executions, declining poll support, and state repeals of capital statutes—which reflect the growing weakness of American capital punishment.[21]

The innocence issue has been so powerful because it attaches names and faces to the death penalty's flaws, as illustrated by the evocative 1998 Northwestern University advertisement for the public to "meet" the wrongfully convicted. Issues such as arbitrariness and discrimination, which require detailed knowledge and complicated statistics to appreciate fully (as well as concern for manifestly guilty offenders), have never gained much popular traction. The continuing power of the innocence issue is partly attributable to the ongoing stream of cases involving wrongfully convicted death row inmates. The recent exoneration of Henry McCollum in 2015 was especially poignant because Justice Scalia had used McCollum's case as the poster child for death penalty retention in his counter to Justice Blackmun's declaration that he would "no longer tinker with the machinery of death."[22] Even more troubling and destabilizing are cases in which wrongful convictions have appeared to result in wrongful executions. In Texas, Cameron Todd Willingham was convicted on the basis of junk arson science and many—if not most—observers regard him to have been the victim of a wrongful execution. Because of the extensive posthumous media coverage of his case, Willingham is probably the most well-known person whom Texas has executed in the modern era among a very large (500+) group. It is his name and image, rather than the names and images of clearly guilty murderers, that currently serve as the face of the Texas death penalty. A recent book by James Liebman makes a compelling case that Texas also wrongfully executed Carlos DeLuna more than a decade before Willingham's execution.[23] As more accounts of wrongful executions—not merely wrongful convictions—emerge, the perception of the problem as endemic rather than episodic will likely further weaken the death penalty, even in states uncommonly committed to the practice.

Though the innocence issue might be regarded as something of an unexpected gift to death penalty opponents, it is fairly viewed as a foreseeable by-product of the Court's regulatory efforts. The Court's regulation fueled the creation of a new set of institutional actors committed to capital defense. Regulation ensures that death-sentenced inmates will have representation and resources more or less continually from the time charges are filed until the time of execution. And the existence of the death penalty and its multiple tiers of review increase the likelihood that errors in capital convictions will be identified at some point during the protracted process.[24] Moreover, despite the loss in *Herrera,* the continued pressure of lawyers representing inmates in state postconviction proceedings has caused many states to suspend or limit procedural obstacles to the review of claims of innocence advanced by death-sentenced inmates.[25] Without the presence of an institutionalized postconviction bar, it is unlikely that post-trial claims of innocence would command as much attention and resources as they currently receive.

Just as importantly, the visibility and (at least partial) success of the LDF's efforts on behalf of death-sentenced inmates laid the groundwork for the emergence of numerous nonprofits devoted to the concerns of American prisoners. The LDF's death penalty work illustrates the potential for small numbers of lawyers to promote meaningful change. The central players in the "innocence movement," organizations like Northwestern University's Center on Wrongful Convictions and Scheck and Neufeld's Innocence Project, bring important energy and expertise to the enterprise, making it much more likely that wrongful convictions will be exposed. Moreover, the collection of nonprofits focused exclusively or primarily on American capital punishment, such as the Death Penalty Information Center, the Southern Center for Human Rights, the Eighth Amendment Project, and the Equal Justice Initiative, ensure that the issue of wrongful convictions remains prominent in the public's eye. These latter groups are in some meaningful sense the descendants of the LDF, and institutionalized advocacy on behalf of capital inmates has been an essential feature of the current successes of the innocence revolution.

Another destabilizing event over the past several decades has been the widespread, indeed universal, embrace of life without possibility of parole (LWOP) as an alternative to the death penalty. As LWOP has eased pressures on prosecutors to seek, and jurors to return, death verdicts, it has no doubt contributed in some measure to the steep drop in death sentences in recent years. The politics behind the growth of LWOP are complex, and the story of its adoption varies from state to state. But in many jurisdictions, concerns about the Court's increasing regulation and potential abolition of the death penalty undeniably fueled states to embrace LWOP. Many states embraced LWOP for the first time in direct response to *Furman* and the prospect that the death penalty would not be revived.[26] Ironically, many of the institutional actors on the defense side that emerged as a result of the Court's regulation actively supported LWOP's adoption for an entirely different reason—because of their well-founded assumption that LWOP would induce a sharp drop in capital sentencing. A pro-LWOP alliance was forged between tough-on-crime politicians who feared the death penalty's demise and abolitionists who actively sought it. The legacy of LWOP is yet to be written. It may, in the end, be the development that most directly accounts for the decline in capital sentences and subsequent abolition of capital punishment; it may also become the most prominent symbol of America's excessive punitiveness given its promiscuous application outside of the capital sphere. But whatever the future for LWOP, it currently stands as yet another unanticipated by-product of the Court's regulation that has contributed to the stunning fragility of American capital punishment.

The project of constitutional regulation has destabilized the death penalty in one final and predictable way: by generating increased expectations about its administration and providing a yardstick for gauging its success. Prior to the 1960s, there were few hints that the Court or anyone else regarded the American death penalty as deeply flawed, much less constitutionally infirm. The rarity of Court decisions pointing to defects in capital cases made the *Furman* intervention that much more surprising and contributed to its fleeting nature. Now, though, the Court has spent more than four decades identifying and trying to solve numerous problems surrounding the death penalty's administration. The Court has essentially communicated to the world that the American death penalty must comport with certain fundamental standards of fairness and reliability in order to remain a constitutionally available punishment. That message in the short term had a soothing and legitimating effect by highlighting the Court's oversight over the capital system. But over the long haul, the Court's constitutional regulation must deliver, and its failure to do so increases the prospects for constitutional abolition. This dynamic is evident in the number of Supreme Court justices who initially supported the regulatory enterprise only later to move to the abolitionist camp. These justices worked within the regulatory framework until they concluded that the problems identified by the Court were irremediable: given the Court's commitment to curing those ills, these justices all arrived at the position that failure (and therefore retention) is not an option. Regulation can improve a practice to the point that constitutional doubts are assuaged. Or it can reveal the unsettling truth that a particular practice is beyond constitutional repair. The Court's experience with constitutional regulation of the death penalty appears to be headed down the latter path.

The New Fragility

Signs of the increasing fragility of the American death penalty abound. Most media accounts focus on the decline in executions nationwide because of the drama and power of executions in signaling support (or lack thereof) for capital punishment. The execution decline is impressive, with only 28 executions in 2015, the lowest number since 1991 and less than half the total of 2005. Equally impressive is the fact that executions were carried out in just 6 states, and only 3 of those states (Texas, Missouri, and Georgia) executed more than 2 inmates. Executions are decreasing while also becoming more concentrated geographically; if Texas were removed from the mix, the national total of executions would be 15—an astonishingly low number given that nearly 100 executions were carried out as recently as 1999.[27]

Executions, though, require the coordination of numerous actors, and a decline in executions does not necessarily reflect broader attitudes about the punishment. Some of the decline in executions, for example, is attributable to continuing problems with lethal injection, including the lack of availability of necessary drugs and judicial or administrative barriers to existing (or contemplated) protocols. These problems might themselves be traceable to popular discomfort with the death penalty, but the difficulties states are encountering in consummating death sentences with executions make executions an imprecise measure of current support.

Accordingly, the number of new death sentences nationwide is the best evidence of the prevailing commitment to the practice, because that total reflects the considered choices of prosecutors and jurors when faced with the concrete choice of death or life imprisonment. And this evidence also happens to be the most dramatic. In 2015, states produced 49 new death sentences, by far the lowest total in the modern era. At the height of the post-*Furman* era, in the mid-1990s, the nation produced about 300 death sentences per year on average; even the first decade of the twenty-first century saw an average of about 146 death sentences annually.[28] The 2015 total of 49 translates into fewer than two death sentences per capital jurisdiction and represents considerably less than 1 percent of homicides committed in the course of the year. Although homicide rates have dropped modestly over the past two decades, that decline cannot account for the much more significant decline in death sentences.[29]

Results at the state level are equally revealing and extraordinary. Texas, which produced more than 40 death sentences per year in the late 1990s, produced only 2 new death sentences in 2015, the lowest total since the adoption of its post-*Furman* statute. Virginia and Georgia, two of the death penalty powerhouses in the modern era (with more than 160 executions between them) did not produce any death sentences at all. The rarity of death sentences even in the buckle of the death belt suggests significant weakness in the practice. In addition, the decline in death sentences not only provides a snapshot of prevailing attitudes, but serves as something of a leading indicator of future practices; significantly fewer death sentences today portend a significant decline in executions down the road.

The number of capital jurisdictions has also shrunk over the past decade, as seven states rejected the death penalty. This flurry of repeals suggests that opposition to the death penalty is no longer regarded as political suicide. In the first two decades post-*Furman*, Governor Mario Cuomo's opposition to the death penalty might have cost him the election for Mayor of New York City and his re-election bid for his fourth term as governor (his opponent, George Pataki, signed a bill reinstating the death penalty when he assumed office in 1995).[30] But by 2007, there was insufficient support in the New York legislature to reinstate the death penalty after New York's highest court found remediable defects in the state's capital statute. The addition of Nebraska to the ranks of abolitionist states is particularly noteworthy. The abolition occurred in the American heartland, in a red state dominated by a Republican legislature that overrode a gubernatorial veto by a count of 32–15 (though the abolition is tentative, as the governor is leading efforts to repeal the repeal via a statewide referendum which will be held in November 2016). The politics of the death penalty have clearly shifted, and even candidates seeking national office, including the presidency—Rand Paul and Jeb Bush on the Republican side and Hillary Clinton and Bernie Sanders on the Democratic side—have been willing to express considerable skepticism about, if not complete opposition to, capital punishment.[31] This willingness to be skeptical stands in sharp contrast to then-governor Bill Clinton's eagerness to show his support for the death penalty by rushing home to Arkansas during his 1992 presidential primary campaign to preside over the execution of a mentally compromised inmate.[32]

Unsurprisingly, this shift in political behavior comes at a time when opinion polls show significantly weakened public commitment to capital punishment. The 2015 Gallup and Pew Research Center polls indicate a weak majority (56–61 percent) supporting capital punishment in the abstract, and the 2015 American Values Survey reports a majority *opposing* the death penalty compared to the choice of LWOP. These numbers reflect a notable decline from the 75 to 80 percent level of support reflected in Gallup Polls from the late-1980s through the mid-1990s, exactly the time frame of the Cuomo and (Bill) Clinton campaigns.[33]

Apart from these quantifiable measurements—executions, death sentences, retentionist jurisdictions, and polling data—there are less empirical yet still revealing indicia of the state of the American death penalty. The last two decades have witnessed a decline in vocal demonstrations of support for the death penalty by victims' rights organizations. In the 1980s and 1990s, such organizations were frequently mobilized to see pro–death penalty initiatives make their way through state legislatures and were a reliable presence at executions. Today, the relatives and friends of victims no longer speak with one voice about the death penalty. The number of victims' groups speaking in support of the death penalty is now rivaled by newly created groups on the other side. In Kansas, for example, a group called "Murder Victims' Families for Reconciliation" recently published a collection of personal stories of family members struggling with the loss of murdered relatives and expressing their concerns about "the ways that the death penalty fails as a response to such tragedy."[34] Along similar lines, Denise and Bill Richard, the parents of the youngest victim of the Boston Marathon bombing and who were also injured in the blast, have been outspoken opponents of the use of the death penalty in response to that crime. They unsuccessfully pleaded with federal authorities to take death off the table. Whereas prosecutors in the past routinely consulted with victims' family members in making the decision to seek death and relied on those relatives to provide victim-impact testimony at trial, the emergence of a significant number of family members opposed to the use of the death penalty has disrupted those practices. The fading of the seemingly monolithic front of family support for the death penalty has thus weakened a previously powerful dynamic in capital prosecutions.

Opposition to the death penalty has also begun to cross party, ideological, and religious lines. Prominent conservative George Will recently offered the "conservative case" against capital punishment in an editorial, arguing that the death penalty inappropriately "cloaks government with a majesty and infallibility discordant with conservatism," risks error by virtue of being a "government program," and is unlikely to deter because it is so infrequently administered.[35] Anti-death penalty positions have likewise emerged in hitherto unlikely places, such as the recent rejection of capital punishment by the Kansas Federation of College Republicans.[36] Even evangelical groups, traditionally ardent supporters of the death penalty, are no longer in accord on the issue, with at least one such group officially registering its opposition to the death penalty and a national evangelical organization registering its divided views.[37]

Perhaps the strongest "lagging" indicator of the death penalty's declining status in the United States can be found in the constant stream of media obituaries announcing its impending demise—or at least flagging that possibility. In fact, 2015 was a banner year for such reports, given the extraordinary lows in executions and death sentences. What is strikingly absent from these pieces is the typically balanced expression of pro- and anti–death penalty voices in reaction to the reporters' musings. One suspects that the nearly universal articulation of anti–death penalty opinions in these articles reflects not ideologically predisposed journalism, but the genuine difficulty in locating strong pro–death penalty advocates in the face of the death penalty's evident decline. Not only does the death penalty appear to be headed toward its grave, nobody seems particularly inclined to give it a respectful burial.

CHAPTER SEVEN

Recurring Patterns in
Constitutional Regulation

THE SUPREME COURT'S more than forty-year experiment with
regulating capital punishment has been a massive undertaking,
utterly transforming a practice that was rooted in local and state prerogative into one that is dominated by federal constitutional law.
Today, it is taken for granted that virtually every contested death
penalty case will wend its way through the federal courts and make
a final stop in the marble temple that houses the U.S. Supreme Court.
The Court's attempt to constitutionally reform the practice of capital
punishment is instructive about the nature and challenges of the
American death penalty—its deep historical connections to distinctive
American practices like slavery and lynching, its complex problems
of administration, and its resistance to top-down rationalization.[1]

But just as the Court's work offers a good medium for examining
the distinctiveness and current shape of the American death penalty,
it also offers an opportunity for exploring the promises and pitfalls
of constitutional regulation more generally. Close attention to the
Court's decades-long regulation of the death penalty reveals some
generalizable features that can be observed in other contexts of
constitutional regulation. Identification of these recurring patterns
highlights similarities in widely disparate areas of constitutional

law. Such a bird's-eye comparative view may offer fresh understandings of particular constitutional controversies and may provide some sobering food for thought for future constitutional litigants as well as for courts.

There are too many features of the death penalty story that can be traced in some other constitutional context to explore them all in depth. Consequently, we focus on four of the most interesting and generalizable aspects of the Court's regulation of capital punishment—political backlash, legitimating effects, remedial constraints, and discourse shaping. For each one, we trace its manifestation in both the death penalty context and in some other area of constitutional regulation—abortion, police practices, voting rights, and same-sex marriage. As particular and idiosyncratic as the death penalty's legal odyssey has been, it also turns out to have some widely shared characteristics that help illuminate the limits, as well as the potential power, of constitutional regulation.

Political Backlash

Many observers of constitutional litigation have questioned whether the Supreme Court can ever effectively lead the polity on controversial issues, arguing for some version of the old quip that "the Court follows the election returns."[2] Such skeptics often point to the major court interventions for social change of the past century—with regard to civil rights, abortion, and, of course, the death penalty—as proof that courts cannot get too far ahead of majoritarian sentiment.[3] According to these skeptical accounts, judicial decisions in each of these areas were of limited efficacy because of the primary check on court-driven social change—political backlash, through which disgruntled majorities reassert their preferences.

The Court's bold abolition of the death penalty in *Furman* followed by its chastened reauthorization of a new era of capital punishment four years later in *Gregg* certainly fits the classic backlash story. *Furman*'s announcement was greeted with outrage and resistance from many quarters, most vehemently in the South. Public opinion in support of capital punishment, which had been trending downward—reaching the lowest point ever recorded in American history in 1966, when a Gallup Poll revealed that more people opposed than supported the death penalty for murder—bumped up sharply immediately after *Furman,* almost certainly in response to the decision.[4] The strongest indicator of the public's rejection of *Furman*'s abolition was the overwhelming support for passage of new death penalty statutes: thirty-five states and the federal government passed such legislation in the four years between *Furman* and *Gregg.*[5] As the Supreme Court itself noted in *Gregg:* "The most marked indication of society's endorsement of the death penalty for murder is the legislative response to *Furman.*"[6] Even Justice Thurgood Marshall, who had argued in *Furman* that the death penalty was "morally unacceptable to the people of the United States at this time in their history,"[7] admitted in his dissenting opinion in *Gregg* that "I would be less than candid if I did not acknowledge that these developments have a significant bearing on a realistic assessment of the moral acceptability of the death penalty to the American people."[8]

The Court's journey from *Furman* to *Gregg,* however, offers more than a simple textbook illustration of political backlash. The death penalty story, when considered more fully in context, offers some important nuances to the simple schematic of the backlash thesis. The Court's death penalty trajectory highlights a number of specific factors that influenced the intensity of the political response to its constitutional intervention. Many, though not all, of these factors are also observable to a degree in the political response to another decision that is often offered as an example of the backlash thesis—the Court's expansion of abortion rights in *Roe v. Wade,* decided just one year after *Furman.*[9] The specific modes of political resistance that the Court's regulation in both the death penalty and abortion contexts engendered over time also share some similar and generalizable features. A comparison of political backlash and resistance in these two contexts demonstrates that the nuanced dynamics of political backlash in the death penalty story are not unique, but rather observable more broadly.

The backlash phenomenon in the death penalty context demonstrates the difficulty of accurately gauging the future trajectory of public opinion. At the time of the decision in *Furman,* the Court as a whole, and in particular the key swing justices Byron White and Potter Stewart, had some powerful reasons to think that the tide of public opinion was turning against the death penalty. There was, of course, the groundbreaking 1966 Gallup Poll in which more opposed than supported the death penalty for murder. In addition, members of the media from both the left and the right, along with academic observers, described "mounting zeal for abolition" and predicted the eventual success of the abolition movement.[10] According to Evan Mandery's behind-the-scenes account of the *Furman* decision, it was this apparent surge of public opinion against the death penalty that moved Stewart to agree with White to make up the *Furman* bare majority, and that would also move Stewart years later to express anger at how wrong the expert reports about the trajectory of public opinion had turned out to be.[11] The possibility of this kind of predictive error is especially strong with regard to issues, like capital punishment, about which public opinion tends to fluctuate significantly over time.

A feature of the death penalty context that may help to explain the unexpected intensity of the backlash that *Furman* engendered, especially in the South, is the significance of the decision's messenger—that is, the lawyers that litigated and won *Furman* and its companion cases in 1972. The LDF was the same organization that had litigated *Brown v. Board of Education,* and later (only one year prior to *Furman*) *Swann v. Charlotte-Mecklenburg Board of Education,* which upheld a controversial court-ordered busing plan to desegregate a North Carolina school district.[12] The continuing Southern resistance to school integration likely helped to fuel anger toward the LDF's parallel constitutional litigation targeting capital punishment. It surely did not help that the death penalty litigation had an apparent Southern focus: two of the three cases decided in 1972 were from Georgia and one was from Texas, while a fourth case in the initial litigation involving a California defendant was mooted before the *Furman* decision by the California Supreme Court's invalidation of that state's death penalty.[13] Not only was the *Furman* decision heralded by a hated messenger, but the litigation also had a barely submerged subtext of racial equality. The death penalty context suggests that risk of political backlash is stronger when the controversial subject of litigation is yoked, either explicitly or implicitly, to other hotly contested issues.

Another contributor to the strength of the *Furman* backlash was the weakness of the Court's majority. Not only was the decision that of a bare majority, but quite unusually, there was no majority opinion or even plurality opinion. Rather, each of the five justices in the majority wrote his own opinion, and none of them joined any of the others' opinions. As a consequence, it was difficult to discern the essential grounds for the Court's judgment, and the decision lacked the moral authority that a strong majority would have carried. Indeed, the decision had the very opposite of moral authority as a consequence of its patently political underpinnings. The four dissenters were all recent Nixon appointees, and their voting as a bloc was significant enough to make a *New York Times* headline.[14] The politics of the voting pattern underscored a theme that the dissenters all pressed in various ways in their four dissents—that the decision to strike down the death penalty was based on the policy preferences of the justices in the majority rather than compelled by the Constitution.

The Court's decision in *Furman* created an opportunity for those running for office, especially in the South. The Republican Party, prior to *Furman*, had already begun to deploy its so-called Southern Strategy of attempting to convince white Southern Democrats who were conservative on social issues to switch party affiliation.[15] Criminal justice issues proved to be a powerful component of the Southern Strategy, not least because of the ways in which concerns about crime dovetailed with resentments and fears about race.[16] Within the realm of criminal justice, the death penalty was an issue of extremely high salience, and it worked as effective shorthand for "tough-on-crime" politics. The death penalty's power as a political issue for many years following *Furman* can be traced at all levels of government. Perhaps the most striking example is the death penalty's role in the defeat of Governor Michael Dukakis in his 1988 presidential bid; during a televised debate, Dukakis unemotionally reiterated his abolitionist stance in response to the question whether he would favor the death penalty if his wife Kitty were raped and murdered.[17] In short, in the death penalty context, backlash did not just spontaneously occur;

rather, the flames of resistance were fanned by political actors who found in *Furman*'s flaws a campaign gift.

A final factor that made the death penalty even more salient as a political issue, and thus helped to fuel the backlash to *Furman,* was the timing of the decision. Although the death penalty had been on the Supreme Court's radar since at least 1963, when Justice Goldberg penned his galvanizing dissent from denial of review, the decade that passed between 1963 and *Furman*'s constitutional abolition in 1972 produced two developments that undermined acceptance of the decision. The first was the Court's controversial criminal procedure revolution, in which it broadly enforced the right to exclude illegally seized evidence, the right to counsel, and restrictions on police interrogations, among other interventions.[18] These rulings engendered significant backlash from the law enforcement community and from tough-on-crime politicians—a wave of organized resistance that gave *Furman*'s backlash the momentum of a running start. The second development was the precipitous rise in crime rates throughout the 1960s and early 1970s, a development that increased public fears and enhanced incentives for politicians to promote tough-on-crime policies. The Court's decision in *Furman* prompted the highly visible release of close to six hundred feared and despised death row prisoners into the ordinary prison population, including mass murderer Richard Speck, among others.[19] Charles Manson and Sirhan Sirhan had won their reprieves from California's death row by the California Supreme Court's decision invalidating the state's death penalty while the *Furman* decision was pending.[20] The direct impact of criminal justice decisions on the fates of individual defendants is thus a double-edged sword: the Court is uniquely powerful in the criminal context with its direct authority to reverse convictions or sentences, but the Court is also uniquely accountable for these results. Given the intensity of public fears about violent crime in the early 1970s, one has to wonder whether the backlash against constitutional abolition of the death penalty would have been as intense had the decision occurred five to ten years earlier.

Many of these same factors were at work in the political response to the Court's ruling protecting the right of women to choose to terminate a pregnancy in *Roe v. Wade*, issued one year after *Furman*. The abortion context is often urged as a prime example of the backlash thesis. The most extreme claim about the effect of *Roe* on American politics is from columnist David Brooks: "Justice Harry Blackmun [the author of the Court's decision in *Roe*] did more inadvertent damage to our democracy than any other 20th-century American. When he and his Supreme Court colleagues issued the *Roe v. Wade* decision, they set off a cycle of political viciousness and counter-viciousness that has poisoned public life ever since."[21] Poison aside, it remains the conventional understanding of *Roe* that it precipitated a backlash, intensifying right-to-life opposition to abortion rights while also demobilizing pro-choice activists. This view is held not only by right-wing critics of *Roe* but also by left-wing supporters of abortion rights. Justice Ruth Bader Ginsburg, herself a major figure in the Women's Rights Movement in the 1970s, has endorsed the backlash thesis: "In one fell swoop, the Court made unconstitutional every abortion law in the country . . . so . . . the people who were advocating for a woman's ability to control her own destiny, they retired, while the opposition mounted."[22]

In recent years, some scholars have cast doubt on the conventional backlash thesis with regard to *Roe*, arguing that societal and political polarization on the issue of abortion had commenced prior to the Court's intervention.[23] This skepticism is helpful, because it introduces an important caution that should accompany the backlash thesis. It is often impossible to know how much of the political mobilization that occurs after a major Supreme Court decision is a product of the Court's controversial intervention, as opposed to a product of the controversy that brought the issue to the Court in the first place. In the death penalty context, it is possible that even absent any intervention by the Court, the death penalty would have seen a resurgence and become an important shorthand for tough-on-crime politics in the 1970s and 1980s, given the general trajectory of the politics of crime during that time period. However, the speed and intensity of the death penalty's resurgence, as well as the court-centric focus of the contro-versy for decades to come, were likely products of the Court's inter-vention in *Furman*. Although the Court did not immediately back-track from its decision in *Roe*—it was not until 1989 that the Court formally abandoned *Roe*'s strong scrutiny of abortion restrictions prior to fetal viability unless they were for the protection of maternal health—the same conclusion is likely true in this context as well.[24] That is, the Court's intervention in *Roe* promoted the speed and in-tensity with which right-to-life opposition coalesced, as well as the court-centric focus of the abortion controversy in the decades that followed.

Turning to the factors that contributed to the intensity of the back-lash to *Furman,* the difficulty of gauging public opinion with regard to the death penalty was also present with regard to abortion. Justice Blackmun, like Justices White and Stewart in the death penalty con-text, *thought* he knew where public opinion was trending; in his case file on *Roe* was a newspaper column reporting a Gallup Poll con-ducted in 1972 indicating that a substantial majority of those sur-veyed believed that "the decision to have an abortion should be made solely by a woman and her physician."[25] However, public opinion turned out to be highly context dependent. In polls that disaggre-gated abortion decisions into different contexts, the results were decidedly more ambiguous. Whereas there was strong support for legalized abortion when the mother's health was at stake, in cases of rape, or if serious birth defects were diagnosed, support fell off con-siderably when the reasons for abortion were the mother's low in-come, unmarried status, or desire not to have any more children (if married). Only a minority of those polled approved of abortion "on demand" or under all circumstances.[26] Blackmun's framework pro-tecting abortion for any reason prior to viability therefore proved to be out of step with the more ambivalent views of the public. As con-stitutional scholar Michael Klarman put it: "*Roe* put the Court on the wrong side of public opinion by extending the right beyond what the public was willing to accept."[27]

Roe also shared, albeit to a lesser degree, *Furman*'s "messenger" problem. Just as the LDF lawyers in *Furman* were associated with the desegregation goals of the Civil Rights Movement, the lawyers in *Roe* were associated with the Women's Rights Movement. Sarah Weddington and Linda Coffee, who litigated *Roe* on behalf of a group of plaintiffs challenging Texas's restrictive abortion law, were recent law school graduates under the age of thirty; both had been involved with the National Organization for Women (NOW) and the feminist movement more generally.[28] Unlike the LDF, however, Weddington and Coffee were by no stretch of the imagination in charge of a coordinated constitutional litigation campaign. Rather, the abortion rights movement "failed to coalesce behind a particular legal strategy" in large part because of "the lack of leadership by a single attorney or group organizing litigation efforts."[29] The large field of abortion rights cases wending their way through the courts in the five years leading up to *Roe* were litigated by a mix of private counsel, American Civil Liberties Union (ACLU) lawyers, and other "movement attorneys."[30] Most of the private counsel cases were brought on behalf of doctors convicted of performing illegal abortions—cases that would have had less of a "messenger" problem had they been the vehicle for the Court's ruling, because doctors' prerogatives did not tap into the culture wars of the early 1970s in the same way as women's rights. Even though Weddington and Coffee were not the face of abortion litigation in the way that LDF lawyers were for death penalty litigation, their connection to the Women's Rights Movement played into Republican attempts to cast the abortion issue as part of a feminist political platform.[31]

The one factor contributing to death penalty backlash that was essentially absent in the abortion context was a weak majority divided along clear political lines. Unlike *Furman*, *Roe* commanded a substantial majority of the Court, with seven justices in the majority, including Nixon appointee Chief Justice Warren Burger. The dissenting justices in *Roe* were also appointed by presidents from different political parties—Byron White by John F. Kennedy, and William Rehnquist by Richard Nixon. Despite the absence of *Furman*'s clear signals of vulnerability, *Roe* nonetheless invited further litigation because of the many questions about the permissible scope of state abortion regulations left open by the decision. In the years immediately following *Roe,* there was wide discussion and debate about the permissibility of parental or spousal consent requirements, restrictions on the use of Medicaid funds for abortions, and regulations of clinics and hospitals that perform abortions.[32] All of these issues would eventually find their way to the courts and, indeed, they continue to be litigated today.

Perhaps the strongest similarity between *Furman* and *Roe* with respect to backlash lies in the political incentives both decisions created going forward. *Roe* no less than *Furman* played into the Republican Southern Strategy by alienating white Southern Democrats who were conservative on social issues. While *Furman* tapped into the racial politics of crime, *Roe* tapped into the cultural politics that swirled around newly permissive attitudes about sex, the role of women in marriage and broader social life, and out-of-wedlock births.[33] Although the decision in *Roe* did not have the same effect of shifting public opinion that *Furman* did in the death penalty context, *Roe* did have a polarizing effect by intensifying individual preferences (rather than changing them). That is, "if one was pro-choice before the decision, one became even more so after; the same held true for pro-lifers."[34] *Roe* created incentives for politicians on *both* sides of the political aisle to use the intensified polarization with regard to abortion for their own political ends.[35]

In a similar vein, the backlash to *Roe,* like the backlash to *Furman,* was intensified by the timing of the decision. The revolution in sexual attitudes and women's roles that we currently identify with the decade of "the sixties" actually occurred later than this convenient labeling—more like 1965 to 1975. After all, Betty Friedan's *The Feminine Mystique* was not published until 1963; the birth control pill, although approved by the U.S. Food and Drug Administration (FDA) in 1960, was not required to be accessible to unmarried women until 1972; and the Equal Rights Amendment was not approved by the House and Senate and sent to the states for ratification until 1972.[36] Hence, at the time of the *Roe* decision in 1973, these cultural changes were still peaking, and anxieties around them were peaking as well. In addition to playing on these anxieties as part of its Southern Strategy, the Republican Party had begun to use the same concerns to woo Roman Catholic voters. The rise of the religious right and of powerful Catholic voices in the Republican Party—such as Phyllis Schlafly, introduced to a national audience during Barry Goldwater's 1964 campaign—created potent opportunities to capitalize on the post-*Roe* political polarization.[37] The congruities between backlash in the death penalty and abortion contexts are not perfect; each story is too particular and complex for any such neat overlay. However, many similar factors likely influenced the extent of political backlash in each context. The dynamics of death penalty backlash should be of general interest for what they can show us about recurring features of constitutional litigation.

There are also similarities in the specific modes of political resistance that arose in response to the Court's interventions in the death penalty and abortion contexts. The initial constitutional abolition of capital punishment in *Furman* was driven by concerns about capital sentencing *outcomes*—the rarity and apparent arbitrariness and discrimination that characterized the use of the death penalty prior to 1972. The thirty-five states that wished to retain capital punishment responded by modifying the *procedures* by which capital sentences were to be imposed, leading to the Court's revival of capital punishment in 1976. This is a common legal phenomenon, in which concerns about substantive outcomes are addressed indirectly by modifying the procedures that lead to those outcomes. However, when the Court eventually imposed some substantive limits on death penalty outcomes, some states responded by undercutting those limits with procedural impediments. Just as procedural interventions can attempt to *fix* substantive problems, procedural restrictions can also *undermine* substantive rights.

The best example of procedure undercutting substance in the death penalty context is the procedural implementation of the Court's substantive constitutional ban on the execution of intellectually disabled offenders.[38] Despite the clarity of the 2002 ruling, the Court left to the states "the task of developing appropriate ways to enforce the constitutional restriction."[39] Some of the ways in which state legislation has enforced the constitutional restriction are so demanding that they make it virtually impossible for defendants to establish their intellectual disability, despite substantial evidence of impairment. For example, whereas most states require that defendants demonstrate their disability by a preponderance of the evidence—that is, by proving that it is "more likely than not" that they are disabled—Georgia requires that defendants prove their disability "beyond a reasonable doubt," the daunting standard that is used in criminal trials for proof of guilt.[40] Such a standard means in practice that if even one state-appointed expert finds that the defendant's IQ is above the statutory threshold, the state can argue that such a finding creates a "reasonable doubt" as to the defendant's disability, regardless of how many other experts disagree or how powerful other evidence of the defendant's impairment might be. For another example, whereas most states have trial judges make the determination about a defendant's intellectual disability before the trial begins, Texas gives the decision to the sentencing jury, to be made at the same time that jury is deliberating about life or death. By this time, jurors will have been exposed to all of the gory details of the offense and the suffering caused by it; they may well have strong leanings toward a sentence of death based on these factors. A decision made at this point about whether the defendant is intellectually disabled—and thus exempt from execution—is unlikely to be as dispassionate as a decision by a trial judge in advance of trial. The Texas courts have also developed and applied their own nonclinical standards for judging intellectual disability. These standards have led them to uphold jury determinations that capital defendants are not intellectually disabled when such defendants almost certainly would have been deemed disabled in other states based on widely accepted clinical standards.

One sees a similar mode of resistance in the abortion context. In states where there is strong opposition to the substantive right protected by *Roe*, lawmakers have promulgated a variety of procedural restrictions that undercut that right. Immediately after *Roe*, states implemented a variety of abortion restrictions, including requiring parental, spousal, or prospective-father consent for abortions, limiting abortion services performed by public hospitals, and eliminating or limiting payment for abortion services by Medicaid or other public assistance plans.[41] States turned to other modes of restriction as well, including waiting periods for abortions, required in-person counseling for women seeking abortions, and limitations on "partial birth" abortions as well as on the availability of medication-induced (as opposed to surgical) abortions. In recent years, states have promulgated tight restrictions on the facilities in which abortion services are offered; such laws are known as TRAP laws, for "targeted regulation of abortion providers."[42] In Texas, for example, a 2013 law requires abortion clinics to meet the same building, equipment, and staffing standards as ambulatory surgical centers and also requires doctors who perform abortions to have admitting privileges at a hospital within thirty miles of the clinic. The law resulted in the closing of about half of the preexisting abortion clinics in Texas, forcing many women to travel hundreds of miles to obtain abortion services. The Court agreed to hear a challenge to the Texas law in its 2015–2016 term, a case that was predicted to be an important reconsideration of the scope of the substantive right protected by *Roe*, at least before the death of Justice Antonin Scalia in February 2016.[43] None of these laws directly challenge the right of a woman to choose abortion prior to viability; rather, as in the context of death penalty eligibility, these laws work indirectly around the edges, undercutting the substantive right by controlling the means by which it is secured.

Procedural undermining of substantive rights also contributes to unequal protection of those rights. As top-down regulation is filtered through state and local institutions and actors, it opens up the possibility of resistance that is geographically diverse and episodic, rather than uniform and predictable. Backlash is not a single action in a discrete moment of time, but often a longer-term phenomenon. Direct resistance to constitutional rulings may often be infeasible or unseemly. Consequently, backlash often manifests itself in multifaceted efforts to "undo" despised decisions through indirect or gradual undercutting, like the imposition of procedural obstacles to securing constitutional entitlements. Just as substantive problems can often be remedied by fixing procedures, procedural restrictions can be deployed to undermine substantive rights, as illustrated by the uncertainty in practice of the constitutional ban on the execution of intellectually disabled offenders and the constitutional right of women to terminate a pregnancy prior to fetal viability.

Legitimating Effects

Another recurring feature of constitutional regulation is the way in which the Supreme Court's intervention in an area of law can serve to legitimate practices that were previously contested, by inducing false or exaggerated faith that the actors being regulated are following rules that will prevent abuses and ensure fairness. The Court's constitutional regulation of the death penalty helped, albeit unintentionally, to legitimate the underlying practice of capital punishment. By taming the existential moment of decision in the capital sentencing process, the Court's Eighth Amendment jurisprudence helped to reduce the anxiety that judges and juries feel about exercising their sentencing power. By requiring more extensive appellate and post-conviction review of capital verdicts, the Court's regulation diluted capital sentencers' sense of ultimate responsibility for imposing the death penalty. These effects carried over to other actors within the capital system, such as prosecutors and governors, and to the public at large, whose hazy knowledge of the capital process left it with the impression of intensive judicial regulation despite its virtual absence—thus leading the public to conclude that any death sentences that made it through the review process were the product of a rigorous, even *too* rigorous, system of constitutional constraints. Only when the advent of DNA evidence revealed that an unexpectedly large number of innocent defendants had been sentenced to death did the legitimating effects of the Court's constitutional regulation of capital punishment dissipate.

A similar legitimating effect can be observed in the Court's constitutional regulation of police practices under the Fourth, Fifth, and Sixth Amendments. Each of these amendments has been construed to impose constitutional limits on police investigative practices—such as the Fourth Amendment's requirement of judicial warrants or probable cause for most police searches or seizures, the Fifth Amendment's requirement of *Miranda* warnings before police custodial interrogations, and the Sixth Amendment's limits on police elicitation of incriminating statements from defendants after a formal charging decision. Each of these rules is enforced with the special judicial remedy of constitutional exclusion—if the police are found to have obtained evidence from a defendant in violation of the Constitution, the evidence will be excluded from the defendant's criminal trial. In the years since the Warren Court's expansion of these rights in the 1960s during its criminal procedure revolution, the Burger and Rehnquist Courts have sharply curtailed them. It is the manner in which this later retrenchment occurred that has produced a legitimating effect with regard to the general public similar to the one we observed with regard to capital punishment.

As the death penalty context illustrates, legitimation requires that constitutional regulation create a *misleading* impression about the nature or effectiveness of its demands. The Court's death penalty regulation was too complex for its workings to be well understood by the public. What *was* visible to the public—the multiple opportunities for judicial review and the resulting lengthy delays between sentence and execution—created the misleading sense that the death penalty was intensively, even exhaustively, regulated, when in fact the Court's doctrine imposed fairly minimal demands on state capital processes. In the context of police practices, the Court's doctrine has created a misleading impression of intensive regulation in a slightly different way, by speaking to the public and to the police in two different voices about the nature of its constitutional requirements. The decisions retreating from the Warren Court's demanding constitutional regulation of the police changed the *consequences* of violating constitutional norms more than they changed the *content* of the norms. The Court minimized the consequences of constitutional violations committed by the police by promulgating a profusion of what might be called "inclusionary rules"—rules that permit the use at trial of admittedly unconstitutionally obtained evidence or that let stand criminal convictions based on such evidence.[44] The content of constitutional norms—like the famous *Miranda* rights—are much more accessible to the general public than the highly technical workings of inclusionary rules. But these latter rules are communicated clearly to the law enforcement community through training and on-the-job experience. As a result, sophisticated law enforcement agents will see incentives to violate constitutional norms when no court-imposed sanction will follow. At the same time, the public's lack of access to the workings of inclusionary rules will lead it to overestimate the extent of court-imposed constraints on the police.

The constitutional rules for when and how the police may interrogate suspects, promulgated by the Warren Court in the 1960s, have remained surprisingly unscathed in the retrenchment of the following decades. Under the Sixth Amendment right to counsel, the Court forbade government agents from deliberately eliciting incriminating statements from a defendant after the formal charging decision unless the defendant explicitly waived the right to counsel.[45] Under the Fifth Amendment right to be free from compelled self-incrimination, the Court forbade police interrogations of suspects in custody prior to a formal charging decision unless the suspects waived the rights elaborated in *Miranda*.[46] Although prosecutors repeatedly asked the Court to curtail or abandon both of these rules, the Court declined. Indeed, the Burger Court actually strengthened the Warren Court's Sixth Amendment rule in multiple ways: it set a high standard for waiver of the right; it established a broad definition of what constitutes "deliberate elicitation" of incriminating statements; and it clarified that formal charging of the defendant gave rise to the right to counsel regardless of whether the defendant was, in fact, represented by appointed or retained counsel at the time the government sought to elicit incriminating statements.[47] Although the Burger Court did permit some retrenchment from the *Miranda* ruling—most notably by permitting custodial interrogation without *Miranda* warnings when "public safety" demands it—the Court also bolstered *Miranda* by establishing fairly broad definitions of "interrogation" and "custody" and by requiring the police to "scrupulously honor" a suspect's assertion of his right to silence.[48]

The Court's continued adherence to Fourth Amendment limitations on police searches and seizures has been more mixed. Here, the Burger and Rehnquist Courts did generate a number of new and more forgiving constitutional norms for the police: these Courts created an expansive definition of "consent" to police searches; they crafted a narrow definition of "reasonable expectations of privacy"; they developed a category of searches reflecting "special needs" that render the warrant requirement inapplicable; they allowed a defendant's flight from the police in a high crime area to suffice as justification for a police stop; and they refused to treat racially motivated stops as "unreasonable" under the Fourth Amendment as long as legitimate grounds for the stop existed (even if those grounds were not the reason for the police action).[49] Despite these significant changes in Fourth Amendment constitutional norms, the Burger and Rehnquist Courts nonetheless held the line with regard to much of the Warren Court's rulebook for police searches and seizures. Most notably, the requirement that searches of a home be authorized by a judicial warrant was reinforced and strengthened by the Burger and Rehnquist Courts.[50] Moreover, the Rehnquist and Roberts Courts have adhered to the Warren Court's rubric for dealing with technological innovation. Just as the Warren Court rejected the government's bugging of a public telephone booth without a warrant, the Rehnquist Court rejected the warrantless use of a thermal imaging device by police to uncover the use of heat lamps for marijuana cultivation in a home.[51] Similarly, the Roberts Court rejected the warrantless attachment of a GPS device to a suspect's car, as well as the warrantless search of the information on an arrestee's cell phone.[52]

Contrast the relative stability of the Court's constitutional norms regarding police practices with the enormous changes in the consequences for violations of those norms. First, the Burger and Rehnquist Courts created a vast array of new rules that permit the government to avoid the exclusion of evidence at trial even when police violate constitutional norms. With regard to the Fourth Amendment, such rules include a narrowed definition of who has "standing" to seek the remedy of exclusion; the development of a "good faith" exception to the warrant requirement; the granting of permission to use unconstitutionally seized evidence at trial when it would have been "inevitably discovered" by legal means; and the creation of an "impeachment" exception to the exclusionary rule, whereby unconstitutionally seized evidence can be used to challenge a defendant's credibility as a witness at trial.[53] Perhaps the greatest evisceration of the Warren Court's exclusionary rule regime is the Roberts Court's more recent ruling that requires a heightened level of government malfeasance—reaching the point of "systemic error or reckless disregard of constitutional requirements"—before a Fourth Amendment violation will lead to evidentiary exclusion. The Court explained: "To trigger the exclusionary rule, police conduct must be sufficiently deliberate that exclusion can meaningfully deter it, and sufficiently culpable that such deterrence is worth the price paid by the justice system."[54] This is the Court's most skeptical statement yet regarding the appropriateness of the remedy of evidentiary exclusion, and it has sent a strong signal to trial courts about their greater discretion to withhold such a remedy. The Court has similarly developed powerful inclusionary rules with regard to Fifth and Sixth Amendment violations, departing from the Warren Court's baseline by treating exclusion in these contexts as a judicially created remedy that can be narrowed at will, rather than as part and parcel of the constitutional rights themselves.[55]

In addition to the rules of inclusion at trial, the Court has also developed rules governing judicial review and reversal of criminal convictions that permit courts to uphold convictions despite the erroneous admission of unconstitutionally obtained evidence at trial. While these latter rules are "inclusionary" in a less direct way than are the former, they nonetheless have the same consequence of permitting the government to reap the benefit of prior police misconduct without incurring any judicially imposed penalty. For example, the Court watered down the standard of "harmless error" review for appellate and postconviction courts, making it easier for such courts to overlook trial judges' mistakes in admitting evidence that should have been excluded.[56] The Court ruled that Fourth Amendment claims may not be considered at all by federal courts on habeas corpus review, denying federal review to the very class of cases in which the temptation of (often elected) state court judges to tolerate police misconduct is probably the strongest.[57] The Court has also developed other, more general limitations on the availability of the federal habeas corpus remedy, including much tougher standards for litigants who procedurally defaulted their claims in state court and for litigants seeking the retroactive application of new rules of constitutional law.[58]

If these rules sound highly technical, that is precisely the point. Inclusionary rules are complex and legalistic; they do not make good copy and therefore are rarely reported in the press. It is fair to say that the public has little to no knowledge about them, whereas every first-year law student can recite the *Miranda* warnings prior to any instruction on the topic. From media news stories, television shows, films, and even "street law clinics" that teach residents about their constitutional rights vis-à-vis the police, the general public has a fair amount of access to the constitutional norms that are supposed to constrain police practices. In contrast, members of the law enforcement community—not surprisingly—have a more accurate and sophisticated understanding of the technical rules that govern the consequences of their actions. Police officers are trained by their departments about the Supreme Court's directives and what the consequences of failure to comply will be—whether those consequences involve the exclusion of evidence, personal civil liability, or internal discipline. Police officers also obtain important information about the trial consequences of violating constitutional prohibitions through their interactions with prosecutors and their experience as witnesses in constitutional suppression hearings.

When the police, as sophisticated criminal justice insiders, are able to predict that their violations of constitutional norms will not result in the exclusion of evidence, they undoubtedly will become more willing to flout those norms. Indeed, one study of police attitudes regarding the Fourth Amendment exclusionary rule revealed that police officers generally did not regard constitutional norms as binding *unless* they were enforced by evidentiary exclusion.[59] Reported cases are rife with examples of police officers strategically violating constitutional norms when they know that the evidence they obtain will be admissible pursuant to some legal exception.[60] Meanwhile, the public is likely to continue to take constitutional norms at face value, unaware that their enforcement is undermined by a hollowed-out remedial scheme. For decades following the Warren Court era, the public routinely indicated that it believed that the police were over-constrained, even "handcuffed," by the constitutional norms announced by the Supreme Court.[61] Public opinion polls routinely reported that the public had enormous faith in law enforcement as an institution and relatively little fear of police overreaching.[62] As in the death penalty context, these views likely reflected a misguided belief in the intensity and efficacy of the Court's constitutional regulation.

In the death penalty context, the legitimating power of the Court's constitutional regulation was finally weakened by the DNA revolution, which shook the public's faith in the reliability of the capital justice system. In the context of the constitutional regulation of police practices, that crisis of faith is happening at the time of this writing. Just as the technology of DNA was able to prove the disturbing frequency of wrongful convictions in capital cases, the technology of video cameras is now proving the disturbing frequency of unjustified police violence on the streets, especially in interactions with black men. As a consequence, there is a groundswell of concern about police misconduct that is fueling demands from many quarters for much greater regulation of the police. That these demands are arising only now, and not decades ago, is at least partly a consequence of the legitimating power of the Court's constitutional regulation of police practices, which was far less constraining than the public long believed.

Remedial Constraints

Another common feature of constitutional regulation is the tendency of the Court to retreat from acknowledged or apparent constitutional norms when it regards remedial choices as unworkable or unattractive. In the capital context, the absence of workable remedies contributed to the failures to protect capital defendants at two crucial moments: the Court's reluctance to protect capital defendants in the first century following the Reconstruction Amendments, and its subsequent refusal to grant relief of any kind in response to post-*Furman* studies showing continuing race discrimination in the modern era of the death penalty. These denials of relief find striking parallels in the Court's approach to voting rights issues in roughly the same eras. The Court's concerns about the limits of its remedial power caused it to step aside when blacks challenged their disenfranchisement in the early twentieth century, despite a clear constitutional imperative protecting their right to vote in the Fifteenth Amendment.[63] When the Court subsequently entered the political thicket in the early 1960s and undertook constitutional regulation of states' election practices, it protected important constitutional values where clear procedural remedies were at hand. But when faced with ubiquitous problems of partisan vote dilution, which implicate similar concerns about fairness and potential legislative abuse, the Court declined to intervene because of inadequate remedial tools.

After the Civil War, the Constitution was amended to protect individuals against state deprivations of rights, with new language declaring that "no State" shall deny to any person the rights associated with the guarantees of "due process" and "equal protection." This marked a radical departure from the original constitutional structure, in which most of the protections for individuals were designed to restrain only federal actors. Early in the post-bellum era, the Court recognized that these new guarantees would not tolerate caste systems of criminal justice and invalidated the death sentence of a West Virginian inmate where state law excluded blacks from serving as jurors in criminal cases.[64] But almost immediately, many states defied the underlying norm of equal treatment and employed a variety of clever and not-so-clever means of excluding blacks from jury service.

Though the violation of constitutional norms was readily apparent, the Court faced significant remedial obstacles. As illustrated in the trial and subsequent lynching of Ed Johnson in Tennessee, the Court had no reason to expect that a decision requiring blacks to serve on juries would be obeyed. In 1906, Johnson challenged the obvious defects in his capital trial, including the exclusion of all blacks from the jury pool, and Justice Harlan subsequently issued a writ of habeas corpus so that the Court could hear that challenge. In response to Harlan's intervention, a mob lynched Johnson, and the questions surrounding his trial became moot.[65] The message was clear: the Court could issue paper rulings, but it lacked the power to compel compliance. Though the Court was willing to pursue contempt charges against the sheriff and jail officials who had facilitated the lynching of Johnson, the Court remained remarkably quiet for many decades about the continuing, transparent, wholesale exclusion of blacks from jury service in the South. The Court's intervention in the Scottsboro Boys case was aberrational, and, for much of the twentieth century, black men were almost uniformly sentenced to die in the South by all-white juries in conformity with what everyone (judges, prosecutors, defense counsel, and the general public) understood to be an unannounced but powerful rule of Southern justice. Had the Court been motivated to solve the problem of widespread exclusion, its remedial choices were unattractive. How could the Court police the complicated political, prosecutorial, and judicial decisions implicated in the selection of jurors? It was easy for the Court to invalidate a statute that said on its face that no blacks could serve on juries; it was (and remains) much more difficult for the Court to review other, non-racially discriminatory means of preventing blacks from serving. Even today, the Court refuses to require measures that would severely limit the exclusion of jurors on a racial basis, such as invalidating the use of peremptory challenges (which permit lawyers to strike prospective jurors based on hunches and intuitions rather than articulable cause).[66] From the Court's perspective, such a limit would intrude too far into state and local prerogatives, even though it might represent the most promising means of limiting racial discrimination in jury selection.

Fast forward to the modern era. *Furman* declared that the risk of arbitrariness and discrimination in capital cases was intolerable and that states could no longer operate schemes characterized by standardless discretion. States revamped their statutes, sought to confine discretion by enumerating aggravating and mitigating factors, and added other safeguards (such as mandatory appellate review and comparative proportionality review) to limit arbitrariness and discrimination. But these interventions could not and did not eliminate the influence of race in capital decision making. The Baldus study documented the continuing role of race—particularly the race of victims—in the distribution of capital sentences.

The findings of the Baldus study seemed particularly important given the rationale for the Court's prior regulatory interventions. If states could be required to recraft their statutes in light of fears of arbitrary and discriminatory applications of the death penalty (or largely anecdotal evidence of such problems), surely rigorous empirical proof of pervasive race discrimination would require additional court relief. But that logic did not prevail in *McCleskey* in large part because of the difficulty of identifying an appropriate remedy.

The major thrust of the Baldus study was the persistent failure to treat minority-victim murders as seriously as white-victim murders. For opponents of the death penalty, the obvious response was for the Court to declare that Georgia had forfeited its ability to punish offenders with death; if the death penalty could not be administered in a racially evenhanded manner, it should not be a penal option. But this remedy posed problems of its own. As an initial matter, how much discrimination was enough to trigger this drastic response? It is one thing to mandate procedures to combat the risk of discrimination; it is quite another to police outcomes and to insist that some quantifiable level of discrimination requires abandoning a practice altogether. Any statistical standard embraced by the Court would inevitably be arbitrary, and the enforcement of that standard would require evaluating Baldus-type studies for other states that would eventually come down the road. Such analyses would take the Court far outside of its competence and comfort zone.

The Baldus study also revealed varying race effects in different parts of the state. Why should the presence of race discrimination in some regions of a state condemn the practice statewide? For abolitionists who saw this litigation as the potential end of the death penalty nationwide, why should demonstrable discrimination within one state (or even several states) provide a ground for denying other states (perhaps more homogenous ones without any significant history of race disparities in their administration of capital punishment) the ability to use the death penalty? Though the litigators in *McCleskey* viewed the Baldus findings as a scathing indictment of American capital punishment and a reason for the Court to reevaluate its constitutionality, it was difficult to see how those findings could serve as the basis for a landmark, nationwide ruling.

There were also problems with structuring a narrow remedy for McCleskey himself. McCleskey's showing that Georgia devalued minority victims did not suggest that he was undeserving of the death penalty, or that he would have been spared had Georgia implemented its capital law in an evenhanded manner. McCleskey's proof of generalized discrimination—where the discriminatory actors (presumably prosecutors and jurors) were spread throughout many counties and often involved in only a very small number of cases— did not fairly establish that McCleskey's own trial was tainted by racial bias, a consideration that the Court highlighted in rejecting McCleskey's claim.[67]

The ability of the Court to remedy the race discrimination documented by the Baldus study was complicated by an additional consideration. If Georgia consistently underprotects minority victims by not securing capital verdicts in minority-victim cases, how would withholding the death penalty in white-victim cases be responsive to the "real" underlying problem—the seeming indifference of prosecutors and jurors to minority victims?[68] The more appropriate response to such indifference would be to compel greater regard for minority victims, which would require *increased* application of the death penalty. That remedy, too, poses problems, because the failure to seek or secure death sentences in minority-victim cases is attributable to institutionally irreducible exercises of discretion. Prosecutorial discretion to reject capital charges is widely regarded as essential to fairness and a defining feature of our system of checks and balances, and courts (rightly) lack the power to command executive officials to seek death in particular cases. Sentencer discretion to return non-death verdicts is one of the central pillars of contemporary death penalty jurisprudence—an essential corollary to the idea that defendants must be able to present, and sentencers must be able to credit, any mitigating evidence that calls for a sentence less than death.

Ultimately, *McCleskey* reveals the limits of constitutional regulation to respond to the failure of its own interventions. Concerns about race discrimination were undoubtedly central to the Court's decision to embark on the regulatory enterprise. The shape of the Court's early regulatory efforts—mandating that states adopt standards identifying the "worst" offenses—reflected the Court's concern that the death penalty not be administered in a racially discriminatory fashion. But having gone down this path, the Court was ill-equipped to regulate further when the procedural reforms proved unsuccessful. Rigorous empirical demonstration of the influence of race in capital decision making cried out for a judicial response, especially after the Court had concluded that the possibility of race discrimination justified invalidating all prevailing capital statutes. The Court, though, was much better equipped to demand procedural reform than to insist upon substantive equality. Where states had not even tried to rationalize their capital systems, the Court was on strong ground in demanding that they rework their antiquated statutes. Once their reforms were in place, though, the Court lacked clear tools to confront the reality of persisting discrimination. Abolition seemed like an extreme remedy, as well as unresponsive to the "underenforcement" dimension of the problem. Individual relief to death-sentenced offenders who killed white victims likewise appeared to be ill-matched to the race-of-the-victim discrimination, as well as potentially unjustified from a culpability perspective. Efforts to protect minority victims through court-mandated vigorous use of the death penalty in minority-victim cases seemed impractical at best and dangerous at worst. In short, regulation of the death penalty soon revealed the enormous limits of the regulatory enterprise and generated the uncomfortable paradox that the Court is often better suited to address the risk of evil than evil itself.

During the same era in which a mob lynched Johnson on a Tennessee bridge, political actors across the South were seeking to disenfranchise black voters. In Alabama, the effort was spectacularly successful: the state's new 1901 constitution used a wide array of measures, including a poll tax, a grandfather clause, literacy tests, property provisions, and criminal disenfranchisement provisions, to ensure an almost exclusively white electorate.[69] The purposes animating Alabama's constitutional convention were not concealed; as convention president John B. Knox unabashedly declared: "And what is it that we want to do? Why it is within the limits imposed by the Federal Constitution, to establish white supremacy in this State."[70] Just prior to the new provisions, Alabama had 181,471 eligible black voters; in 1903, just after their enactment, the number of registered black voters was 2,980.[71] In response to Alabama's transparent scheme to deny voting rights to its black citizens, a group of black plaintiffs sued the board of registrars to include them in the voting rolls. The case landed in the Supreme Court, and in its resulting decision, *Giles v. Harris,* the Court laid out in detail the new constitutional provisions as well as the black plaintiffs' allegation that the Alabama officials administering those provisions were conspiring to deny blacks the right to vote.[72]

Justice Holmes, writing for the Court, denied the claim. He did not deny that the new Alabama Constitution and the officials charged with enforcing it were committed to preventing blacks from voting. Rather, in what stands as one of the most remarkable and revealing decisions in Supreme Court history, Holmes denied that the Court could do anything about it. According to Holmes:

> The bill imports that the great mass of the white population intends to keep the blacks from voting. To meet such an intent something more than ordering the plaintiff's name to be inscribed upon the lists of 1902 will be needed. If the conspiracy and the intent exist, a name on a piece of paper will not defeat them. Unless we are prepared to supervise the voting in that state by officers of the court, it seems to us that all that the plaintiff could get from equity would be an empty form.[73]

In short, Justice Holmes did not dispute (though nor did he acknowledge) that the administration of the Alabama scheme violated the Fifteenth Amendment's guarantee of voting rights without regard to race. Instead, Holmes insisted that the Court's inability to enforce a remedy—to ensure that blacks would actually be able to vote in Alabama—was reason enough to not issue an order compelling state officials to allow blacks to do so. This decision effectively took the Court out of the business of protecting minority voters for at least a half century and ensured that relief would come, if at all, through the political branches. The rest of the story is familiar. The right of blacks to vote in the South was secured not through Court enforcement of the straightforward language of the Fifteenth Amendment, but through the social and political mobilization culminating in the federal Voting Rights Act of 1965.

Giles stands as the most conspicuous and candid example of the perceived inadequacy of remedies causing the Court not to recognize constitutional rights. In retrospect, scholars dispute whether Holmes was accurate in his assessment of the Court's powerlessness to protect black voting rights. Rick Pildes, a scholar of the law of democracy, argues that Holmes's extreme "realism" about the Court's impotence probably overstated the Court's inability to counter disenfranchisement in the South, particularly in jurisdictions where there was greater ambivalence about the disenfranchisement project (such as in North Carolina).[74] But the *Giles* episode, like the Court's reluctance to intervene in capital trials when mobs with ropes loomed in the background, illustrates the limits of court-centered strategies when the Court doubts its own capacity to enforce its decisions.

Six decades after *Giles,* the Court changed course and began to assume a more robust role in overseeing a variety of states' voting practices. The most substantial intervention involved malapportioned legislatures. In its first landmark apportionment case, the Court rejected the view that apportionment challenges implicate "political questions" that should be left for the political branches.[75] The challenge involved Tennessee's legislative districts, which afforded rural districts much greater representation in the state senate and house than their populations alone would have suggested. Because the districts had been drawn in 1901 and shifts in population had been dramatic, by 1961 about 40 percent of the states' voters elected almost two-thirds of the state senators and representatives.[76] Opponents to the Court's intervention argued that the Court lacked manageable standards for assessing whether state apportionment schemes undermined equality. But the majority insisted that the Court should not shy away from the litigation merely because it implicated the allocation of political power within a state. Two years later, the Court ruled on the merits of an apportionment challenge, holding that Alabama's apportionment denied equal protection because of the disparate sizes of the state's legislative districts.[77] So was born the "one person, one vote" principle that has been a staple of American election law ever since. The Court has since vigorously enforced the principle in districting for both state and federal offices and tolerated few departures from absolute mathematical equality in the size of such districts.[78]

The Court's apportionment decisions are analogous to the Court's intervention in *Furman*. In both circumstances, the Court was faced with what appeared to be an outdated and anachronistic practice: states had failed to attend to their apportionment schemes in much the same way as they had declined to update their capital statutes. Both prevailing practices also seemed to invite arbitrariness and inequality. Just as standardless discretion in the capital realm ensured discordant results, the indiscriminate districting in apportionment schemes generated palpable inequality with few observable benefits.

But there were deep objections on the other side. As Justice Harlan argued in dissent in both areas, the Court was ill-equipped to regulate apportionment or the death penalty because it was not clear either practice could be improved by virtue of the Court's intervention. In the capital context, Harlan argued, the search for guidance was illusory. The Court could not require states to improve their capital statutes because the death penalty decision could not be tamed. In the apportionment context, the "one person, one vote" principle was not obviously better than other principles in districting, such as honoring historical boundaries, balancing economic or other interest groups, or ensuring representation of disparate voices. The Court's insistence on equally populous districts amounted to taking sides in a complicated debate about representational theory.

In the end, the Court undoubtedly viewed itself as capturing the low-hanging fruit. Telling states to at least attempt to draft capital statutes would be an improvement over the evidently unreflective status quo. And enforcing "one person, one vote" was a quick and easy improvement over the manifest injustice produced by outdated district lines. In both areas, though, Justice Harlan proved prescient in viewing these "easy" fixes as wrought with peril. The effort to tame the death penalty decision led to unintended and, in many respects, unwelcome consequences. In the voting rights context, it soon became apparent that legislatures could accomplish much mischief even if—perhaps especially if—they were constantly required to ensure population balance in their districts. By packing one's opponents into a few districts, legislators can ensure political power for their parties disproportionate to their number of voters. These efforts triggered constitutional challenges to the practice of diluting the political strength of opponents in the drawing of district lines.

Partisan vote dilution of this sort raises important questions of equality and fairness. It is very unseemly for politicians to be selecting their voters, rather than the other way around, especially if that selection process is intended to lock in their prevailing power. Had the Court not entered the political thicket, the problem might be viewed as one of policy. But having decided that voters have a constitutional interest in their voting strength (apart from merely the right to cast a ballot), the Court seemed to invite constitutional litigation challenging partisan gerrymandering.

But the Court's ultimate response—similar to its response in *McCleskey*—has been to shrink away from claims of partisan vote dilution. Although the Court has ruled such claims "justiciable" (capable of being asserted in court) for the moment, it has yet to embrace such a claim on the merits.[79] The Court has erected a virtually impossible standard for plaintiffs, requiring that they demonstrate that challenged practices unfairly dilute their voting strength as well as "consistently degrade" their group's influence in the political process.[80] Several justices have expressed a willingness to reconsider the federal courts' power even to hear such claims, which would render the prevailing partisan vote dilution doctrine a dead letter.[81] The reasons for the Court's retreat are similar to those in *McCleskey*. Although partisan efforts to impair the voting strength of opponents are deeply threatening to constitutional values identified by the Court, it is difficult to calibrate how much diminution requires constitutional intervention. The Court is unwilling to demand absolute equality of outcomes, and even if it were so willing, the attractive mathematical precision of the one person, one vote doctrine is simply unattainable in the partisan vote dilution context. The best cure—mandating the use of independent, nonpartisan districting commissions—seems like an extraordinary intrusion on state and local prerogatives. Just

246 | COURTING DEATH

as the Court is unwilling to take charging decisions away from individual prosecutors to reduce the influence of race (by moving them to an independent entity or a statewide prosecutorial team), so too is the Court reluctant to deny legislators their traditional responsibility to decide communities of political interest.

The Court's enthusiastic efforts to advance norms of constitutional equality in both the voting and capital contexts encountered sobering remedial constraints that limited the Court's eventual success. The experiences in both fields of constitutional regulation reflect the long-observed truth that constitutional rights are only as powerful as the remedies that can be offered to enforce them.

Discourse Shaping

Constitutional decision making is always in conversation with wider public discourse. It seems obvious that the Court's framing and articulation of its constitutional decisions will necessarily reflect the way in which a controversy is presented to it and the general ways of thinking about the issue that are prevalent at the time. What is less obvious and worth unearthing is the way in which constitutional regulation may not only mirror but also shift the nature of public discourse. One can trace such impacts on public discourse from the Court's constitutional regulation of capital punishment and from more recent constitutional decision making around same-sex marriage.

In the death penalty context, the most striking shift in public discourse from the period immediately preceding *Furman* to the present has been the virtual disappearance of arguments against the death penalty premised on its fundamental immorality, such as claims about its essential barbarity, its denial of human dignity, or its incompatibility with civilized society. Rather, the overwhelming flavor of current public debates about capital punishment is relentlessly pragmatic, focused on whether the death penalty's benefits are worth its extravagant cost and whether problems in its administration are fixable. Today, opponents of the death penalty tend to highlight long-standing problems of arbitrariness and discrimination, or they

highlight newer problems like delays between sentence and execution and the difficulty of obtaining lethal injection drugs. But almost no one speaks primarily in the language that Justices Brennan
and Marshall invoked in their categorical opinions in *Furman,* where
Brennan pronounced the death penalty "degrading to the dignity of
human beings" and Marshall celebrated the Court's abolition as "a
major milestone in the long road up from barbarism."[82]

One reason for the declining focus on human dignity in debates
surrounding the American death penalty was the movement of the
issue into the courts in the 1960s. Prior to the LDF's sustained legal
attack on the death penalty, anti-death penalty advocacy was primarily the province of religious and moral opponents of the practice,
who gave voice to their categorical objections to the death penalty in
the political realm. When the issue entered the courts, the legal
attacks on the death penalty understandably focused primarily on
its administration rather than its overarching morality given perceptions about the types of arguments that would resonate in the judicial
forum. The enormous energy devoted to capital litigation tended to
crowd out the more absolutist voices in the anti-death penalty movement as the LDF became the primary face of the American anti-death
penalty movement

The Court's own work reviving and regulating capital punishment
commencing with *Gregg* in 1976 contributed to this substantial shift
in discourse in several ways. While Brennan and Marshall were
important voices in the majority in *Furman* in 1972, they were the
sole dissenters in *Gregg* in 1976—reflecting the extent to which their
views were those of an increasingly marginalized left wing on criminal justice issues, both on the Court and in public discourse more
generally. The rising crime rates of the 1970s and 1980s gave arguments about the need for deterrence new plausibility, a rationale that
the *Gregg* Court enshrined, along with retribution, as one of the
principle justifications for capital punishment. The years following
Furman saw a revival of retributivism as a central theory of criminal
punishment in the United States, both among scholars and the public.[83]
Retributivism's insistence on proportional punishment as a matter
of the offender's "just deserts" offers powerful support to death penalty

proponents, who maintain that only death is a sufficiently severe punishment for heinous murders. Retributive theory itself is arguably rooted in the value of dignity: inflicting proportional punishment on an offender respects the offender's dignity by treating the offender as an autonomous author of his own punishment, and it respects the dignity of victims by balancing or annulling the offender's degrading act.[84] The turn to retributivism sapped appeals to dignity of their abolitionist force by investing them with countervailing punitive force. The Court's marginalization of Brennan's "human dignity" argument in 1976 both reflected and reinforced this accelerating change in the valence of appeals to dignity.

The Court's constitutional regulation of capital punishment also reduced the likelihood that the United States would join in the eventual European consensus that the death penalty was an issue of international human rights. Partly, this was because the human rights approach shared Brennan's focus on human dignity, as reflected in a 1997 Resolution of the United Nations High Commission for Human Rights asserting that the "abolition of the death penalty contributes to the enhancement of human dignity and to the progressive development of human rights."[85] But the failure of a human rights approach to capital punishment to take hold in the United States was also a product of the fact that the Supreme Court held that the death penalty was consistent with the values enshrined in our foundational national document. The U.S. Constitution holds a place in the American public imagination as the locus of all essential rights and freedoms—what one commentator has called a kind of "civil religion" of "Constitution worship."[86] It is therefore hard for American political leaders to articulate, or for members of the American public to accept, that our much vaunted Constitution could validate something that was inconsistent with universally accepted human rights.

However, the most profound impact of the Court's constitutional regulation of capital punishment on public discourse has been the product of regulation's tendency to vastly increase the financial cost of the death penalty. Until quite recently, it seemed obvious that executing offenders was cheaper than incarcerating them for life; the cost argument was always invoked by supporters of capital punishment rather than by abolitionists. Only in the post-*Gregg* era did compliance with the Court's regulatory framework raise the cost of capital trials while simultaneously delaying executions by a lengthy review process, thus requiring long and costly incarceration on death row. The change in valence of the cost argument permitted abolitionists to reframe the prevailing discourse around capital punishment. Instead of being forced into "soft-on-crime" expressions of sympathy for the dignity of heinous murderers, abolitionists were able to use the cost argument to make a sharp rhetorical turn away from the humanitarian cast of their prior arguments. Instead of premising the abolitionist case on the cruelty or unfairness of capital punishment to convicted murderers, abolitionists could focus on the interests of the collective by emphasizing the necessity of cost-cutting and the alternative collective goods that inevitably compete with capital punishment for funding.

The 2009 abolitionist effort in Colorado, which failed by a single vote, made this trade-off explicit by seeking to tie the savings that would be produced by legislative repeal of the death penalty to increased funding for the investigation of unsolved murders ("cold cases"). Similarly, abolitionists have long focused on the cruelty to condemned inmates of lengthy and uncertain stays on death row; now, however, the length of stays on death row has become as much an argument about the often substantial cost differential between incarceration on death row and in the general population. The enormous size of the overall cost differential between capital and noncapital sentencing allows abolitionists to argue, with some plausibility, that alternative deployment of the funds currently used to support capital punishment may not only offer necessary cost-savings, but may also produce *better* outcomes in terms of crime control and prevention. Abolitionists have taken to noting that police chiefs are ten times more likely to cite "lack of law enforcement resources" than "insufficient use of the death penalty" in their response to the question "What interferes with effective law enforcement?"[87]

In an ironic turnabout, proponents of capital punishment often find themselves responding to such utilitarian arguments by resorting to the essentially moral or retributivist argument that only the death penalty is an appropriately severe response to the worst crimes. As one proponent of capital punishment explained: "The death penalty should not be a utilitarian issue in terms of weighing the costs against the benefits, but rather an issue simply of justice, of who deserves it."[88] In light of the current enormous costs of the death penalty, proponents are placed in the tenuous position of arguing that no price is too high for the "justice" of capital punishment. As a result, the rhetorical positions of abolitionists and retentionists in previous debates have flipped: abolitionists get to shed the unattractive cloak of soft sentimentality and don the mantle of efficient crime control, while retentionists now have to rebut charges that their attachment to the death penalty is a form of unworldly moralism. This striking about-face is wholly a product of the new financial realities of capital punishment, which themselves are the product of the Court's constitutional regulation.

In a similar manner, constitutional rulings about same-sex marriage by the U.S. Supreme Court as well as other federal and state courts have altered the discourse around gay rights. Interestingly, the shift in this context also involved a move from moral to utilitarian concerns, as the constitutional battle shifted the terrain from the morality of gay sex to the costs and benefits of gay marriage. The first major constitutional ruling in this area was the Supreme Court's 1986 decision upholding the constitutionality of statutes criminalizing consensual same-sex sodomy. The Court's description of the issue in that case—"whether the Federal Constitution confers a fundamental right upon homosexuals to engage in sodomy"—suggested that the Gay Rights Movement was primarily a movement about gay *sex*, a formulation that emphasized the most transgressive aspect of claims for protection of sexual orientation.[89] More than fifteen years later, the Court would overrule that holding and in doing so reflect and reinforce a new understanding that was being pressed by litigants and advocates in the broader public sphere. The Court explained that its prior decision had failed "to appreciate the extent of the liberty at stake" because the criminal sodomy laws "have more far-reaching consequences" affecting "the most private human conduct, sexual behavior, and in the most private of places, the home," and seeking "to control personal relationship[s]."[90] The introduction of the concepts of "home" and "relationships" to the Court's analysis of statutes that prohibited discrete sex acts profoundly shifted the framework of discussion and seemed to invite future litigation around the issue of marriage. Indeed, less than six months later, the Massachusetts Supreme Judicial Court ruled in favor of marriage equality under the Massachusetts Constitution in the pathbreaking *Goodridge* decision, authored by Chief Justice Margaret Marshall.[91]

In its decision striking down criminal sodomy statutes, the U.S. Supreme Court made a key doctrinal move that would shape both the marriage litigation to come and the wider public discourse. Both Justice Kennedy's majority opinion based on the Due Process Clause and Justice O'Connor's concurrence based on the Equal Protection Clause agreed that "the fact that the governing majority . . . has traditionally viewed a particular practice as immoral is not a sufficient reason for upholding a law prohibiting the practice."[92] The import of this holding meant that, going forward, opponents of marriage equality would have to identify harms—*other than personal revulsion or moral outrage*—that would flow from recognizing same-sex marriage in order to defeat due process and equal protection challenges in the courts.

The attempts of the opponents of same-sex marriage to rise to this challenge provided moments of absurdist theater that were a gift to the proponents of marriage equality, who easily demolished the attempted demonstrations of purported harms that recognition of marriage equality would produce. In the lengthy trial challenging California's ban on same-sex marriage passed by Proposition 8, the defenders of Prop 8 relied heavily on the testimony of marriage "expert" David Blankenhorn, a former amateur boxer who was forced to do some verbal bobbing and weaving on the witness stand.[93] On direct examination, Blankenhorn emphasized harm to children of same-sex unions, arguing that the main purpose of marriage was the protection of children within a family, and that "the two-biological-parent, married-couple home . . . is the best model from the child's point of view." Blankenhorn went on to opine that extending marriage rights to same-sex couples would harm not only children, but also the institution of marriage itself. In his view, marriage equality would create a process of "deinstitutionalization" because it would make the rules governing marriage "less comprehensible and clear and . . . less authoritative." Instead of expanding that circle of marriage, extending rights to same-sex couples would result in "kind of a shrinking process."[94]

Star litigator David Boies patiently and humorously decimated Blankenhorn on the stand, eventually eliciting substantial retrenchment on Blankenhorn's central points. Boies destroyed Blankenhorn's "expert" qualifications by establishing that he had no relevant academic degrees, that he had never taught a course in any college or university on marriage, fatherhood, or family structure, and that he had never conducted independent research on the effects of permitting same-sex marriage. In the prolonged cross-examination that followed, Blankenhorn's uncertain and evasive answers elicited frequent laughter from the courtroom, leading the presiding judge, Vaughn Walker, to try to reassure the witness that Boies wasn't laughing at him: "He's amused at the back-and-forth, as I think many of us who are observing this are." Blankenhorn eventually stated that he believed that "adopting same-sex marriage would be likely to improve the well-being of gay and lesbian households and their children," and also conceded that none of the scholars whose work he cited had predicted that same-sex marriage would damage heterosexual marriage.[95]

In a somewhat different vein, defenders of same-sex marriage bans in Wisconsin and Indiana argued that the extension of marriage rights to same-sex couples would fail to promote the central purpose of marriage—which was "to try to channel unintentionally procreative sex into a legal regime in which the biological father is required to assume parental responsibility." Judge Richard Posner derided this argument as "so full of holes that it cannot be taken seriously," noting that "if channeling procreative sex into marriage were the only reason that Indiana recognizes marriage, the state would not allow an infertile person to marry . . . [and] it would make marriage licenses expire when one of the spouses (fertile upon marriage) became infertile because of age or disease."[96] At oral argument in the case,

Posner repeatedly asked for examples of concrete harmful consequences that would flow from recognizing same-sex marriage, without getting a straightforward answer. He finally gave up and asked the Wisconsin attorney to "speculate" about what the harms might be. "The harmful possibilities are, 'We don't know,'" came the reply, prompting a caustic riposte from Posner: "You don't have any sort of empirical or even conjectural basis for your law. Funny."[97]

During oral argument before the Supreme Court in the landmark case of *Obergefell v. Hodges,* which ruled that the Constitution protected marriage equality, Mary Bonauto (often referred to as the Thurgood Marshall of the Gay Rights Movement) pressed the same point.[98] In response to questions from the justices about the long tradition of the institution of marriage excluding gays and lesbians, Bonauto insisted that opponents of marriage equality had to offer some basis other than what Kennedy had called "personal revulsion or moral outrage" for that long history of exclusion. Bonauto maintained that "the Court still needs *a reason* to maintain that tradition."[99]

The Prop 8 trial, the Posner oral argument, and the Supreme Court case were all extensively covered and widely quoted in the press, focusing public attention on the issue of the concrete harms (or lack of them) threatened by same-sex marriage. This focus was not entirely fair to the anti–marriage equality camp. Their harm arguments were lame because they weren't the *real* reasons behind opposition to same-sex marriage, which were entirely moral in character. But the Supreme Court had taken morality off the table with regard to the relevant constitutional rubrics. As a consequence, the highly publicized journey to constitutional recognition of same-sex marriage turned into an extended exegesis of how cost-benefit analysis supported the case for marriage equality.

The Supreme Court's opinion in *Obergefell* also played a role in shifting public discourse, but along a different dimension. Justice Kennedy's opinion for the Court was not so much a dismantling of arguments about the purported harms of same-sex marriage as it was a paean to marriage itself. Marriage, he explained, is a fundamental right because it "is essential to our most profound hopes and aspirations." In the most soaring language of the opinion, Kennedy concluded: "No union is more profound than marriage, for it embodies the highest ideals of love, fidelity, devotion, sacrifice, and family. In forming a marital union, two people become something greater than once they were. . . . [M]arriage embodies a love that may endure even past death."[100] Both the decision within the gay rights community to focus on marriage rights and Kennedy's encomium to marriage in *Obergefell* reflect an essentially conservative impulse to turn away from the transgressive aspects of gay life and culture, to insist that gay people are—or should be—"just like" everyone else.[101] This constitutional recasting of the movement for gay equality is finding its way into mainstream culture in an unusual, but maybe also highly predictable way—through the reading of judicial decisions at marriage ceremonies. It turns out that marrying couples, both gay and straight, are turning to Justice Kennedy's opinion (as well as Chief Justice Margaret Marshall's opinion in the Massachusetts case and Judge Vaughn Walker's opinion from the Prop 8 trial) to help them consecrate their vows.[102] What better proof of the penetration of constitutional law into public discourse could there be?

"Death is different," the Supreme Court has often intoned, expressing the uniqueness of capital punishment and its need for special constitutional treatment. Yet it turns out that death is not so different when it comes to constitutional regulation, in that many characteristics of the regulatory enterprise that seem particular to the death penalty context can be traced in other, widely divergent areas of constitutional law. These commonalities suggest that both constitutional litigants and courts would do well to attend to the recurring features of constitutional regulation that the death penalty story, among others, brings to vivid life.

CHAPTER EIGHT

The Future of the
American Death Penalty

THE AMERICAN DEATH PENALTY is currently more vulnerable than it has been at any point since its revival in 1976. The profound shifts in the law, practice, institutions, and politics of capital punishment have mutually reinforced one another, creating increasing momentum toward marginalization of the death penalty. For the first time since the late 1960s, nationwide abolition seems achievable in the foreseeable future—a possibility that might have been dismissed out of hand as recently as the early 2000s. The media is abuzz with predictions of the death penalty's demise. In June 2015, *Time* magazine ran a cover story entitled "The Death of the Death Penalty," and three months later, *USA Today* ran a multipart story on why the death penalty is "on life support."[1]

Consideration of the various possible mechanisms for nationwide abolition reveals that the path to abolition in the United States will be as distinctive, and as distinctively constitutional, as the American choice to regulate capital punishment rather than merely retain or abolish it. Contrary to the abolition of the death penalty achieved by most of our peer countries, American abolition almost certainly will arrive, if it does, by constitutional ruling rather than legislative repeal. In most of the countries in Western Europe, abolition of the death penalty has occurred through legislation. Portugal and the Netherlands initiated abolition of the death penalty for ordinary crimes in the mid-nineteenth century, and the Scandinavian countries followed in the first few decades of the twentieth. Germany and Italy abolished capital punishment for ordinary crimes in their postwar constitutions after surrendering to the Allied powers in 1945. But the phenomenon called "European abolition" was largely accomplished during the last quarter of the twentieth century, when virtually all of Europe completely abolished the death penalty not only for ordinary crimes like murder, but for all crimes (including military crimes, treason, and terrorism). This abolition was almost always the consequence of legislative action, either through the passage of ordinary legislation or the legislature's approval of constitutional provisions.

Although the United States has seen a powerful surge of state legislative repeal of the death penalty in recent years, nationwide abolition cannot reasonably be expected through legislative means, either on the state or federal level. At the state level, it is likely that the surge of legislative repeal is not over, as a number of states recently have come extremely close to repealing the death penalty.[2] But American federalism cedes primary authority over criminal justice matters to individual states and permits—indeed, celebrates—wide variation among the states, which serve, as Justice Louis Brandeis evocatively suggested, as "laboratories of democracy."[3] And among those laboratories are jurisdictions—such as Texas and Alabama, among others—in which legislative repeal is simply a political nonstarter for the foreseeable future. These states may become increasingly marginalized as legislative repeal gains ground elsewhere; moreover, capital punishment may become increasingly marginalized *within* these states as fewer counties seek or impose death sentences. But while capital punishment may substantially decrease in scope through a combination of legislative repeal and local restraint, it will not disappear as an American institution anytime soon through unanimous state legislative action.[4]

Nor is federal legislative action a likely route to nationwide abolition. Although the matter is not settled, the Constitution may well prevent Congress from abolishing capital punishment in the states, even if Congress wanted to do so. In the early 1970s, congressional hearings addressed the constitutionality of potential top-down abolition (as well as a more limited proposal to stay executions), and some scholars opined that such a path might be open to Congress.[5] But a series of Supreme Court decisions since then has imposed limits on federal power that make such a course more doubtful today.[6] It is unlikely that Congress could use its otherwise broad power to regulate interstate commerce to override states' choice to retain the death penalty, given the remote connection between the death penalty and commerce and the prerogative of states (protected by the Tenth Amendment) to choose their own criminal justice policies.[7] Congress might also be precluded from using its enforcement powers under the Fourteenth Amendment to achieve abolition. Unless the Supreme Court itself were to embrace the view that state capital punishment practices are constitutionally problematic, congressional abolition might not satisfy the Court's increasingly restrictive test for appropriate Fourteenth Amendment legislation. Perhaps Congress could use its spending power to condition receipt of targeted federal funds on states' willingness to abandon the death penalty (such as funds for indigent defense), but that type of legislation could only encourage, and not command, state abolition across the board.

Even if congressional abolition were constitutionally permissible, its political prospects appear remote. Congress has the power to reform or abolish its own capital provisions, but there have been no significant initiatives to withdraw the federal death penalty. The federal government—with its small number of death sentences, death row prisoners, and executions—may seem to have more in common with states considering repeal than those actively engaged in executions. Despite these similarities, friction between the federal government and the states regarding the death penalty in recent times has come not from the federal government trying to inhibit states' use of the death penalty, but rather from the federal government seeking to impose the death penalty for a federal crime committed in an abolitionist jurisdiction, such as the recent capital prosecution of Dzhokhar Tsarnaev in Massachusetts for the 2013 Boston Marathon

attack. The Tsarnaev case illustrates the unique federal considerations that support retention: the view that the death penalty might
be essential to punish extraordinary crimes such as treason, espionage, military offenses, or terrorism. Experience in Europe and elsewhere demonstrates that these uses of the death penalty tend to be
the last to be repealed, representing the final step toward full abolition. Accordingly, Congress is an unlikely candidate to initiate (much
less complete) the process of American death penalty abolition.

Consequently, if truly nationwide abolition is to occur in the foreseeable future, it must come by means of a federal constitutional
ruling—a "Furman II." Given the close divide on the Court on this
and other contested social issues, much depends on the Court's
changing composition. The death of Justice Antonin Scalia in February of 2016 underscored how crucial the next Supreme Court
appointment will be in either maintaining or shifting the current
balance on the death penalty. But the consistent movement of justices
toward abolition and the creation of a doctrinal "blueprint" for abolition under the Eighth Amendment suggest that the moment may
be coming, and coming sooner rather than later. The possibility of
an imminent "Furman II" has engendered speculation and debate
even among those who would be expected to welcome it, as abolitionist lawyers ponder the tactics of constitutional litigation under
conditions of uncertainty.

The Marshall Hypothesis and Movement on the High Court

When we law clerks would ask Justice Thurgood Marshall indig-
nantly how the Court could issue what we viewed as an objectionable ruling, Marshall would respond by holding up his hand with the
fingers spread out. "Five," he would answer with a shake of his head.
"Five votes—that's how." Marshall's simple pragmatism is every
lawyer's catechism: legal change happens only when there are enough
votes to make it happen. Might there be five votes on the Supreme
Court to make a "Furman II"—that is, to constitutionally abolish
capital punishment in America? Seven justices since *Furman* have indicated that they think capital punishment should be ruled categori-

cally unconstitutional: Justices Brennan and Marshall in *Furman* it-self and Justices Powell, Blackmun, Stevens, Breyer, and Ginsburg in the decades since. However, only two of them (Breyer and Ginsburg) currently sit on the Court. Despite the small number of current jus-tices who have already indicated their willingness to invalidate cap-ital punishment, the consistent movement of justices over time toward constitutional skepticism of capital punishment is instruc-tive. Indeed, no other body of constitutional law has been so severely criticized—and, indeed, abandoned—by so many of the justices who created it and attempted in good faith to apply it.

Two of the seven justices who have declared the American death penalty categorically unconstitutional, William Brennan and Thur-good Marshall, did so as members of the five-justice majority in *Furman* in 1972. Their views, expressed separately in their individual concurring opinions, reflected a criticism of capital punishment that was widespread in the 1960s but is much less commonly voiced today—that the infliction of the death penalty is inconsistent with fundamental moral principles enshrined in the Constitution. Brennan opined that the death penalty was "cruel and unusual" under the Eighth Amendment because it was "uncivilized and inhuman" and inconsistent with respect for the "intrinsic worth" and "dignity" of human beings.[8] Marshall expressed a similar view that the death penalty paid insufficient regard to "the humanity of our fellow be-ings" and was "morally unacceptable to the people of the United States at this time in their history."[9] Brennan and Marshall are not exemplars either of justices' changing views over time (because their views remained static) or of the reasons for such changing views (which have been concerns about the application in practice rather than the fundamental morality of capital punishment). But they are important because of Marshall's theory about how to gauge societal acceptance of the death penalty. Marshall explained that societal ac-ceptance of the death penalty should not be measured by such things as legislative enactments or even public opinion polls; rather, he as-serted that "the question with which we must deal is not whether a substantial proportion of American citizens would today, if polled, opine that capital punishment is barbarously cruel, but whether they would find it to be so in the light of all information presently available."[10]

Marshall offered a long list of facts that would influence an "informed" citizen's attitude toward the death penalty, including information on the penalty's lack of deterrent effect, the good behavior of most convicted murderers in prison and their low recidivism rates upon release, and the higher cost of capital punishment as compared with life imprisonment, among other things. Such facts would convince the average citizen that the death penalty was "unwise," in Marshall's view. But Marshall then identified further considerations that would convince "even the most hesitant of citizens" that the death penalty was "morally reprehensible"—namely, that "capital punishment is imposed discriminatorily against certain identifiable classes of people; there is evidence that innocent people have been executed before their innocence can be proved; and the death penalty wreaks havoc with our entire criminal justice system."[11]

This prediction about what the American public would believe about the death penalty, if fully informed, has become known as "the Marshall hypothesis." In the decades following *Furman*, numerous social scientists conducted a variety of studies seeking to determine whether subjects' reported attitudes about the death penalty changed in response to the subjects' exposure to the kind of information that Marshall predicted would move them to oppose the death penalty. Some of the studies found that at least some people, in some settings, may be moved by the transmission of such information, at least temporarily. But other studies found that exposing subjects to information produced only short-term changes in beliefs ("rebound") or even intensification of subjects' preexisting beliefs about the death penalty ("polarization"). These latter findings reflect the likelihood that, for many people, emotional or cultural influences on death penalty attitudes outweigh purely cognitive input. For this reason, death penalty attitudes may well be more resistant to lasting change through rational argument than the Marshall hypothesis allows.[12]

Despite the at-best modest success of the Marshall hypothesis in the laboratory of social science research, the Marshall hypothesis has had rather stunning success among Marshall's colleagues on the

Court. Arguably, the justices of the Supreme Court are an excellent sample to study the effect of information on death penalty attitudes. The justices, who generally serve for a substantial number of years, get a very detailed and panoramic view of the administration of capital punishment across the country, because every contested death sentence makes its way to the Court before the execution may be carried out. The justices are forced to reflect upon and articulate their own views about capital punishment because the Eighth Amendment calls upon the Court to decide whether the administration of the death penalty in any particular context conforms to the "evolving standards of decency that mark the progress of a maturing society," which in turn requires the Court to consider not only evidence of societal consensus but also its "own judgment."[13] The experience of reviewing capital cases from around the country over the course of decades has led five justices—all of whom voted to uphold many death sentences during their tenures on the Court—eventually to view capital punishment as categorically unconstitutional. Strikingly, three of these justices originally disagreed with Marshall in *Furman* or *Gregg* (or both)—the Court's foundational death penalty cases. The remaining two were not on the Court at the time of *Furman* and *Gregg*, but rather sit on the Court today and represent the ongoing power of the Marshall hypothesis. Consideration of the ways in which these various justices evolved in their views over time offers substantial grounds to predict an eventual majority on the Court for constitutional abolition.

The most surprising repudiation of the Court's death penalty jurisprudence was by Justice Lewis Powell, who was a steady and central player in the defense of the death penalty during the tumultuous years in which the Court evaluated categorical challenges to its constitutionality. In 1972, Powell was one of the block of four Nixon appointees who dissented in *Furman* from the Court's invalidation of the death penalty. Four years later, Powell, along with Justices Potter Stewart and John Paul Stevens, coauthored the plurality opinions reinstating the death penalty in *Gregg* and its companion cases. Powell was the only one of the later death penalty critics who both dissented in *Furman* and formed part of the key plurality in *Gregg*.

In *Furman,* Powell authored the longest and most comprehensive of the four dissents, methodically rejecting all of the various arguments made in the five different majority opinions against the constitutionality of capital punishment. In response to arguments about the discriminatory application of the death penalty, emphasized by both Marshall and Justice William O. Douglas, Powell expressed confidence that "standards of criminal justice have 'evolved' in a manner favorable to the accused" and concluded that therefore "discriminatory imposition of capital punishment is far less likely today than in the past."[14] The plurality opinions reinstating the death penalty in *Gregg* and its companion cases similarly expressed faith in the efficacy of the procedures mandated by the new statutes passed in response to *Furman.* Powell and his plurality colleagues explained that "the concerns expressed in *Furman* that the penalty of death not be imposed in an arbitrary or capricious manner can be met by a carefully drafted statute that ensures that the sentencing authority is given adequate information and guidance."[15]

Powell's views on the issue of discrimination in the imposition of capital punishment took center stage a decade later, when the Court finally reviewed a challenge to the death penalty based on empirical evidence of the effects of race on capital sentencing. In *McCleskey v. Kemp,* Powell cast the crucial fifth vote to reject the constitutional challenge, and he authored the majority opinion for the Court.[16] Powell accepted for the sake of argument the validity of the empirical study that showed that both the race of the perpetrator and the race of the victim had played statistically significant roles in the distribution of death sentences in the jurisdiction in which McCleskey, a black man, had been sentenced to death for the murder of a white police officer; the study showed that the killers of white victims, especially if they were black, faced heightened chances of a death verdict. Nonetheless, Powell concluded that such findings did not undermine the constitutional validity of McCleskey's death sentence. Powell reasoned that the defense had shown only that race effects were prevalent in the jurisdiction in which McCleskey was sentenced, not that his particular jury had actually been motivated by either his (black) race or the (white) race of his victim. The Court's ruling in

McCleskey effectively foreclosed future challenges to racial discrimination in the imposition of the death penalty because the available evidence of such discrimination tends to be historical or statistical evidence of race effects over time, rather than the sort of "smoking gun" evidence about a specific jury that Powell's opinion for the Court seemed to require.

Powell, unlike the other four justices who would later change their views on the death penalty, did not express any change of heart while sitting on the Court. Indeed, he retired from the Court very shortly after authoring the majority opinion in *McCleskey.* However, several years after his retirement, Powell's official biographer, John Jeffries Jr., asked him in an interview if there were any votes that he would change from his tenure on the Court, and Powell responded, "Yes, *McCleskey v. Kemp.*" Powell's reconsideration of the death penalty went beyond McCleskey's particular case to the underlying constitutionality of capital punishment in general; Powell explained to Jeffries that he had come to believe that the death penalty cannot be enforced fairly and therefore that it "brings discredit on the whole legal system."[17]

Justice Harry Blackmun had a similar epiphany, but his occurred shortly before, rather than after, he retired from the Court. Blackmun's repudiation of the constitutionality of the death penalty is less surprising than Powell's in light of the intense personal distaste expressed by Blackmun for capital punishment. Like Powell, Blackmun was one of the four Nixon appointees who dissented in *Furman,* but his dissent was a far cry from Powell's lengthy, point-by-point refutation of the arguments against the constitutionality of the death penalty made by the justices in the majority. Rather, Blackmun's dissent described the "excruciating agony of the spirit" that he suffered in facing the clash between his personal beliefs about capital punishment and his views about the limits of the judicial role. Wrote Blackmun, "I yield to no one in the depth of my distaste, antipathy, and, indeed, abhorrence for the death penalty. . . . For me, it violates childhood's training and life's experiences."[18] Despite these strong feelings, Blackmun concluded in *Furman,* "Although personally I may rejoice at the Court's result, I find it difficult to accept or to justify as a matter of history, of law, or of constitutional pronouncement. I fear the Court has overstepped."[19] Blackmun's conviction that the issue of capital punishment lay within the purview of the political branches of government rather than the judiciary led him to join the majority in reviving capital punishment in 1976 and in upholding numerous capital convictions against constitutional challenges in years that followed, though with increasing reservations (for example, Blackmun dissented from Powell's majority opinion in *McCleskey*).

Blackmun's reservations about capital punishment coalesced into a categorical constitutional position that he expressed in a lengthy and impassioned dissent from denial of review in a capital case in 1994, shortly before his retirement from the Court. Blackmun explained that a fundamental contradiction lay at the heart of the capital jurisprudence that the Court, with his assistance, had developed since the 1970s. The Court's constitutional command that capital sentencing discretion must be legislatively guided to avoid arbitrary sentencing, he wrote, could not be reconciled with its mandate that all potentially mitigating evidence must be considered to promote individualized sentencing. Because proper legislative guidance and sufficient individualized consideration were both crucial to the administration of capital punishment and yet could not simultaneously be achieved, Blackmun concluded that the death penalty could not stand: "Experience has taught us that the constitutional goal of eliminating arbitrariness and discrimination from the administration of death can never be achieved without compromising an equally essential component of fundamental fairness—individualized sentencing." Like Powell, Blackmun saw the question as one of fundamental fairness: "The death penalty must be imposed fairly, and with reasonable consistency, or not at all."[20]

Blackmun went the furthest of any of the retracting justices by not merely announcing his new, categorical view on the unconstitutionality of capital punishment, but also applying that view during the brief remainder of his tenure on the Court. Blackmun dramatically proclaimed, "From this day forward, I no longer shall tinker with the machinery of death."[21] As Marshall and Brennan had done after their dissents to the reinstatement of capital punishment in *Gregg* and its companion cases, Blackmun refused to vote to uphold any further death sentences. In every subsequent capital case that came before the Court, Blackmun voted to stay the execution, grant review, and vacate the death sentence. Indeed, a search of the Supreme Court's database for the phrase "Adhering to my view" in proximity to "death penalty" turns up not only Marshall and Brennan's decades of dissents in all of the Court's capital cases from the post-*Gregg* era, but also Blackmun's dozens of dissents from the latter part of the 1993–1994 term of the Court—articulated, no doubt self-consciously, in the same language as that of the original dissenting duo.

Justice Stevens is the third of Marshall's contemporaries to change course on the constitutionality of capital punishment. Although Stevens was not yet on the Court at the time of the decision in *Furman,* he was appointed (like Powell and Blackmun, by a Republican president) in time to join Powell as one of the three justices in the plurality that wrote the 1976 opinions reinstating the death penalty. Stevens's journey from architect of the death penalty's revival to constitutional abolitionist was the longest of any of the justices who changed their minds, taking more than three decades. Although Stevens voted to uphold numerous death sentences against constitutional challenges in the 1970s, 1980s, and 1990s, he, like Blackmun, became a more and more frequent dissenter. Like Blackmun, Stevens dissented from Powell's majority opinion in *McCleskey.* Moreover, Stevens joined all three of the Court's opinions, issued long after the retirements of Powell and Blackmun, cutting back on the scope of the death penalty by invalidating it for intellectually disabled and juvenile offenders and for the crime of child rape.[22] In the same year that he joined the majority to invalidate the death penalty for child rape, Stevens wrote a solo concurrence in another capital case, announcing that he had come to the conclusion that the death penalty could no longer be constitutionally tolerated.

Stevens placed responsibility for his change of heart squarely on his long tenure on the Court spent reviewing large numbers of capital cases. Stevens explained that after "extensive exposure to countless cases for which death is the authorized penalty," he came to the conclusion on the basis of his "own experience" that the Court's original decision in *Furman* had been correct and that the death penalty is "patently excessive and cruel and unusual punishment violative of the Eighth Amendment."[23] Stevens first grounded his rejection of the death penalty in its failure to contribute measurably to the goals of either deterrence or retribution. But he went on to explain that of "decisive importance" to his judgment that the death penalty was unconstitutional was its irrevocability, which renders the legal system unable to respond to the problem of "the real risk of error" in its application. This risk, Stevens argued, is exacerbated by the inadequacy of current procedures to guarantee fairly representative capital juries, to protect against emotion overcoming reason in capital deliberations, or to prevent discriminatory application of the death penalty.[24] However, unlike Blackmun (or Marshall and Brennan), Stevens explained that he felt bound to continue to apply the Court's existing death penalty doctrine out of respect for precedent, and he did so until his retirement from the Court two years later in 2010. Indeed, Stevens voted to uphold the defendant's death sentence in the very case in which he announced his rejection of the death penalty's constitutionality.

Seven years after Stevens's announcement of his changed view on capital punishment, and five years after his retirement, a new pair of justices came to a similar conclusion, echoing Stevens's concerns about innocence and discrimination and adding new considerations. In 2015, the Court split five to four in upholding Oklahoma's use of the controversial drug midazolam for lethal injections. In addition to joining Justice Sonia Sotomayor's dissent on the lethal injection issue, Justice Stephen Breyer wrote for himself and Justice Ruth Bader Ginsburg, both Clinton appointees, to express the view that "the death penalty, in and of itself, now likely constitutes a legally prohibited 'cruel and unusual punishment.'" By using the qualifier "likely" (and later "highly likely"), Breyer stopped short of the categorical stance embraced by Powell, Blackmun, and Stevens; rather, he called for the Court to ask for full briefing on the question "whether the death penalty violates the Constitution."[25] However, Breyer's lengthy dissent, with its exhaustive marshalling of empirical evidence, leaves little doubt as to how he and Ginsburg would resolve the ultimate issue. Breyer took the unusual step of reading his dissent aloud from the bench, which intensified media attention to its content.[26]

Breyer's concerns about the death penalty, like those of all of the justices who followed Marshall and Brennan in rejecting the constitutionality of capital punishment, focused on its administration rather than its underlying morality. Breyer explained that the Court's original view in 1976 that "the death penalty could be healed" was undermined by almost "40 years of studies, surveys, and experience." He listed three "fundamental constitutional defects" in the administration of the death penalty and then added a fourth consideration—the fact that "most places within the United States have abandoned its use."[27]

Breyer's first fundamental defect tracked the factor that Stevens had identified as of "decisive importance"—the problem of lack of reliability, or possible innocence. Breyer took the bold step of identifying cases in recent decades in which "researchers have found convincing evidence that . . . innocent people have been executed." He also noted the larger number of people (over a hundred) who had been sentenced to die but who were later completely exonerated before their scheduled executions. Breyer considered possible explanations for these disturbing figures and concluded that capital defendants face "a greater likelihood of an initial wrongful conviction" than noncapital defendants—a risk that researchers have identified as "about 4 percent," or one out of twenty-five. Reasons for this higher risk of error in capital cases, explained Breyer, include greater pressure on law enforcement to close such cases, skewed capital juries created by the exclusion of those opposed to the death penalty, flawed forensic testimony, and legal error by courts. On the innocence issue, Breyer concluded, "Unlike 40 years ago, we now have plausible *evidence* of unreliability that (perhaps due to DNA evidence) is stronger than the evidence we had before."[28]

Breyer's second fundamental defect also aligned with a central concern of Stevens and Powell—arbitrariness in the imposition of the death penalty. What Breyer added to previous considerations of this problem was evidence, based on an exhaustive study of the Connecticut death penalty, that the "egregiousness" of a capital defendant's conduct was not well correlated, or even correlated at all, with the likelihood of a death sentence. On the other hand, characteristics such as the race of murder victims, the gender of defendants and victims, and the geographic location of a murder within a state *were* correlated with the likelihood of capital sentences. Breyer, unlike Powell, Blackmun, and Stevens, did not treat the problem of racial discrimination as distinctive, but rather folded it into other "irrelevant" factors—thus returning to *Furman*'s primary focus on arbitrariness rather than discrimination. Breyer concluded that "after considering thousands of death penalty cases and last-minute petitions over the course of more than 20 years[,] I see discrepancies for which I can find no rational explanations."[29]

Breyer's third and final fundamental defect was one that he had noted in previous cases—the "excessively long periods of time that individuals typically spend on death row," periods that now average "nearly 18 years." Such lengthy stays on death row are cruel in their own right, explained Breyer, because almost all states keep death row inmates in solitary confinement for most of their incarceration, and these inmates endure both extended isolation and an agonizing uncertainty as to whether and when a death sentence will in fact be carried out. Moreover, lengthy delay between sentence and execution "undermines the death penalty's penological rationale." Reiterating the Court's frequently made observation that the primary purposes of capital punishment are deterrence and retribution, Breyer concluded that executions that take place decades after the offense (if they even take place at all) are exceedingly unlikely to contribute measurably to either goal. Breyer explained that the problem cannot be solved by shortening the time between sentence and execution, because the delays that currently exist are the product of the courts' appropriate attempts to ensure reliability and fairness in the administration of the ultimate punishment. Breyer crisply concluded that "we can have a death penalty that at least arguably serves legitimate penological purposes *or* we can have a procedural system that at least arguably seeks reliability and fairness in the death penalty's application. We cannot have both."[30]

Beyond presenting evidence of fundamental flaws in the administration of capital punishment, Breyer also chronicled the extraordinary recent decline in the use of the death penalty, measured along many dimensions. Breyer noted diminishing death sentences and executions, increasing state legislative repeals (and near-miss attempted repeals), and the growing geographic concentration of death sentencing and executions on both state and county levels. Breyer added a wholly new metric by using population data to calculate the percentage of Americans who live in a state that conducted an execution within the prior three years, noting that this percentage dropped from 54 percent to 33 percent between 1994 and 2014. In a nod to the Eighth Amendment analysis used by the Court to reject the death penalty for intellectually disabled and juvenile offenders and for the crime of rape, Breyer also observed the consistency of the direction of change in death penalty practices, public opinion polling that reflects a preference for life without possibility of parole over the death penalty, and the isolation of the United States in the world community as one of only eight countries that continues to execute a significant number of people.

Justice Antonin Scalia penned a forceful and sarcastic concurring opinion, joined by Justice Clarence Thomas, responding specifically to Breyer's dissent. What is striking for our purposes is Scalia's opening line: "Welcome to Groundhog Day." By this Scalia was referring to the 1993 film of the same name in which a TV weatherman is forced to relive the same day over and over again. Scalia went on to chide Breyer for making "familiar" arguments as he "takes on the role of the abolitionists" in the Court's "long-running drama."[31] Scalia's response highlights the validity of Justice Marshall's hypothesis regarding the effect of information on attitudes about the death penalty, at least with regard to the Court itself. Over and over again, justices who have reviewed hundreds or thousands of capital cases from around the country have come to the conclusion that the process for administering the death penalty is so flawed that the practice can no longer be considered constitutional, while no justices have changed their views about the death penalty in the other direction.

The sheer repetition of this unidirectional phenomenon, though it struck Scalia as occasion for derision, offers substantial grounds for predicting its repeated occurrence in the future, especially if new evidence of wrongful convictions, arbitrariness, discrimination, delays, and marginalization of the practice of capital punishment continues to mount.

Of course, it will take five members of the Court to reach this conclusion at the same time in order for a "Furman II" ruling to issue. Although they are relatively new to the Court and have not yet had many opportunities to write death penalty opinions (or decades to become disillusioned with the project of constitutional regulation), Justices Sonia Sotomayor and Elena Kagan, both Obama appointees, seem like plausible future candidates for joining Breyer and Ginsburg in such a ruling. Although Sotomayor and Kagan did not join Breyer's separate dissent on the ultimate issue of the death penalty's categorical constitutionality, they both dissented in that case on the narrower lethal injection issue in a hard-hitting opinion that cast some doubt on whether other lethal injection protocols or other modes of execution are constitutional.[32] Both Sotomayor and Kagan have endorsed the methodology that was used before they joined the Court to preclude the death penalty for intellectually disabled and juvenile offenders and for the crime of child rape—a methodology that may yet be used to preclude the death penalty altogether. If the vacancy created by the death of Justice Scalia is filled by someone who is a liberal on criminal justice issues, that justice might provide the necessary fifth vote for constitutional abolition. But even in the absence of a shift in the balance on the Court, a fifth vote for abolition might come from Justice Anthony Kennedy—the swing justice on many hotly contested social issues. Although Kennedy, too, has not (yet) abandoned the Court's Eighth Amendment jurisprudence, he has played a large role in developing the doctrine that has limited it, and in doing so has expressed some skepticism about the success of the Court's project of constitutional regulation of capital punishment.

In 2002, Kennedy joined a six-justice majority in the first case limiting the substantive scope of the death penalty since the 1980s, holding that intellectually disabled offenders cannot constitutionally be put to death.[33] In 2005 and 2008, Kennedy provided the crucial fifth vote and wrote the opinions for the Court in two further cases precluding the death penalty for juvenile offenders and for the crime of child rape.[34] In the third of these three cases, Kennedy not only wrote the Court's opinion limiting the death penalty, but offered some general observations about the shortcomings of the Court's death penalty jurisprudence. Echoing Blackmun's critique of the fundamental contradiction at the heart of the Court's Eighth Amendment doctrine, Kennedy wrote: "The tension between general rules and case-specific circumstances has produced results *not altogether satisfactory.*"[35] He went on to observe that the Court's "response to this case law, which is still in search of a unifying principle, has been to insist upon confining the instances in which capital punishment may be imposed."[36] Kennedy seems to be suggesting that the inadequacy of the Court's constitutional regulation of capital punishment should lead the Court to scale back the American death penalty. It is not a giant step from reduction to wholesale rejection, especially if the results of the Court's regulatory project continue to be "not altogether satisfactory."

What may be even more important than Kennedy's expressed skepticism about the Court's regulatory project is the constitutional doctrine that he played such a key role in developing. The cases limiting the scope of the death penalty for certain offenders and offenses developed a detailed methodology that offers a potential blueprint for a more general constitutional abolition.

A Blueprint for Constitutional Abolition

One can find a wide variety of approaches to the issue of constitutional abolition of capital punishment in the opinions of Supreme Court justices, as well as in opinions of judges from other courts, both federal and state.[37] Given the many defects identified over time in the administration of the death penalty, there is a broad menu of arguments that could be marshalled, individually or in combination, to support a categorical constitutional ban. But though there are multiple possible paths to the same destination, one in particular is both broader and better traveled than the others. This path also has the virtues of having been forged by the key swing justice on the current Court and used repeatedly in the past ten to fifteen years to limit the death penalty. It is this constitutional doctrine—what the Court has called the "proportionality" principle of the Eighth Amendment—that seems most likely to produce a "Furman II" ruling.

Before turning to the proportionality principle as a path to constitutional abolition, we first consider some of the alternative paths and their limitations. Most obviously, concerns about the risk of executing the innocent have taken on new force in the past few decades as the introduction of DNA testing uncovered numerous instances of wrongful conviction in both capital and noncapital cases. Both Stevens and Breyer placed this issue foremost in their broader critiques of the American death penalty. Justice David Souter also expressed serious concern about wrongful capital convictions before he left the Court, writing in a dissenting opinion in a closely divided capital case: "Today, a new body of fact must be accounted for in deciding what, in practical terms, the Eighth Amendment guarantees should tolerate, for the period starting in 1989 has seen repeated exonerations of convicts under death sentences, in numbers never imagined before the development of DNA tests." However, Souter cautioned that "it is far too soon for any generalization about the soundness of capital sentencing across the country."[38]

Arguments for constitutional abolition of the death penalty based on the problem of conviction of the innocent must grapple with the difficulty of finding an agreed upon definition of "innocence." Must there be clear-cut proof that the defendant did not commit the crime? Or must there only be a serious defect in the affirmative case that the defendant did commit the crime? In both the public sphere and on the Court, opponents have vociferously disagreed about the scope of the problem of innocent defendants being convicted and sentenced to death, precisely because of their disagreement about definitions. In response to Souter's voicing of his concerns about innocence in capital cases, Scalia faulted him for relying on an empirical study with a "distorted concept of what constitutes 'exoneration.'" Scalia argued that the fact that a conviction is reversed for legal error does not constitute proof of the defendant's innocence and maintained that "mischaracterization of reversible error as actual innocence is endemic in abolitionist rhetoric."[39] Souter and Scalia's dueling opinions cite a variety of competing sources that reflect the lack of consensus about how to define—and therefore how to count—exonerations of the innocent.

We do not have to imagine what a constitutional invalidation of capital punishment based solely on the innocence issue might look like, because federal trial court judge Jed Rakoff issued just such a ruling in 2002, striking down the federal death penalty on this ground. Rakoff noted, like Souter, the growing body of evidence of wrongful capital convictions: "We now know, in a way almost unthinkable even a decade ago, that our system of criminal justice, for all its protections, is sufficiently fallible that innocent people are convicted of capital crimes with some frequency." To give this newly pressing concern a foundation in constitutional law, Rakoff explained that capital defendants are deprived of "due process of law" when there exists "an undue risk that a meaningful number of innocent persons, by being put to death before the emergence of the techniques or evidence that will establish their innocence, are thereby effectively deprived of the opportunity to prove their innocence."[40] This ruling was promptly reversed by a federal appeals court—not on the ground that Rakoff had used a faulty definition of innocence, but rather on the ground that there was no Supreme Court law that suggested a right "to a continued opportunity for exoneration throughout the course of one's natural life."[41] The appeals court pointed to a Supreme Court precedent that seemed to suggest exactly the opposite—a decision in which the Court refused to endorse a constitutional right for death-sentenced inmates to present newly discovered evidence of innocence.[42] Powerful as the innocence issue may be as a policy concern, the lack of precedent supporting the argument likely undermines its use as the sole ground for a constitutional attack on the death penalty.

Concerns about racial discrimination and more general arbitrariness in capital sentencing are also major themes in the opinions of many of the justices who have found the death penalty to be unconstitutional. However, the Court has a long history of avoiding or deflecting the race issue in capital cases, and a sudden change of course does not seem likely. Breyer's dissent calling for full briefing on the constitutionality of the death penalty itself downplayed the issue, treating race as only one of several "irrelevant" factors that appear to influence capital sentencing. The more general "arbitrariness" argument holds more promise, and, indeed, it convinced the key swing justices in *Furman* itself, Byron White and Potter Stewart, to vote to invalidate the death penalty in that case. However, the success of such a claim today, as Breyer's dissent illustrated, may well depend on assessment of empirical studies—a mode of analysis that the Court also has often sought to avoid because of the limitations of its own institutional competence.

Even if the Court could be persuaded to consider empirical evidence of arbitrariness or discrimination in the application of the death penalty, further difficulties arise. Empirical evidence is extraordinarily costly and time-consuming to collect, and therefore it is likely that such evidence will be limited in scope, both geographically and temporally. If such evidence is available for only some states, or for only some counties within any given state, it is questionable whether inferences could be drawn from it that are broad enough to support a nationwide abolition. Similarly, as demographic and other conditions change in states and localities, empirical studies conducted in the past may not reflect more current circumstances. These difficulties suggest that it would be extremely challenging to mount a successful case for constitutional abolition based on arbitrariness and discrimination in the application of the death penalty.

Breyer's dissent also noted his long-standing concern about lengthy delays between sentence and execution. This ground formed the sole basis for a decision by federal trial court judge Cormac Carney that ruled California's death penalty unconstitutional in 2014, a ruling later reversed on appeal.[43] Both Breyer and Carney argued that rare and long-delayed executions are unlikely to make any measurable contributions to the death penalty's penological purposes, echoing Justice White's grounds for supporting *Furman*'s ruling in 1972. As Carney explained, delays in California are so extreme that they have "quietly transformed" a sentence of death into a sentence that "no rational jury or legislature could ever impose: life in prison, with the remote possibility of death." In such a system, Carney concluded, the "random few" who actually do eventually get executed "will have languished for so long on Death Row that their execution will serve no retributive or deterrent purpose."[44] The problem with relying on lengthy delays alone to support a constitutional argument against the death penalty is that states vary widely in how long it takes to convert death sentences to executions. The cruelty of death row conditions—especially solitary confinement on death row, which Breyer also relied upon and which Kennedy has expressed grave concern about—also varies from state to state.[45] A further problem with the argument about cruelty is that prison conditions, including the use of solitary confinement, are far more easily remedied than procedural delays, which Breyer argued are necessary to promote reliability and fairness. These difficulties suggest that arguments based on lengthy delays on death row are unlikely by themselves to achieve a categorical constitutional ban.

There are undoubtedly additional challenges that could be brought that might serve, alone or in combination, as grounds for a categorical constitutional ruling against capital punishment. Nonetheless, the foregoing approaches seem to be the most obvious rivals to the proportionality approach to which we will turn in a moment. Among the many advantages of the Court's proportionality doctrine as a vehicle for constitutional abolition is its capaciousness, such that each of the challenges surveyed above can be subsumed within it, thus adding to the cumulative power of the ultimate argument.

Perhaps the greatest attraction of the Court's proportionality doctrine as a vehicle for constitutional abolition is its relatively long usage within the Court's Eighth Amendment jurisprudence. As early as 1976, when the Court revived the death penalty in *Gregg* and its companion cases, the Court explained why the death penalty did not violate "evolving standards of decency" with reference first to legislative enactments (thirty-five states and the federal government had reenacted death penalty statutes since 1972) and jury verdicts (more than 450 death sentences had been imposed under the new statutes), and second to the twin purposes of capital punishment (deterrence and retribution), which the Court believed could be served by the practice.[46]

Just one year later, the Court used the Eighth Amendment methodology it had inaugurated in *Gregg* to strike down Georgia's death penalty for the crime of rape of an adult because it was "grossly disproportionate and excessive punishment" for such a crime. The Court started with what it called "objective evidence of the country's present judgment concerning the acceptability of death as a penalty" in such cases. The Court noted that Georgia was the only state in the post-*Gregg* world to authorize the death penalty for rape and that Georgia juries had returned relatively few death sentences for rapists in recent years, both in absolute numbers and especially as a percentage of those eligible for such sentences. Moreover, the Court explained that "the Constitution contemplates that in the end our own judgment will be brought to bear on the question of the acceptability of the death penalty under the Eighth Amendment."[47] By "our own judgment," the Court did not mean that the justices were to consult their individual moral or policy views on capital punishment. Rather, the Court explained that the justices should consider, as the *Gregg* Court had done, whether the challenged practice promoted the deterrent and retributive purposes of capital punishment. With regard to capital punishment for the crime of rape, the Court addressed only the question of retribution and concluded that the punishment of death was simply disproportionate when the defendant had not taken a life, suggesting without explicitly holding that the absence of *either* justification would invalidate a challenged practice under the Eighth Amendment.

The Court used the same methodology five years later to strike down a death sentence imposed on a defendant who had served as a getaway driver for an armed robbery, remaining in the car while two others approached a home to rob an elderly couple, ultimately killing them when the couple resisted. Although the defendant was technically guilty of "felony murder" because of his participation in the underlying felony (armed robbery) that resulted in death, the Court concluded that a death sentence was "disproportionate" for someone "who neither took life, attempted to take life, nor intended to take life."[48] Though the Court would later narrow its felony murder limitation,[49] its reasoning continued to track the proportionality approach it had used to strike down the death penalty for rape—considering first "objective evidence" of society's views like legislative decisions and jury verdicts, followed by the Court's "own judgment" with regard to whether the purposes of deterrence and retribution are served. In the context of felony murder, the one notable addition to the Court's analysis was the inclusion of prosecutorial decisions, along with those of legislatures and juries, as objective evidence of society's views. Although good data on prosecutorial charging decisions in felony murder cases was not available, the Court explained that "it would be relevant if prosecutors rarely sought the death penalty for accomplice felony murder, for it would tend to indicate that prosecutors, who represent society's interest in punishing crime, consider the death penalty excessive" for such crimes.[50]

In two key rulings in 1989, the Court declined to find capital punishment disproportionate either for intellectually disabled offenders or juvenile offenders.[51] Following these rulings, the Court did not invoke its capital proportionality jurisprudence for more than a decade, leading many to think that the doctrine was moribund. But in three cases decided over a period of six years, the Court not only applied but also expanded its proportionality approach, using it to strike down the death penalty for intellectually disabled and juvenile offenders and for the crime of child rape (and other nonhomicidal offenses). It is these three decisions—two of which were authored by Justice Kennedy—that flesh out the Court's proportionality doctrine as a potential blueprint for a categorical constitutional ruling.

In 2002, in the decision striking down the death penalty for intellectually disabled offenders (and thus overturning its 1989 decision to the contrary), the Court added some new considerations both to the "objective evidence" and "our own judgment" prongs of its proportionality doctrine. With regard to objective evidence of societal consensus, Justice Stevens observed in his opinion for the Court that a total of eighteen states had specifically outlawed the death penalty for intellectually disabled offenders, sixteen of them having passed such legislation since 1989. Eighteen may seem like an unprepossessing number out of a total of fifty states, but Stevens bolstered the count in several ways. First, he noted that ultimately unsuccessful bills had passed at least one house of the legislature in two additional states, and that a gubernatorial commission had recommended adoption of such a bill in a third state. Second, he noted the "overwhelming" voting margins by which successful legislation passed. And finally, he argued that the twelve abolitionist states that did not permit the death penalty at all should be counted along with the states that had specifically exempted intellectually disabled offenders, bumping the figure of eighteen up to a more impressive majority of thirty. Stevens emphasized that when it came to legislative enactments, counting noses was not the only consideration: "It is not so much the number of [states exempting intellectually disabled offenders] that is significant, but the consistency of the direction of change." In addition, Stevens observed that the sixteen new state enactments restricting the scope of the death penalty should be considered "powerful" evidence of societal consensus in light of the unpopularity of legislation protective of "persons guilty of violent crime."[52] This objective evidence of legislative opinion was bolstered by the fact that the Court identified only a handful of intellectually disabled offenders who had been executed in the period since 1989.

The most controversial new move that Stevens made in addressing objective evidence of societal consensus was his marshalling of evidence of "a much broader societal and professional consensus." Stevens noted that this evidence, which he listed in a footnote, was "by no means dispositive." But he maintained that its "consistency with the legislative evidence" lent support to the Court's conclusion about societal consensus. Specifically, Stevens noted that expert organizations on the topic of intellectual disability supported the exemption of such offenders from the death penalty, as did representatives of diverse religious communities. The world community, especially our peer countries, had expressed overwhelming disapproval of execution of such offenders. Polling data, too, indicated a widespread consensus against such executions, even among those who favored the death penalty. This footnote vastly expanded the universe of information relevant to establishing a societal consensus and in doing so gave the Court much greater latitude to reject death penalty practices that are widely authorized by existing state legislation.[53]

Even though he relegated it to a footnote, Stevens's move drew fire from the dissenting justices. Chief Justice Rehnquist dissented specifically "to call attention to the defects in the Court's decision to place weight on foreign laws, the views of professional and religious organizations, and opinion polls in reaching its conclusion."[54] Justice Scalia was more apoplectic in his response to Stevens's analysis, to the point of bestowing upon it a sarcastic award: "the Prize for the Court's Most Feeble Effort to fabricate 'national consensus' must go to its appeal (deservedly relegated to a footnote) to the views of assorted professional and religious organizations, members of the so-called 'world community,' and respondents to opinion polls."[55]

Despite the intensity of the dissenting justices' reactions to Stevens's analysis, Justice Kennedy adopted and bolstered it three years later when he wrote the opinion for the Court striking down the death penalty as "a disproportionate punishment for juveniles." The numbers in the case were similar to those regarding intellectually disabled offenders: eighteen state legislatures explicitly prohibited the execution of juvenile offenders, and the addition of the twelve abolitionist states again yielded the number thirty. Moreover, a similarly small number of juvenile offenders had been executed in recent years. But the case for a juvenile exemption was a little trickier because there had been less state movement on the issue than on intellectual disability since the Court had rejected both claims in 1989: only five states (as opposed to sixteen) had recently changed their laws to exempt juvenile offenders. The Court bolstered its analysis in the juvenile context, as it had with regard to intellectual disability, by reference to the consistency of the direction of change and by the unpopularity of legislation that might be viewed as soft on crime. However, the centerpiece of the Court's analysis was its reference to extensive expert opinion, presented in "scientific and sociological studies," about adolescents' relative lack of maturity and self-control, their susceptibility to peer influences, and their still malleable personality traits. These qualities both reduced the culpability of juveniles for their offenses, undermining the goal of retribution, and made it less likely that juveniles would be susceptible to additional deterrence from the threat of the death penalty over life imprisonment.[56]

In addition to giving pride of place to "expert" scientific conclusions, Kennedy concluded his opinion with a defense of the views of the world community. He noted "the stark reality that the United States is the only country in the world that continues to give official sanction to the juvenile death penalty." For Kennedy, our isolation on this issue, especially among our peer nations, was important enough to take out of a footnote and to highlight in dramatic language at the very close of his opinion: "It does not lessen our fidelity to the Constitution or our pride in its origins to acknowledge that the express affirmation of certain fundamental rights by other nations and peoples simply underscores the centrality of those same rights within our own heritage of freedom."[57]

Kennedy wrote a third opinion restricting the scope of the death penalty by invalidating it for the crime of child rape (and for any other interpersonal crime in which life is not taken). A handful of states had begun passing laws adding child rape to the list of capital offenses, and Louisiana had sentenced two separate defendants to death for such crimes. The Court granted review on one of these two cases and struck down the death sentence under its proportionality doctrine. The analysis in this case was easier on the "objective evidence" prong because the numbers were so lopsided—only six states had passed such legislation, leaving an overwhelming majority on the other side of the issue. Moreover, among the states that had authorized the death penalty for child rape, Louisiana was the only state that had actually sentenced anyone to death for such a crime since 1976. In addition, the Court noted that no one had been executed for the rape of a child—or an adult, for that matter—since 1964, and no one had been executed for any other nonhomicide offense since 1963.

Although the raw numbers of statutes, death sentences, and executions made the case relatively easy to dispose of under the Court's proportionality doctrine, Kennedy nonetheless added some new considerations to the analysis. He noted the large number of people who potentially could be executed under the new laws, pointing out that more than 5,000 child rapes were reported nationwide in 2005. This expansion could not be reconciled with the need to "constrain the use of the death penalty"—a need that Kennedy linked to the Court's "not altogether satisfactory" capital jurisprudence, which had been unable to fully eradicate the "inconsistency of application" that had motivated the doctrine in the first place. In addition, the Court reiterated a concern that it had raised in the context of intellectually disabled offenders: the possibility that there might be a heightened risk of wrongful conviction. In the case of offenders with intellectual disability, the risk derived from the limited ability of such defendants to consult with counsel and to present an appropriate affect to the jury; in the case of defendants accused of child rape, the risk derived from the fact that "children are highly susceptible to suggestive questioning techniques" and that rape prosecutions depend heavily on the child's testimony.[58]

The Court has expanded the ambit of its capital proportionality doctrine by applying it to *non*capital cases involving the imposition of sentences of life without possibility of parole (LWOP) imposed on juvenile offenders. In this context, the Court—again, per Justice Kennedy—concluded that LWOP sentences are unconstitutionally disproportionate for juveniles who have not committed homicide offenses. In doing so, the Court faced a more difficult argument on the "objective evidence" prong because a substantial number of juveniles were serving LWOP sentences nationwide—123 to be precise—a figure much larger than that in any of the preceding capital proportionality cases. To deal with this large number, Kennedy added two new and interesting considerations to the Court's analysis of "objective evidence." First, he noted not merely the raw number of juvenile LWOP sentences, but also their *distribution,* observing that seventy-seven of the sentences were in Florida alone, and the rest were concentrated in only ten states. Second, Kennedy treated the raw number of juvenile LWOP sentences as the numerator in a fraction and noted the importance of the denominator—that is, the number of juveniles who were *eligible* for LWOP sentences for nonhomicide offenses in the period of time that produced the existing juvenile LWOP sentences. In light of the hundreds of thousands of nonhomicide offenses committed by juveniles every year, Kennedy concluded that the sentence of LWOP for a juvenile nonhomicide offender was exceedingly rare "in proportion to the opportunities for its imposition."[59]

The Court's long and expansive development of its Eighth Amendment proportionality doctrine provides a detailed blueprint for a potential categorical constitutional challenge to the American death penalty. The various elements that the Court has added over time to its proportionality doctrine allow for consideration of virtually all of the most powerful current concerns about the death penalty, including the concerns that motivated the alternative constitutional challenges mounted by various justices and judges.

Start with the "objective evidence" prong of the Court's proportionality doctrine. The Court always begins this analysis with a legislative head count. Currently, nineteen states have abolished capital punishment—not in itself a particularly impressive number. However, as Breyer noted in his dissent calling for full briefing on the constitutionality of the death penalty, another eleven states have not carried out an execution in more than eight years.[60] If we treat these states as de facto abolitionist states, the number rises to thirty—a key number in the Court's capital proportionality cases, because it is the number of states that the Court found sufficient to establish a consensus against the death penalty for intellectually disabled and juvenile offenders. Moreover, the raw legislative head count is not necessarily dispositive; rather, the Court has also considered both the speed and the consistency of the direction of change. Seven states have abolished the death penalty in the past decade, one of the most active periods of legislative abolition in the nation's history, and no abolitionist states have reinstated the penalty in more than two decades. As Breyer also noted, a number of other states have come extremely close to achieving abolition in recent years. In addition to counting legislatures, the Court counts jury verdicts and actual executions, both of which have fallen dramatically over the past fifteen years to modern-era lows. Governors and prosecutors, as elected officials, should also count as "objective evidence" of societal consensus (indeed, the Court has explicitly noted that prosecutors do), and several governors in key states have imposed moratoria on executions, while prosecutors have declined to seek the death penalty in increasing numbers of cases. As it explained in the juvenile LWOP context, the Court considers not just the number but also the distribution of sentences, and the death penalty has become increasingly concentrated in fewer states, and in fewer counties within those states. As Breyer noted in his dissent, the percentage of the U.S. population that lives in a state that has conducted an execution in the past three years has fallen to well below fifty percent over the past two decades. Another gloss on the raw numbers, aside from distribution, is the ratio of death sentences imposed to death sentences authorized by law. Viewed through this lens, the "numerator" of those sentenced to death—twenty-eight in 2015—is tiny compared with the denominator of those eligible for capital murder, who likely number in the thousands.[61]

In addition to "objective evidence" based on the numbers of statutes, sentences, and executions, the evidence of "a much broader societal and professional consensus" against the death penalty is likewise strong. Expert legal organizations have taken highly skeptical positions with regard to the American death penalty. In 1997, the American Bar Association's House of Delegates passed a resolution, which remains in force today, by a more than two-to-one margin calling for a moratorium on executions in the United States until courts across the country can ensure that such cases are "administered fairly and impartially, in accordance with due process," and with minimum risk of executing innocent people.[62] And in 2009, the American Law Institute withdrew the model death penalty provisions from its Model Penal Code—which had served as a template for the revised statutes approved by the Court in 1976—because of "current intractable institutional and structural obstacles to ensuring a minimally adequate system for administering capital punishment."[63] Leaders of diverse religious communities oppose the death penalty; indeed, in 2015, Pope Francis used his landmark appearance before Congress to urge the abolition of the American death penalty.[64] The world community has overwhelmingly moved to abandon the death penalty, and our peer countries—other Western democracies—are unanimous in this regard. The United States is not only alone among its peers, but its distinction as one of the world's top five executing nations places it in the company of countries that are among the least democratic and the worst human rights abusers in the world.[65] Public opinion polling in the United States has shown decreasing levels of support for the death penalty, especially in comparison with the option of life without possibility of parole.[66]

It is through the application of the Court's "own judgment" to the Eighth Amendment question that concerns about innocence, racial discrimination, arbitrariness, and lengthy delays on death row can all be brought to bear. With regard to both intellectually disabled defendants and those accused of raping a child, the Court noted that concerns about heightened risks of wrongful conviction played a role in its own judgment on the Eighth Amendment issue. While it is hard to find precedent for a constitutional challenge to the death penalty based solely on the issue of innocence, that concern has an established home in the Court's proportionality doctrine. And as many justices and judges have observed, there is increasing evidence of wrongful convictions generally—and *especially* with regard to capital cases.[67] As for the issues of racial discrimination and arbitrariness, the failure of capital sentences to capture "the worst of the worst" undercuts the retributive purpose of the death penalty.[68] Justice Kennedy specifically noted "inconsistency of application" of the death penalty as a reason to limit its scope under the Court's proportionality doctrine—a reason that could support the more drastic limitation of wholesale abolition if evidence of inconsistent application of the penalty continues to mount. Finally, lengthy delays undercut *both* the retributive and the deterrent purposes of the death penalty, as Justice Breyer and Judge Carney each observed. Given that evaluation of these purposes is the primary focus of the justices' "own judgment," the concern about delays also has a clear home in the Court's Eighth Amendment jurisprudence.

Although the Court's established Eighth Amendment doctrine permits the marshaling of a strong case for a categorical constitutional abolition of the death penalty, constitutional doctrines do not drive outcomes in any mechanistic way. Constitutional doctrines are many, overlapping, contested, ambiguous, and sometimes inconsistent with each other (and internally). They do not often clearly compel results, especially not on highly contested issues like the death penalty, which has spawned a great multitude of highly contested constitutional doctrines, both large and small. Constitutional doctrines are merely tools, but powerful tools can be put to powerful use both by advocates before the Court and by the justices themselves. The Court's proportionality doctrine offers advocates an approach that is extremely capacious, allowing them to raise many of the most compelling concerns about the death penalty's current operation as matters of constitutional law. Moreover, the doctrine gives the justices a means to abolish the death penalty that is rooted in decades of Court precedent, offering some insulation from claims that such a decision would be too "activist" or "political." To be sure, such claims will undoubtedly be made should the Court issue a "Furman II" ruling, but the Court's long adherence to and lengthy elaboration of its proportionality doctrine would provide a rejoinder to such charges.

Anticipation and Anxiety

Breyer's call for full briefing on the constitutionality of capital punishment in 2015 is an eerie echo of Goldberg's similar call for Court review in 1963. (Breyer clerked for Goldberg during the 1964 term and reports learning from Goldberg not to be discouraged by being in the minority on opinions: "I can hear Goldberg saying . . . 'Keep going. Maybe they didn't agree yesterday. Maybe they'll agree tomorrow.'"[69]) Goldberg's dissent inspired a concerted strategy of constitutional litigation that brought about *Furman*'s (temporary) abolition of the death penalty in 1972. Breyer's dissent has similarly energized many in the capital defense bar to develop, individually and in concert, ambitious constitutional challenges to the death penalty in hopes of generating a "Furman II" ruling. However, Breyer's dissent also has inspired caution in the very same quarters— hesitancy no doubt born of the hindsight offered by the *Furman* litigation and its aftermath. As both anticipation and anxiety mount among sophisticated abolitionist lawyers, which sentiment should prevail?

The chances for a successful and enduring constitutional abolition may be better now than they were in the 1960s because much greater infrastructure currently exists to facilitate a concerted constitutional litigation campaign. We now have a specialized capital defense bar, which arose in response to the development of the Court's complex capital jurisprudence. Prior to 1976, there was no need for lawyers representing defendants in capital cases to have specialized knowledge or training, as such cases were tried in much the same way as noncapital criminal cases. Today, there are legions of dedicated capital defense lawyers who often know each other through training and resource-sharing networks, and they have the capacity for long-term, coordinated strategic planning. We now also have nonprofit organizations dedicated to abolitionist strategy, including litigation. Organizations like the National Coalition to Abolish the Death Penalty and the Eighth Amendment Project had no analog in the 1960s. While there were nonprofits opposed to the death penalty, the litigation piece of the abolitionist project was virtually nonexistent until it was taken up by the LDF, an organization that up to that point had been dedicated to racial justice but not abolition of the death penalty.

While this new and extensive infrastructure is probably to the overall benefit of a constitutional litigation campaign, it also presents some challenges. The existence of a specialized capital defense bar means that almost all of the most sophisticated lawyers on capital issues are trained and view themselves as individual representatives of their clients rather than as "cause" lawyers. This self-conception entails an obligation to put individual client goals ahead of collective strategic goals. As a consequence, capital defense attorneys may feel compelled to push issues on behalf of individual clients before the timing for consideration is optimal, or in cases that have less-than-optimal facts or procedural postures, or in hostile courts that may not provide sufficient leeway to develop the record. The specialized and well-resourced nonprofits that are attempting to coordinate a litigation strategy are limited in their ability to choose the timing, facts, procedural posture, and courts for test cases, because they cannot call off "lone wolves" who are simply doing their best to advocate for their clients. In the 1960s, the LDF lawyers viewed themselves and operated more as "cause" lawyers than as client-centered lawyers. For example, when *Furman*, a murder case, was consolidated with two other cases that involved death sentences for the crime of rape, the LDF made the choice to decline to ask the Court to strike down the death penalty for rape and not for murder, in order to avoid presenting the Court with an attractive compromise short of blanket abolition.[70] Although the LDF may have operated on a limited budget, it was able to keep much tighter control over litigation strategy than is possible today.

Despite these limitations, there appears to be some enthusiasm in the nonprofit world for moving ahead with a coordinated constitutional litigation campaign to abolish the death penalty.[71] Tempering that enthusiasm is anxiety that the Court's intervention might invite a backlash—that a "Furman II" would be superseded by a "Gregg II" if the public mood shifted or the Court's personnel changed. Some feel that it might be a safer and more enduring strategy to let the death penalty die a slower, quieter death as it becomes more and more marginalized, rather than to seek its sudden death by constitutional decree. Although there is little doubt that *Furman* sparked a powerful backlash that helped to overturn it four years later, a similar response would be less likely should a "Furman II" issue today or in the near future. One of the primary drivers of the public's reaction to *Furman* was the rising rate of violent crime across the country, an upward trajectory that had begun more than a decade before *Furman* was decided and that would not begin to reverse itself until the 1990s.[72] Today, we have enjoyed a more than two-decades-long downward curve in violent crime, with homicide rates reaching lows not seen since the 1960s.[73] Another difference between the era of *Furman* and the present is that concerns about problems in the administration of the death penalty had barely begun to be addressed when the Supreme Court struck it down in 1972. Today, we have reached the forty-year mark of the Court's "mend-it-don't-end-it" regulatory approach—with dismal success, as explained by a seemingly never-ending stream of dissenting justices who tried in good faith to "patch up the death penalty's legal wounds" before calling for abolition.[74] The growing consensus about the failures of the Court's interventions would help to blunt the force of backlash to a "Furman II." A further change lies in the overwhelming international consensus that has developed against the death penalty since the 1970s, especially among our peer nations. Constitutional abolition would no doubt evoke strong foreign approval—including the illumination of the Coliseum in Rome, a symbolic gesture of support that has greeted state legislative repeals.[75] And retreat from abolition would no doubt evoke equally strong disapproval and even possible repercussions for joint criminal justice endeavors with abolitionist allies.

While abolitionist anxiety about backlash is exaggerated, another source of anxiety seems better founded. If a concerted constitutional litigation campaign "jumps the gun" and gets a categorical challenge to the Court before it is ready to issue a "Furman II" ruling, the precedent set by the failure of such a claim would likely delay an ultimate constitutional victory more than if the Court had not considered the issue at all. Justices tend to be especially reluctant to overrule very recent decisions out of respect for precedent; Stevens continued to apply the Court's death penalty law, even after concluding that it should be abandoned, for just this reason. Willingness to jettison recent precedent leads to claims like the one leveled by Marshall when the Court cast aside a then recent five-to-four death penalty decision by Brennan shortly after Brennan's retirement from the Court: "Power, not reason, is the new currency of this Court's decisionmaking."[76] Thus, there are dangers in seeking the "full briefing" that Breyer called for on the constitutionality of the death penalty. Perhaps Breyer's call should be read as reflecting his belief that there are currently five votes on the Court for this result. But perhaps not; maybe Breyer's dissent is better understood, in Scalia's words, as Groundhog Day—the latest in a long line of death penalty disavowals from justices nearing retirement.

Yet, there are also dangers in waiting for just the right moment to bring a constitutional claim—in this litigation context or any other when the Supreme Court is closely divided politically, as is the current Court. If Justice Breyer's call for a full briefing does mean that there are five justices ready to abolish the death penalty, but the challenge is not brought to the Court before one of those five leaves the Court, a constitutional victory may be delayed or even defeated (or, conversely, ensured) by a change in the balance on the Court. Justice Scalia was not among the five justices who some speculate might be ready to abolish the death penalty, so his replacement can only make a "Furman II" ruling more rather than less likely. However, three of the five "speculative" justices—Breyer, Ginsburg, and Kennedy—are over seventy-five years old, so the possibility remains of retirements in the near future that might shift the balance against constitutional abolition.

These uncertainties attend all constitutional litigation campaigns. Advocates who win landmark decisions are often hailed as prescient geniuses, while those who lose are sometimes dismissed as fools. The truth of the matter is more complicated, because informed guesswork is a large part of the strategy of any constitutional litigation campaign, and serendipity is a large part of the outcome. As anyone who plays fantasy football knows, you can make choices based on reams of player information, but there are no guarantees that you will win big as opposed to lose your shirt. Yogi Berra said it best: "It's tough to make predictions, especially about the future." The many unanticipated consequences produced in the past by the convoluted path of the Supreme Court's interventions in capital punishment offer ample reason to be cautious in predicting the death penalty's future. Nonetheless, a "Furman II" seems likely in the coming decade or two—but only if justices who leave the current Court are replaced with justices who hold similar or more liberal views. A doctrinal blueprint is available in the Court's proportionality jurisprudence, and current conditions on the ground may provide the necessary building blocks for an enduring constitutional edifice rejecting the death penalty once and for all.

CHAPTER NINE

Life after Death

I F THE SUPREME COURT does abolish the death penalty nationwide through a categorical constitutional ruling, what then? Of course, death rows across the country will be emptied, as they were at the time of *Furman,* and those spaces and the resources that sustain them will be repurposed to serve other criminal justice or social needs.[1] But what broader effects on the larger criminal justice system are likely in the wake of such a ruling?

The most welcome result of constitutional abolition will be the elimination of the distorting effects that the existence of capital punishment currently imposes on the larger criminal justice system. However, abolition of the death penalty also will remove the dramatic "spotlight" that capital cases shine on the American criminal justice system; it may become harder to attract and sustain attention to the many problems of the wider system when lives are not so clearly on the line. The central legal question posed by constitutional abolition is the afterlife of the Court's Eighth Amendment death penalty doctrine. Already, the Court has given some indications that this body of law may extend beyond capital punishment and provide a continuing resource for reviewing and revising other troubling criminal justice practices, such as the escalating use of sentences of life without possibility of parole. At a broader level, abolition of the American death penalty will have salutary consequences for the politics of criminal justice, both within the United States and between the United States and the rest of the world. Most broadly, the fact of constitutional abolition will be incorporated into America's ever-evolving political self-conception—though national mythmaking may obscure the truer, darker story of the death penalty's demise.

The Distorting Effects of Death

Justice Marshall argued in his solo concurring opinion in *Furman* that "even the most hesitant of citizens" would reject the death penalty if they were informed about its actual operation, including the fact that "the death penalty wreaks havoc with our entire criminal justice system."[2] The distorting effects of capital cases on the broader criminal justice system are more pronounced now than they were at the time Marshall wrote in *Furman*—partly as a result of *Furman*'s inauguration of constitutional regulation of capital punishment. The special procedures required in capital cases have drained resources away from the much larger and perpetually underresourced noncapital justice system. The long delays between sentence and execution that are produced by constitutional review have led to the passage of sweeping limits on federal oversight of state criminal convictions in order to speed executions, but with major consequences for noncapital cases as well. The revival of robust capital sentencing practices, which were encouraged by the Court's seemingly intrusive (but in fact largely ineffectual) constitutional oversight, led death penalty opponents to join "tough-on-crime" politicians to promote the adoption of life without possibility of parole statutes— statutes that have affected far more defendants in the noncapital system than in capital cases. Quite apart from the consequences of the Court's regulation, capital punishment has tended to normalize other extremely severe punishments and marginalize consideration of criminal justice issues that affect far more people, such as the enormous increase in incarceration rates over the past forty years. Finally, the availability of the death penalty currently creates incentives for prosecutors to pursue capital charges for strategic reasons rather than for the genuine purpose of achieving a death sentence. The abolition of the death penalty would have the salutary effect of minimizing these distortions by reallocating resources more sensibly within the criminal justice system, reorienting debates about criminal justice policy and reform, and eliminating perverse prosecutorial incentives.

Consider the distorting effect of capital punishment on the distribution of resources in the criminal justice system. Although death row inmates are a very small fraction of the overall prison population, the death penalty extracts a disproportionately large share of resources at every stage of the proceedings. Indeed, the total costs of capital prosecutions are considerably greater than those of noncapital cases that result in sentences of life imprisonment (or other lengthy prison terms), even when the costs of incarceration are included.[3] Capital trials are much more expensive than their noncapital counterparts because of their complexity, staffing needs, investigative demands, and the requirement of separate trial and penalty phases. In most states, these costs are primarily borne by local jurisdictions, while prisons are funded by state budgets. As a result, a prosecutor's decision to seek the death penalty often has significant financial consequences for the local jurisdiction in which the case is tried. Indigent defense is notoriously underfunded in both capital and noncapital cases, and the resources devoted to the capital side often come directly at the expense of the rest of the indigent defense budget. In the capital prosecution in 2008 of Brian Nichols for an infamous courthouse shooting and escape in Atlanta that killed a judge, a court reporter, a sheriff's deputy, and a federal agent, the investigative phase of the case generated defense costs that wiped out the remainder of Georgia's indigent defense budget and required postponement of the trial.[4] Death penalty prosecutions thus compromise already overburdened and underfunded indigent defense systems, in addition to imposing daunting costs on prosecutors and their budgets.

The political pressures and high emotions in capital cases can sometimes overwhelm sober assessments about resource allocation. For example, one capital defendant in Texas was tried three times before prosecutors finally accepted his offer to plead guilty to a life sentence (after three reversals of his death sentences) in proceedings that cost the prosecuting county millions of dollars. Following the Supreme Court's reversal of the first sentence, the local district attorney announced his intention to retry the issue whatever the cost, declaring to the press, "if I have to bankrupt this county, we're going to bow up and see that justice is served."[5] More recently, an assessment by the American Bar Association of Florida's capital justice system led the chair of the Florida Assessment Team to report that "all members of the Assessment Team, including those representing the state, were deeply worried that the expenditure of resources on capital cases significantly detracts from Florida's ability to render justice in *non*capital cases."[6]

In addition to the financial costs of prosecuting and defending capital trials, the death penalty places enormous burdens on state and federal judicial resources. In some states, such as California, the burdens imposed by capital cases on appellate courts compromise the ability of those courts to manage their competing commitments in ordinary criminal (and civil) cases. Such burdens are not merely a function of the sheer time required for capital litigation; rather, the frenetic nature of last-minute litigation in active executing states no doubt exacts its own toll on judges and court personnel and likely negatively affects the courts' ability to fulfill their noncapital obligations.[7] The Supreme Court's constitutional regulation of capital punishment has made capital cases far more legally complex than they were in the pre-*Furman* era. As a consequence, the pleadings filed on appeal and in postconviction review can be extraordinarily lengthy and can require courts to address them in judicial opinions that are also far lengthier than those issued in ordinary criminal cases; these opinions often total hundreds of pages before the review of a capital case is concluded. While noncapital criminal defendants have no constitutional or statutory right to counsel after their first appeal, almost every death penalty state provides for court-appointed counsel for indigent capital defendants in postconviction review by state courts, and Congress has also mandated counsel for indigent capital defendants in postconviction review in federal courts. These provisions—which reflect the unique severity and finality of a death sentence—add substantially to the financial costs of capital prosecutions, as well as to the length and complexity of postconviction challenges.

The intensive legal attention that capital cases receive, along with the complex and continually changing body of constitutional law that must be applied in such cases, has substantially extended the time between sentence and execution as the judicial review process runs its course. These delays have drawn criticism both from the right, which claims that justice for murder victims is too long deferred, and from the left, which claims that lengthy stays on death row are cruel to inmates. In the wake of the Oklahoma City bombing and the arrest of suspects Timothy McVeigh and Terry Nichols, right-wing critics of death penalty delays secured enough votes in Congress to pass a sweeping reform bill that substantially cut back on federal postconviction review through habeas corpus, the traditional means by which federal courts are empowered to oversee state criminal convictions to ensure compliance with the federal Constitution. The title of the new federal statute—the Antiterrorism and Effective Death Penalty Act of 1996 (AEDPA)—revealed its political origins in frustration with delays in capital cases. To address these delays, AEDPA imposed a slew of new restrictions on federal review of state convictions and sentences. A few of the law's key provisions include a one-year statute of limitations for filing a petition for federal review, a sharp limit on the power of federal courts to hear new factual evidence, and a deferential standard of review that requires federal courts to uphold state court decisions even when they are wrong, as long as they are "reasonable."[8]

Whatever one thinks about the desirability of shortening the time between death sentences and executions, AEDPA went far beyond that goal by changing the process of federal review for *all* criminal defendants. The drafters of the law were obviously well aware of this fact; they were able to use the high salience of the death penalty, especially in the wake of a horrific act of domestic terrorism, to push for sweeping new limitations on the power of federal courts to review criminal cases—limitations that right-wing reformers had sought for years prior to AEDPA without success.[9] These changes fell like an "atomic bomb" on the federal judiciary, decimating its ability to hear and redress claims of federal constitutional violations.[10] Noncapital defendants in particular bore the brunt of the new restrictions, because they were forced to navigate AEDPA's procedural minefield without the assistance of appointed counsel. After AEDPA, the already extremely low rate of success of ordinary criminal defendants seeking federal redress fell to microscopic levels, rendering federal habeas corpus review "utterly worthless to the vast majority of state criminal defendants."[11] The rewriting of the law of habeas corpus has had an enormous impact on the entire criminal justice system. While constitutional abolition of the death penalty would not also abolish AEDPA—only Congress can do that—the absence of the death penalty would eliminate the distorting incentives that capital punishment creates for lawmakers and the general public to "reform" the entire criminal justice process in order to promote swifter, surer executions in a few cases.

Just as increasingly delayed executions prompted death penalty supporters to promote law reform limiting judicial review, increasingly frequent death sentences prompted death penalty opponents to promote law reform offering an attractive alternative to capital sentences—namely, life without possibility of parole (LWOP) sentences. As in the case of AEDPA, the widespread adoption of LWOP has affected far more defendants in *non*capital cases than in capital cases. At the time *Furman* was decided, only seven states in the United States had LWOP statutes.[12] Just two years after *Furman*, the Supreme Court upheld the constitutionality of LWOP sentences, clearing the way for their further adoption.[13] After the Court revived capital punishment in 1976, death sentencing rates began to climb, as did general support for capital punishment, which was reflected not only in increasing numbers of death sentences but also in public opinion polls. However, polling also showed that the widespread support that capital punishment enjoyed dropped significantly when people were asked about their preference between a death sentence and LWOP. One nationwide poll in the early 1990s indicated that while 77 percent of respondents said that they supported the death penalty in the abstract, support fell to 49 percent when respondents were given the alternative of LWOP (and to 41 percent when LWOP was combined with restitution for victims).[14]

As a result, many death penalty opponents, who otherwise may have had reservations about promoting LWOP sentences outside of the capital context, supported such statutes. As crime continued to rise in the post-*Furman* era, politicians supporting tough-on-crime policies increasingly promoted the introduction and expansion of LWOP. Instead of opposing such statutes, many criminal justice liberals either passively acquiesced or actively collaborated in promoting LWOP because of its power as an alternative to capital punishment.[15] By the mid-1990s, LWOP was available as a penalty for murder in about half the states, and today it is authorized in every death penalty state (and indeed, in every state in the United States with the exception of Alaska, though the maximum punishment there is ninety-nine years of imprisonment).[16]

It is difficult to establish whether death penalty abolitionists' support for LWOP was essential to its stunning spread across the United States. Rising crime rates and the tough-on-crime rhetoric that dominated the political sphere for more than a generation permitted get-tough politicians to pass many harsh criminal policies without any help from anti–death penalty forces. However, it is clear that in some states the adoption of LWOP was driven primarily, if not exclusively, by death penalty politics. For example, Alabama, Illinois, and Louisiana each adopted LWOP statutes for the first time in response to *Furman,* fearing that the abolition of the death penalty would leave no other means of protecting the community from dangerous murderers.[17] In Texas, the adoption of LWOP also came about as a result of the Supreme Court's regulation of capital punishment. Death penalty supporters in Texas had long opposed LWOP as an alternative to the death penalty for the same reason that death penalty opponents supported it—the shared belief that the availability of LWOP as an alternative would make Texas sentencing juries less likely to return death verdicts. Only after the Supreme Court invalidated the death penalty for juveniles did death penalty supporters agree to make LWOP a sentencing alternative for murder, because with the death penalty off the table for juveniles, the introduction of LWOP had the effect of increasing, rather than decreasing, the maximum punishment available for juvenile murderers. Texas's experience with LWOP suggests that the spread of such a new and extreme penalty was facilitated in part by the muting of left-wing opposition—the result of the left's prioritization of eliminating the death penalty at all costs.

Abolitionists were not misguided in their hope that the availability of LWOP would drive down death sentencing. By ensuring that murderers will never be released from prison, LWOP gives prosecutors cover for declining to seek capital charges and gives jurors comfort in voting against death even when prosecutors seek it. Therefore, it is reasonable to assume at least some of the steep decline in death sentences since 2000 is a result of the availability of LWOP, though it is unclear just how much. But even if the *entire* decline in death sentencing were (implausibly) attributed to LWOP, the number of capital defendants affected by LWOP's introduction would still be dwarfed by the number of noncapital defendants affected by its widespread adoption and use. Between 2001 and 2013, the number of inmates sentenced to death totaled around 1,600, roughly 2,000 fewer than were sentenced to death in the equivalent period prior to 2001.[18] Meanwhile, in the five years between 2008 and 2013 alone, the number of inmates serving LWOP sentences increased by nearly 9,000, from approximately 40,000 to approximately 49,000.[19] This steep growth is only the most recent manifestation of a longer-term trend of rising LWOP sentences, in both absolute and proportional terms. Between 1992 and 2012, the LWOP population in American prisons quadrupled; as of 2013, one in every nine inmates was serving a life sentence, with one-third of that group ineligible for parole or release.[20] In short, while LWOP has helped some escape the death penalty, it has also caused many others who would have received sentences with parole eligibility to instead be sentenced to die in prison. The passage of LWOP statutes around the country, like the passage of AEDPA in Congress, was fueled by the existence of capital punishment but was most significant for its impact on the broader criminal justice system.

Capital punishment also has a distorting effect on criminal justice because the availability of death as a punishment exerts upward pressure on other sentences in order to maintain proportionality in the scale of sentences. Regardless of whether sentences of many decades or life imprisonment are ever appropriate, they will seem necessary to fill in the gap between lesser penalties at the bottom and death at the top of the sentencing range. Penalties short of death, however severe, do not draw the criticism they fairly deserve because the death penalty, with its high drama and political salience, exerts a gravitational pull on the attention of reformers, the media, the public, and the courts. The tendency of capital punishment to become a focal point of concern tends to normalize other serious punishments. Justice Scalia made a version of this point in responding to Justice Breyer's call for abolition of the death penalty based on concerns about wrongful capital convictions. Scalia noted that death-sentenced inmates are much better off than those sentenced to life because of all the attention that their death sentences receive: "The capital convict will obtain endless legal assistance from the abolition lobby (and legal favoritism from abolitionist judges), while the lifer languishes unnoticed behind bars."[21] The ease with which juvenile LWOP passed in Texas after the Supreme Court outlawed the death penalty for juvenile murderers is a good example of the way in which the death penalty can normalize other punishments: the fact that death was still an option that was regularly imposed on adults convicted of murder in Texas made LWOP seem at the time like a boon to juvenile offenders rather than an innovative and extraordinarily severe punishment (Texas has since abandoned juvenile LWOP). The same dynamic holds for LWOP more generally, as applied to any offenders. Because LWOP is not the most severe sentence available in most state criminal justice systems, and because an LWOP sentence is often celebrated as a tremendous victory in hard-fought capital trials, it is hard for the public to appreciate the extent to which LWOP is "an extreme and excruciating punishment."[22]

In addition to normalizing severe sanctions short of death, capital punishment can detract attention from other major dysfunctions in the criminal justice system. As the nation's most extreme punishment and the clearest symbol of state authority, the death penalty is the obvious target of reformist efforts. Over the same four decades in which the Supreme Court intensively regulated capital punishment under the Constitution, the American incarceration rate rose inexorably to reach heights unique in our country's history and in the world. Yet, only in recent years have concerns about "mass incarceration" become widely discussed, because it takes decades of exponential prison growth to match the drama of even a few executions. As one commentator noted, "Prison cells don't attract many spectators, but executions have always drawn crowds."[23] The Court's project of constitutional regulation of capital punishment itself has contributed to the marginalization of concerns about the scale of incarceration. The Court's insistence in its Eighth Amendment jurisprudence that "death is different" reflects the implicit conclusion that lengthy imprisonment is *not* different and is not worthy of serious scrutiny, judicial or otherwise.

In debates between supporters and opponents of the death penalty, it is common for supporters to argue that opponents will never stop at abolishing the death penalty, but will turn their attention next to repealing authorization for the same LWOP sentences that they supported in the past as an alternative to capital punishment. There is surely some truth in this prediction, but it should be a welcome truth. Debates about criminal justice policy—with regard to the proper scope of federal judicial review, the wisdom of LWOP sentences, or the nature of the most important problems in our criminal justice system—have been distorted by the overwhelming power of death as a punishment. A categorical constitutional abolition of capital punishment would eliminate this distortion and allow franker and more accurate appraisals of criminal justice law and policy on their own terms, rather than in the shadow of death.

Finally, the availability of the death penalty creates some perverse incentives for prosecutors to threaten or initiate capital charges for reasons other than the genuine pursuit of a death sentence. In murder cases in which prosecutors believe that a sentence of life without possibility of parole is the appropriate sentence, prosecutors may nonetheless threaten capital charges in order to induce defendants to waive trial and plead guilty in order to avoid the possibility of a death sentence. Recent empirical research suggests that the threat of capital punishment does impact the likelihood of plea agreements to sentences less than death.[24] Moreover, the availability of death qualification in capital cases, which allows prosecutors to eliminate many prospective jurors opposed to the death penalty, has been shown to yield juries that are more prosecution-prone on the issue of guilt (quite apart from the issue of sentence). The prospect of such a result "may invite prosecutorial gamesmanship, tempting prosecutors to charge cases as capital crimes solely to produce a friendlier jury."[25] These distorting incentives would disappear with the end of capital punishment. Despite the welcome elimination of the distorting effects of death on criminal justice policies and prosecutions, the abolition of capital punishment would also eliminate the powerful spotlight that capital cases shine on the workings of the criminal justice system. The severity and irrevocability of death naturally evokes heightened concerns about the possibility of unfairness and miscarriages of justice in capital cases. Combine these concerns with the high drama of capital cases, from initial crime reporting through trial and execution, and the result is public and media attention to problems in the criminal justice system that might otherwise fly below the radar of public attention. Courts, too, currently give disproportionate consideration to generally applicable legal issues in the context of capital cases—issues that might not otherwise make it onto their noncapital dockets. Although death penalty opponents would clearly have reason to rejoice at nationwide abolition, criminal justice reformers (who often overlap with death penalty opponents) might have some reason to mourn the loss of the death penalty's compelling power.

The distinctive capacity of capital punishment to command public attention is best illustrated by the response to evidence of wrongful convictions in death penalty cases. The discovery that more than a dozen innocent people had been erroneously convicted and sentenced to death in Illinois led to a sustained period of public debate, media attention, and political response. In 1999, a pair of investigative reporters published a five-part series in the *Chicago Tribune,* concluding:

"Capital punishment in Illinois is a system so riddled with faulty evidence, unscrupulous trial tactics and legal incompetence that justice has been forsaken."[26] In 2000, Republican Governor George Ryan declared a moratorium on further executions, and in 2003, he commuted the sentences of the 167 inmates on Illinois's death row—the largest mass clemency in American history.[27] Ryan appointed a commission to study the causes of wrongful capital convictions, and the group ultimately recommended a variety of reforms to death penalty processes and the broader criminal justice system. Many of these proposed reforms foundered in the state legislature. But a number were successful, including a 2003 bill, spearheaded by then-State Senator Barack Obama, requiring the videotaping of police interrogations in homicide cases—making Illinois the first state in the country to pass such a law. In the years that followed, many other states have passed similar or even more expansive laws, which obviously affect many defendants outside the capital justice system.[28] Similar media attention and reform proposals followed in the wake of other high-profile capital cases, such as the 2004 execution of Cameron Todd Willingham in Texas for an apparent arson that prosecutors alleged was intended to take the lives of his three daughters. Willingham's trial was dominated by expert testimony that is now widely viewed to have been the product of "junk" fire science. The case inspired a *New Yorker* article, a *Nightline* news report, and a *Frontline* documentary; it also prompted proposals, in Texas and beyond, for forensic science reform.[29] Although evidence of wrongful convictions in noncapital cases sometimes evokes public concern and calls for reform, the degree of media attention, public outrage, and political response to such evidence in death penalty cases is of a different order of magnitude. This attention has been a powerful force for highlighting problems in the justice system that might never otherwise have seen the light of day.

The disproportionate attention garnered by capital cases is perhaps even stronger in the courts than in the forum of public opinion. Judicial attention to capital cases is driven partly by institutional arrangements. One reason for the relative costliness of capital prosecutions is the fact that states give capital defendants—and only capital defendants—the right at several different stages to challenge their convictions and sentences. Whereas noncapital defendants are usually afforded only discretionary review to the highest state court on direct appeal, capital inmates have a right to such review. Moreover, whereas indigent noncapital inmates have no right to counsel in state postconviction review and federal habeas corpus review (and thus generally must represent themselves at these stages), indigent death-sentenced inmates are generally provided with counsel in both state and federal postconviction proceedings.

The docket of the U.S. Supreme Court disproportionately addresses capital cases because of the same institutional arrangements that drive state and lower federal court review, and because of the Court's ongoing project of constitutional regulation of capital punishment. Whereas capital defendants account for considerably less than one-tenth of 1 percent of criminal defendants prosecuted for crime in any given year, capital cases have occupied somewhere between one-quarter and one-half of the state criminal cases on the Supreme Court's docket in recent years. If one's exposure to the American criminal justice system were confined to attending arguments and reading opinions of the nation's highest court, one might believe that capital prosecutions greatly outnumber speeding violations, burglaries, or drug offenses. As a consequence, much of the constitutional law that affects the general operation of the criminal justice system is made in the context of capital cases.

Some of this generally applicable law is made incidentally, when the Supreme Court makes rulings that are relevant to the broader criminal justice system in decisions that primarily advance the Court's constitutional regulation of capital cases. In a series of opinions addressing the duties of capital defense lawyers to investigate and present mitigating evidence to sentencing juries, the Court elaborated on the evaluation of constitutional claims of "ineffective assistance of counsel" under the Sixth Amendment, which are frequently asserted by capital and noncapital defendants alike. One question addressed by the Court in these opinions was the relevance of bar standards to the constitutional evaluation of reasonably effective representation; another was the relevance of the defendant's own statements to counsel's duty to conduct a reasonable investigation.[30] Without the death penalty driving the Court to develop constitutional standards for the special context of capital cases, there would be fewer opportunities for such incidental development of constitutional law in the more general criminal justice context.

Sometimes the Court chooses to decide general criminal justice issues in capital cases that do not present any questions specific to capital punishment. For example, the Court has addressed the persistent problem of racial discrimination in the selection of criminal juries by granting review in a series of capital cases in which black defendants were convicted and sentenced to death by juries from which all, or almost all, black prospective jurors had been eliminated by the prosecution through the exercise of discretionary strikes.[31] Racial discrimination in jury selection is a problem that extends well beyond the narrow band of capital cases. However, the Court's decisions addressing this problem have dealt disproportionately with capital prosecutions, probably because the disquieting optics of all-white juries condemning black defendants to death heighten the concerns about the perceived legitimacy of the criminal justice system that motivate the constitutional law in this area. The Court has observed that "the very integrity of the courts is jeopardized when a prosecutor's discrimination invites cynicism respecting the jury's neutrality and undermines public confidence in adjudication."[32] In cases like these, in which the high stakes of capital cases drive the Court's granting of review and scrutiny of generally applicable issues of criminal justice, the death penalty helps to produce more constitutional law than otherwise would exist, and it also likely helps to produce law that is more solicitous of the rights of criminal defendants. Capital punishment prompts the Court, no less than the public, to see more clearly and consider more carefully problems in the broader criminal justice system that might not otherwise claim its serious attention. The welcome elimination of distortions that abolition of the death penalty would produce thus must be qualified by recognition of the loss of the power of death to command attention to the serious defects of the broader criminal justice system.

Legacies of Death Penalty Law

The Supreme Court has spent more than forty years developing an intricate body of law addressing death penalty practices under the Eighth Amendment. The language of the Eighth Amendment itself, however, makes no distinction between capital and noncapital cases; rather, it merely forbids "cruel and unusual punishments." In the wake of a categorical constitutional abolition of capital punishment, will the Court's death penalty doctrine be rendered a dead letter, or will it find continuing life as a resource for considering Eighth Amendment challenges to noncapital practices? Until recently, the Court's capital and noncapital Eighth Amendment doctrines were walled off from each other. But a few recent cases, inaugurated by key swing Justice Anthony Kennedy, have breached the divide, suggesting an ongoing role for the Court's Eighth Amendment law forged in capital cases even in the wake of capital punishment's eventual demise. This law offers the Court tools, if it wishes to use them, to address some of the most extreme practices short of death in the criminal justice system, such as LWOP, mandatory sentencing, and solitary confinement.

For most of the forty years following the revival of capital punishment in 1976, the Court treated Eighth Amendment challenges to noncapital punishments under an entirely separate constitutional rubric. For example, the Court found no need in noncapital sentencing to import its capital sentencing requirement that defendants be afforded individualized consideration of "compassionate or mitigating factors stemming from the diverse frailties of humankind." Rather, the Court observed that while "Consideration of both the offender and the offense in order to arrive at a just and appropriate sentence has been viewed as a progressive and humanizing development," in noncapital cases such a practice "generally reflects simply enlightened policy rather than a constitutional imperative."[33] As a consequence, mandatory sentencing has flourished in the broader criminal justice system in both state and federal courts; mandatory minimum sentences are authorized for a wide range of crimes from drug and gun possession to crimes of violence; and "three-strikes-you're-out" regimes mandate lengthy sentence enhancements for repeat offenders, without any consideration of the individual circumstances of such offenders beyond the offenses they committed.

Similarly, the Court's treatment of proportionality challenges to harsh sentences that stopped short of death took an entirely different constitutional path from the proportionality doctrine it developed in the capital context. In a series of cases from the early 1980s to the early 2000s—the very same time it was developing its capital proportionality doctrine—the Court developed a noncapital proportionality doctrine that made it essentially impossible for any sentence of incarceration to be deemed constitutionally excessive. In its initial forays in this area in the early 1980s, the Court permitted states wide leeway to impose extremely lengthy sentences without constitutional constraint. In 1980, the Court upheld a mandatory sentence of life (with the possibility of parole) that was imposed for the theft of $120 by false pretenses when the crime was the defendant's third such offense, thus triggering the application of a Texas recidivism statute.[34] The defendant's prior two offenses had been the fraudulent use of a credit card for $80 and the passing of a forged check in the amount of $28.36. The Court appeared confident that few, if any, sentences of incarceration would run afoul of the Constitution, noting that the proportionality principle would come into play only "in the extreme example . . . if a legislature made overtime parking a felony punishable by life imprisonment."[35] Two years later, the Court upheld a sentence totaling forty years imprisonment for the offenses of possession with intent to distribute of nine ounces of marijuana and distribution of marijuana.[36]

However, in 1983, the Court seemed to indicate that the Constitution did place an outside limit on incarceration when, for the first time, it struck down a sentence of incarceration as disproportionate to a crime under the Eighth Amendment. By a slim five-to-four majority, the Court threw out a sentence of life *without* the possibility of parole that was imposed on Jerry Helm under a South Dakota recidivism statute for Helm's crime of passing a bad $100 check, his seventh nonviolent felony conviction.[37] The Court struck down Helm's LWOP sentence after considering not only the harshness of the punishment in relation to the gravity of the offense, but also two further things: the fact that Helm's sentence was the longest that the state could have imposed on any criminal for any crime, and the fact that South Dakota was one of only two states in the country that authorized an LWOP sentence for an offender in Helm's situation. These intra- and interjurisdictional comparisons added weight to the Court's initial intuition that Helm's punishment was "significantly disproportionate to his crime."[38]

The Court did not return to the question of the proportionality of sentences of incarceration until the early 1990s. At that point, a new configuration of justices upheld, also by a five-to-four vote, a mandatory LWOP sentence imposed on Ronald Harmelin, a first-time offender convicted under Michigan law of possessing 672 grams of cocaine found in the trunk of his car after it was stopped and searched when he ran a red light.[39] In Harmelin's case, even more than in Helm's, intra- and interjurisdictional comparisons suggested that his LWOP sentence was disproportionate. Michigan, unlike South Dakota at the time of Helm's prosecution, did not have the death penalty, and thus LWOP was the harshest punishment of any kind that could be imposed in that state; as the sentence imposed on mass murderers, it seemed an incongruous punishment for first-time drug offenders. Moreover, no other jurisdiction in the country permitted the imposition of a punishment nearly as severe as LWOP for possession of the amount of drugs at issue in Harmelin's case. For example, if Harmelin had been prosecuted by federal rather than Michigan officials, his sentence would have been only ten years. Nonetheless, a plurality of the Court, in an opinion authored by Justice Kennedy, changed the constitutional analysis that had been used in Helm's case. Instead, Kennedy explained that intra- and interjurisdictional comparisons are "not always relevant" to a court's Eighth Amendment analysis and should be considered "only in the rare case in which a threshold comparison of the crime committed and the sentence imposed leads to an inference of gross disproportionality." As for Harmelin's situation, the plurality concluded that his was *not* the "rare case" in which an inference of "gross disproportionality" was appropriate because of the serious harms caused by drug offenses. The Court explained: "Possession, use, and distribution of illegal drugs represent one of the greatest problems affecting the health and welfare of our population."[40]

The *Harmelin* Court's prediction that successful Eighth Amendment challenges to sentences of incarceration would be "rare" was confirmed by two cases in the early 2000s that seemed to be the end of the road for the Court's noncapital proportionality doctrine. In 2003, the Court reviewed two challenges to California's "three strikes" statute. In one case, the defendant had been sentenced to twenty-five years to life for stealing three golf clubs from a pro shop; the defendant's record, which included several burglaries, a robbery, a car theft, and a battery along with some petty offenses, triggered the application of the California recidivist statute.[41] In the second case, the defendant had been sentenced to fifty years to life for stealing nine videos from K-Mart; his record of numerous petty offenses and three burglaries likewise triggered the California recidivist statute.[42]

As in the *Harmelin* case, intra- and interjurisdictional comparisons suggested that these two defendants' sentences were seriously out of whack. Within California, sentences of twenty-five or fifty years to life were greater than those typically imposed on far more serious offenders, including first-degree murderers. Outside of California, such sentences were virtually unique in their harshness, even in other states with "three strikes" laws. Nonetheless, the Court never reached such comparative analysis, because a plurality, again including Justice Kennedy, found that neither case crossed the threshold of "gross disproportionality." Applying the Court's "traditional deference to legislative policy choices," the plurality acceded to the California legislature's "judgment that protecting the public safety requires incapacitating criminals who have already been convicted of at least one serious or violent crime."[43] To underscore just how difficult its analysis was intended to be, the plurality reached back more than two decades to repeat approvingly the Court's earlier observation that its proportionality principle would be applied to incarceration challenges only in "extreme" cases like life imprisonment for overtime parking.[44]

In the aftermath of these decisions upholding California's "three strikes" law, there seemed to be little remaining hope that any sentences of incarceration would be deemed disproportionate under the Eighth Amendment. If a state's interest in "incapacitating criminals" can serve to block the required inference of gross disproportionality, such an interest arguably exists in virtually every case. The fairest reading of the Court's approach to Eighth Amendment proportionality challenges to sentences of incarceration seemed to be that only overtime parkers serving lifetime sentences need apply. Judges in state and lower federal courts got the message. When inmates raised proportionality challenges to their sentences of incarceration, courts tended to reject them "without extended discussion," citing the Court's decisions in the California cases.[45]

In the decade following these decisions, however, the legal and political *zeitgeist* began to turn in the direction of questioning the American practice of what began to be called "mass incarceration." Interestingly, many identify the commencement of this shift with a speech given by Justice Kennedy at the American Bar Association's annual meeting in 2003, just a few months after he joined the majority in upholding California's "three strikes" law. Kennedy lamented the scale of imprisonment, stating bluntly: "Our resources are misspent, our punishments too severe, our sentences too long."[46] He called on the ABA to recommend the repeal of the mandatory minimum sentencing schemes, the reinvigoration of executive clemency, and the improvement of prison conditions. The political shift that Kennedy's speech reflected and helped to promote would ultimately lead California voters (rather than the courts) to modify the harshness of their state's "three strikes" law. In 2012, Proposition 36 radically cut back on the harshness of the law; the ballot initiative was approved by an overwhelming margin.[47]

In this changing national climate, it is perhaps not surprising that Kennedy led the Court to revisit the virtually absolute bar that its Eighth Amendment law seemed to pose to challenges to sentences of incarceration. What *was* surprising was that the Court did not revise the methodology that it had established in *Harmelin* and applied in the California "three strikes" cases. Rather, the Court for the first time applied the much more accommodating and flexible proportionality analysis *from its capital cases* to a challenge to a *non*capital sentence. In *Graham v. Florida,* the Court considered an Eighth Amendment challenge to a sentence of LWOP imposed on Terrance Graham for violating his parole for a burglary that he committed when he was sixteen years old.[48] Kennedy wrote the opinion for the Court striking down Graham's sentence and invalidating LWOP sentences for any juvenile offenders convicted of nonhomicide crimes. Perhaps recognizing that the Court's *Harmelin* methodology posed an insurmountable bar to relief, Kennedy turned to the capital proportionality cases that had been used to strike down the death penalty for (some) felony murderers, for juvenile and intellectually disabled offenders, and for the offense of rape (of adults or children). Kennedy recast these decisions as involving *categorical,* rather than *capital,* challenges; in each of the successful death penalty cases, Kennedy maintained, the challenge had been to an entire category of sentences, based on offender or offense attributes. The impossible *Harmelin* methodology, in contrast, had been used to address *non*-categorical claims by individuals to their particular sentences. Having established the relevance of the Court's capital proportionality decisions to the noncapital context, Kennedy considered the relative rarity (and concentration in Florida) of juvenile LWOP sentences for nonhomicide offenders as "objective evidence" of a consensus against the practice. He then turned to the Court's "own judgment" and emphasized both the special conditions of youth that had led the Court to abolish the juvenile death penalty and the diminished culpability of those who did not kill that had led the Court to limit the death penalty for felony murderers. Kennedy emphasized the extreme severity of LWOP as a sentence: "It deprives the convict of the most basic liberties without giving hope of restoration, except perhaps by executive clemency—the remote possibility of which does not mitigate the harshness of the sentence."[49] Concluding that the traditional purposes of punishment would not be served by LWOP sentences for juveniles in nonhomicide cases, Kennedy explained that the practice was "categorically" banned by the Eighth Amendment.

Kennedy's revisionist recasting of more than thirty years of Eighth Amendment decisions was both controversial and confusing. The dissenting justices, led by Clarence Thomas, emphasized the majority's departure from what had appeared to be a settled capital/noncapital divide: "The Court's departure from the 'death is different' distinction is especially mystifying when one considers how long it has resisted crossing that divide."[50] Chief Justice John Roberts, too, though he concurred in the result, observed, "I see no need to invent a new constitutional rule of dubious provenance."[51] Moreover, the future application of the new categorical/non-categorical distinction in other contexts remains murky, as many challenges could be fairly viewed as belonging on either side of the line. For example, Harmelin—the first-time offender sentenced to LWOP for drug possession—was assumed by Kennedy to have made a non-categorical challenge to his particular sentence. But why was his challenge not properly viewed as a categorical one based on Harmelin's status as a first-time offender or based on the offense of drug possession?

Despite these difficulties, the Court two years later applied its capital proportionality cases yet again to noncapital cases—again involving juveniles sentenced to LWOP. In *Miller v. Alabama*, Justice Elena Kagan wrote for the Court in striking down mandatory LWOP sentences imposed in two separate cases on fourteen-year-olds convicted of murder, ruling that even juvenile *homicide* offenders could not receive LWOP sentences as mandatory punishment for their offenses.[52] The Court drew on two distinct lines of its formerly capital Eighth Amendment jurisprudence: its consideration of the special characteristics of youth that led it to reject the juvenile death penalty, and its insistence on individualized, nonmandatory sentencing in capital cases. The Court explained that because LWOP is the most severe punishment available for juvenile offenders, it should be treated as "analogous to capital punishment" in juvenile Eighth Amendment challenges. Kagan limited the Court's holding to striking down *mandatory* LWOP sentences for juveniles, but hinted at a more wholesale skepticism: "given all we have said . . . about children's diminished culpability and heightened capacity for change, we think appropriate occasions for sentencing juveniles to this harshest possible penalty will be uncommon."[53]

The Court's repurposing of its capital cases in *Graham* and *Miller* to apply to noncapital constitutional challenges is the strongest indication that its death penalty jurisprudence may have continuing life even after a categorical constitutional abolition. How far the Court will be willing to go in regulating noncapital punishments under the Eighth Amendment remains to be seen. As with the potential categorical abolition of the death penalty, much will depend on the composition of the Court and trends in punishment practices on the ground. On the one hand, the decisions in *Graham* and *Miller* could simply be the end of the line for the constitutional regulation of noncapital punishments; they could be read to mark only a small, discrete exception to otherwise boundless judicial deference to legislative judgment in this area. On the other hand, the Court's capital jurisprudence offers potentially powerful tools to address significant issues in the broader criminal justice system, such as juvenile sentencing, LWOP, mandatory minimums, and solitary confinement (among other harsh prison conditions).

Graham and *Miller* were, first and foremost, decisions about juvenile offenders, whose special characteristics the Court addressed most comprehensively in its 2002 decision abolishing the juvenile death penalty. The Court's consideration of evidence about the development of the adolescent brain and its effects on the capacities of young people led it to conclude that "the distinctive attributes of youth diminish the penological justifications for imposing the harshest sentences on juvenile offenders, even when they commit terrible crimes."[54] The Court may well conclude that the "harshest sentences" that are inappropriate for juveniles go beyond what the Court has already outlawed. The Court might well take the step that it hinted at in *Miller* and abolish LWOP for juveniles, period—not merely *mandatory* LWOP—as numerous states have done in the wake of *Miller*.[55] Beyond LWOP, life sentences *with* the possibility of parole and sentences of multiple decades of incarceration also rank among the harshest sentences and will undoubtedly lead to challenges when imposed on juveniles, especially if they are imposed for nonviolent or less serious crimes—or even for more serious crimes in which the juvenile played a relatively minor role. Challenges to LWOP and other harsh sentences will likely be made on behalf of young people over the age of current "juvenile" status (and challenges to the death penalty for such young adults no doubt will be made while capital punishment continues).[56]

The success of challenges such as these to juvenile sentences will depend partly on the direction of punishment practices on the ground—the "objective" evidence that the Court addresses first under its capital/categorical proportionality analysis. If LWOP or other harsh sentences for juveniles continue to be outlawed or restricted by legislatures, and if such sentences become increasingly rare in practice, the case for an emerging consensus against such practices becomes stronger. As the science of adolescent brain development evolves, it may inform the Court's "own judgment" as to the permissibility of a variety of harsh punishments on juveniles or on youths over the age of eighteen but not yet fully mature, an analysis that turns on whether such punishments promote the retributive and deterrent purposes of capital punishment.[57] The (generally much milder) treatment of juvenile offenders abroad may also inform the Court's consideration of challenges to juvenile sentencing practices in the United States.[58] The Court's capital/categorical proportionality doctrine thus allows for considerations that may well powerfully support further constitutional restrictions on juvenile sentencing.

However, such constitutional challenges raise a ubiquitous question: where to draw the line? In *Graham* and *Miller*, the Court was able to rely on two very bright lines: the well-recognized age of eighteen as the line for juvenile status and the clear distinction between LWOP and other sentences. With the exception of completely abolishing LWOP for all juvenile offenders, the rest of the potential rulings canvassed above would require the Court (and the state or lower federal courts that would first assess such challenges) to progress down the slippery slope of incremental differences in both age and sentence length. The absence of an easy stopping point might thus inhibit any attempt to extend *Graham* and *Miller* to address sentences beyond LWOP for juveniles or for a larger category of youths that would include young adults.

Some but not all of the same considerations apply to potential challenges to LWOP outside of the juvenile or youth context. In the absence of the death penalty, LWOP would ascend to the position of the harshest legally available punishment, and as such it would likely become the target of the same kinds of Eighth Amendment challenges that the death penalty invited. One can already see the death penalty analogy emerging in advocacy against LWOP, when the sentence is described as "a living death" or "death in prison."[59] One likely constitutional challenge LWOP will face is an attack on the scope of its application, given the current imposition of LWOP for many offenses other than homicide.[60] The continued availability of LWOP for nonhomicide offenses (and even for nonviolent crimes pursuant to some recidivism and drug laws) will depend, as in the juvenile context, on "objective evidence" of an emerging consensus against such uses, as seen in state legislative enactments and in the numbers of defendants actually sentenced. As for the Court's "own judgment," it will likely be influenced by advances in empirical understanding of the effectiveness (or ineffectiveness) of LWOP sentences in reducing crime, and possibly by public opinion polling on the relative harshness of LWOP compared to death.[61] As in the juvenile context, one of the strongest arguments for limiting LWOP sentences will be the Court's consideration of LWOP's authorization and use abroad (where to date it is extraordinarily rare).[62]

A second likely challenge to LWOP in the wake of death penalty abolition is an attack on its mandatory imposition under a number of current homicide and recidivism statutes. Once again, the trend in numbers will be important, as will the Court's "own judgment" about the importance of individualized sentencing outside of the capital or juvenile context. The LWOP challenges do not present the same "slippery slope" problem as do the attempted extensions of the Court's juvenile sentence rulings, because LWOP as a punishment is sufficiently distinctive that it may come to be viewed, as advocates already contend, as equivalent to death. As a result, the challenge to mandatory LWOP sentences, like the challenge to LWOP's broad scope, may hold more promise for advocates. Should a challenge to mandatory LWOP sentences succeed, other defendants would undoubtedly seek to extend such a ruling to challenge mandatory sentencing more broadly. Here, the "slippery slope" problem would again arise, as it is hard to find a principled stopping point between LWOP and *any* mandatory minimum sentence, however modest.

Another significant problematic practice in the criminal justice system that might be addressed by the Court's formerly capital Eighth Amendment jurisprudence is the extensive use of solitary confinement. Part of this problem would disappear with the death penalty itself, as capital inmates are the only ones who are held in solitary confinement as a function of their sentences (rather than as a function of incidents within the prison environment). Indeed, the Court's Eighth Amendment doctrine may well be deployed *before* any successful categorical challenge to the death penalty to try to change the ubiquitous use of solitary confinement on death row. But even in the wake of death penalty abolition, the extended solitary confinement of noncapital inmates, either as punishment for misbehavior in prison or for their own protection, would remain a troubling issue.[63] Here, too, legislative movement toward restricting use of solitary confinement will be of primary significance to the Court's Eighth Amendment analysis.[64] In addition, the Court would likely consider the growing medical and psychological literature on the impact of extended solitary confinement, as well as expert assessments of its necessity as a tool of prison management. Moreover, the nature and use of solitary confinement abroad, which is generally less extreme than in American prisons, would likely also inform the Court's "own judgment" in its Eighth Amendment analysis.[65]

Although solitary confinement has not been questioned directly by the Court's precedents (in contrast to juvenile LWOP and mandatory sentencing), there is nonetheless some reason to think that the Court might be willing to apply its Eighth Amendment doctrine to this new context. Justice Breyer, writing for himself and Justice Ginsburg, cited the cruelty of extended solitary confinement on death row as one reason to question the constitutionality of the death penalty. Presumably, these justices' concerns would extend to lengthy solitary confinement outside the confines of death row as well.[66] Justice Kennedy has added his important weight to the issue by raising it at oral argument and then writing a separate concurring opinion in a case in which it had not even been raised by the parties. Kennedy wrote movingly of the "human toll wrought by extended terms of isolation" and called upon the legal community to give the issue continued consideration. He concluded by invoking Dostoyevsky's apt admonition: "The degree of civilization in a society can be judged by entering its prisons."[67] Although Kennedy did not invoke the concept of dignity in his brief concurrence, as he has in many other contexts, it is not far-fetched to see the harms inflicted on inmates held in extended solitary confinement as dignitary ones. After all, the Court itself has proclaimed: "The basic concept underlying the Eighth Amendment is nothing less than the dignity of man."[68] There is strong reason to think that Kennedy will be open to Eighth Amendment challenges to extended solitary confinement.

The challenge for the Court's capital jurisprudence in the solitary confinement context, as in the juvenile context, is a line-drawing one. There is extensive evidence that even outside the context of death row, many inmates spend lengthy periods of time—measured in years rather than weeks or months—in solitary confinement.[69] However, despite the horror of some of these extremes, prison officials will argue that they need to use solitary confinement in at least some instances for a variety of important purposes, such as preventing violence, punishing misbehavior, protecting vulnerable inmates, or dealing with security risks. The "slippery slope" problem here is the same as in the context of limiting sentences short of LWOP—time is incremental. Just as it would be hard to pinpoint which sentences short of LWOP are disproportionate for juveniles, it would be hard to pinpoint when solitary confinement becomes so "extended" as to violate the Eighth Amendment. Despite apparent interest on the Court in addressing the problem of solitary confinement, on death row and beyond, the difficulty of articulating a categorical rule may pose an impediment to the application of the Court's Eighth Amendment precedents in this area.

The "slippery slope" problem points to a more general limitation of the Court's extension of its capital Eighth Amendment jurisprudence to noncapital sentencing. The Court's capital proportionality doctrine, though it has the powerful potential to bring about a categorical constitutional abolition of the death penalty, is unlikely to do much more than permit limited attacks against discrete noncapital punishments, such as LWOP or solitary confinement. These discrete attacks, even if wildly successful, would do little to address the biggest problem in the American criminal justice system—namely, the scale of imprisonment. The Eighth Amendment simply does not offer the necessary tools to reverse the phenomenon of mass incarceration, which is the product of numerous intersecting policies, including law enforcement strategies, prosecutorial charging decisions, legislative sentencing authorizations, and executive practices limiting parole and clemency. Ultimately, the difference between the death penalty and large-scale incarceration is similar to the difference between smoking and obesity. The constitutional attack against the death penalty is premised on the assertion that the death penalty is unnecessary and our society would be best served by abolishing it altogether. As with smoking, we can just kick the habit. But incarceration is more like food, with every society needing some level of imprisonment to deter crime and incapacitate dangerous offenders. Moreover, there remains wide disagreement about what a healthy diet of incarceration looks like. Is the proper baseline found in the relatively low rates of incarceration prevailing in places like the Netherlands and Switzerland—approximately 80 per 100,000—or in the relatively high rates found in places like Russia, Cuba, and the United States— ranging from approximately 500 to 700 per 100,000?[70] Even if the various jurisdictions within the United States committed themselves to reducing their incarceration rates, the path toward that end is not obvious. The perception that the United States currently has too much incarceration calls for controversial and complicated interventions. Constitutional proportionality doctrine does not offer a wholesale approach to the problem, and judicial intervention on a case-by-case basis is too discrete a remedy to be an effective means of addressing the enormous scale of American imprisonment.

Thus, the prognosis for the future vitality of the Court's capital Eighth Amendment jurisprudence is mixed. This body of law may well have a robust "life after death" and provide tools for courts to diagnose and treat some significant pathologies in the broader criminal justice system. However, a clear-eyed assessment of the magnitude of the problems afflicting the American criminal justice system should make us wary of viewing the Eighth Amendment as a panacea.

The Politics of Criminal Justice after Abolition

A categorical constitutional abolition will have consequences beyond the legal sphere in the broader realm of politics. The death penalty plays an outsized role in public discourse about criminal justice because of its powerful drama and symbolism. The removal of the death penalty from political play likely will tone down criminal justice debates while also extending them: without the death penalty as shorthand, political candidates will have to say more about their criminal justice policies in order to communicate with voters. Even if pro-death penalty politicians urge resistance in the wake of an announcement of constitutional abolition (much the way some opponents have resisted the constitutional mandate recognizing same-sex marriage), eventually the issue will be settled, and the criminal justice conversation will focus on other issues. Nationwide abolition will also eliminate political conflicts between the federal government and abolitionist states over federal death penalty prosecutions in those states. Finally, the end of the American death penalty will remove an impediment to international criminal justice collaborations with our abolitionist allies and also bring the United States closer to the rest of our peer nations by allowing us to view the practice through a shared human rights lens.

Despite its minor role relative to incarceration as a criminal sanction, the death penalty is a substantial force on the political stage. Elected judges and district attorneys, as well as governors and presidents, often have campaigned—or been attacked by political rivals—on their death penalty positions. Given the extremely small contribution that the federal government makes to the American death penalty (only three of the more than 1,400 executions since 1976 have been at the hands of the federal government), and the negligible role that the president plays in supervising the federal death penalty, the emphasis that presidential candidates, among others, place on capital punishment is clearly symbolic.

What does the death penalty symbolize? First and foremost, it is shorthand for a "tough on crime" stance, which had great political resonance in the 1980s and 1990s, though less today in an era of much lower crime rates. But the death penalty has salience beyond crime policy; it has become one of the key issues in the "culture wars" that divide South from North, red states from blue states, and the religiously observant from the nonobservant. The map of active death penalty states illustrates the profound regional division on this issue.[71] Even within geographic regions, polling shows that that the death penalty is more popular among Protestants and even Catholics than among those who are religiously unaffiliated. It is also a race and gender issue, as the death penalty is more popular among whites than blacks, and among men than women.[72] As a result, the death penalty has worked as a political wedge issue whose invocation speaks simultaneously to the cluster of demographic divisions that shape the partisan political dichotomy.

The death penalty's power as political shorthand lies in its capacity to appeal to these many different audiences in a visceral, emotional way. But the ability of the death penalty to move people seems to be contingent on its continued existence within a political community. In other Western democracies, popular majorities generally supported the death penalty at the time of abolition; only after abolition did public support wane to the low levels that exist today.[73] If the experience of our peer countries is any guide, support for the death penalty will fall in the United States in the wake of constitutional abolition and tensions over the issue will dissipate. The death penalty's absence will also likely lower the temperature of criminal justice debates. Without the possibility of reviving capital punishment through politics (short of constitutional amendment), heinous crimes will not lead to dramatic gestures like Donald Trump's full-page ad in four New York City newspapers to "Bring Back the Death Penalty" in response to the infamous attack in 1989 on a Central Park jogger (whose alleged assailants were exonerated long after their convictions and paid more than 40 million dollars in compensation for their wrongful incarceration).[74] Instead of short, hot, slogan-driven appeals, criminal justice debates will have to be longer and cooler engagements on a broader range of issues, as no other single issue has the same shorthand power as the death penalty.

Constitutional abolition of the death penalty will moderate the tone of disagreement among states, as well as among political rivals. Just as the constitutional mandate that same-sex marriage be recognized in every state eliminated that issue as one of state identity, so too will constitutional abolition retire the label of "death penalty state" from the lexicon of state differentiation. The red state/blue state divide will not disappear anytime soon, but the disappearance of the death penalty along with restrictions on same-sex marriage from the internal map of the United States will allow for more purple than would otherwise exist.

In addition to easing tensions among states, constitutional abolition of the death penalty will eliminate a recurring irritant in federal/state relations. When the federal government pursues a death penalty prosecution in an abolitionist state (or territory like Puerto Rico), it is often controversial, no matter how heinous the crime. Attorney General John Ashcroft, who served under President George W. Bush, drew criticism for "making an end run around local laws and customs" when he instituted a policy of affirmatively seeking federal capital prosecutions in abolitionist states.[75] Because anyone who sits as a juror in a capital case must not be unalterably opposed to the death penalty, federal capital juries in abolitionist states tend to be drawn from a minority of the state's population with views unrepresentative of the larger political community. The prosecution of Boston Marathon bomber Dzhokhar Tsarnaev in federal court in 2015 was a case in point. Despite the horror of Tsarnaev's crimes and defense attempts to move the trial outside of Boston for fear of bias against their client, polls during the trial showed that residents of Boston (and Massachusetts more generally) overwhelmingly favored a life sentence.[76] But the Tsarnaev jurors, seated on the condition that they could consider a death sentence, unanimously voted for death. Such results can generate concerns about jury bias and even charges of "show trials."[77]

Constitutional abolition of the death penalty will also reduce tension between the United States and its international peers. Joint criminal justice initiatives with our abolitionist allies will no longer be shadowed by the concern that extradition to the United States may be refused because of the possibility of a capital prosecution.[78] On a broader level, the United States will no longer have reason to reject the consensus that capital punishment is a human rights issue rather than one of domestic criminal justice policy. Adopting a shared human rights lens with our allies will reduce the friction that our fundamentally different conception of the issue currently generates. No longer will earnest young human rights activists from Paris, Geneva, and Stockholm seek internships in capital defense organizations in Texas and Alabama. No longer will the U.N. Special Rapporteur on extrajudicial, summary or arbitrary executions file reports to the Commission on Human Rights about defects in death penalty processes in the United States.[79] Such changes are not merely symbolic; more pragmatically, they will permit the United States to avoid claims of hypocrisy when it dons the mantle of a global human rights leader and seeks to take other countries, like China, to task for their human rights failings.

A categorical constitutional abolition of the death penalty obviously will render the criminal justice system less harsh. But it will also likely produce a less divisive criminal justice politics, both domestically and internationally.

Abolition and American Ideals

As we approach what may be the final chapter of the American death penalty story, we are struck by the odd and exceptional path capital punishment has traveled to the present moment.

Given the prominence of Enlightenment ideas at our country's birth and the sympathetic reading of Cesare Beccaria's abolitionist tract by many of our most prominent founders, one might have expected the United States to have been among the first rather than last of nations to jettison what many of the founders viewed as the "sanguinary" old-world practice of capital punishment. But it is important to remember that several American states—Michigan, Wisconsin, and Rhode Island—were among the world's first abolitionist jurisdictions, abandoning the death penalty in the mid-nineteenth century. The persistence of capital punishment in the United States is fundamentally a state-by-state affair, reflecting deep regional differences that have existed since the colonial era. That fact stands as a reminder that our constitutional inheritance combines two separate, powerful commitments: an abstract belief in the fundamental rights of life and liberty, on the one hand, and a political structure that assigns most important policy choices to state and local rather than national actors, on the other. The history of the United States is in many respects a history of how these two commitments have come into conflict, as the struggles over slavery, lynching, Jim Crow, and the death penalty (among many other practices) frequently involved a choice between claims of state and local prerogatives and claims of fundamental justice.

Ironically, the battle over the American death penalty seems no longer to be waged in terms of its potential tension with fundamental rights and Enlightenment ideals. Instead, the modern era of constitutional regulation has altered the death penalty in ways that simultaneously increase its cost and reduce its efficacy. As a result, capital punishment has become increasingly vulnerable to the more prosaic charge that it is simply bad policy. That shift in emphasis from principle to pragmatism in the court of public opinion is reflected in, and reinforced by, a similar shift in emphasis among the death penalty's detractors on the Supreme Court. Rather than declare the death penalty a violation of human dignity, these justices tend to focus on its prevailing inadequate administration—its declining use, its unreliability, and its delays (which in turn undermine its deterrent and retributive value).

If and when abolition finally comes, it is likely to arrive in the form of a Supreme Court opinion declaring that the death penalty no longer serves its avowed purposes. Although we would certainly welcome such a result, we worry that the final word on the American death penalty will not fully acknowledge or record the darker sides of the American death penalty—particularly the extent to which the resonance of the practice and its continued use have been inseparably connected to race. We also wonder whether, regardless of what the Court says, Americans will eventually reimagine the death penalty's demise as reflecting our deep, even exceptional, regard for human dignity as reflected in our founding documents. The incentive to adopt the human rights lens of our peer countries on the issue will likely speed this revisionism. It will no doubt be easier and more comforting to believe that the Supreme Court abolished capital punishment because of our profound respect for human life and "who we are as a people," than to face the more complicated, though more accurate, truth that the death penalty simply could not survive the uniquely American project to attempt to cure its many ills through judicial regulation.

Justice Marshall, believing that the Court's decision in *Furman* had sealed the fate of the death penalty, wrote in that case to defend the result against a charge of judicial activism. "In striking down capital punishment," Marshall argued, "this Court does not malign our system of government." Rather, by "recognizing the humanity of our fellow beings, we pay ourselves the highest tribute. We achieve 'a major milestone in the long road up from barbarism.'" Marshall's image of a universal road elevating humanity toward civilization is a powerful one, suggesting that the death penalty is one of those practices that societies inevitably discard as they achieve a greater measure of moral progress. The proposition that civilization and the death penalty are incompatible might be accurate, but the American experience with capital punishment over the past forty years has been more messy and complicated than the image suggests. The United States has not traveled along a well-trod path toward a predetermined destination. The American road has been marked by rises and descents and sudden curves. If the United States arrives at abolition, it will do so not primarily because of noble considerations marking moral advancement but rather because of particular features of the American terrain, most notably the failed and perhaps impossible effort to improve capital punishment with the lofty but limited power of the Constitution.

Notes

Acknowledgments

Index

Notes

Introduction

1. Jones v. Chappell, 31 F. Supp. 3d 1050, 1053 (C.D. Cal. 2014), rev'd, Jones v. Davis, 806 F.3d 538, 553 (9th Cir. 2015) (emphasis in original).
2. Phillip Reese, "How California Death Row Inmates Die," *Sacramento Bee,* September 21, 2015, http://www.sacbee.com/site-services/databases /article35995422.html.
3. Tara Murtha, "Capital Punishment is Hard to Abolish. Pennsylvania's Death Penalty Battle Shows Why," *New Republic,* June 29, 2015, https://newrepublic .com/article/122199/capital-punishment-hard-abolish.
4. Frank Thompson, "Life without Parole a Better Choice than Death Penalty," *Statesman Journal,* December 3, 2015, http://www.statesmanjournal.com/story /opinion/readers/2015/12/03/life-without-parole-better-choice-death-penalty /76745524/.
5. Glossip v. Gross, 135 S. Ct. 2726, 2768 (2015) (Breyer, J., dissenting) (citing sources).
6. Jones v. Chappell, 1053.
7. Furman v. Georgia, 408 U.S. 238, 309–310 (1972) (Stewart, J., concurring).
8. National Weather Service, "U.S. Lightning Fatalities Since the 1940s," http://www.nws.noaa.gov/om/hazstats/resources/weather_fatalities.pdf.
9. Callins v. Collins, 510 U.S. 1141, 1145 (1994) (Blackmun, J., dissenting from denial of certiorari).

1. Before Constitutional Regulation

1. Howard Pyle, *Mary Dyer Being Led to the Scaffold,* ca. 1905, image reproduced in Ruth S. Taylor, "Connected to the Past: Objects from the Collections of the Newport Historical Society," *Antiques & Fine Art Magazine* (2016), http://www .antiquesandfineart.com/articles/article.cfm?request=899.

2. An image of the statue of Mary Dyer is available at http://www.publicartboston .com/content/mary-dyer.

3. Daniel J. Boorstin, *The Americans: The Colonial Experience* (New York: Random House, 1958), 3, 38.

4. Ibid., 35–40.

5. Ibid., 28.

6. "The English tradition of selectively enforcing capital statutes was also a feature of Massachusetts law. Many sexual crimes that carried the penalty of death were not enforced with any degree of regularity." Patrick Callaway, "Fear, Capital Punishment, and Order: The Construction and Use of Capital Punishment Statutes in Early Modern England and Seventeenth-Century New England," in *Invitation to an Execution: A History of the Death Penalty in the United States,* ed. Gordon Morris Bakken (Albuquerque: University of New Mexico Press, 2010), 47, 56.

7. Caleb Johnson, "Crime and Punishment in Plymouth Colony," *Caleb Johnson's Mayflower History* (1994–2016), http://mayflowerhistory.com/crime.

8. Lisa M. Lauria, "Sexual Misconduct in Plymouth Colony," *The Plymouth Colony Archive Project* (1998), http://www.histarch.illinois.edu/plymouth /Lauria1.html.

9. M. Watt Espy and John Ortiz Smykla, *Executions in the United States, 1608–2002: The ESPY File,* 4th ed. (Ann Arbor, MI: Inter-university Consortium for Political and Social Research [producer and distributor], 2004), http://doi.org/10.3886 /ICPSR08451.v4.

10. Stuart Banner, *The Death Penalty: An American History* (Cambridge, MA: Harvard University Press, 2002), 8–9.

11. Howard W. Allen and Jerome M. Clubb, *Race, Class, and the Death Penalty: Capital Punishment in American History* (Albany: SUNY Press, 2008), 45.

12. Banner, *Death Penalty,* 72–75.

13. "Treason denoted 'not only offences against the king and government,' explained William Blackstone, but also crimes 'proceeding from the same principle of treachery in private life.'" Ibid., 71, quoting William Blackstone, *Commentaries on the Laws of England* (1765–1769), 9th ed. (London: W. Strahan et al., 1783), 4:75.

14. Philip Dray, *At the Hands of Persons Unknown: The Lynching of Black America* (New York: Random House, 2002), 26. For a more in-depth treatment of the Stono slave rebellion, see Mark Michael Smith, ed., *Stono: Documenting and Interpreting a Southern Slave Revolt* (Columbia: University of South Carolina Press, 2005). "How many, if any, of the 'executions' of slaves [who participated in the Stono rebellion] involved any form of judicial proceeding . . . is unclear.

Some were certainly put to death without trial or other legal process." Allen and Clubb, *Race, Class, and the Death Penalty,* 35–36.

15. Death Penalty Information Center, *Number of Executions by State and Region since 1976* (2016), http://www.deathpenaltyinfo.org/number-executions-state-and-region-1976.

16. Frank McLynn, *Crime and Punishment in Eighteenth-Century England* (New York: Oxford University Press, 1991), ix–x.

17. During the nineteenth century, both England and continental Europe saw the narrowing of formerly broad capital statutes. "The nineteenth century would become the age of the penitentiary, and . . . long-term imprisonment eventually replaced death on the scaffold as the punishment for all but the most serious criminals." David Garland, *Peculiar Institution: America's Death Penalty in an Age of Abolition* (Cambridge, MA: Belknap Press of Harvard University Press, 2010), 88.

18. John D. Bessler, *The Birth of American Law: An Italian Philosopher and the American Revolution* (Durham, NC: Carolina Academic Press, 2014), 290.

19. Cesare Beccaria, *On Crimes and Punishments,* trans. Jane Grigson (New York: Marsilio Publishers, 1996). Beccaria's critique of capital punishment appears on pages 52–61 of this edition.

20. Banner, *Death Penalty,* 91.

21. Jeffrey L. Kirchmeier, *Imprisoned by the Past: Warren McCleskey and the American Death Penalty* (New York: Oxford University Press, 2015), 47.

22. Banner, *Death Penalty,* 95–96.

23. Bessler, *Birth of American Law,* 270.

24. Banner, *Death Penalty,* 98.

25. Ibid., 98–99, 131.

26. "Condemnations of the death penalty marked the emergence of a new understanding of crime and punishment. Essayists argued that social influences, not depravity, caused crime and that reformation, not retribution, should govern punishments." Louis P. Masur, *Rites of Execution: Capital Punishment and the Transformation of American Culture 1776–1865* (New York: Oxford University Press, 1989), 5.

27. Banner, *Death Penalty,* 131.

28. See Hugo Adam Bedau, *The Death Penalty in America: Current Controversies* (New York: Oxford University Press, 1997), 8. Bedau lists the date of Michigan's abolition as 1847, which is when the abolition bill passed in 1846 took effect.

29. "By the Civil War capital punishment for whites was, with a few exceptions, in practice reserved for murder throughout the South nearly as much as in the North." Banner, *Death Penalty,* 139.

30. Philip English Mackey, "The Inutility of Mandatory Capital Punishment: An Historical Note," in *Capital Punishment in the United States,* eds. Hugo Adam Bedau and Chester M. Pierce (New York: AMS Press, 1976), 49, 49–51.

31. Bedau, *Current Controversies,* 5–6. The case that finally put to rest the possibility of any mandatory death penalty was Sumner v. Shuman, 483 U.S. 66 (1987), which rejected a mandatory death sentence even for an aggravated

murder committed by a prison inmate serving a sentence of life without possibility of parole.

32. John D. Bessler, *Death in the Dark: Midnight Executions in America* (Boston: Northeastern University Press, 1997), 46. Bessler finds evidence in legislative reports from the 1830s through the 1850s for the "original intent" of private execution laws: "One Massachusetts report, penned in 1836, states that '[t]he spectacle of capital punishments is most barbarizing, and promotive of cruelty and a disregard for life.' It concludes that, after public executions, 'the spectators go away with their virtuous sensibility lessened, their hearts more callous, and with less power of resistance, if any strong temptation shall urge them to a deed of blood.' . . . An 1835 legislative report from Maine also complained about the 'drunkenness and profanity' at public executions and the persons 'who came to profit by the solemn scene' of such spectacles." Ibid., 43–44.

33. Brett Barrouquere, "Nation's Last Public Execution, 75 Years Ago, Still Haunts Town," *Associated Press,* August 14, 2011, http://www.boston.com/news/nation/articles/2011/08/14/after_75_years_last_public_hanging_haunts_city. For the most complete account of the 1936 execution in Kentucky, see Perry T. Ryan, *The Last Public Execution in America* (Lexington, KY: Alexandria Printing, 1992).

34. Bessler, *Death in the Dark,* 44–45.

35. Ibid., 71.

36. For a description of the birth of the "modern mode" of capital punishment in the nineteenth century, see Garland, *Peculiar Institution,* 87–96.

37. Bessler, *Death in the Dark,* 65–66.

38. Technically, England temporarily suspended the death penalty for murder in 1965 and made that suspension permanent in 1969. Parliament finally abolished the death penalty for all crimes (including treason and war crimes) in 1998, but no executions took place anywhere in the United Kingdom after 1965.

39. Austin Sarat, *Gruesome Spectacles: Botched Executions and America's Death Penalty* (Stanford, CA: Stanford University Press, 2014), 42, quoting "A Gallows Butchery, Three Bald Knob Murderers Hanged at Ozark, Missouri," *Philadelphia Inquirer,* May 11, 1889, p. 6.

40. Sarat, *Gruesome Spectacles,* 54, 58–59.

41. Banner, *Death Penalty,* 189; Craig Brandon, *The Electric Chair: An Unnatural American History* (Jefferson, NC: McFarland & Company, 1999), 205–206.

42. Sarat, *Gruesome Spectacles,* 73–74.

43. Ibid., 81–83.

44. Scott Christianson, *The Last Gasp: The Rise and Fall of the American Gas Chamber* (Berkeley: University of California Press, 2010), 1–3, 227.

45. Sarat, *Gruesome Spectacles,* 96, 100–102, 106, 112.

46. A study of all executions in America from 1890–2010 found a botch rate of 3 percent, whereas executions by lethal injection are botched in 7 percent of cases—more than double the overall rate. Ibid., 5, 120. Sarat concedes in the note to this point that "identifying a botched lethal injection is somewhat

problematic because the medicalization of the process and the three-drug protocol, which until recently has been the standard, work to prevent the body from registering signs of suffering." Ibid., 244n28.

47. Ross Levitt and Deborah Feyerick, "Death Penalty States Scramble for Lethal Injection Drugs," *CNN News,* November 16, 2013, http://www.cnn.com/2013/11 /15/justice/states-lethal-injection-drugs/index.html.

48. Corinna Barrett Lain, "The Politics of Botched Executions," *University of Richmond Law Review* 49 (2015): 827–834.

49. In 2008, the Supreme Court rejected a challenge to Kentucky's three-drug lethal injection protocol, which was also widely used by other executing states. Baze v. Rees, 553 U.S. 35 (2008). In 2015, the Court rejected a challenge to Oklahoma's substitution of the sedative midazolam for the now unavailable sedative used in the three-drug protocol approved in *Baze.* Glossip v. Gross, 135 S. Ct. 2726 (2015). These unfavorable rulings have not quelled lethal injection litigation, however, and executions have been put on hold as lethal injection drugs and processes are further scrutinized. Manny Fernandez, "Delays as Death-Penalty States Scramble for Execution Drugs," *New York Times,* October 8, 2015, http://www.nytimes.com/2015/10/09/us/death-penalty -lethal-injection.html?ref=topics.

50. Josh Sanburn, "The Dawn of a New Form of Capital Punishment," *Time,* April 17, 2015, http://time.com/3749879/nitrogen-gas-execution-oklahoma -lethal-injection/.

51. Jason Millman, "Another Reason Firing Squads Could See a Comeback," *Washington Post Wonkblog,* March 24, 2015, http://www.washingtonpost.com /blogs/wonkblog/wp/2015/03/24/another-reason-firing-squads-could-see-a -comeback/.

52. Franklin E. Zimring, *The Contradictions of American Capital Punishment* (New York: Oxford University Press, 2003), 66.

53. The ten inactive death penalty states (the states that currently retain the death penalty but have conducted no more than three executions since 1976) are Colorado, Idaho, Kansas, Kentucky, Montana, New Hampshire, Oregon, Pennsylvania, South Dakota, and Wyoming. Death Penalty Information Center, *Number of Executions by State and Region since 1976.*

54. Comprehensive statistics on the number of executions carried out in each region of the country from the seventeenth to the twenty-first century reveal the significant discrepancy in executions between the North and South. Allen and Clubb, *Race, Class, and the Death Penalty,* 34, 50, 53, 70, 76, 84, 97, 101, 105, 121, 133, 172.

55. Carol S. Steiker and Jordan M. Steiker, "The American Death Penalty and the (In)Visibility of Race," *University of Chicago Law Review* 82 (2015): 245.

56. Marvin L. Michael Kay and Lorin Lee Cary, "'The Planters Suffer Little or Nothing': North Carolina Compensations for Executed Slaves, 1748–1772," *Science & Society* 40 (1976): 288–306.

57. "From the perspective of slaveowners, harsh punishments were necessary to manage such large captive populations." Banner, *Death Penalty,* 142.

58. Stephen John Hartnett, *Executing Democracy* (vol. 1): *Capital Punishment & the Making of America, 1683–1807* (East Lansing: Michigan State University Press, 2010), 20.

59. Zimring, *Contradictions,* 89–118.

60. Garland, *Peculiar Institution,* 253.

61. Sheri Lynn Johnson, "*Coker v. Georgia:* Of Rape, Race, and Burying the Past," in *Death Penalty Stories,* eds. John H. Blume and Jordan M. Steiker (New York: Thomson Reuters/Foundation Press, 2009), 191.

62. George M. Stroud, *A Sketch of the Laws Relating to Slavery in the Several States of the United States of America* (Philadelphia: Kimber and Sharpless, 1827), 107.

63. Banner, *Death Penalty,* 139 (emphasis added).

64. Garland, *Peculiar Institution,* 124; Bedau, *Current Controversies,* 5–6.

65. Banner, *Death Penalty,* 142–143. For a discussion of the earliest proposals for abolition of the death penalty, which uniformly occurred in the North or Midwest, see Philip English Mackey, ed., *Voices against Death: American Opposition to Capital Punishment, 1787–1975* (New York: Burt Franklin, 1976), xxviii.

66. Eugene G. Wanger, "Michigan Constitutional History," *Michigan Bar Journal* 81 (2002): 38.

67. Amnesty International, "Death Sentences and Executions 2014," March 31, 2015, http://www.amnestyusa.org/research/reports/death-sentences-and-executions-2014.

68. Banner, *Death Penalty,* 228.

69. William D. Carrigan, *The Making of a Lynching Culture: Violence and Vigilantism in Central Texas, 1836–1916* (Urbana: University of Illinois Press, 2004), 153.

70. Ibid., 112–113. Another scholar describes the charge of rape by a black man of a white woman as "the most emotionally potent excuse" for lynchings in the postbellum South. Randall Kennedy, *Race, Crime, and the Law* (New York: Pantheon Books, 1997), 45.

71. Garland, *Peculiar Institution,* 124.

72. Banner, *Death Penalty,* 229.

73. Jennifer Wriggins, "Race, Racism, and the Law," *Harvard Women's Law Journal* 6 (1983): 109. The attorney's quotation that is paraphrased is found in State v. Petit, 119 La. 1013, 1016 (1907): "Now, don't you know that, if this nigger had committed such a crime, he never would have been brought here and tried . . . he would have been lynched."

74. John F. Galliher, Gregory Ray, and Brent Cook, "Abolition and Reinstatement of Capital Punishment during the Progressive Era and Early 20th Century," *Journal of Criminal Law and Criminology* 83 (1992): 574.

75. Ibid., 557. A popular *Debater's Handbook* on capital punishment, of which five editions were published between 1909 and 1925, contained numerous references to the anti-lynching argument in favor of retaining the death penalty. Carol S. Steiker and Jordan M. Steiker, "Capital Punishment: A Century of Discontinuous Debate," *Journal of Criminal Law and Criminology* 100 (2010): 653.

76. Banner, *Death Penalty,* 221–222.

77. "The desire to watch executions was strong with both whites and blacks in the South." Michael A. Trotti, "The Scaffold's Revival: Race and Public Execution in the South," *Journal of Social History* 45 (2011): 203.

78. Banner, *Death Penalty*, 155.

79. Trotti, "The Scaffold's Revival," 203.

80. Zimring, *Contradictions*, 99.

81. Trotti, "The Scaffold's Revival," 209.

82. Ibid., 202–203.

83. Ibid., 207.

84. Ibid.

85. Carol S. Steiker and Jordan M. Steiker, "Entrenchment and/or Destabilization? Reflections on (Another) Two Decades of Constitutional Regulation of Capital Punishment," *Law and Inequality* 30 (2012): 219.

86. Dray, *Persons Unknown*, 30, 81, 94.

87. Associated Press, "Vote for Firing Squad Shows Frustration with Drug Shortages," *New York Times*, March 11, 2015, http://www.nytimes.com /aponline/2015/03/11/us/ap-us-utah-firing-squad.html. Sarah Parvini, "Q&A: Why Utah Wants to Revive Execution by Firing Squad," *Los Angeles Times*, March 12, 2015, http://www.latimes.com/nation/la-na-firing-squad-qa -20150312-story.html.

88. Wilkerson v. Utah, 99 U.S. 130, 136 (1878).

89. Gilbert King, "Cruel and Unusual History," *New York Times*, April 23, 2008, http://www.nytimes.com/2008/04/23/opinion/23king.html.

90. Mark Essig, *Edison & the Electric Chair: A Story of Light and Death* (New York: Walker & Company, 2003), 2–3.

91. Brandon, *Electric Chair*, 8–9.

92. Ibid., 110–111.

93. Ibid., 121–122 (testimony of Dr. Alphonse D. Rockwell).

94. Ibid., 137, 155.

95. The Eighth Amendment was held to apply to the states in Robinson v. California, 370 U.S. 660 (1962).

96. In re Kemmler, 136 U.S. 436, 444, 447, 449 (1890).

97. Brandon, *Electric Chair*, 176–179.

98. Sarat, *Gruesome Spectacles*, 150–151.

99. Louisiana ex rel. Francis v. Resweber, 329 U.S. 459, 464 (1947).

100. Ibid., 473–474 (Burton, J., dissenting).

101. Ibid., 470–471 (Frankfurter, J., concurring).

102. Hurtado v. California, 110 U.S. 516, 521 (1884).

103. Dray, *Persons Unknown*, 211.

104. Frank v. Mangum, 237 U.S. 309, 337–338 (1915).

105. Ibid., 347 (Holmes, J., dissenting).

106. Mark Curriden, "A Supreme Case of Contempt," *ABA Journal*, June 2, 2009, http://www.abajournal.com/magazine/article/a_supreme_case_of_contempt.

107. Michael J. Klarman, *From Jim Crow to Civil Rights: The Supreme Court and the Struggle for Racial Equality* (New York: Oxford University Press, 2004), 98.

108. Moore v. Dempsey, 261 U.S. 86, 89–90, 91, 92 (1923).

109. Brown v. Mississippi, 297 U.S. 278, 282, 285, 285–86 (1936).

110. Verna Gates, "Alabama Pardons Scottsboro Boys in 1931 Rape Case," *Reuters,* November 21, 2013, http://www.reuters.com/article/us-usa-alabama-scottsboro -idUSBRE9AK0X720131121. One of the Scottsboro Boys, Clarence Norris, had already been pardoned by Governor George Wallace in 1976.

111. Powell v. Alabama, 287 U.S. 45 (1932); Gideon v. Wainright, 372 U.S. 335 (1963).

112. Klarman, *Jim Crow,* 118.

113. Ibid., 118–119.

2. The Supreme Court Steps In

1. Alexander M. Bickel, *The Least Dangerous Branch: The Supreme Court at the Bar of Politics* (Indianapolis: Bobbs-Merrill, 1962), 240, 242.

2. Evan J. Mandery, *A Wild Justice: The Death and Resurrection of Capital Punishment in America* (New York: W. W. Norton, 2013), ix.

3. Petition for Writ of Certiorari to the Supreme Court of the State of Alabama, Rudolph v. Alabama, No. 308 (filed June 28, 1963), 2.

4. Lucas A. Powe, Jr., *The Warren Court and American Politics* (Cambridge, MA: Harvard University Press, 2000), 212.

5. Mark V. Tushnet, *Making Civil Rights Law: Thurgood Marshall and the Supreme Court, 1936–1961* (New York: Oxford University Press, 1994), 50, 55.

6. Gilbert King, *Devil in the Grove* (New York: Harper Perennial, 2012), 5.

7. Michael Meltsner, *Cruel and Unusual: The Supreme Court and Capital Punishment* (New York: Random House, 1973), 107.

8. For example, the Ohio jury instruction read, "If you find the defendant guilty of murder in the first degree, the punishment is death, unless you recommend mercy, in which event the punishment is imprisonment in the penitentiary during life." McGautha v. California, 402 U.S. 183, 194 (1971).

9. William J. Bowers, *Executions in America* (Lexington, MA: Lexington Books, 1974), 113.

10. In addition, some states with unitary proceedings actually precluded defendants from offering mitigating evidence unless it directly bore on the question of guilt or innocence.

11. Witherspoon v. Illinois, 391 U.S. 510, 514, 522 (1968).

12. Maxwell v. Bishop, 393 U.S. 997, 997–998 (1968); Boykin v. Alabama, 395 U.S. 238 (1969).

13. Meltsner, *Cruel and Unusual,* 120–122.

14. McGautha v. California, 190, 204, 208.

15. Mandery, *A Wild Justice,* 115.

16. Brief for Respondent at 5, 8 citing Appendix at 47, 54–55 in Furman v. Georgia, 408 U.S. 238 (1972) (No. 69–5003); Brief for Petitioner at 7, 9 citing Appendix at 62–63 in Furman v. Georgia, 408 U.S. 238 (1972) (No. 69–5003).

17. Furman v. Georgia, 239–240, 255, 291, 309–311, 369.

18. Ibid., 369, 371.

19. Mandery, *A Wild Justice,* 242.

20. Robinson v. California, 370 U.S. 660, 666–667 (1962).

21. Trop v. Dulles, 356 U.S. 86, 99–101 (1958).

22. Meltsner, *Cruel and Unusual,* 55.

23. Mark Tushnet, "*Brown v. Board* and Its Legacy: A Tribute to Justice Thurgood Marshall, Public Law Litigation and the Ambiguities of *Brown,*" *Fordham Law Review* 61 (1992): 26–28; Meltsner, *Cruel and Unusual,* 130.

24. Mandery, *A Wild Justice,* 42.

25. Brief for the NAACP Legal Defense and Educational Fund, Inc. as *Amicus Curiae,* Gregg v. Georgia, No. 74–6257 (filed Feb. 25, 1976) (available on Westlaw at 1976 WL 178715), 23–24.

26. Arthur J. Goldberg, "Death and the Supreme Court," *Hastings Constitutional Law Quarterly* 15 (1987): 1.

27. Roger Hood and Carolyn Hoyle, *The Death Penalty: A Worldwide Perspective* (New York: Oxford University Press, 2015), 49, 50, 70.

28. Ibid., 14, 53–55.

29. Gallup, *Death Penalty,* http://www.gallup.com/poll/1606/death-penalty.aspx.

30. Bowers, *Executions in America,* 23.

31. Bickel, *The Least Dangerous Branch,* 243.

32. Carol S. Steiker and Jordan M. Steiker, "No More Tinkering: The American Law Institute and the Death Penalty Provisions of the Model Penal Code," *Texas Law Review* 89 (2010): 355.

33. William J. Stuntz, *The Collapse of American Criminal Justice* (Cambridge, MA: The Belknap Press of Harvard University Press, 2011), 231, Table 8.

34. Mandery, *A Wild Justice,* 234 (quoting Donald Zoll of the *National Review* and other sources).

35. Carol S. Steiker and Jordan M. Steiker, "Lessons for Law Reform from the American Experiment with Capital Punishment," *Southern California Law Review* 87 (2014): 733, 743; Mandery, *A Wild Justice,* 235.

36. William Robbins, "Nixon Backs Death Penalty for Kidnapping, Hijacking," *New York Times,* June 30, 1972, p. A1.

37. Meltsner, *Cruel and Unusual,* 290.

38. Steiker and Steiker, "No More Tinkering," 356.

39. Gregg v. Georgia, 428 U.S. 153, 179 (1976).

40. Ibid., 183.

41. Ibid., 186–187.

42. Ibid., 199.

43. Ibid., 221 (White, J., concurring).

44. Ibid., 226 (White, J., concurring).

45. Furman v. Georgia, 405 (Blackmun, J., dissenting).

46. Gregg v. Georgia, 428 U.S. 227, 232 (1976) (Marshall, J., dissenting).

47. Woodson v. North Carolina, 428 U.S. 280, 293, 302–304 (1976).

48. Franklin E. Zimring, "The Scale of Imprisonment in the United States: Twentieth Century Patterns and Twenty-First Century Prospects," *Journal of Criminal Law and Criminology* 100 (2010): 1225, 1228.

49. See, for example, Michael Tonry, "Determinants of Penal Policies," in *Crime, Punishment, and Politics in Comparative Perspective,* ed. Michael Tonry (Chicago: University of Chicago Press, 2007), 381.

50. Franklin E. Zimring, *The Contradictions of American Capital Punishment* (New York: Oxford University Press, 2003), 89–92.

51. David Garland, *Peculiar Institution: America's Death Penalty in an Age of Abolition* (Cambridge, MA: Harvard University Press, 2010), 155, 157, 166, 175.

52. Moshik Temkin attempts to explain the permanence of abolition in European countries through an illuminating account of the role of human rights principles in European politics, including domestic policy making, as compared to the more limited role of human rights discourse in U.S. domestic law. Moshik Temkin, "The Great Divergence: The Death Penalty in the United States and the Failure of Abolition in Transatlantic Perspective," HKS Faculty Research Working Paper Series RWP15–037, July 2015. Available at https://research.hks.harvard.edu/publications/workingpapers/citation.aspx?PubId=978 5&type=WPN.

53. Stuart Banner, *The Death Penalty: An American History* (Cambridge, MA: Harvard University Press, 2003), 239.

54. Abe Fortas, "The Case Against Capital Punishment," *New York Times Magazine,* January 23, 1977.

3. The Invisibility of Race in the Constitutional Revolution

1. "The justices' unanimity in all three 1950 race cases—an impressive accomplishment for this ordinarily splintered Court—is most plausibly attributable to the Cold War imperative." Michael J. Klarman, *From Jim Crow to Civil Rights: The Supreme Court and the Struggle for Racial Equality* (New York: Oxford University Press, 2004), 210.

2. David Alan Sklansky, "'One Train May Hide Another': *Katz,* Stonewall, and the Secret Subtext of Criminal Procedure," *University of California Davis Law Review* 41 (2008): 875, 880, 897–900 (contending that the Supreme Court's landmark decision in Katz v. United States, 389 U.S. 347 [1967], and the Fourth Amendment jurisprudence that flowed from it were influenced by the justices' anxieties, perhaps unconscious, about the use of peepholes and undercover decoys to police gay men's encounters in public lavatories).

3. Brown v. Board of Education, 347 U.S. 483 (1954).

4. Rudolph v. Alabama, 375 U.S. 889, 889–891 (1963) (Goldberg, J., dissenting from the denial of certiorari). The Chief Justice permitted Justice Goldberg to retain a footnote to a United Nations Report on Capital Punishment, which itself included data on racial discrimination, and both Goldberg and Dershowitz "hoped that this oblique reference would be enough to suggest the race argument." Evan J. Mandery, *A Wild Justice: The Death and Resurrection of Capital Punishment in America* (New York: W.W. Norton, 2013), 29.

5. Mark V. Tushnet, *Making Civil Rights Law: Thurgood Marshall and the Supreme Court, 1936–1961* (New York: Oxford University Press, 1994), 56–57.

6. Michael Meltsner, *Cruel and Unusual: The Supreme Court and Capital Punishment* (New York: Random House, 1973), 78, 86–88.

7. For an first-person account that explicitly links the LDF's death penalty research in the South to the broader work of the Civil Rights Movement, see Barrett J. Foerster, *Race, Rape, and Injustice: Documenting and Challenging Death Penalty Cases in the Civil Rights Era*, ed. Michael Meltsner (Knoxville: University of Tennessee Press, 2012). Foerster was one of the student researchers who went South, and Meltsner was one of the LDF lawyers who sent him.

8. Marvin E. Wolfgang and Marc Riedel, "Rape, Racial Discrimination, and the Death Penalty," in *Capital Punishment in the United States*, eds. Hugo Adam Bedau and Chester M. Pierce (New York: AMS Press, 1976), 99–121.

9. Maxwell v. Bishop, 398 F.2d 138, 148 (8th Cir. 1968).

10. Meltsner, *Cruel and Unusual,* 71, 106–107.

11. Ibid., 108.

12. Petition for a Writ of Certiorari to the United States Court of Appeals for the Eighth Circuit, Maxwell v. Bishop, No. 622–13 (filed Oct. 9, 1968), 35–36, 42.

13. Brief *Amici Curiae* of the Synagogue Council of America and Its Constituents (The Central Conference of American Rabbis, the Rabbinical Assembly of America, the Rabbinical Council of America, the Union of American Hebrew Congregations, the Union of Orthodox Jewish Congregations of America, the United Synagogue of America) and the American Jewish Congress, Maxwell v. Bishop, No. 622–13 (filed Sept. 15, 1969) (available on Westlaw at 1969 WL 136886), 26–30.

14. Brief *Amici Curiae* of Berl I. Bernhard, William Coleman, Samuel Dash, John W. Douglas, Steven Duke, William T. Gossett, John Griffiths, Rita Hauser, George N. Lindsay, Burke Marshall, Monrad S. Paulsen, Steven R. Rivkin, Whitney North Seymour, Jerome J. Shestack, and Cyrus R. Vance, Urging Reversal, Maxwell v. Bishop, No. 622–13 (filed Oct. 24, 1969) (available on Westlaw at 1969 WL 1184278), 6–7.

15. Witherspoon v. Illinois, 391 U.S. 510 (1968).

16. Supplemental Brief for Petitioner, Maxwell v. Bishop, No. 622–13 (filed September 17, 1969) (available on Westlaw at 1969 WL 120077), 31, 1 n.1.

17. Maxwell v. Bishop, 398 U.S. 262, 264, 265–266, 267 n.4 (1970). Prior to the decision to reverse Maxwell's conviction on *Witherspoon* grounds, both Justices Douglas and Brennan drafted opinions (neither of which was ever published) addressing the claims regarding Arkansas's unitary proceedings and the jury's standardless discretion in imposing death. Both justices noted the possibility that standardless discretion could result in racially discriminatory decision making, though neither ventured an opinion on the racial distribution of capital verdicts in Arkansas rape cases. Maxwell v. Bishop, No. 622–13 (1970) (draft opinion of Douglas) (on file with the Library of Congress), 8; Maxwell v. Bishop, No. 622–13 (1970) (draft concurrence of Brennan) (on file with the Library of Congress), 5.

18. Petitioner's Brief, Witherspoon v. Illinois, No. 1015 (filed Mar. 11, 1968) (available on Westlaw at 1968 WL 112521), 17–20.

19. Motion for Leave to File Brief *Amici Curiae* and Brief *Amici Curiae* of the NAACP Legal Defense and Educational Fund, Inc., and the National Office for the Rights of the Indigent, Witherspoon v. Illinois, No. 1015 (filed Mar. 12, 1968) (available on Westlaw at 1968 WL 129362), 3, 28, 38–39.

20. Brief of the Illinois Division, American Civil Liberties Union, as *Amicus Curiae,* Witherspoon v. Illinois, No. 1015 (filed Mar. 1, 1968) (available on Westlaw at 1968 WL 112520), 17.

21. Witherspoon v. Illinois, 513–514, 520.

22. McGautha v. California, 402 U.S. 183 (1971); Furman v. Georgia, 408 U.S. 238 (1972).

23. For example, see Brief for Petitioner, McGautha v. California, No. 203 (filed Aug. 4, 1970) (available on Westlaw at 1970 WL 122021), 18.

24. For example, see ibid., 25.

25. Respondent's Brief, McGautha v. California, No. 203 (filed Sept. 25, 1970) (available on Westlaw at 1970 WL 122022), 74.

26. Mandery, *A Wild Justice,* 111–112, 114 (describing the LDF's disappointment with the decision in *McGautha* and Justice Brennan's belief that the decision meant the end of the dispute over the death penalty's constitutionality).

27. Brief for Petitioner, Aikens v. California, No. 68–5027 (filed Sept. 10, 1971) (available on Westlaw at 1971 WL 134168), 22, 51 (footnote omitted).

28. Brief for Petitioner, Furman v. Georgia, No. 69–5003 (filed Sept. 9, 1971) (available on Westlaw at 1971 WL 134167), 8, 12.

29. Brief for Respondent, Furman v. Georgia, No. 69–5003 (filed Sept. 24, 1971) (available on Westlaw at 1971 WL 126674), 79. In suggesting that the overrepresentation of blacks on death row was caused by higher black homicide rates, Georgia cited 1970 Atlanta police statistics indicating that 187 murders were committed by black offenders compared to fifty-five murders committed by white offenders. Ibid., 80.

30. Brief *Amici Curiae* and Motion for Leave to File Brief *Amici Curiae* of the Synagogue Council of America and Its Constituents (The Central Conference of American Rabbis, the Rabbinical Assembly of America, the Rabbinical Council of America, the Union of American Hebrew Congregations, the Union of Orthodox Jewish Congregations of America, the United Synagogue of America) and the American Jewish Congress, Furman v. Georgia, No. 69–5003 (filed Sept. 9, 1971) (available on Westlaw at 1971 WL 134169), 29–34.

31. Motion for Leave to File Brief as *Amici Curiae* and Brief *Amici Curiae* of the National Association for the Advancement of Colored People, National Urban League, Southern Christian Leadership Conference, Mexican-American Legal Defense and Educational Fund, and the National Council of Negro Women, Furman v. Georgia, No. 69–5003 (filed Aug. 31, 1971) (available on Westlaw at 1971 WL 134376), 7, 13 (comma omitted).

32. Brief *Amici Curiae* of the West Virginia Council of Churches, Christian Church (Disciples) in West Virginia, and United Methodist Church, West Virginia Conference, Furman v. Georgia, No. 69–5003 (filed Aug. 26, 1971), 11.

33. Furman v. Georgia, 249–250, 253, 256–257 (Douglas, J., concurring) (quotation marks omitted).

34. Ibid., 310 (Stewart, J., concurring) (quotation marks omitted).

35. Ibid., 362, 363, 363–364 (Marshall, J., concurring). Remarking on the relative disadvantage of those sentenced to death, Justice Marshall observed, "Their impotence leaves them victims of a sanction that the wealthier, better-represented, just-as-guilty person can escape." Ibid., 366.

36. In his discussion of *Furman,* Professor Evan Mandery argues that, "whatever the justices may have intended, everyone understood *Furman* as having been about race." Mandery, *A Wild Justice,* 276.

37. For a discussion criticizing the mild tone of *Brown* and the Court's failure to speak more clearly and forthrightly about the "true" meaning of racial segregation, see Jordan Steiker, "American Icon: Does It Matter What the Court Said in *Brown?,*" review of *What* Brown v. Board of Education *Should Have Said,* by Jack M. Balkin, ed., *Texas Law Review* 81 (2002): 305, 312–315.

38. The brief challenging Georgia's nonmandatory statute noted: "The sentencing stage is only one of the many stages in the criminal process subject to unrestrained and arbitrary discretion." Brief for Petitioner, Gregg v. Georgia, No. 74–6257 (filed Feb. 26, 1976) (available on Westlaw at 1976 WL 194055), 13. The brief challenging Louisiana's purportedly mandatory statute explained that "death is not by any means the inevitable or predictable outcome of the case" even after a conviction of capital murder, and argued: "Discretion permeates the entire criminal justice system, from police detection and arrest, through prosecutorial charging and plea negotiation, to jury deliberation, appellate reconsideration, and executive pardon." Brief for Petitioner, Roberts v. Louisiana, No. 75–5844 (filed Feb. 25, 1976) (available on Westlaw at 1976 WL 194475), 37.

39. For example, see Brief for Petitioner in *Gregg,* 25a n.50.

40. Meltsner, *Cruel and Unusual,* 76–78.

41. Brief for Petitioner in *Gregg,* 25a n.50, 28a n.51.

42. See, for example, Brief for Petitioner, Jurek v. Texas, No. 75–5394 (filed Feb. 26, 1976) (available on Westlaw at 1976 WL 181478), Appendix 1.

43. Brief for Petitioner in *Gregg,* 25a n.50.

44. Ibid., 27a–28a; Brief for Petitioner in *Jurek,* 82–83.

45. Brief for the NAACP Legal Defense and Educational Fund, Inc. as *Amicus Curiae,* Gregg v. Georgia, No. 74–6257 (filed Feb. 25, 1967) (available on Westlaw at 1976 WL 178715), 1, 1–2.

46. Motion for Leave to File Brief of *Amicus Curiae* and Brief of Amnesty International as *Amicus Curiae,* Gregg v. Georgia, No. 74–6257 (filed Feb. 25, 1976) (available on Westlaw at 1976 WL 178716), 3.

47. Brief for the United States as *Amicus Curiae,* Gregg v. Georgia, No. 74–6257 (filed Mar. 25, 1976) (available on Westlaw at 1976 WL 194056), 65.

48. Ibid., 66, 4a–5a, 68.

49. Stuart Banner, *The Death Penalty: An American History* (Cambridge, MA: Harvard University Press, 2002), 274–275.

50. Gregg v. Georgia, 179, 182–186, 203.

51. Mandery, *A Wild Justice,* 345.

52. Ibid., 344.

53. Sheri Lynn Johnson, "*Coker v. Georgia:* Of Rape, Race, and Burying the Past," in *Death Penalty Stories,* eds. John H. Blume and Jordan M. Steiker (New York: Thomson Reuters/Foundation Press, 2009), 171, 194–195.

54. Brief for Petitioner, Coker v. Georgia, No. 75–5444 (filed Dec. 9, 1976) (available on Westlaw at 1976 WL 181481), 52, 54, 55–56, 56.

55. Brief *Amicus Curiae* of the American Civil Liberties Union, the Center for Constitutional Rights, the National Organization for Women Legal Defense and Education Fund, the Women's Law Project, and the Center for Women Policy Studies, the Women's Legal Defense Fund, and Equal Rights Advocates, Inc., Coker v. Georgia, No. 75–5444 (filed Dec. 3, 1976) (available on Westlaw at 1976 WL 181482), 6, 10, 11, 16–19, 19.

56. Brief for Respondent in Coker v. Georgia, No. 75–5444 (filed Jan. 14, 1977) (available on Westlaw at 1977 WL 189754), 12, 23, 24.

57. Coker v. Georgia, 433 U.S. 584, 592, 594–597, 598 (1977) (plurality opinion). The Court noted that only six death sentences had been returned in the sixty-three rape convictions reviewed by the Georgia Supreme Court since 1973. Ibid., 596–597.

58. Furman v. Georgia, 310 (Stewart, J., concurring).

59. The "Brown II" case was Brown v. Board of Education, 349 U.S. 294 (1955).

60. Green v. County School Board, 391 U.S. 430 (1968).

61. Swann v. Charlotte-Mecklenburg Board of Education, 402 U.S. 1 (1971).

62. For a discussion of the political climate with respect to school desegregation in the 1960s, see Klarman, *Jim Crow,* 341–343.

63. Mandery, *A Wild Justice,* 28. The case that invalidated laws prohibiting interracial marriage was Loving v. Virginia, 388 U.S. 1 (1967).

64. David Garland, *Peculiar Institution: America's Death Penalty in an Age of Abolition* (Cambridge, MA: Belknap Press of Harvard University Press, 2010), 222–223, 234–236.

65. Aikens v. California, 406 U.S. 813 (1972) (dismissing the case as moot in light of the California Supreme Court's decision striking down the California death penalty in People v. Anderson, 493 P.2d 880 [Cal. 1972]).

66. Some Black Power leaders, for example, defended the "use of violence as a legitimate means of influencing the system." This rhetoric, in turn, produced an "indiscriminate crack-down" on the part of law enforcement who claimed the "ready excuse of restoring law and order." Yohuru Williams, "'A Red, Black, and Green Liberation Jumpsuit': Roy Wilkins, the Black Panthers, and the Conundrum of Black Power," in *The Black Power Movement: Rethinking the Civil Rights-Black Power Era,* ed. Peniel E. Joseph (New York: Routledge, 2006), 167, 175–176.

67. Garland, *Peculiar Institution,* 238–244.

68. Respondent's Brief in *McGautha,* 74; Brief for the United States in *Gregg,* 66–67.

69. Brief for Petitioner in *Gregg,* 25a n.50. To make its argument regarding racial discrimination in murder cases, the LDF was left to extrapolate from Wolfgang's rape analysis and to suggest what would become apparent only a decade later, after David Baldus's statistical analysis of capital murder that was presented to the Court in *McCleskey*—that the lack of strikingly apparent discrimination in the murder context was largely attributable to a strong race-of-the-*victim* bias. The bias toward capital prosecutions when murder victims were white tended to counterbalance the bias toward prosecutions of black murder defendants, given the intra-racial nature of most homicides.

70. Brief for Respondent in *Furman,* 80–81.

71. McCleskey v. Kemp, 481 U.S. 279 (1987).

72. Justice Lewis Powell, Memorandum to Law Clerk (Sept. 16, 1986), 27, http://perma.cc/2F2T-DBQZ.

73. For example, the Court made a similar move in the extended litigation about the practice of death-qualifying juries. In *Witherspoon,* the Court put off until another day the question of the adequacy of the statistical proof that death-qualified juries were skewed toward conviction. When the Court finally addressed the issue, it assumed for the sake of argument that the statistical proof was valid but decided the case on legal rather than statistical grounds. Lockhart v. McCree, 476 U.S. 162, 173 (1986).

74. Scott E. Sundby, "The Loss of Constitutional Faith: *McCleskey v. Kemp* and the Dark Side of Procedure," *Ohio State Journal of Criminal Law* 10 (2012): 1, 14.

75. Ibid., 13; see also McCleskey v. Kemp, 297.

76. Professor Alexander Bickel mounted one of the most rigorous criticisms of the Warren Court's judicial activism in Alexander M. Bickel, *The Least Dangerous Branch: The Supreme Court at the Bar of Politics,* 2nd ed. (New Haven, CT: Yale University Press, 1986).

77. See, for example, Furman v. Georgia, 403–405 (Burger, C. J., dissenting).

78. State v. Makwanyane and Another, 1995 (3) SA 391 (CC) (South Africa).

79. Owen Roberts, "Race-Blind Abolition: *Makwanyane*'s Unused Inequality Argument" (unpublished manuscript, April 2014, on file with authors), 24–26.

80. The best example of this avoidance is the Court's decision in Duncan v. Louisiana, 391 U.S. 145 (1968), the case that incorporated the right to trial by jury to apply to the states. The opinion speaks in broad terms about the abstract value of juries, even while the accused was a black teenager charged with criminal assault for slapping the arm of one of a group of four white boys who were harassing two black schoolchildren; this altercation took place in the midst of a highly contested school desegregation fight in one of the most racially divided parishes in Louisiana. Nancy J. King, "*Duncan v. Louisiana:* How Bigotry in the Bayou Led to the Federal Regulation of State Juries," in *Criminal Procedure Stories,* ed. Carol S. Steiker (New York: Foundation Press, 2006), 261–293.

81. For a description and critique of the procedural focus of the Bill of Rights, see William J. Stuntz, *The Collapse of American Criminal Justice* (Cambridge, MA: The Belknap Press of Harvard University Press, 2011), 74–85.

82. Swann v. Charlotte-Mecklenburg Board of Education, 27.

83. The Court's initial decision striking down racial quotas but upholding diversity-based affirmative action in university admissions was Regents of the University of California v. Bakke, 438 U.S. 265, 369 (1978). Justice O'Connor's call for a time limit on such policies appeared in Grutter v. Bollinger, 539 U.S. 306, 342–343 (2003).

84. Brief for Respondent in *Furman*, 80.

85. Brief for the United States as *Amicus Curiae* in *Gregg*, 66.

86. Roberts, "Race-Blind Abolition," 27, 28 (quotation marks omitted), citing *Makwanyane* at ¶ 185 (Didcott, J., concurring).

87. McCleskey v. Kemp, 313.

88. Batson v. Kentucky, 476 U.S. 79 (1986).

89. Snyder v. Louisiana, 552 U.S. 472 (2008); Miller-El v. Dretke, 545 U.S. 231 (2005).

90. William J. Bowers, et al., "Death Sentencing in Black and White: An Empirical Analysis of the Role of Jurors' Race and Jury Racial Composition," *University of Pennsylvania Journal of Constitutional Law* 3 (2001): 171.

91. McCleskey v. Kemp, 314–315.

92. Justice Antonin Scalia, Memorandum to the Conference Re: No. 84–6811—McCleskey v. Kemp (Jan. 6, 1987), available at Library of Congress, Thurgood Marshall Papers, McCleskey v. Kemp file.

93. Frank R. Baumgartner and Tim Lyman, "Louisiana Death-Sentenced Cases and Their Reversals, 1976–2015," *Journal of Race, Gender, and Poverty* 7 (2016): 58.

94. Lincoln Caplan, "Racial Discrimination and Capital Punishment: The Indefensible Death Sentence of Duane Buck," *New Yorker*, April 20, 2016, http://www.newyorker.com/news/news-desk/racial-discrimination-and-capital-punishment-the-indefensible-death-sentence-of-duane-buck.

95. Andrew Cohen, "A Judge Overturned a Death Sentence Because the Prosecutor Compared a Black Defendant to King Kong," *Marshall Project*, March 28, 2016, https://www.themarshallproject.org/2016/03/28/a-judge-overturned-a-death-sentence-because-the-prosecutor-compared-a-black-defendant-to-king-kong#.L3TkiLKLG.

96. Matt Ford, "A Tainted Execution in Georgia," *The Atlantic*, April 12, 2016, http://www.theatlantic.com/politics/archive/2016/04/kenneth-fults-execution-georgia/477969/.

97. Johnson, "Of Rape, Race, and Burying the Past," 196–200.

98. McCleskey v. Kemp, 279.

99. Johnson, "Of Rape, Race, and Burying the Past," 200.

100. Carol S. Steiker and Jordan M. Steiker, "Entrenchment and/or Destabilization? Reflections on (Another) Two Decades of Constitutional Regulation of Capital Punishment," *Law and Inequality* 30 (2012): 211, 231–233.

101. Coker v. Georgia, 592.

102. Stanford v. Kentucky, 492 U.S. 361 (1989) (upholding capital punishment for some juvenile offenders); Penry v. Lynaugh, 492 U.S. 302 (1989) (upholding capital punishment for offenders with intellectual disabilities); Enmund v.

Florida, 458 U.S. 782 (1982) (prohibiting capital punishment for some defendants convicted of felony murder who did not themselves kill); Tison v. Arizona, 481 U.S. 137 (1987) (narrowing the exemption created in *Enmund*).

103. Roper v. Simmons, 543 U.S. 551 (2005) (prohibiting capital punishment for all juvenile offenders); Atkins v. Virginia, 536 U.S. 304 (2002) (prohibiting capital punishment for offenders with intellectual disabilities); Kennedy v. Louisiana, 554 U.S. 407 (2008) (prohibiting capital punishment for offenders who commit ordinary crimes other than murder).

104. Paul Brest et al., *Processes of Constitutional Decisionmaking: Cases and Materials,* 5th ed. (New York: Aspen Publishers, 2006), 309.

105. Ibid., 302.

106. Andrew Krull, *The Color-Blind Constitution* (Cambridge, MA: Harvard University Press, 1992), 76–79.

107. The cost here might be overstated, given that the explicit guarantee of racial equality in the context of voting that was enacted in the Fifteenth Amendment did little to protect that right until congressional intervention in the 1960s. See Klarman, *Jim Crow,* 253. Nonetheless, it is not fanciful to think that the Fourteenth Amendment's race-neutral language contributed to the long delay in dismantling formal, state-sponsored segregation.

4. Between the Supreme Court and the States

1. Stuart Banner, *The Death Penalty: An American History* (Cambridge, MA: Harvard University Press, 2002), 5, 53–54, 68–69.

2. Ibid., 62, 245–246.

3. Douglas Hay, "Property, Authority and the Criminal Law," in *Albion's Fatal Tree: Crime and Society in Eighteenth-Century England,* eds. Douglas Hay et al. (New York: Pantheon, 1975), 17, 55.

4. Death Penalty Information Center, *Number of Executions by State and Region since 1976,* http://www.deathpenaltyinfo.org/number-executions-state-and-region-1976; Death Penalty Information Center, *Information on Defendants Who Were Executed since 1976 and Designated as "Volunteers,"* http://www.deathpenaltyinfo.org/information-defendants-who-were-executed-1976-and-designated-volunteers.

5. Death Penalty Information Center, *Death Sentencing Rates by State, 1977–1999,* http://www.deathpenaltyinfo.org/death-sentencing-rate-state-1977-1999; James Liebman et al., *A Broken System, Part II: Why There Is So Much Error in Capital Cases, and What Can Be Done About It* (2002), 305 (showing that Harris County registered 19 death verdicts per 1,000 homicides, compared to Philadelphia County's 27), http://www2.law.columbia.edu/brokensystem2/report.pdf; Death Penalty Information Center, *Number of Executions by State and Region since 1976;* Death Penalty Information Center, *Information on Defendants Who Were Executed since 1976 and Designated as "Volunteers";* Death Penalty Information Center, *Death Row Inmates by State,* http://www.deathpenaltyinfo.org/death-row-inmates-state-and-size-death-row-year.

6. Death Penalty Information Center, *Executions per Death Sentence*, http://www
.deathpenaltyinfo.org/executions-death-sentence; Death Penalty Information
Center, *Death Sentences in the United States from 1977 by State and by Year*,
http://www.deathpenaltyinfo.org/death-sentences-united-states-1977–2008;
Death Penalty Information Center, *Number of Executions by State and Region
since 1976*; William J. Bowers, *Executions in America* (Lexington, MA:
Lexington Books, 1974), 33–35 (detailing the numbers of individuals executed
before the modern era); Sam Brock, "Future of CA Death Penalty on Trial,"
NBC Bay Area, September 2, 2015, http://www.nbcbayarea.com/news/Future
-of-CA-Death-Penalty-on-Trial-324016821.html (discussing the various causes
of death on California's death row).

7. Godfrey v. Georgia, 446 U.S. 420 (1980) (finding one of Georgia's aggravating
factors unconstitutional because it was insufficiently narrow); Lockett v. Ohio,
438 U.S. 586 (1978) (finding Ohio's statute unconstitutional because it limited
the types of mitigating evidence the jury could consider); Caldwell v. Mississippi, 472 U.S. 320 (1985) (finding improper a prosecutor's misleading statement to jurors that their imposition of a death sentence would be reviewed by a
higher court); Witherspoon v. State of Illinois, 391 U.S. 510 (1968) (holding that
potential jurors cannot be struck solely because they have moral qualms about
the death penalty); Morgan v. Illinois, 504 U.S. 719 (1992) (holding that jurors
must be excluded if they would automatically impose death upon a finding of
guilt); Payne v. Tennessee, 501 U.S. 808 (1991) (eliminating a per se ban on
the introduction of victim-impact evidence at capital sentencings); Booth v.
Maryland, 482 U.S. 496 (1987) (imposing limits on the use of victim-impact
evidence); South Carolina v. Gathers, 490 U.S. 805 (1989) (imposing limits on
testimony about the victim's qualities); Eddings v. Oklahoma, 455 U.S. 104
(1982) (holding that defendants must be able to present mitigating evidence,
even if it is unrelated to the crime); Simmons v. South Carolina, 512 U.S. 154
(1994) (allowing a defendant to introduce evidence regarding the true meaning
of a life sentence).

8. Gregg v. Georgia, 428 U.S. 153, 162–167 (1976) (describing the Georgia capital
statute).

9. Liebman et al., *A Broken System, Part II*, Table A-1.

10. Ibid.

11. Texas Code of Criminal Procedure, Article 37.071; Penry v. Lynaugh, 832 F.2d
915, 926 (5th Cir. 1987) (upholding the Texas statute).

12. Penry v. Lynaugh, 492 U.S. 302 (1989) (finding the Texas statute unconstitutional as applied to a defendant with a history of abuse and intellectual
disability); William R. Long, "A Time to Kill? Reflections on the Oregon Death
Penalty," *Oregon State Bar Bulletin*, April 2002, https://www.osbar.org
/publications/bulletin/02apr/kill.htm (describing Oregon's reaction to *Penry*);
Death Penalty Information Center, *Number of Executions by State and Region
since 1976*; Abdul-Kabir v. Quarterman, 550 U.S. 233, 246 (2007) (reversing the
CCA's interpretation of *Penry* as unreasonably wrong); Brewer v. Quarterman,
550 U.S. 286, 289 (2007) (same).

13. Strickland v. Washington, 466 U.S. 668, 687 (1984).

14. *Ex parte* Burdine, 901 S.W.2d 456, 457–458 (Maloney, J., dissenting) (describing the behavior of a lawyer who was found adequate, which included sleeping during the trial); Texas Defender Service, *Lethal Indifference* (2002), vii, http://texasdefender.org/wp-content/uploads/Lethal-Indiff_web.pdf (describing lawyers who conducted no investigation); Romero v. Lynaugh, 884 F.2d 871, 875 (1989) (holding that a lawyer who put on no case during sentencing was not ineffective); see *Ex parte* Guzmon 730 S.W.2d 724, 733 (1987) (finding a lawyer effective despite referring to his client in a racially derogatory manner during trial); see also Banda v. State, 768 S.W.2d 294, 297 (1989) (Teague, J., dissenting) (describing how the lawyer made no argument on behalf of his client's life to the jury).

15. Williams v. Taylor, 529 U.S. 362 (2000); Wiggins v. Smith, 539 U.S. 510 (2003).

16. See Bobby v. Van Hook, 558 U.S. 4 (2009); Wong v. Belmontes, 558 U.S. 15 (2009).

17. John Hanna, "Kansas Court's Approval of Death Sentence Not Seen As Shift," *San Francisco Gate,* November 15, 2015, http://www.sfgate.com/news/crime/article/Kansas-court-s-approval-of-death-sentence-not-6633873.php; see Kansas v. Marsh, 548 U.S. 163 (2006) (reversing a lower court's grant of relief); Kansas v. Cheever, 134 S. Ct. 596 (2013) (same); Kansas v. Carr, 135 S. Ct. 1698 (2015) (indicating that the Supreme Court would take the case).

18. Penry v. Lynaugh, 302 (declining to categorically exclude intellectually disabled individuals from the death penalty); Atkins v. Virginia, 536 U.S. 304, 321 (2002) (finding a national consensus against executing intellectually disabled individuals); *Ex parte* Briseno, 135 S.W.3d 1 (Tex. Crim. App. 2004) (interpreting *Atkins* for Texas).

19. *Ex parte* Briseno, 6.

20. *Ex parte* Briseno, 6, 8; see John H. Blume et al., "A Tale of Two (and Possibly Three) *Atkins:* Intellectual Disability and Capital Punishment Twelve Years After the Supreme Court's Creation of a Categorical Bar," *William & Mary Bill of Rights Journal* 23 (2014); Hensleigh Crowell, "The Writing Is on the Wall: How the *Briseno* Factors Create an Unacceptable Risk of Executing Individuals with Intellectual Disability," *Texas Law Review* 94 (2016).

21. Blume et al., "A Tale of Two (and Possibly Three) *Atkins,*" 393, 397 (finding that the average national success rate for *Atkins* claims is 55 percent while the success rate in Texas is only 17 percent).

22. Hall v. Florida, 134 S. Ct. 1986 (2014) (finding Florida's interpretation of the IQ cutoff unconstitutional); Mays v. Stephens, 757 F.3d 211, 2188 (5th Cir. 2014) (holding that *Hall* does not affect Texas's interpretation of *Atkins*).

23. Texas Defender Service, *Lethal Indifference,* 38 ("As often is the case, the trial lawyer was appointed to represent [the defendant] in his direct appeal."); California Rules of Court 76.6 (describing the appellate proficiency required of attorneys appointed for direct capital appeals in California).

24. Compare California Rules of Court 36(b)(3)(A)–(B) (limiting appellate briefs to 280 pages and 140 pages for a reply), with Texas Rules of Appellate Procedure

71.1 (limiting briefs to the Court of Criminal Appeals to 125 pages); People v. Brown, 862 P.2d 710, 722 (Cal. 1993) ("Based on this court's own practice and experience . . . we know that tentative written determinations prepared prior to argument are both helpful to the court in collecting and organizing its thoughts, and not infrequently altered or even reversed after argument and further reflection.").

25. California Rules of Court 35.1, 35.2 (establishing the process for certifying the trial record in capital cases as complete and accurate); Texas Rules of Appellate Procedure 37.3(a)(2) ("If the clerk's record or reporter's record has not been timely filed, the appellate court clerk must refer the matter to the appellate court. The court must make whatever order is appropriate to avoid further delay and to preserve the parties' rights.").

26. See Clive A. Stafford Smith and Rémy Voisin Starns, "Folly by Fiat: Pretending that Death Row Inmates Can Represent Themselves in State Capital Post-Conviction Proceedings," Loyola Law Review 45 (1999): 108 ("Indeed, the California Appellate Project is an extremely effective and well-funded resource for appointed lawyers.").

27. Bob Egelko, "State's Chief Justice Praises Long Appeals Process: 'We Don't Turn Them Out Like Texas,' He Says," San Francisco Chronicle, December 15, 2004, A21; Gerald Eulmen et al., Final Report, California Commission on the Fair Administration of Justice (2008), 122, http://www.ccfaj.org/documents/CCFAJFinalReport.pdf (describing the lack of counsel for death-sentenced inmates in California).

28. Texas Code of Criminal Procedure, Article 4.04; Eulmen et al., Final Report, 114–115 ("California's death penalty system is dysfunctional. The system is plagued with excessive delay in the appointments of counsel for direct appeals and habeas corpus petitions, and a severe backlog in the review of appeals and habeas petitions before the California Supreme Court."); Jones v. Chappell, 31 F. Supp. 3d 1050, 1057 (2014) (describing the delays in California's direct appeal process); Death Penalty Information Center, State Execution Rates, http://www.deathpenaltyinfo.org/state-execution-rates.

29. Carlos Sanchez, "House Approves Bill to Refine Death Row Appeals, Cut Delays," Fort Worth Star-Telegram, May 19, 1995, 34.

30. One example is the case of Robert Black. Black's direct appeal was denied on May 29, 1991, Black v. State, 816 S.W.2d 350, 365 (Tex. Crim. App. 1991), and the Fifth Circuit opinion denying habeas relief was issued less than a year later, on May 21, 1992, Black v. Collins, 962 F.2d 394, 409 (5th Cir. 1992). Black was then executed the next day, May 22, 1992, although his petition for review in the U.S. Supreme Court was not denied until June 15, 1992; Justice Blackmun noted that the petition should have been dismissed as moot, Black v. Collins, 504 U.S. 992 (1992); Texas Department of Criminal Justice, Executed Offenders, https://www.tdcj.state.tx.us/death_row/dr_executed_offenders.html.

31. Death Penalty Information Center, Searchable Executions Database, http://www.deathpenaltyinfo.org/views-executions; Death Penalty Information Center, Executions by Year, http://www.deathpenaltyinfo.org/executions-year.

32. Texas Defender Service, *Lethal Indifference*, 13; Steve Mills, "Texas Judges Attack Decision Leading to Execution," *Chicago Tribune*, February 13, 2013, http://articles.chicagotribune.com/2003-02-13/news/0302130346_1_criminal-appeals-habeas-corpus-appeal-texas-court; see Wilson v. Cockrell, 70 F. App'x 219, 221–222 (5th Cir. 2003).

33. Death Penalty Information Center, *Executions by State and Year*, http://www.deathpenaltyinfo.org/node/5741#TX.

34. See North Carolina General Statute § 15A-1415(f) ("The State, to the extent allowed by law, shall make available to the capital defendant's counsel the complete files of all law enforcement and prosecutorial agencies involved in the investigation of the crimes committed or the prosecution of the defendant.").

35. 28 U.S.C. § 2254(f) (2012).

36. See Clark v. Johnson, 202 F.3d 760, 766 (5th Cir. 2000) ("we have repeatedly found that a paper hearing [in state court] is sufficient to afford a petitioner a full and fair hearing on the factual issues").

37. Death Penalty Information Center, *Texas Newspaper Studies State's Death Penalty Appeals Process*, http://www.deathpenaltyinfo.org/node/1838.

38. California Supreme Court, *Supreme Court Policies Regarding Cases Arising from Judgments of Death* (amended January 1, 2008), http://www.courts.ca.gov/documents/PoliciesMar2012.pdf.

39. Eulmen et al., *Final Report*, 122; Death Penalty Information Center, *Death Row Inmates by State*, http://www.deathpenaltyinfo.org/death-row-inmates-state-and-size-death-row-year; California Appellate Court Case Information, People v. Masters Docket, 6, 13, http://tompainetoo.com/docs/Death%20Penalty/Appeal/Appeal%20docket%20sheet.pdf.

40. See McFarland v. Collins, 7 F.3d 47, 48 (5th Cir. 1993) (denying a stay where "The only postconviction relief petitioner has sought in state court has been a number of motions to stay court ordered executions to permit the petitioner to obtain habeas counsel").

41. Antiterrorism and Effective Death Penalty Act of 1996, Public Law 104–132, 110 Stat. 1214; Ibid., § 2254(d)(1), § 2254(d)(2); Randy Hertz and James S. Liebman, *Federal Habeas Corpus Practice and Procedure*, 6th ed., Vol. I (New Providence, NJ: LexisNexis, 2011), 126 (describing the decrease in federal habeas reversals following the enactment of AEDPA); Death Penalty Information Center, *Executions by Year*.

42. Alicia Bannon, *The Impact of Judicial Vacancies on Judicial Trial Courts* (New York: Brennan Center for Justice, 2014), 4 (describing California federal court docket loads); Sandhya Bathija, "Texas, Where Are the Judges?," *Center for American Progress*, April 2, 2014, https://www.americanprogress.org/issues/civil-liberties/report/2014/04/02/86910/texas-where-are-the-judges/ (describing Texas federal court docket loads); Holiday v. Stephens, 136 S. Ct. 387 (2015) (Sotomayor, J., statement respecting the application for stay of execution and denial of certiorari).

43. Evan Caminker and Erwin Chemerinsky, "The Lawless Execution of Robert Alton Harris," *Yale Law Journal* 102 (1992): 225–226 (describing the litigation

leading up to Harris's execution); Vasquez v. Harris, 503 U.S. 1000 (1992) (the Supreme Court order barring future stays of execution).

44. Mark Berman, "Pennsylvania's Governor Suspends the Death Penalty," *Washington Post,* February 13, 2015, https://www.washingtonpost.com/news /post-nation/wp/2015/02/13/pennsylvania-suspends-the-death-penalty/; Ian Lovett, "Executions are Suspended by Governor in Washington," *New York Times,* February 11, 2014, http://www.nytimes.com/2014/02/12/us/washington -governor-jay-inslee-suspends-death-penalty.html?_r=0; Shelby Sebens, "New Oregon Governor Kate Brown to Extend Death Penalty Moratorium," *Reuters,* February 20, 2015, http://www.reuters.com/article/2015/02/20/us-usa-politics -oregon-idUSKBN0LO2E420150220#r0l2R8tqIh4uSXUZ.97; James Marquet et al., *The Rope, The Chair, and The Needle: Capital Punishment in Texas, 1923–1990* (Austin: University of Texas Press, 1998), 24 (describing the rate of commutations in Texas before the modern era); Richard C. Dieter, Death Penalty Information Center, *The Future of the Death Penalty in the U.S.: A Texas-Sized Crisis,* http://www.deathpenaltyinfo.org/the-future-of-the-death -penalty#sxn7 (describing the rate of commutations in Texas in the modern era); Governor's Office Press Release, "Governor Ryan Declares Moratorium on Executions, Will Appoint Commission to Review Capital Punishment System," *Illinois Government News Network,* January 31, 2000, http://www3.illinois.gov /PressReleases/showpressrelease.cfm?subjectid=3&recnum=359; Jodi Wilgoren, "Citing Issues of Fairness, Governor Clears Out Death Row in Illinois," *New York Times,* January 12, 2003, http://www.nytimes.com/2003/01/12/us/citing -issue-of-fairness-governor-clears-out-death-row-in-illinois.html; "Illinois Abolishes Death Penalty, Clears Death Row," *Associated Press,* March 9, 2011, http://www.cbsnews.com/news/illinois-ends-death-penalty-clears-death-row/.

45. Baze v. Rees, 553 U.S. 35 (2008).

46. Jerry Markon, "Virginia Executes Man, Ending De Facto Moratorium," *Washington Post,* May 28, 2008, http://www.washingtonpost.com/wp-dyn /content/article/2008/05/27/AR2008052702257.html.

47. Julia Cheever, "Court in SF Hears Bid to Reinstate Lethal Injection Protocol," *San Francisco Appeal,* April 16, 2013, http://sfappeal.com/2013/04/court-in-sf -hears-bid-to-reinstate-lethal-injectionprotocol/.

48. Nathan Koppel, "Drug Halt Hinders Executions in the U.S.," *Wall Street Journal,* January 22, 2011, http://www.wsj.com/articles/SB100014240527487047 543045760959807901296 92; Jeffrey Stern, "The Cruel and Unusual Execution of Clayton Lockett," *The Atlantic,* June 2015, http://www.theatlantic.com /magazine/archive/2015/06/execution-clayton-lockett/392069/; David Jolly, "Danish Company Blocks Sale of Drugs for U.S. Executions," *New York Times,* July 1, 2011, http://www.nytimes.com/2011/07/02/world/europe/02execute .html.

49. Stern, "The Cruel and Unusual Execution of Clayton Lockett."

50. Matt Ford, "Clayton Lockett and the World's Deepening Death Penalty Divide," *The Atlantic,* May 1, 2014, http://www.theatlantic.com/international /archive/2014/05/clayton-lockett-and-the-worlds-deepening-death-penalty

-divide/361482/ (describing the use of compounding pharmacies); "Texas Prison Officials Send Virginia Sought-After Drug for Execution This Week," *Associated Press,* September 26, 2015, http://www.nytimes.com/2015/09/27 /us/texas-prison-officials-send-virginia-sought-after-drug-for-execution -this-week.html; Stern, "The Cruel and Unusual Execution of Clayton Lockett" (describing the e-mail exchange between Texas and Oklahoma officials).

51. The Williams case dominated the television and print media in the days leading up to and including his execution. See Sarah Kershaw, "California Gang Founder Loses Death Row Appeal," *New York Times,* December 13, 2005, A27; Sarah Kershaw, "Execution Ignites New Fire in Death Penalty Debate," *New York Times,* December 14, 2005, A30.

52. Carol Towarnicky, "Mumia Story Properly Getting Moldy," *Philadelphia Daily News,* October 25, 2005, 17.

53. Ronald F. Wright, "Sentencing Commissions as Provocateurs of Prosecutorial Self-Regulation," *Columbia Law Review* 105 (2005): 1022.

54. Franklin E. Zimring, *The Contradictions of American Capital Punishment* (New York: Oxford University Press, 2003), 82.

55. Frank E. Zimring, "Postscript: The Peculiar Present of American Capital Punishment," in *Beyond Repair? America's Death Penalty,* ed. Stephen P. Garvey (Durham: Duke University Press, 2003), 229.

56. Carol Steiker, "Introduction," in *Criminal Procedure Stories,* ed. Carol Steiker (New York: Foundation Press, 2006), vii, viii–ix.

57. Stephen B. Bright, "Sleeping on the Job," *National Law Journal,* December 4, 2000, A26; Bruce Shapiro, "Sleeping Lawyer Syndrome: Murder Case in Texas, During Which the Defendant's Lawyer Was Observed Sleeping," *The Nation,* April 7, 1997, 27.

58. This account departs slightly from Frank Zimring's provocative emphasis on "vigilante values" in executing jurisdictions as the most promising explanation for the execution gap. Zimring, *The Contradictions of American Capital Punishment,* 98 (asserting that a "high historical commitment to vigilante justice may be a necessary but not sufficient condition for a social and governmental climate that generates high levels of official execution in the late twentieth century"). Zimring's thesis is interesting and powerful, but fails to capture the relative newness of the execution divide; like most scholars who engage the divide, Zimring views the high level of executions in executing states as the phenomenon in need of explanation, and does not fully account for the dramatic shift of most symbolic states—such as New York, California, and Pennsylvania—from being robustly executing states in the first half of the twentieth century to becoming symbolic states in the second half. That development seems to call for an explanation more focused on the 1960s and 1970s than rooted in deep cultural differences that extend back another century.

59. David McCord, "Afterword: If Capital Punishment Were Subject to Consumer Protection Laws," *Judicature* 89 (2005): 305.

60. John Kaplan, "Administering Capital Punishment," *University of Florida Law Review* 36 (1984): 183.

61. Soering v. United Kingdom, 161 Eur. Ct. H.R., 44–45 (1989) (denying an extradition from the United Kingdom to the United States because of the likelihood that the man sought would suffer "death row phenomenon" in the prolonged and uncertain wait for his execution, which would violate the European Convention on Human Rights); Pratt & Morgan v. Attorney-Gen. for Jamaica, 2 A.C. 1, 35 (1993) (appeal taken from Jamaica) ("in any case in which execution is to take place more than five years after sentence there will be strong grounds for believing that the delay is such as to constitute 'inhuman or degrading punishment or other treatment.'").

62. Jones v. Chappell, 31 F. Supp. 3d 1050 (C.D. Cal. 2014).

63. Ibid., 1053 (emphasis omitted).

64. Jones v. Davis, 806 F.3d 538 (9th Cir. 2015) (focusing on the *Teague* issue).

65. Glossip v. Gross, 135 S. Ct. 2726, 2764–2768 (2015) (Breyer, J., dissenting).

66. Davis v. Ayala, 135 S. Ct. 2187, 2208, 2210 (2015) (Kennedy, J., concurring).

67. Banner, *Death Penalty*, 62.

5. The Failures of Regulation

1. United States v. Garson, 291 F. 646, 649 (1923) (criticizing constitutional criminal procedure generally).

2. Furman v. Georgia, 408 U.S. 238, 308 (1972); Baugus v. State, 141 So. 2d 264, 266 (Fla. 1962).

3. Furman v. Georgia, 249–253, 255, 257.

4. Gregg v. Georgia, 428 U.S. 153, 161; Model Penal Code § 210.6(3)(h) (1980).

5. Godfrey v. Georgia, 446 U.S. 420, 427 (1980) (finding one of Georgia's aggravating factors unconstitutional because it was insufficiently narrow); Walton v. Arizona, 497 U.S. 639, 643 (1990) (upholding the application of an Arizona aggravating factor involving whether the murder was committed in an "especially heinous, cruel, or depraved" manner); Lewis v. Jeffers, 497 U.S. 764, 779 (1990) (same); Arave v. Creech, 507 U.S. 463, 465 (1993) (upholding the application of Idaho's "utter disregard for human life" aggravating factor).

6. James S. Liebman and Lawrence C. Marshall, "Less Is Better: Justice Stevens and the Narrowed Death Penalty," *Fordham Law Review* 74 (2006): 1669.

7. Edwin Colfax, "Fairness in the Application of the Death Penalty Code: The Massachusetts Governor's Council Report. Panel One—The Capital Crime," *Indiana Law Journal* 80 (2005): 35; Scott Turow, *Ultimate Punishment: A Lawyer's Reflections on Dealing with the Death Penalty* (New York: Farrar, Straus and Giroux, 2003), 114.

8. David C. Baldus et al., *Equal Justice and the Death Penalty: A Legal and Empirical Analysis* (Boston: Northeastern University Press, 1990), 102–103, 268n31.

9. Zant v. Stephens, 462 U.S. 862 (1983) (upholding the imposition of a sentence resting in part on an invalid aggravating factor); Clemons v. Mississippi,

494 U.S. 738 (1990) (requiring "reweighing" or harmless error analysis after a jury's reliance on an invalid aggravating factor); Brown v. Sanders, 546 U.S. 212 (2006) (adopting a new approach to sentences resting in part on invalid aggravating factors).

10. Coker v. Georgia, 433 U.S. 584, 617 (1977).

11. Enmund v. Florida, 458 U.S. 782 (1982) (prohibiting the imposition of the death penalty on individuals who did not take a life, attempt to take a life, or intend to take a life); Tison v. Arizona, 481 U.S. 137 (1987) (qualifying the rule in *Enmund* and allowing the imposition of the death penalty on individuals who were major participants in the underlying felony); Stanford v. Kentucky, 491 U.S. 361 (1989) (declining to categorically exclude juveniles from the death penalty); Penry v. Lynaugh, 492 U.S. 302 (1989) (declining to categorically exclude intellectually disabled individuals from the death penalty).

12. Roper v. Simmons, 543 U.S. 551 (2005) (prohibiting the execution of individuals who were juveniles at the time of the crime); Atkins v. Virginia, 536 U.S. 304 (2002) (finding a national consensus against executing intellectually disabled individuals); Kennedy v. Louisiana, 554 U.S. 407, 437 (2008) (prohibiting the use of the death penalty for the rape of a child).

13. Roper v. Simmons, 575.

14. The court has denied review in numerous cases of inmates presenting compelling claims of intellectual disability. See Lizcano v. Texas, 2015 WL 4365907 (Dec. 7, 2015) (denying a petition for writ of certiorari).

15. American Civil Liberties Union, *Mental Illness and the Death Penalty*, https://www.aclu.org/mental-illness-and-death-penalty.

16. Woodson v. North Carolina, 428 U.S. 280 (1976).

17. Lockett v. Ohio, 438 U.S. 586 (1978) (finding Ohio's statute unconstitutional because it limited what mitigating evidence the jury could consider); Eddings v. Oklahoma, 455 U.S. 104, 112–115 (1982) (holding that defendants must be able to present mitigating evidence, even if it is unrelated to the crime); Skipper v. South Carolina, 476 U.S. 1, 4–5 (1986).

18. Tennard v. Dretke, 542 U.S. 274 (2004).

19. McKoy v. North Carolina, 494 U.S. 434 (1990) (rejecting a unanimity requirement for the consideration of mitigating factors); Johnson v. Texas, 509 U.S. 350 (1993) (finding a former Texas statute adequate for the consideration of mitigating qualities of youth); Brewer v. Quarterman, 550 U.S. 286 (2007) (reversing the Fifth Circuit Court of Appeals's interpretation of *Penry*); Abdul-Kabir v. Quarterman, 550 U.S. 233 (2007) (reversing the Fifth Circuit Court of Appeals's interpretation of *Penry*).

20. Gregg v. Georgia, 190.

21. Gardner v. Florida, 430 U.S. 349, 357–362 (1977) (holding that heightened reliability requires defense access to a presentence report used in sentencing); Turner v. Murray, 476 U.S. 28, 37 (1986) (requiring specific voir dire on possible racial bias in an interracial offense); Caldwell v. Mississippi, 472 U.S. 320, 328–330 (1985) (holding that a jury may not be led to believe that the power of determining the appropriateness of a death penalty rests elsewhere); Simmons

v. South Carolina, 512 U.S. 154 (1994) (allowing a defendant to introduce evidence regarding the real meaning of a life sentence); Beck v. Alabama, 447 U.S. 625, 637–638 (1980) (requiring that a jury be allowed to consider the lesser included offenses of capital murder).

22. Simmons v. South Carolina, 2205 (Scalia, J., dissenting).

23. Strickland v. Washington, 466 U.S. 668, 687, 689–690, 693 (1984).

24. Stephen B. Bright, "Counsel for the Poor: The Death Sentence Not for the Worst Crime but for the Worst Lawyer," *Yale Law Journal* 103 (1994): 1838–1839.

25. Williams v. Taylor, 529 U.S. 362 (2000); Wiggins v. Smith, 529 U.S. 510 (2003); Rompilla v. Beard, 545 U.S. 374 (2005).

26. Wiggins v. Smith, 522; Rompilla v. Beard, 387.

27. Murray v. Giarratano, 492 U.S. 1, 13 (1989) (rejecting a constitutional claim to postconviction counsel for indigent inmates); Pennsylvania v. Finley, 481 U.S. 551, 555–557 (1987) (same).

28. Teague v. Lane, 489 U.S. 288, 309–310 (1991); 28 U.S.C.A. § 2244(b)(1) (1996); 28 U.S.C.A. § 2254.

29. Randy Hertz and James S. Liebman, *Federal Habeas Corpus Practice and Procedure*, 6th ed., Vol. I (New Providence, NJ: LexisNexis, 2011), 126 (describing the decrease in federal habeas reversals following the enactment of the Antiterrorism and Effective Death Penalty Act, or AEDPA). A particularly telling illustration of the consequences of the new deferential standard can be found in a decision by the Fifth Circuit Court of Appeals reversing a grant of habeas relief by a federal district court. Buntion v. Quarterman, 524 F.3d 664 (5th Cir. 2008). In *Buntion*, the state trial judge had declared in open court that he was doing "God's work" to see that the defendant was executed, and he laughed during the testimony of defense witnesses. The Fifth Circuit Court of Appeals found the state trial judge's behavior inappropriate, but held that the federal district court erred in finding a constitutional violation in light of the deference AEDPA affords state court decisions.

30. Herrera v. Collins, 506 U.S. 390 (1993).

31. Kansas v. Marsh, 548 U.S. 163, 208, 210 (2006) (Souter, J., dissenting).

32. McCleskey v. Kemp, 481 U.S. 279 (1987).

33. Furman v. Georgia, 310.

34. McCleskey v. Kemp, 314–315.

35. Ibid., 319 (quoting *Gregg v. Georgia*).

36. Pulley v. Harris, 465 U.S. 37 (1984).

37. Associated Press, "Ginsburg Backs Ending Death Penalty," April 9, 2001. http://www.truthinjustice.org/ginsburg.htm.

38. Barefoot v. Estelle, 463 U.S. 880, 920 (1983) (Blackmun, J., dissenting) (quoting American Psychiatric Association).

39. Barefoot v. Estelle, 899.

40. Brief for the NAACP Legal Defense and Educational Fund, Inc. and the National Office for the Rights of the Indigent as *Amici Curiae*, McGautha v. California, 402 U.S. 183 (1971), No. 71-203, 69.

41. Walton v. Arizona, 639, 661, 664, 673.

42. Callins v. Collins, 510 U.S. 1141, 1149, 1154, 1157 (1994).

43. Walton v. Arizona, 718.

44. McGautha v. California, 402 U.S. 183, 197, 204 (1971).

45. Woodson v. North Carolina, 280, 304 .

46. Justice Antonin Scalia, Memorandum to the Conference Re: No. 84–6811—McCleskey v. Kemp (Jan. 6, 1987), available at Library of Congress, Thurgood Marshall Papers, McCleskey v. Kemp file.

47. The twelve states assessed by the ABA Death Penalty Due Process Review Project are Alabama, Arizona, Florida, Georgia, Indiana, Kentucky, Missouri, Ohio, Pennsylvania, Tennessee, Texas, and Virginia. The reports are available at http://www.americanbar.org/groups/crsj/projects/death_penalty_due _process_review_project/state_death_penalty_assessments.html.

48. Shaila Dewan and Brenda Goodman, "Capital Cases Stall as Costs Grow Daunting," *New York Times,* November 4, 2007, http://www.nytimes.com/2007 /11/04/us/04penalty.html?ex=1351918800&_r=0.

49. Death Penalty Information Center, *The Clustering of the Death Penalty,* http://www.deathpenaltyinfo.org/clustering-death-penalty.

50. Matthew J. Streb, *Running for Judge: The Rising Political, Financial, and Legal Stakes of Judicial Elections* (New York: New York University Press, 2007), 7 (describing the judicial election process); Joseph R. Grodin, "Judicial Elections: The California Experience," *Judicature* 70 (1987): 367 (describing a television spot that encouraged voters to vote "three times for the death penalty; vote no on Bird, Reynoso, Grodin"); Stephen B. Bright, "Political Attacks on the Judiciary: Can Justice Be Done Amid Efforts to Intimidate and Remove Judges from Office for Unpopular Decisions?," *New York University Law Review* 72 (1997): 314 (describing an opposing party's political ad instructing voters to "Vote for Capital Punishment by Voting NO on August 1 for Supreme Court Justice Penny White"); Professor Philip Alston, Press Statement, *United Nations Human Rights Council Special Rapporteur on Extrajudicial, Summary or Arbitrary Executions,* June 30, 2008.

51. Robert Weisberg, "Deregulating Death," *Supreme Court Review* (1983): 342–343, 353, 364, 376, 393.

52. Caldwell v. Mississippi, 320, 329.

53. Hugo Adam Bedau, "The Decline of Executive Clemency in Capital Cases," *New York University Review of Law and Societal Change* 18 (1990–1991): 268; Franklin E. Zimring, "Inheriting the Wind: The Supreme Court and Capital Punishment in the 1990s," *Florida State University Law Review* 20 (1992): 17.

54. Robert Weisberg, "Deregulating Death," 353.

55. Alan Hyde, "The Concept of Legitimation in the Sociology of Law," *Wisconsin Law Review* 379 (1983): 414.

56. Death Penalty Information Center, *Death Sentences by Year since 1976,* http://www.deathpenaltyinfo.org/death-sentences-year-1977-2009; James Dao, "Death Penalty in New York Reinstated After 18 Years; Pataki Sees Justice Served," *New York Times,* March 8, 1995, http://www.nytimes.com/1995/03/08

/nyregion/death-penalty-in-new-york-reinstated-after-18-years-pataki-sees
-justice-served.html; Jeffrey Jones, "Americans' Support for the Death Penalty
Stable," *Gallup,* October 23, 2014, http://www.gallup.com/poll/178790
/americans-support-death-penalty-stable.aspx (showing heightened support for
the death penalty in the 1990s).

6. An Unsustainable System?

1. Death Penalty Information Center, *Death Sentences by Year since 1976,*
   http://www.deathpenaltyinfo.org/death-sentences-year-1977-2009; Death
   Penalty Information Center, *States With and Without the Death Penalty,*
   http://www.deathpenaltyinfo.org/states-and-without-death-penalty; Death
   Penalty Information Center, *Executions by Year,* http://www.deathpenaltyinfo
   .org/executions-year; Death Penalty Information Center, *The Death Penalty in
   2015: Year End Report,* http://www.deathpenaltyinfo.org
   /YearEnd2015#graphic.
2. Welsh S. White, *The Death Penalty in the Nineties: An Examination of the
   Modern System of Capital Punishment* (Ann Arbor: University of Michigan
   Press, 1991), 74.
3. Williams v. Taylor, 529 U.S. 362 (2000).
4. Foster v. Humphrey, 135 S. Ct. 2349 (2015); Ian Millhiser, "The Supreme Court
   Will Hear An Almost Comically Egregious Case of Race Discrimination,"
   Think Progress, May 26, 2015, http://thinkprogress.org/justice/2015/05/26
   /3662697/supreme-court-will-hear-almost-comically-egregious-case-race
   -discrimination/.
5. Wainwright v. Witt, 469 U.S. 412 (1985) (limiting the scope of Witherspoon);
   White v. Wheeler, 136 S. Ct. 456 (2015) (summarily reversing a Sixth Circuit
   case that granted relief based on the improper exclusion of a juror); Christopher Letkewicz, "Stacking the Deck in Favor of Death: The Illinois Supreme
   Court's Misinterpretation of *Morgan v. Illinois,*" *DePaul Journal for Social
   Justice* 2 (2009): 224–226.
6. 18 U.S.C. § 3599.
7. Stephen B. Bright, "Counsel for the Poor: The Death Sentence Not for the Worst
   Crime but for the Worst Lawyer," *Yale Law Journal* 103 (1994): 1838–1841.
8. Antiterrorism and Effective Death Penalty Act of 1996, Public Law 104–132,
   110 Stat. 1214; 28 U.S.C. § 2254(d)(1), § 2254(d)(2) (creating a deferential
   standard of review); U.S.C. § 2244(d)(1) (creating a one-year statute of
   limitations).
9. United States v. MacCollom, 426 U.S. 317, 319 (1976) (finding no right to state
   postconviction proceedings); Murray v. Giarratano, 492 U.S. 1, 3–4 (1989)
   (finding no right to the appointment of counsel for state postconviction
   proceedings); see generally Williams v. Taylor (upholding AEDPA and
   interpreting several of its provisions); Cullen v. Pinholster, 563 U.S. 170,
   181–182 (2011) (holding that federal habeas review of state court proceedings is
   limited to the record before the state court).

10. Colton Lochhead, "Audit: Death Penalty Nearly Doubles Cost of Nevada Murder Cases," *Las Vegas Review-Journal,* December 2, 2014, http://www .reviewjournal.com/news/nevada/audit-death-penalty-nearly-doubles-cost -nevada-murder-cases; Legislative Services Agency, "Fiscal Impact Statement for SB 43," January 6, 2010, http://www.deathpenaltyinfo.org/documents /INCostAssess.pdf; Philip J. Cook, "Potential Savings from Abolition of the Death Penalty in North Carolina," *American Law and Economics Review* (2009); Judge Arthur L. Alarcón and Paula M. Mitchell, "Executing the Will of the Voters?: A Roadmap to Mend or End the California Legislature's Multi-Billion-Dollar Death Penalty Debacle," *Loyola of Los Angeles Law Review* 44 (2011).

11. David Pittman, "Murder Trial Costs Gray County A Lot," *Lubbock Avalanche-Journal,* October 20, 2009, http://lubbockonline.com/stories/102009/loc _506696310.shtml#.VoLjlsArIUs.

12. Russell Berman, "How Nebraska Abolished the Death Penalty," *The Atlantic,* May 27, 2015, http://www.theatlantic.com/politics/archive/2015/05/how -nebraska-banned-the-death-penalty/394271/.

13. Editorial, "High Cost of Death Row," *New York Times,* September 27, 2009, http://www.nytimes.com/2009/09/28/opinion/28mon3.html?_r=0.

14. Death Penalty Information Center, *Time on Death Row,* http://www .deathpenaltyinfo.org/time-death-row.

15. Johnson v. Bredesen, 558 U.S. 1067 (2009) (Stevens, J., joined by Breyer, J., statement respecting denial of certiorari).

16. Sandra Chereb, "Nevada Pursues Death Chamber, Controversial Drug," *Las Vegas Review-Journal,* July 13, 2015, http://www.reviewjournal.com/news /nevada/nevada-pursues-death-chamber-controversial-drug-0; Sean Waley, "Panel Rejects Construction of a New Nevada Execution Chamber," *Las Vegas Review-Journal,* May 22, 2013, http://www.reviewjournal.com/news/nevada -legislature/panel-rejects-construction-new-nevada-execution-chamber.

17. Herrera v. Collins, 506 U.S. 390 (1993).

18. Ronald J. Tabak, "Finality Without Fairness: Why We are Moving Towards Moratoria on Executions, and the Potential Abolition of Capital Punishment," *Connecticut Law Review* 33 (2001): 739–741.

19. Don Terry, "Survivors Make Case Against Death Row," *New York Times,* November 16, 1998, http://www.nytimes.com/1998/11/16/us/survivors-make -the-case-against-death-row.html; conference poster on file with authors.

20. Press Release, "Governor Ryan Declares Moratorium on Executions, Will Appoint Commission to Review Capital Punishment System," *Illinois Govern-ment News Network,* January 31, 2000, http://www3.illinois.gov/PressReleases /showpressrelease.cfm?subjectid=3&recnum=359; "Illinois Ends Death Penalty, Clears Death Row," *Associated Press,* March 9, 2011, http://www.cbsnews.com /news/illinois-ends-death-penalty-clears-death-row/.

21. Jim Dwyer et al., *Actual Innocence: Five Days to Execution and Other Dis-patches from the Wrongly Convicted* (New York: Doubleday, 2000).

22. Callins v. Collins, 510 U.S. 1141, 1145 (1994) (Blackmun, J., dissenting); ibid., 1143 (Scalia, J., concurring); Dahlia Lithwick, "N.C. Governor Pardons

Brothers Imprisoned Three Decades for Murder They Did Not Commit," *Slate,* June 5, 2015, http://www.slate.com/blogs/the_slatest/2015/06/05/henry _mccollum_and_leon_brown_pardoned_after_dna_exoneration_and_30 _years.html.

23. James S. Liebman, *The Wrong Carlos: Anatomy of a Wrongful Execution* (New York: Columbia University Press, 2014), 2. DeLuna was executed in 1989.

24. Kansas v. Marsh, 548 U.S. 163, 199 (2006) (Scalia, J., concurring).

25. *Ex parte* Elizondo, 947 S.W.2d 202 (Tex. Crim. App. 1996) (en banc) (holding that a bare innocence claim suffices as a constitutional challenge to an otherwise constitutional trial or guilty plea).

26. See Note, "A Matter of Life and Death: The Effect of Life-Without-Parole Statutes on Capital Punishment," *Harvard Law Review* 119 (2006): 1838, 1841.

27. Death Penalty Information Center, *The Death Penalty in 2015: Year End Report,* http://www.deathpenaltyinfo.org/YearEnd2015#graphic.

28. Death Penalty Information Center, *Death Sentences by Year since 1976.*

29. See Inimai M. Chettiar, "The Many Causes of America's Decline in Crime," *The Atlantic,* February 11, 2015, http://www.theatlantic.com/politics/archive/2015 /02/the-many-causes-of-americas-decline-in-crime/385364/.

30. Adam Nagourney, "Mario Cuomo, Ex-New York Governor and Liberal Beacon, Dies at 82," *New York Times,* January 1, 2015, http://www.nytimes.com/2015/01 /02/nyregion/mario-cuomo-new-york-governor-and-liberal-beacon-dies-at-82 .html?_r=0; James Dao, "Death Penalty in New York Reinstated After 18 Years; Pataki Sees Justice Served," *New York Times,* March 8, 1995, http://www .nytimes.com/1995/03/08/nyregion/death-penalty-in-new-york-reinstated-after -18-years-pataki-sees-justice-served.html.

31. James Hohmann, "In Iowa, Rand Paul Sticks With Death Penalty Skepticism," *Washington Post,* May 28, 2015, https://www.washingtonpost.com/news/post -politics/wp/2015/05/28/in-iowa-rand-paul-sticks-with-death-penalty -skepticism/; Ed O'Keefe, "Jeb Bush Feels 'Conflicted' About the Death Penalty," *Washington Post,* November 1, 2015, https://www.washingtonpost .com/news/post-politics/wp/2015/11/01/jeb-bush-conflicted-about-the-death -penalty/; Amy Choznick, "Hillary Clinton Comes Out Against Abolishing the Death Penalty," *New York Times,* October 28, 2015, http://www.nytimes.com /politics/first-draft/2015/10/28/hillary-clinton-comes-out-against-abolishing -the-death-penalty/ (quoting Hillary Clinton as saying the use of the death penalty should be "very limited and rare"); Mollie Reilly, "Bernie Sanders Speaks Out Against the Death Penalty After Hillary Clinton Stands By It," *Huffpost Politics,* October 29, 2015, http://www.huffingtonpost.com/entry /bernie-sanders-death-penalty_56326622e4b00aa54a4d48ff.

32. Marshall Frady, "Death in Arkansas," *New Yorker,* February 22, 1993, http:// archives.newyorker.com/?i=1993-02-22#folio=104.

33. Gallup, *Death Penalty,* http://www.gallup.com/poll/1606/death-penalty.aspx; Public Religion Research Institute, *Anxiety, Nostalgia, and Mistrust: Findings from the 2015 American Values Survey,* http://publicreligion.org/site/wp -content/uploads/2015/11/PRRI-AVS-2015.pdf.

34. Murder Victims' Families for Reconciliation, *Voices of Kansas: Murder Victims' Families Speak Out Against the Death Penalty,* http://ksabolition.org/wp-content/uploads/2015/04/MVFR_KansasVoices_Pages_Spring2015.pdf.
35. George Will, "Capital Punishment's Slow Death," *Washington Post,* May 20, 2015, https://www.washingtonpost.com/opinions/capital-punishments-slow-death/2015/05/20/f3c14d32-fe4f-11e4-8b6c-0dcce21e223d_story.html.
36. Kim Bellware, "Kansas College Republicans Latest Conservative Group to Oppose the Death Penalty," *Huffpost Politics,* August 25, 2015, http://www.huffingtonpost.com/entry/kansas-college-republicans-death-penalty_55db5192e4b04ae49703d63d.
37. Ruth Gledhill, "NaLEC Becomes First Major Evangelical Group to Oppose Death Penalty," *Christianity Today,* March 28, 2015, http://www.christiantoday.com/article/nalec.becomes.first.major.evangelical.group.to.oppose.death.penalty/50933.htm; Sarah Eekhoff Zylstra, "Evangelicals Now Officially Divided on the Death Penalty," *Christianity Today,* October 19, 2015, http://www.christianitytoday.com/gleanings/2015/october/evangelicals-divided-death-penalty-nae-capital-punishment.html.

7. Recurring Patterns in Constitutional Regulation

1. In announcing his rejection of the constitutionality of the death penalty near the end of his more than twenty-year tenure on the Supreme Court, Justice Harry Blackmun stated, "I feel morally and intellectually obligated simply to concede that the death penalty experiment has failed." Callins v. Collins, 510 U.S. 1141, 1145 (1994) (Blackmun, J., dissenting from denial of certiorari).
2. Robert Dahl argued in the mid-twentieth century that empirical data demonstrated that "the policy views dominant on the Court are never for long out of line with the policy views dominant among the lawmaking majorities of the United States." Robert A. Dahl, "Decision-Making in a Democracy: The Supreme Court as a National Policy-Maker," *Journal of Public Law* 6 (1957): 285. See also Barry Friedman, *The Will of the People: How Public Opinion Has Influenced the Supreme Court and Shaped the Meaning of the Constitution* (New York: Farrar, Straus and Giroux, 2009), 15 (arguing that "over time . . . the Court and the public will come into basic alliance with each other"); Gerald N. Rosenberg, *The Hollow Hope: Can Courts Bring About Social Change?* (Chicago: University of Chicago Press, 1991), 336–343 (concluding that American courts are incapable of effecting social change without the support of the people).
3. See Lee Epstein and Joseph F. Kobylka, *The Supreme Court and Legal Change: Abortion and the Death Penalty* (Chapel Hill: University of North Carolina Press, 1992), 82–90, 202, 207–210 (describing backlash to *Furman v. Georgia* and *Roe v. Wade*); Michael J. Klarman, *From Jim Crow to Civil Rights: The Supreme Court and the Struggle for Racial Equality* (New York: Oxford University Press, 2004), 344–363 (describing local resistance to the implementation of the Court's desegregation decisions in the aftermath of *Brown v. Board of Education*).

4. The Gallup Poll conducted in 1966 revealed that 47 percent opposed and 42 percent favored the death penalty for murder, while 11 percent were undecided. Robert M. Bohm, "American Death Penalty Opinion, 1936–1986: A Critical Examination of the Gallup Polls," in *The Death Penalty in America: Current Research*, ed. Robert M. Bohm (Cincinnati: Anderson Publishing, 1991), 113, 116.

5. Gregg v. Georgia, 428 U.S. 153, 179–180 (1976).

6. Ibid., 179.

7. Furman v. Georgia, 408 U.S. 238, 360 (1972) (Marshall, J., concurring).

8. Gregg v. Georgia, 232 (Marshall, J., dissenting).

9. Roe v. Wade, 410 U.S. 113 (1973).

10. Evan Mandery, *A Wild Justice: The Death and Resurrection of Capital Punishment in America* (New York: W. W. Norton, 2013), 234 (quoting Professor Donald Zoll in the *National Review* and citing other sources).

11. Ibid., 235.

12. Brown v. Board of Education, 347 U.S. 483 (1954); Swann v. Charlotte-Mecklenburg Board of Education, 402 U.S. 1 (1971).

13. The California Supreme Court's decision invalidating the state's death penalty under the California constitution, People v. Anderson, 493 P.2d 880 (Cal. 1972), was overturned later in the same year by the passage of Proposition 17, which amended the California Constitution to permit capital punishment. This episode offers a state-level example of political backlash in response to a high court decision out-of-step with public opinion.

14. Fred P. Graham, "Court Spares 600: 4 Justices Named by Nixon All Dissent in Historic Decision," *New York Times,* June 30, 1972, 1.

15. See David Garland, *Peculiar Institution: America's Death Penalty in an Age of Abolition* (Cambridge, MA: Belknap Press of Harvard University Press, 2010), 238–244 (describing the development and deployment of the Republican Party's "Southern Strategy").

16. Ibid., 240 ("Crime became a short-hand *signal,* to crucial numbers of white voters, of broader issues of social disorder, tapping powerful ideas about authority, status, morality, self-control and race.") (quoting Thomas Byrne Edsall with Mary D. Edsall, *Chain Reaction: The Impact of Race, Rights, and Taxes on American Politics* [New York: W. W. Norton, 1991], 224) (italics in original; internal quotation marks omitted).

17. For a general discussion of the effects of *Furman* on public sentiment and politics, see Marie Gottschalk, *The Prison and the Gallows: The Politics of Mass Incarceration in America* (New York: Cambridge University Press, 2006), 216–217. For an account of Dukakis's disastrous televised debate in which his response to the death penalty question was credited as a turning point in his presidential campaign, see the first chapter (entitled "A Killer Question") in Jack W. Germond and Jules Witcover's book about the 1988 election, *Whose Broad Stripes and Bright Stars? The Trivial Pursuit of the Presidency 1988* (New York: Warner Books, 1989), 10, 16.

18. Mapp v. Ohio, 367 U.S. 643 (1961) (applying the Fourth Amendment's exclusionary rule to state proceedings); Gideon v. Wainwright, 372 U.S. 335 (1963) (extending the right to counsel for indigent criminal defendants); Miranda v. Arizona, 384 U.S. 436 (1966) (regulating custodial interrogations by the police).

19. There is disagreement over the exact number of those released from death row by the *Furman* decision, with estimates ranging from 589 to 633. See Carol S. Steiker, "*Furman v. Georgia*: Not an End, But a Beginning," in *Death Penalty Stories*, eds. John H. Blume and Jordan M. Steiker (Foundation Press: 2009), 97 n.9.

20. Joan M. Cheever, *Back from the Dead: One Woman's Search for the Men Who Walked off America's Death Row* (Chichester, UK: John Wiley & Sons, 2006), 36, 52.

21. David Brooks, "Roe's Birth, and Death," *New York Times*, April 21, 2005, http://www.nytimes.com/2005/04/21/opinion/roes-birth-and-death.html.

22. Colleen Walsh, "Honoring Ruth Bader Ginsburg," *Harvard Gazette*, May 29, 2015, http://news.harvard.edu/gazette/story/2015/05/honoring-ruth-bader -ginsburg/. See also Michael J. Klarman, "Fidelity, Indeterminacy, and the Problem of Constitutional Evil," *Fordham Law Review* 65 (1997): 1751 (ex-plaining that the "conventional understanding" of *Roe* is that it prompted an anti-abortion backlash).

23. Linda Greenhouse and Reva B. Siegel, "Before (and After) *Roe v. Wade*: New Questions About Backlash," *Yale Law Journal* 120 (2011): 2032 (adding new arguments to "a small but growing body of scholarship questioning whether abortion backlash has been provoked primarily by adjudication").

24. The Court backtracked from *Roe* in Webster v. Reproductive Health Services, 492 U.S. 490 (1989), in which Justice Sandra Day O'Connor introduced the now-controlling constitutional rubric for addressing abortion restrictions, under which such restrictions are permitted unless they place an "undue burden" on women's right to choose an abortion prior to viability. O'Connor later explained that an abortion restriction creates an "undue burden" when it "has the purpose or effect of placing a substantial obstacle in the path of a woman seeking an abortion of a nonviable fetus." Planned Parenthood of Southeastern Pennsylvania v. Casey, 505 U.S. 833, 877 (1992) (plurality opinion).

25. Greenhouse and Siegel, "Before (and After) *Roe*," 2031 (quoting George Gallup, "Abortion Seen Up to Woman, Doctor," *Washington Post*, August 25, 1972, A2).

26. Epstein and Kobylka, *Abortion and the Death Penalty*, 188 (reporting 1972 polling data).

27. "Backlash from Roe v. Wade Continues to Shape Public Discourse, Says Klarman," *Harvard Law Today*, March 25, 2013, http://today.law.harvard.edu /backlash-from-roe-v-wade-continues-to-shape-public-discourse-says -klarman/.

28. Epstein and Kobylka, *Abortion and the Death Penalty*, 167–168. Margie Hames, the lead counsel in *Roe*'s companion case from Georgia, Doe v. Bolton, 410 U.S.

179 (1973), also was likely viewed as part of the Women's Rights Movement. Hames was a female attorney who was a board member of the national ACLU and vice president of the Georgia affiliate. Ibid., 167.

29. Ibid., 161.

30. Ibid., 164–166 (listing abortion rights cases and their counsel).

31. Greenhouse and Siegel, "Before (and After) *Roe*," 2080 (noting that Republican attempts to cast abortion as a feminist issue preceded the Court's decision in *Roe*).

32. Epstein and Kobylka, *Abortion and the Death Penalty,* 205.

33. Garland, *Peculiar Institution,* 241 (arguing that these cultural anxieties were targeted by the Republican Southern Strategy).

34. Epstein and Kobylka, *Abortion and the Death Penalty,* 203.

35. See Mary Ziegler, *After Roe: The Lost History of the Abortion Debate* (Cambridge, MA: Harvard University Press, 2015) (tracing the ways in which different social movements deployed *Roe* to promote their political ends in the decade following the decision).

36. Eisenstadt v. Baird, 405 U.S. 438 (1972) (ruling that unmarried people were constitutionally entitled to the same access to contraception as married people).

37. Donald T. Critchlow, *Phyllis Schlafly and Grassroots Conservatism: A Woman's Crusade* (Princeton, NJ: Princeton University Press, 2005), 110.

38. Atkins v. Virginia, 536 U.S. 304 (2002).

39. Ibid., 317 (internal quotation marks omitted).

40. Georgia was the first state to exempt offenders with intellectual disability from the death penalty, acting more than a decade before the Court's decision barring such executions under the Eighth Amendment. But even after the right was recognized by the Court, Georgia adhered to its extremely demanding standard of proof, which has the effect of denying the exemption to offenders whose intellectual disability is not obvious or unquestioned.

41. Epstein and Kobylka, *Abortion and the Death Penalty,* 214–215 (charting legal challenges to state abortion restrictions after *Roe*).

42. Editorial, "The Reproductive Rights Rollback of 2015," *New York Times,* December 19, 2015, http://www.nytimes.com/2015/12/20/opinion/sunday/the -reproductive-rights-rollback-of-2015.html.

43. Adam Liptak, "Supreme Court to Hear Texas Abortion Law Case," *New York Times,* November 13, 2015, http://www.nytimes.com/2015/11/14/us/politics /supreme-court-accepts-texas-abortion-law-case.html.

44. Carol S. Steiker, "Counter-Revolution in Constitutional Criminal Procedure? Two Audiences, Two Answers," *Michigan Law Review* 94 (1996): 2469.

45. Massiah v. United States, 377 U.S. 201 (1964).

46. Miranda v. Arizona, 436.

47. Steiker, "Counter-Revolution," 2475–2479 (describing cases strengthening the Warren Court's Sixth Amendment *Massiah* rule). One of the Burger Court's cases strengthening the Warren Court's *Massiah* rule, Michigan v. Jackson, 475 U.S. 625 (1986), was overruled by the Roberts Court in Montejo v. Loui-

siana, 556 U.S. 778 (2009). Despite this backtracking, it remains the case that Sixth Amendment norms (and other constitutional norms for police) have been far more stable than the consequences of violating them.

48. New York v. Quarles, 467 U.S. 649 (1984) (establishing the "public safety" exception to *Miranda*); Michigan v. Mosley, 423 U.S. 96, 104 (1975) (holding that the police must "scrupulously honor" a suspect's assertion of his right to silence) (internal quotation marks omitted); see also Steiker, "Counter-Revolution," 2480–2485 (discussing Burger and Rehnquist Court cases that addressed the meaning and scope of *Miranda*).

49. Steiker, "Counter-Revolution," 2490–2500 (describing Fourth Amendment cases addressing consent to search, reasonable expectations of privacy, and special needs); see also Illinois v. Wardlow, 528 U.S. 119 (2000) (holding that a suspect's flight from police in a high crime area justified stop); Whren v. United States, 517 U.S. 806 (1996) (holding that a pretextual stop does not violate the Fourth Amendment as long as it is objectively reasonable).

50. Steiker, "Counter-Revolution," 2486–2488 (describing cases bolstering the warrant requirement for home searches).

51. Katz v. United States, 389 U.S. 347 (1967) (rejecting the warrantless bugging of a telephone booth); Kyllo v. United States, 533 U.S. 27 (2001) (rejecting the warrantless use of a thermal imaging device on a home).

52. United States v. Jones, 132 S. Ct. 945 (2012) (rejecting the warrantless attachment of a GPS device to a suspect's car); Riley v. California, 134 S. Ct. 2473 (2014) (rejecting the warrantless search of an arrestee's cell phone).

53. Steiker, "Counter-Revolution," 2505–2532 (describing cases creating new rules that allow the government to use unconstitutionally seized evidence at trial).

54. Herring v. United States, 555 U.S. 135, 144 (2009).

55. Steiker, "Counter-Revolution," 2521–2527 (describing Fifth and Sixth Amendment cases restricting evidentiary exclusion).

56. See Harry T. Edwards, "To Err is Human, But Not Always Harmless: When Should Legal Error Be Tolerated?," *New York University Law Review* 70 (1995): 1176 (noting that the Burger and Rehnquist Courts "dramatically expanded the list of constitutional violations that are subject to harmless-error analysis, while adding few to . . . the list of violations that are per se reversible"); Arizona v. Fulminante, 499 U.S. 279 (1991) (holding that coerced confessions are not per se reversible, but instead are subject to harmless error review); Brecht v. Abrahamson, 507 U.S. 619 (1993) (watering down the harmless error standard for constitutional errors on federal habeas corpus review).

57. Stone v. Powell, 428 U.S. 465 (1976).

58. Wainwright v. Sykes, 433 U.S. 72 (1977) (announcing a tougher standard for excusing state procedural defaults on federal habeas review); Teague v. Lane, 489 U.S. 288 (1989) (announcing a tougher standard for retroactive application of new constitutional rules on federal habeas review).

59. Milton A. Loewenthal, "Evaluating the Exclusionary Rule in Search and Seizure," *University of Missouri-Kansas City Law Review* 49 (1980): 29 (finding that "most police officers interpret the *Wolf* case [which declined to extend the

federal Fourth Amendment exclusionary rule to the states in 1949] as not having imposed any legal obligation on the police since, under that decision, the evidence would still be admissible no matter how it was obtained").

60. For example, federal agents burglarized a bank officer's hotel room in order to obtain a bank client's financial records, knowing that the client did not have "standing" to object to the search and therefore could not exclude the records from his criminal trial. United States v. Payner, 447 U.S. 727 (1980).

61. In the wake of the Court's decision in *Miranda,* former Attorney General Nicholas Katzenbach called claims that the Supreme Court's decisions were "handcuffing" the police "emotional nonsense." "Katzenbach Puts Down Police Criticism of Supreme Court," *Chicago Daily Defender,* March 29, 1967, 3. Nonetheless, polls continued to show that this view was widely held among the general public. For example, a 1982 poll revealed that more than two-thirds of those polled agreed with the statement: "The police can't really do much about crime because the courts have put too many restrictions on the police." U.S. Department of Justice, Bureau of Justice Statistics, *Sourcebook of Criminal Justice Statistics* (1983), 236, Table 2.46, http://bjs.gov/content/pub/pdf/scjs83.pdf.

62. Steiker, "Counter-Revolution," 2549nn369–371 (citing polls). More recent polls continue to show high levels of public confidence in the police, with more than half reporting a "Great deal" or "Quite a lot" of confidence in the police every year for the past two decades—much more confidence than was expressed in the criminal justice system or the Supreme Court. Gallup Historical Trends, *Confidence in Institutions* (2015), http://www.gallup.com/poll/1597/confidence -institutions.aspx.

63. "The right of citizens of the United States to vote shall not be denied or abridged by the United States or any State on account of race, color, or previous condition of servitude." U.S. Constitution, Amendment XV, §1.

64. Strauder v. West Virginia, 100 U.S. 303 (1879).

65. Mark Curriden, "A Supreme Case of Contempt," *ABA Journal* 95, no. 6 (2009): 34–42, http://www.abajournal.com/magazine/article/a_supreme_case_of _contempt.

66. Batson v. Kentucky, 476 U.S. 79, 102–103 (1986) (Marshall, J., concurring) (urging the Court to abolish peremptory challenges).

67. McCleskey v. Kemp, 481 U.S. 279, 292–293 (1987). ("Thus, to prevail under the Equal Protection Clause, McCleskey must prove that the decisionmakers in *his* case acted with discriminatory purpose. He offers no evidence specific to his own case that would support an inference that racial considerations played a part in his sentence.")

68. See Randall L. Kennedy, "*McCleskey v. Kemp*: Race, Capital Punishment, and the Supreme Court," *Harvard Law Review* 101 (1988): 1388–1443 (discussing the difficulties surrounding the remediation of race-of-the-victim discrimination).

69. Richard H. Pildes, "Democracy, Anti-Democracy and the Canon," *Constitutional Commentary* 17 (2000): 302–303.

70. Hunter v. Underwood, 471 U.S. 222, 229 (1985).

71. Pildes, "Democracy, Anti-Democracy and the Canon," 303–304n38.

72. Giles v. Harris, 189 U.S. 475, 482–484 (1903).

73. Ibid., 488.

74. Pildes, "Democracy, Anti-Democracy and the Canon," 311–317.

75. Baker v. Carr, 369 U.S. 186 (1962).

76. Ibid., 192; ibid., 253 (Clark, J., concurring).

77. Reynolds v. Sims, 377 U.S. 533 (1964).

78. See, for example, Karcher v Daggett, 462 U.S. 725 (1983).

79. Davis v. Bandemer, 478 U.S. 109 (1986); Vieth v. Jubelirer, 541 U.S. 267 (2004).

80. Davis v. Bandemer, 143.

81. Vieth v. Jubelirer, 281.

82. Furman v. Georgia, 271 (Brennan, J., concurring); ibid., 371 (Marshall, J., concurring) (internal quotation marks and citation omitted).

83. David Dolinko, "Three Mistakes of Retributivism," *University of California Los Angeles Law Review* 39 (1992): 1623 (describing the "vigorous . . . revival" of retributivism to dominance as a theory of criminal punishment in the 1970s and beyond).

84. Jeffrey H. Reiman, "Justice, Civilization, and the Death Penalty: Answering Ernest van den Haag," *Philosophy and Public Affairs* 14 (1985): 122–125 (tracing Hegelian and Kantian conceptions of retributivism).

85. United Nations High Commission for Human Rights Resolution, E/CN.4/1997/12 (April 3, 1997).

86. Sanford Levinson, "Pledging Faith in the Civil Religion; Or, Would You Sign the Constitution?," *William and Mary Law Review* 29 (1987): 115.

87. Death Penalty Information Center, *Facts about the Death Penalty* (February, 2016), http://www.deathpenaltyinfo.org/documents/FactSheet.pdf.

88. Jon Herskovitz, "U.S. Death Penalties, Executions Slow as Capital Punishment is Squeezed," *Reuters,* November 15, 2015 (quoting law professor Robert Blecker), http://www.reuters.com/article/us-usa-execution -idUSKCN0T40OV20151115.

89. Bowers v. Hardwick, 478 U.S. 186, 190 (1986).

90. Lawrence v. Texas, 539 U.S. 558, 567 (2003).

91. Goodridge v. Department of Public Health, 798 N.E.2d 941 (Mass. 2003).

92. Lawrence v. Texas, 577 (internal quotation marks and citation omitted).

93. Kenji Yoshino, *Speak Now: Marriage Equality on Trial* (New York: Broadway Books, 2015), 110.

94. David Boies and Theodore B. Olson, *Redeeming the Dream: Proposition 8 and the Struggle for Marriage Equality* (New York: Penguin Group, 2014), 153–154.

95. Ibid., 157–159, 166.

96. Baskin v. Bogan, 766 F.3d 648, 656, 660, 661 (7th Cir. 2014).

97. Dale Carpenter, "The Posner Treatment," *Washington Post: Volokh Conspiracy,* August 28, 2014, https://www.washingtonpost.com/news/volokh-conspiracy /wp/2014/08/28/gay-marriage-bans-get-the-posner-treatment/.

98. Obergefell v. Hodges, 135 S. Ct. 2584 (2015). See Michael Levenson, "Mary Bonauto Set to Argue for Gay Marriage before Supreme Court," *Boston Globe,*

April 28, 2015, https://www.bostonglobe.com/metro/2015/04/27/mary-bonauto-argues-pivotal-same-sex-marriage-case-before-supreme-court/gykuFXcQ2ei0nk2MF41a3K/story.html.

99. Transcript of oral argument, Obergefell v. Hodges, No. 14–556, April 28, 2015, 12 (emphasis added), http://www.supremecourt.gov/oral_arguments/argument_transcripts/14-556q1_7l48.pdf.

100. Obergefell v. Hodges, 2594, 2608.

101. Louis Michael Seidman, "The Triumph of Gay Marriage and the Failure of Constitutional Law," *Supreme Court Review* (forthcoming 2016), http://papers.ssrn.com/sol3/papers.cfm?abstract_id=2636386## (describing Kennedy's "valorization of marriage" as "deeply reactionary"); Noah Feldman, "A Momentous, Yet Conservative, Win for Gay Rights," *Bloomberg View,* December 21, 2015, http://www.bloombergview.com/articles/2015-12-21/a-momentous-yet-conservative-win-for-gay-rights (describing Kennedy's opinion as "fundamentally conservative").

102. Natalie Schachar, "Justice Kennedy's Gay Marriage Opinion is Celebrated Again—in Wedding Vows," *Los Angeles Times,* August 28, 2015, http://www.latimes.com/nation/la-na-couples-justice-kennedy-20150828-story.html.

8. The Future of the American Death Penalty

1. David Von Drehle, "The Death of the Death Penalty," *Time,* June 8, 2015, http://time.com/deathpenalty/; Richard Wolf and Kevin Johnson, "Courts, States Put Death Penalty on Life Support," *USA Today,* September 14, 2015, http://www.usatoday.com/story/news/nation/2015/09/14/death-penalty-execution-supreme-court-lethal-injection/32425015/.

2. See Glossip v. Gross, 135 S. Ct. 2726, 2774–2775 (2015) (Breyer, J., dissenting) (listing New Hampshire, Montana, and Delaware as states that came close to repealing the death penalty in 2014 or 2015). In 2016, Utah came very close to abolishing its death penalty statute, with a repeal bill making it through both the state Senate and a key committee in the House of Representatives before falling short. Mark Berman, "Utah Will Keep the Death Penalty After All," *Washington Post*, March 11, 2016, https://www.washingtonpost.com/news/post-nation/wp/2016/03/11/utah-will-keep-the-death-penalty-after-all/.

3. New State Ice Company v. Liebmann, 285 U.S. 262, 311 (1932) (Brandeis, J., dissenting) ("It is one of the happy incidents of the federal system that a single courageous state may, if its citizens choose, serve as a laboratory; and try novel social and economic experiments without risk to the rest of the country.").

4. For the same political reasons that preclude unanimous legislative repeal, unanimous executive commutation is not a likely route to nationwide abolition of the death penalty.

5. *Capital Punishment: Hearing on H.R. 12217 Before the House Committee on the Judiciary,* 92nd Cong. 429–434 (1972) (expert letters addressing proposals to stay executions and/or abolish the death penalty nationwide).

6. The Court's decisions limiting congressional power include United States v. Lopez, 514 U.S. 541 (1995) (invalidating a federal statute criminalizing possession of guns in school zones); New York v. United States, 505 U.S. 144 (1992) (striking down a federal statute compelling states to regulate according to congressional direction); City of Boerne v. Flores, 521 U.S. 507 (1997) (limiting Congress's use of its Fourteenth Amendment enforcement power to statutory remedies that are congruent and proportional to Court-identified constitutional violations); and National Federation of Independent Businesses v. Sebelius, 132 S. Ct. 2566 (2012) (limiting Congress's ability to use its spending power to encourage states to embrace Medicaid expansion).

7. The Tenth Amendment provides: "The powers not delegated to the United States by the Constitution, nor prohibited by it to the States, are reserved to the States respectively, or to the people."

8. Furman v. Georgia, 408 U.S. 238, 270 (1972) (Brennan, J., concurring).

9. Ibid., 360, 371 (Marshall, J., concurring).

10. Ibid., 362.

11. Ibid., 362–364.

12. For further discussion of the social scientific testing of the Marshall hypothesis, see Carol S. Steiker, "The Marshall Hypothesis Revisited," *Howard Law Journal* 52 (2009): 530–536.

13. The "evolving standards of decency" formulation of the Eighth Amendment comes from Trop v. Dulles, 356 U.S. 86, 101 (1958) (plurality opinion). The invocation of the Court's "own judgment" with regard to evolving standards of decency was first articulated in Coker v. Georgia, 433 U.S. 584, 597 (1977), and invoked many times over the ensuing decades.

14. Furman v. Georgia, 450 (Powell, J., dissenting).

15. Gregg v. Georgia, 428 U.S. 153, 195 (1976) (plurality opinion).

16. McCleskey v. Kemp, 481 U.S. 279 (1987).

17. David Von Drehle, "Retired Justice Changes Stand on Death Penalty," *Washington Post,* June 10, 1994, A1.

18. Furman v. Georgia, 405 (Blackmun, J., dissenting).

19. Ibid., 414.

20. Callins v. Collins, 510 U.S. 1141, 1144 (1994) (Blackmun, J., dissenting from denial of certiorari). Blackmun retired from the Court at the end of the term in which he dissented in *Callins.*

21. Ibid., 1145.

22. Atkins v. Virginia, 536 U.S. 304 (2002) (ruling the death penalty unconstitutional for intellectually disabled offenders); Roper v. Simmons, 543 U.S. 551 (2005) (ruling the death penalty unconstitutional for juvenile offenders); Kennedy v. Louisiana, 554 U.S. 407 (2008) (ruling the death penalty unconstitutional for the crime of child rape).

23. Baze v. Rees, 553 U.S. 35, 86 (2008) (Stevens, J., concurring).

24. Ibid., 85.

25. Glossip v. Gross, 2726, 2756, 2776 (Breyer, J., dissenting).

26. David G. Savage and Timothy M. Phelps, "Supreme Court Dissenters Signal Historic Challenge to Death Penalty," *L.A. Times,* June 29, 2015, http://www.latimes.com/nation/la-na-supreme-court-lethal-injections-death-penalty-20150629-story.html.

27. Ibid., 2755–2756.

28. Ibid., 2756–2759.

29. Ibid., 2760, 2762–2763.

30. Ibid., 2764–2765, 2772.

31. Ibid., 2746–2747 (Scalia, J., concurring).

32. Ibid., 2796 (Sotomayor, J., dissenting) ("Nor . . . should . . . rapidly changing circumstances give us any greater confidence that the execution methods ultimately selected will be sufficiently humane to satisfy the Eighth Amendment. Quite the contrary. The execution protocols States hurriedly devise as they scramble to locate new and untested drugs . . . are all the more likely to be cruel and unusual—presumably, these drugs would have been the States' first choice were they in fact more effective.").

33. Atkins v. Virginia, 304.

34. Roper v. Simmons, 551; Kennedy v. Louisiana, 407.

35. Kennedy v. Louisiana, 436 (emphasis added).

36. Ibid., 437.

37. For a recent, historic state constitutional ruling abolishing the death penalty in Connecticut, see State v. Santiago, 122 A.3d 1 (Conn. 2015).

38. Kansas v. Marsh, 548 U.S. 163, 207–208, 210 (2006) (Souter, J., dissenting).

39. Ibid., 196–197 (Scalia, J., concurring).

40. United States v. Quinones, 196 F. Supp. 2d 416, 418, 420 & n.6 (S.D.N.Y. 2002).

41. United States v. Quinones, 313 F.3d 49, 52 (2d Cir. 2002).

42. Ibid., 67 (citing Herrera v. Collins, 506 U.S. 390 [1993]).

43. Jones v. Chappell, 31 F. Supp. 3d 1050 (C.D. Cal. 2014).

44. Ibid., 1053 (emphasis omitted).

45. For Justice Kennedy's concerns about solitary confinement, see Davis v. Ayala, 135 S. Ct. 2187, 2209 (2015) (Kennedy, J., concurring) (describing solitary confinement as a punishment that "will bring you to the edge of madness, perhaps to madness itself").

46. Gregg v. Georgia, 173, 179–184.

47. Coker v. Georgia, 593–597.

48. Enmund v. Florida, 458 U.S. 782, 786 & n.2, 787–788 (1982).

49. See Tison v. Arizona, 481 U.S. 137 (1987) (holding that defendants convicted of "felony murder" who did not themselves intend to kill or participate in the killing nonetheless may constitutionally receive a death sentence if they were major participants in the underlying felony and evinced reckless indifference to human life).

50. See Enmund v. Florida, 796.

51. Penry v. Lynaugh, 492 U.S. 302 (1989) (holding that the death penalty is not disproportionate for intellectually disabled offenders); Stanford v. Kentucky,

492 U.S. 361 (1989) (holding that the death penalty is not disproportionate for juvenile offenders).

52. Atkins v. Virginia, 315 & n.17, 316.
53. Ibid., 316 n.21.
54. Ibid., 322 (Rehnquist, C.J., dissenting).
55. Ibid., 347 (Scalia, J., dissenting).
56. Roper v. Simmons, 564–566, 569–570.
57. Ibid., 575, 578.
58. Kennedy v. Louisiana, 4436, 439, 440, 443.
59. Graham v. Florida, 560 U.S. 48, 66 (2010).
60. An alternative accounting of inactive death penalty states would include those that have conducted no more than three executions since 1976—a number that totals ten rather than eleven. See Figure 1 in Chapter 1.
61. Murder and non-negligent homicide rates nationwide have hovered between 14,000 and 15,000 in recent years. See FBI, "Crime in the United States 2014," *Uniform Crime Reports*, https://www.fbi.gov/about-us/cjis/ucr/crime-in-the-u.s /2014/crime-in-the-u.s.-2014/tables/table-1. Because most states have enacted broad eligibility for capital murder (including, for example, all felony murders), a substantial fraction of the murders in any given state would likely be death-eligible.
62. American Bar Association, "Death Penalty Moratorium Resolution" (1997), http://www.americanbar.org/groups/committees/death_penalty _representation/resources/dp-policy/moratorium-1997.html.
63. Adam Liptak, "Group Gives Up Death Penalty Work," *New York Times,* January 4, 2010, http://www.nytimes.com/2010/01/05/us/05bar.html. We coauthored the report that led the American Law Institute to withdraw its support for its model death penalty provisions. See Carol S. Steiker and Jordan M. Steiker, "Report to the ALI Concerning Capital Punishment," *Texas Law Review* 89 (2010): 367–421.
64. Mark Berman, "Pope Francis Tells Congress 'Every Life is Sacred,' Says the Death Penalty Should Be Abolished," *Washington Post,* September 24, 2015, https://www.washingtonpost.com/news/post-nation/wp /2015/09/24/pope-francis-tells-congress-the-death-penalty-should-be -abolished/.
65. The United States ranked fifth among executing nations in 2015, after China, Iran, Saudi Arabia, and Iraq. See Amnesty International, "Death Sentences and Executions 2014," March 31, 2015, http://www.amnestyusa.org/research /reports/death-sentences-and-executions-2014.
66. While most Americans still register support for the death penalty in the abstract, a majority would choose a sentence of life without possibility of parole over the death penalty. See Reid Wilson and Scott Clement, "Support for Death Penalty Still High, But Down," *Washington Post,* June 5, 2014, https://www .washingtonpost.com/blogs/govbeat/wp/2014/06/05/support-for-death-penalty -still-high-but-down/.

67. See Glossip v. Gross, 2757 (Breyer, J., dissenting) (explaining why "exonerations occur far more frequently where capital convictions, rather than ordinary criminal convictions, are at issue").

68. Ibid., 2760.

69. Jeffrey Toobin, "Breyer's Big Idea," *New Yorker,* October 31, 2005, 43.

70. Jack Greenberg, who argued one of the rape cases that was consolidated with *Furman,* maintained that the death penalty was unconstitutional for *all* crimes, not just for rape, despite the fact that his client "would have been entirely satisfied" with a ruling on rape alone. This choice was an example of "the conflict in LDF's roles" that arose from representing multiple defendants in the same litigation campaign. Evan J. Mandery, *A Wild Justice: The Death and Resurrection of Capital Punishment in America* (New York: W. W. Norton, 2013), 164.

71. The nonprofit called The Eighth Amendment Project has described its "ultimate mission" as supporting lawyers who bring cases to the Supreme Court that are aimed at ending the death penalty. See Chris Geidner, "The Most Ambitious Effort Yet to Abolish the Death Penalty is Already Happening," *BuzzFeed News,* November 8, 2015, http://www.buzzfeed.com /chrisgeidner/the-most-ambitious-effort-yet-to-abolish-the-death-penalty.

72. As Bill Stuntz observed: "The decade-long crime drop of the 1990s followed a nearly two-generation-long crime wave." William J. Stuntz, *The Collapse of American Criminal Justice* (Cambridge, MA: Belknap Press of Harvard University Press, 2011), 245.

73. See Inimai M. Chettiar, "The Many Causes of America's Decline in Crime," *The Atlantic,* February 11, 2015, http://www.theatlantic.com/politics/archive/2015 /02/the-many-causes-of-americas-decline-in-crime/385364/; Reid Wilson, "In Major Cities, Murder Rates Drop Precipitously," *Washington Post,* January 2, 2015, https://www.washingtonpost.com/blogs/govbeat/wp/2015/01/02/in-major -cities-murder-rates-drop-precipitously/.

74. Glossip v. Gross, 2755 (Breyer, J., dissenting).

75. See Joanne Young, "Roman Coliseum Honors Nebraska's Repeal of Death Penalty," *Lincoln Journal Star,* July 2, 2015, http://journalstar.com/news/state -and-regional/govt-and-politics/roman-coliseum-honors-nebraska-s-repeal-of -death-penalty/article_a8770ec5-1c95-57cb-84ae-026d61a238c2.html.

76. Payne v. Tennessee, 501 U.S. 808, 844 (1991) (Marshall, J., dissenting).

9. Life after Death

1. Legal journalist Joan Cheever wrote a book about her efforts to track down the roughly 600 people reprieved from death row in 1972 by the Court's decision in *Furman.* Most of those inmates were eventually released from prison, including William Furman himself. See Joan M. Cheever, *Back from the Dead: One Woman's Search for the Men Who Walked off America's Death Row* (Chichester, UK: John Wiley & Sons, 2006). In light of changes in the nature of life sentences in the past four decades, it is highly unlikely that any of the roughly

3,000 people currently on death row would ever be released from prison if their death sentences were commuted by a "Furman II" ruling.

2. Furman v. Georgia, 408 U.S. 238, 364 (1972) (Marshall, J., concurring).
3. Carol S. Steiker and Jordan M. Steiker, "Report to the ALI Concerning Capital Punishment," *Texas Law Review* 89 (2010): 405.
4. Ibid., 407.
5. Steve Brewer, "Penry Likely to Face Retrial, Officials Say," *Huntsville Item,* July 1, 1989, 3A.
6. Christopher Slobogin, "The Death Penalty in Florida," *Elon Law Review* 1 (2009): 62–63.
7. See Jeffrey L. Kirchmeier, *Imprisoned by the Past: Warren McCleskey and the American Death Penalty* (New York: Oxford University Press, 2015), 111 (describing Justice Lewis Powell's frustration with the capital review process that led attorneys to file last-minute appeals).
8. Antiterrorism and Effective Death Penalty Act of 1996, Pub. L. No. 104–132, 110 Stat. 1214 (1996).
9. Wright v. West, 505 U.S. 277, 305 (1992) (O'Connor, J., concurring) (noting the decades of attempts to pass habeas reform bills in Congress prior to the 1990s).
10. Lincoln Caplan, "The Destruction of Defendants' Rights," *New Yorker,* June 21, 2015 (quoting Randy Hertz and James S. Liebman, *Federal Habeas Corpus Practice and Procedure,* 6th ed. (New Providence, NJ: LexisNexis, 2011), http://www.newyorker.com/news/news-desk/the-destruction-of-defendants -rights.
11. Nancy J. King and Joseph L. Hoffmann, *Habeas for the Twenty-First Century: Uses, Abuses, and the Future of the Great Writ* (Chicago: University of Chicago Press, 2011), 169.
12. Roger Hood and Carolyn Hoyle, *The Death Penalty: A Worldwide Perspective,* 5th ed. (New York: Oxford University Press, 2015), 478.
13. Schick v. Reed, 419 U.S. 256, 267 (1974) (holding that a death-sentenced inmate whose sentence was commuted to incarceration without possibility of parole could not constitutionally challenge the no-parole provision because it was similar to sentences imposed under LWOP statutes, which "do not offend the Constitution").
14. Richard C. Dieter, *Sentencing for Life: Americans Embrace Alternatives to the Death Penalty* (Death Penalty Information Center, April, 1993), Fig. 2, http://www.deathpenaltyinfo.org/sentencing-life-americans-embrace -alternatives-death-penalty. See also William J. Bowers and Benjamin D. Steiner, "Death by Default: An Empirical Demonstration of False and Forced Choices in Capital Sentencing," *Texas Law Review* 77 (1999): 645–671 (empirical study of actual capital jurors indicated that the more jurors underestimated the alternative to capital punishment, the more likely they were to vote for a death sentence).
15. Professor Marie Gottschalk has observed: "Over the years, many leading abolitionists have ardently supported LWOP. They have uncritically accepted LWOP as a viable alternative to the death penalty, thus helping to legitimize the

wider use of a sentence that has many features in common with capital punishment." Marie Gottschalk, "Days Without End: Life Sentences and Penal Reform," *Prison Legal News,* January 2012, 14, https://www.prisonlegalnews.org/media/issues/01pln12.pdf.

16. Hood and Hoyle, *Death Penalty,* 478.

17. See Note, "A Matter of Life and Death: The Effect of Life-Without-Parole Statutes on Capital Punishment," *Harvard Law Review* 119 (2006): 1841.

18. See Death Penalty Information Center, *Death Sentences by Year: 1976–2014* (2015), http://www.deathpenaltyinfo.org/death-sentences-year-1977-2009.

19. Hood and Hoyle, *Death Penalty,* 481.

20. Ibid., 479.

21. Glossip v. Gross, 135 S. Ct. 2726, 2747 (2015) (Scalia, J., concurring).

22. Sarah Solon, "The Truth About Choosing Between Life and Death," *ACLU Blog,* January 6, 2014 (arguing that jurors in capital cases should be able to hear testimony about what LWOP is like, because otherwise ordinary people are unable to appreciate its severity), https://www.aclu.org/blog/truth-about-choosing-between-life-and-death.

23. Stephen Lurie, "The Death Penalty is Cruel. But So Is Life Without Parole." *New Republic,* June 16, 2015, https://newrepublic.com/article/121943/death-row-crueler-and-more-unusual-penalty-execution.

24. Sherod Thaxton, "Leveraging Death," *Journal of Criminal Law and Criminology* 103 (2013): 475.

25. Adam Liptak, "Facing a Jury of (Some of) One's Peers," *New York Times,* July 20, 2003, http://www.nytimes.com/2003/07/20/weekinreview/20LIPT.html.

26. Ken Armstrong and Steve Mills, "Part 1: Death Row Justice Derailed," *Chicago Tribune,* November 14, 1999, http://articles.chicagotribune.com/1999-11-14/news/chi-991114deathillinois1_1_capital-punishment-death-row-criminal-justice-system. The entire "Justice Derailed" series is available at http://www.chicagotribune.com/news/watchdog/chi-justicederailed-storygallery-storygallery.html.

27. See Andrew Novak, *Comparative Executive Clemency: The Constitutional Pardon Power and the Prerogative of Mercy in Global Perspective* (New York: Routledge, 2016), 164–165.

28. The Illinois law requiring police to videotape interrogations in homicide cases was expanded to apply a broader array of offenses in 2013, making Illinois the seventeenth state to require videotaping in cases other than homicides. See Dan Hinkel, "Quinn Signs Bill Expanding Recording of Police Interrogations," *Chicago Tribune,* August 26, 2013, http://www.chicagotribune.com/news/ct-met-ct-met-videotaped-interrogations-law-20130827-story.html.

29. See David Grann, "Trial by Fire," *New Yorker,* September 7, 2009, http://www.newyorker.com/magazine/2009/09/07/trial-by-fire; Nightline, "Wrongly Executed?," *ABC News,* September 17, 2009, http://abcnews.go.com/video/playerIndex?id=8608644; Frontline, "Death by Fire," *PBS* video, October 19, 2010, http://www.pbs.org/wgbh/pages/frontline/death-by-fire/.

30. See, for example, Williams v. Taylor, 529 U.S. 362 (2000); Wiggins v. Smith, 539 U.S. 510 (2003); Rompilla v. Beard, 545 U.S. 374 (2005); Bobby v. Van Hook, 558 U.S. 4 (2009) (per curiam); Porter v. McCollum, 558 U.S. 30 (2009) (per curiam).
31. See Miller-El v. Dretke, 545 U.S. 231 (2005) (concerning a black defendant sentenced to death by a jury in which all but one prospective black juror had been struck by the prosecution); Snyder v. Louisiana, 552 U.S. 472 (2008) (concerning a black defendant sentenced to death by a jury in which all prospective black jurors had been struck by the prosecution); Foster v. Chatman, No. 14-8349 (pending in the U.S. Supreme Court) (concerning a black defendant sentenced to death by a jury in which all prospective black jurors had been struck by the prosecution).
32. Miller-El v. Dretke, 238 (quotation marks and citations omitted).
33. Woodson v. North Carolina, 428 U.S. 280, 304 (1976).
34. Rummel v. Estelle, 445 U.S. 263 (1980).
35. Ibid., 274 n.11.
36. Hutto v. Davis, 454 U.S. 370 (1982) (per curiam).
37. Solem v. Helm, 463 U.S. 277 (1983).
38. Ibid., 303.
39. Harmelin v. Michigan, 501 U.S. 957 (1991); People v. Harmelin, 440 N.W.2d 75 (Mich. Ct. App. 1989).
40. Harmelin v. Michigan, 1002, 1005 (quotation marks omitted).
41. Ewing v. California, 538 U.S. 11 (2003).
42. Lockyer v. Andrade, 538 U.S. 63 (2003).
43. Ewing v. California, 25.
44. Ibid., 21.
45. Sara Sun Beale, "The Story of *Ewing:* Three Strikes Laws and the Limits of the Eighth Amendment Proportionality Review," in *Criminal Law Stories,* eds. Donna Coker and Robert Weisberg (New York: Thomson Reuters/Foundation Press, 2013), 458.
46. See Anthony M. Kennedy, "Speech at the American Bar Association Annual Meeting," August 9, 2003, transcript, Supreme Court of the United States, http://www.supremecourt.gov/publicinfo/speeches/sp_08-09-03.html.
47. Tracey Kaplan, "Proposition 36: Voters Overwhelmingly Ease Three Strikes Law," *San Jose Mercury News,* November 6, 2012, http://www.mercurynews.com/ci_21943951/prop-36-huge-lead-early-returns.
48. Graham v. Florida, 560 U.S. 48 (2010).
49. Ibid., 69–70.
50. Ibid., 103 (Thomas, J., dissenting).
51. Ibid., 86 (Roberts, C.J., concurring in the judgment).
52. Miller v. Alabama, 132 S. Ct. 2455 (2012).
53. Ibid., 2467, 2469 (quoting Graham v. Florida, 89 [Roberts, C.J., concurring in the judgment]).
54. Ibid., 2458.

55. In the three years following the *Miller* decision in 2012, nine states have effectively abolished juvenile LWOP and many more have restricted it. Phillips Black Project, *Juvenile Life Without Parole After* Miller v. Alabama (2015), http://www.phillipsblack.org/s/Juvenile-Life-Without-Parole-After-Miller.pdf. An example of constitutional abolition is the decision of the Massachusetts Supreme Judicial Court to completely abolish juvenile LWOP in response to the Court's decision in *Miller,* even though *Miller* required only the abandonment of *mandatory* juvenile LWOP sentences. The Massachusetts SJC concluded that juvenile LWOP violated the federal Constitution and the Massachusetts Constitution, reasoning: "Simply put, because the brain of a juvenile is not fully developed, either structurally or functionally, by the age of eighteen, a judge cannot find with confidence that a particular offender, at that point in time, is irretrievably depraved. Therefore, it follows that the judge cannot ascertain, with any reasonable degree of certainty, whether imposition of this most severe punishment is warranted." Diatchenko v. Suffolk District Attorney, 1 N.E.3d 270, 284 (Mass. 2013) (citations omitted).

56. The case for applying the restrictions on harsh punishments for juveniles to slightly older defendants as well derives from the growing scientific evidence that adolescent brain maturation is not generally complete until the mid-twenties. For a white paper outlining the science and its implications for punishment practices, see Hollis A. Whitson, "The Case Against Execution of People who Were Youths Under the Age of Twenty-One Years Old at the Time of the Offense" (position paper, Death Penalty Information Center, 2014), http://www.deathpenaltyinfo.org/documents/YouthExecutionPositionPaper.pdf.

57. Movement toward raising the age of juvenile status for the purpose of criminal adjudication has already begun. Connecticut Governor Dannel Malloy announced in 2015 that he would like to see the state raise the age of juvenile status from seventeen to twenty. See Jacqueline Rabe Thomas and Mark Pazniokas, "Malloy: Raise the Age for Juvenile Justice System to 20," *Connecticut Mirror,* November 6, 2015, http://ctmirror.org/2015/11/06/malloy-raise-the-age-for-juvenile-justice-system-to-20/.

58. See generally Neal Hazel, *Cross-National Comparison of Youth Justice* (U.K. Youth Justice Board, Cross-National Comparison of Youth Justice, 2008), http://dera.ioe.ac.uk/7996/1/Cross_national_final.pdf.

59. ACLU, *A Living Death: Life Without Parole for Nonviolent Offenses* (2013), https://www.aclu.org/sites/default/files/field_document/111813-lwop-complete-report.pdf; Equal Justice Initiative, *Death in Prison Sentences for Children,* http://www.eji.org/childrenprison/deathinprison.

60. In eight states, more than a third of inmates serving LWOP sentences were convicted of a nonhomicide crime. See The Sentencing Project, *Life Goes On: The Historic Rise in Life Sentences in America* (2013), 8, http://sentencingproject.org/doc/publications/inc_Life%20Goes%20On%202013.pdf.

61. Many prospective jurors in capital cases respond to questioning about their views on the death penalty by opining that LWOP is a harsher sentence. See, for

example, Masha Gessen, "Can Life in Prison Be Worse than Death? Some Tsarnaev Jurors Think So.," *Washington Post,* February 25, 2015, https://www .washingtonpost.com/news/post-nation/wp/2015/02/25/can-life-in-prison -might-be-worse-than-death-some-tsarnaev-jurors-think-so/.

62. Hood and Hoyle, *Death Penalty,* 472 (noting that all but a few countries replaced capital punishment for their most heinous crimes with sentences less than LWOP, which is widely viewed as a "cruel, inhuman, and degrading punishment").

63. See generally Hope Metcalf, Judith Resnik, and Megan Quattlebaum, eds., *Isolation and Reintegration: Punishment Circa 2014* (Seventeenth Annual Liman Colloquium, Yale Law School, April 2014, revised January 2015) (collecting materials that describe current patterns of incarceration and explore interventions designed to reduce the degree to which correctional facilities maintain order through the isolation of prisoners).

64. Ibid., 103–110, 129–137.

65. See Sharon Shalev, "Solitary Confinement: The View from Europe," *Canadian Journal of Human Rights* 4 (2015): 145 (finding that European uses of solitary confinement are on a "smaller scale" and are less "distinctly extreme" than in the United States).

66. Glossip v. Gross, 2765 (Breyer, J., dissenting).

67. Davis v. Ayala, 135 S. Ct. 2187, 2209–2210 (Kennedy, J., concurring) (internal quotation marks omitted).

68. Trop v. Dulles, 356 U.S. 86, 100 (1958) (plurality opinion).

69. Metcalf et al., *Isolation and Reintegration,* 82, 121, 125.

70. Roy Walmsley, *World Prison Population List,* 10th ed. (International Centre for Prison Studies, 2013), http://www.prisonstudies.org/sites/default/files/resources /downloads/wppl_10.pdf.

71. See Figure 1 in Chapter 1.

72. See Pew Research Center, *Less Support for Death Penalty, Especially Among Democrats,* Pew Research Center, U.S. Politics & Policy, April 16, 2015, http://www.people-press.org/2015/04/16/less-support-for-death-penalty -especially-among-democrats/.

73. Death penalty scholars writing in 1986 about abolition in Western democracies observed: "Indeed, there are no examples of abolition occurring at a time when public opinion supported the measure. . . . [But] when a country has been abolitionist in practice for a number of years, controversy tends to end." Franklin E. Zimring and Gordon Hawkins, *Capital Punishment and the American Agenda* (New York: Cambridge University Press, 1986), 22.

74. Matt Ford, "Donald Trump's Racially Charged Advocacy of the Death Penalty," *The Atlantic,* December 18, 2015, http://www.theatlantic.com /politics/archive/2015/12/donald-trump-death-penalty/420069/; Benjamin Weiser, "Settlement Approved in Central Park Jogger Case, but New York Deflects Blame," *New York Times,* September 5, 2014, http://www.nytimes .com/2014/09/06/nyregion/41-million-settlement-for-5-convicted-in-jogger -case-is-approved.html.

75. Richard B. Schmitt, "Ashcroft is Undeterred in Push for Capital Cases," *Los Angeles Times,* September 29, 2004, http://articles.latimes.com/2004/sep/29 /nation/na-death29.

76. Evan Allen, "Few Favor Death for Dzhokhar Tsarnaev, Poll Finds," *Boston Globe,* April 26, 2015, https://www.bostonglobe.com/metro/2015/04/26/globe -poll-shows-diminishing-support-for-death-penalty-for-tsarnaev /S3GMhFlGj5VUkZrmLzh1iN/story.html.

77. See Petra Bartosiewicz, "U.S. Prosecutors Have Risked a Show Trial for the Chance to Execute Dzhokhar Tsarnaev," *New Republic,* April 8, 2015, https:// newrepublic.com/article/121496/prosecutors-may-have-put-boston-through -show-trial-execution.

78. See Ved P. Nanda, "Bases for Refusing International Extradition Requests— Capital Punishment and Torture," *Fordham International Law Journal* 23 (1999): 1369, 1370–1394.

79. See *Special Rapporteur on Extrajudicial, Summary or Arbitrary Executions,* United Nations, Office of the High Commissioner on Human Rights, http://www.ohchr.org/EN/Issues/Executions/Pages/SRExecutionsIndex.aspx.

Acknowledgments

This book is the culmination of more than two decades of joint work on scholarly, litigation, and law reform projects. Too many people to count or name have helped us along the way on one or another of these projects, so the thanks that follow are necessarily underinclusive.

Our time as law clerks with Justice Thurgood Marshall stirred our interest in the death penalty, and his work as a lawyer and judge has been inspirational to us and to all those who care about justice in the United States. Judge Louis Pollak (for whom Jordan served as a law clerk) encouraged us in all of our academic endeavors and was particularly supportive of our work for the American Law Institute concerning the modern administration of the American death penalty.

We are deeply indebted to those colleagues who read the entire manuscript and offered comments and suggestions: Lincoln Caplan, Brandon Garrett, Bernard Harcourt, Sheri Lynn Johnson, Sandy Levinson, Michael Meltsner, Scot Powe, and Michael Radelet. Many other academic colleagues, lawyers, and judges have educated us through their own work and served as sounding boards for our ideas over many years: Tony Amsterdam, David Baldus, Stuart Banner, Rachel Barkow, Hon. David Barron, John Blume, Steve Bright, Dick Burr, Paul Butler, David Cole, Andrew Crespo, Deborah Denno, Alan Dershowitz, John Donohue, Jeff Fagan, Joey Fishkin, Willy Forbath, James Forman Jr., Cary Franklin, Charles Fried, David Garland, Hon. Nancy Gertner, Marie Gottschalk, Sam Gross, Phil Heymann, Hon. Patrick Higginbotham, Joe Hoffmann, Pam Karlan, Kathryn Kase, Randy Kennedy, Nancy King, Michael Klarman, Lee Kovarsky, Corinna Lain, Jennifer Laurin, Jim Liebman, Andrea Lyon, Ken Mack,

Evan Mandery, Larry Marshall, Tracey Meares, Frank Michelman, Charles Ogletree Jr., David Oshinsky, Dan Richman, Austin Sarat, Steve Schulhofer, Mike Seidman, Lis Semel, David Sklansky, Bryan Stevenson, Scott Sundby, Moshik Temkin, Gerald Torres, Larry Tribe, Mark Tushnet, Lloyd Weinreb, Bob Weisberg, Greg Wiercioch, and Frank Zimring.

Three scholars who are no longer with us were especially influential in the development of this book: Hugo Bedau, who put the death penalty on the map as a subject of serious scholarly investigation; Dan Meltzer, whose guidance on our report to the American Law Institute modeled the rigor and sophistication that we aspire to bring to our work; and Bill Stuntz, whose own book, *The Collapse of American Criminal Justice,* was a path-breaking achievement. We wish they were here to see the completion of this project.

Two sets of deans over the past decade have steadfastly encouraged our work: Elena Kagan and Martha Minow at Harvard, and Larry Sager and Ward Farnsworth at the University of Texas. The Radcliffe Institute for Advanced Study offered an invaluable respite and an engaging, wide-ranging group of colleagues to Carol during the 2014–2015 year, when she was the Rita E. Hauser Fellow. Alex Whiting, Larry Schwartztol, and Anna Kastner of the Criminal Justice Policy Program at Harvard Law School were tremendously supportive during that program's inaugural year. Harvard research librarian Claire DeMarco provided speedy and thorough assistance on polling data, and faculty assistants Amanda Cegielski and Maureen Worth at Harvard and Angel Leffingwell at the University of Texas assisted us in countless ways.

Students in our capital punishment courses at both Harvard and the University of Texas have challenged and honed our thinking over the years. Colleagues in the Capital Punishment Center at the University of Texas, including Maurie Levin, Jim Marcus, Rob Owen, Rita Radostitz, Meredith Rountree, Raoul Schonemann, and Mollie Spalding have been exceedingly helpful in thinking through the issues and inspirational in their efforts on behalf of death-sentenced inmates. Student research assistants made many valuable contributions to the production of the book: Alex Blumberg, Alice Cullina, Jake Newman, Sara Nommensen, and Lark Turner from Harvard Law School; Gene Chang, Kyle Kim, and Eva Shang, who served as Radcliffe Research Partners from Harvard College; and Hensleigh Crowell and Anne Swift at the University of Texas School of Law. Hensleigh Crowell, in particular, made enormous contributions over several years.

Joyce Seltzer, our editor at Harvard University Press, shepherded the book from its inception, and we have greatly appreciated her excellent eye and her enthusiastic support for this project.

We are, as always, grateful for our large and loving family. We thank our parents, David and Judy Steiker, to whom this book is dedicated; our brother and sister-in-law, Jim Steiker and Wendy Epstein, who do so much to bring our wonderful extended family together; our cousin, Valerie Steiker, who cheerfully offered professional publishing advice; and our children, Abby, Eliza, Blake, Aaron, and Josh, who grew up with this book. Most of all, we thank our spouses, Lori Holleran Steiker and Paul Holtzman, who have supported this project with unfailing patience and humor and without whom this book, among many other things, would not have been possible.

The closing section of Chapter 2 ("American Exceptionalism and the Death Penalty") borrows brief portions from Carol S. Steiker, "Capital Punishment and Contingency," *Harvard Law Review* 125 (2012): 760–787. Chapter 3 is a slightly revised version of Carol S. Steiker and Jordan M. Steiker, "The American Death Penalty and the (In)Visibility of Race, *University of Chicago Law Review* 82 (2015): 243–294. Chapter 4 expands upon Carol S. Steiker and Jordan M. Steiker, "A Tale of Two Nations: Implementation of the Death Penalty in 'Executing' versus 'Symbolic' States in the United States," *Texas Law Review* 84 (2006): 1869–1927. Chapter 5 combines and expands upon two articles: Carol S. Steiker and Jordan M. Steiker, "Sober Second Thoughts: Reflections on Two Decades of Constitutional Regulation of Capital Punishment," *Harvard Law Review* 109 (1995): 355–438, and Carol S. Steiker and Jordan M. Steiker, "No More Tinkering: The American Law Institute and the Death Penalty Provisions of the Model Penal Code," *Texas Law Review* 89 (2010): 353–421. Chapter 7 incorporates portions of Carol S. Steiker and Jordan M. Steiker, "Lessons for Law Reform from the American Experiment with Capital Punishment," *Southern California Law Review* 87 (2014): 733–784. The opening section of Chapter 8 ("The Marshall Hypothesis and Movement on the High Court") includes some passages from Carol S. Steiker, "The Marshall Hypothesis Revisited," *Howard Law Journal* 52 (2009): 525–555. We are also indebted to the following journals, publishers, and their editors, for providing us with early venues to explore ideas and develop concepts: *American Journal of Criminal Law,* Foundation Press (*Death Penalty Stories,* John Blume and Jordan Steiker, eds.), *Journal of Criminal Law and Criminology, Law and Inequality, Michigan Law Review, University of Chicago Legal Forum, University of Miami Law Review,* and *University of Pennsylvania Journal of Constitutional Law.*

Index

ABA. *See* American Bar Association (ABA)

Abolitionists: privatizing of executions and, 12–13

Abolitionist states, 118

Abolition of capital punishment: American exceptionalism and questions tied to, 71–77; American ideals and, 320–322; anticipation and anxiety over prospect of, 285–289; constitutional, blueprint for, 271–285; Eighth Amendment challenges and, 304–317; lynching and arguments about, 23; Marshall hypothesis, movement on the Supreme Court, and, 258–271; near, road to, 40–51; politics of criminal justice after, 317–320; regulation vs., 60–71; vulnerability of American death penalty and, 255; welcome results of, 290–291. *See also Furman v. Georgia*

Abortion: political backlash thesis and, 218, 223–229; regulation of, 4, 219

Abu-Jamal, Mumia, 145

ACLU. *See* American Civil Liberties Union (ACLU)

Actual Innocence (Dwyer, et al.), 208

ADA. *See* Americans with Disabilities Act (ADA)

Adams, John, 10

Administrative Office of the U.S. Courts, 203

AEDPA. *See* Anti-Terrorism and Effective Death Penalty Act (AEDPA)

Affirmative action: Court's color-blind ideal and, 105

African Americans. *See* Blacks

Aggravating factors, 44; "aggravator creep" and, 161; enumeration of, Supreme Court's regulatory efforts and, 158–163; states, capital decision making, and, 177

Aikens v. California, 87

Alabama: voting rights scheme in, 241–242

ALI. *See* American Law Institute (ALI)

American Bar Association (ABA), 308; Death Penalty Due Process Review Project, 183, 351n47; Florida Assessment Team, 293; Guidelines for the Appointment and Performance of Counsel in Death Penalty Cases, 171; House of Delegates, 283

American Civil Liberties Union (ACLU), 54, 225

American exceptionalism: death penalty and, 71–77

American Law Institute (ALI), 43, 70. *See also* Model Penal Code (MPC)

American Psychiatric Association, 180

American Revolution, 10